Rick S

GERMANY, AUSTRIA & SWITZERLAND
1999

John Muir Publications
Santa Fe, New Mexico

Other JMP travel guidebooks by Rick Steves
Rick Steves' Europe Through the Back Door
Europe 101: History and Art for the Traveler (with Gene Openshaw)
Rick Steves' Postcards from Europe
Rick Steves' Mona Winks: Self-Guided Tours of Europe's Top Museums
   (with Gene Openshaw)
Rick Steves' Best of Europe
Rick Steves' France, Belgium & the Netherlands (with Steve Smith)
Rick Steves' Great Britain & Ireland
Rick Steves' Italy
Rick Steves' Russia & the Baltics (with Ian Watson)
Rick Steves' Scandinavia
Rick Steves' Spain & Portugal
Rick Steves' London (with Gene Openshaw)
Rick Steves' Paris (with Gene Openshaw and Steve Smith)
Rick Steves' Phrase Books: German, French, Italian, Spanish/
   Portuguese, and French/German/Italian
Asia Through the Back Door (with Bob Effertz)

Thanks to my team at Europe Through the Back Door; the readers
who shared experiences from their travels; the Europeans who make
travel such a good living; and to my wife, Anne, for her support.

John Muir Publications, P.O. Box 613, Santa Fe, NM 87504

Printed in the United States of America
Second printing February 1999

For the latest on Rick's lectures, guidebooks, tours, and public television
series, contact Europe Through the Back Door, Box 2009, Edmonds,
WA 98020, tel. 425/771-8303, fax 425/771-0833, Web site: www
.ricksteves.com, or e-mail: rick@ricksteves.com.

ISBN 1-56261-463-0
ISSN 1085-7222

Europe Through the Back Door Editor Risa Laib
John Muir Publications Editors Krista Lyons-Gould, Jill Metzler
Research Brian Carr Smith
Production Rebecca Cook
Design Linda Braun
Cover Design Janine Lehmann
Typesetting Kathleen Sparkes, White Hart Design
Maps David C. Hoerlein
Printer Banta Company
Cover Photo Neuschwanstein Castle, Bavaria, Germany;
   copyright © Blaine Harrington III

Distributed to the book trade by
Publishers Group West
Berkeley, California

W9-AYD-457

CONTENTS

Top Destinations in Germany, Austria, and Switzerland

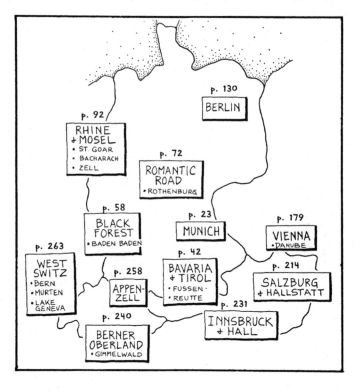

p. 130
BERLIN

p. 92
RHINE
& MOSEL
• ST. GOAR
• BACHARACH
• ZELL

p. 72
ROMANTIC
ROAD
• ROTHENBURG

p. 58
BLACK
FOREST
• BADEN BADEN

p. 23
MUNICH

p. 179
VIENNA
• DANUBE

p. 263
WEST
SWITZ
• BERN
• MURTEN
• LAKE
  GENEVA

p. 258
APPEN-
ZELL

p. 42
BAVARIA
& TIROL
• FUSSEN •
• REUTTE

p. 214
SALZBURG
& HALLSTATT

p. 240
BERNER
OBERLAND
• GIMMELWALD

p. 231
INNSBRUCK
& HALL

INTRODUCTION

This book breaks Germany, Austria, and Switzerland into their top big-city, small-town, and rural destinations. It then gives you all the information and opinions necessary to wring the maximum value out of your limited time and money in each of these destinations.

If you plan a month or less in this region, this lean and mean little book is all you need.

Experiencing this region's culture, people, and natural wonders economically and hassle-free has been my goal for more than 25 years of traveling, tour guiding, and travel writing. With this book, I pass on to you the lessons I've learned, updated for 1999.

Rick Steves' Germany, Austria & Switzerland is your friendly Franconian, your German in a jam, a tour guide in your pocket. The book includes a balance of cities and villages, mountaintop hikes and forgotten Roman ruins, sleepy river cruises, and sky-high gondola rides. It covers the predictable biggies and mixes in a healthy dose of Back Door intimacy. And, with this edition, I've added Prague, the most exciting city in eastern Europe.

Along with visiting Rhine castles, Mozart's house, and the Vienna Opera, you'll ride a thrilling Austrian mountain luge, soak in a Black Forest mineral spa, share a beer with Bavarian monks, and ramble through traffic-free Swiss Alpine towns. I've been selective, including only the most exciting sights. For example, it's redundant to visit both the Matterhorn and the Jungfrau. I take you up and around the better of the two.

The best is, of course, only my opinion. But after more than two busy decades of travel writing, lecturing, and tour guiding, I've developed a sixth sense of what stokes the traveler's wanderlust. Just thinking about the places featured in this book makes me want to slap-dance and yodel.

This Information Is Accurate and Up-to-Date

This book is updated every year. Most publishers of guidebooks that cover a country from top to bottom can afford an update only every two or three years (and even then, it's often by letter). Since this book is selective, covering only the places I think make up the top month or so in Germany, Austria, and Switzerland, I am able to personally update it each year. Even with an annual update, things change. But if you're traveling with the current edition of this book, I guarantee you're using the most up-to-date information available. This book will help you have an inexpensive, hassle-free trip. Use this year's edition. I tell you, you're crazy to save a few bucks by traveling on old information. If you're packing an old book, you'll understand the gravity of your mistake . . . in Europe. Your trip costs about $10 per waking hour. Your time is valuable. This guidebook saves lots of time.

Planning Your Trip

This book is organized by destination. Each destination is covered as a mini-vacation on its own, filled with exciting sights and homey, affordable places to stay. In each chapter you'll find:

Planning Your Time, a suggested schedule with thoughts on how to best use your limited time.

Orientation, including tourist information, city transportation, and an easy-to-read map designed to make the text clear and your arrival smooth.

Sights with ratings: ▲▲▲—Worth getting up early and skipping breakfast for; ▲▲—Worth getting up early for; ▲—Worth seeing if it's convenient; No rating—Worth knowing about.

Sleeping and Eating, with addresses and phone numbers of my favorite budget hotels and restaurants.

Transportation Connections, including nearby destinations serviced by train and route tips for drivers, with recommended roadside attractions along the way.

The Appendix is a traveler's toolkit, with a climate chart, telephone tips, rail routes, and German survival phrases.

Browse through this book, choose your favorite destinations, and link them up. Then have a great trip! You'll travel like a temporary local, getting the absolute most out of every mile, minute, and dollar. You won't waste time on mediocre sights because, unlike other guidebook authors, I cover only the best. Since lousy, expensive hotels are a major financial pitfall, I've worked hard to assemble the best accommodations values for each stop. As you travel the route I know and love, I'm happy you'll be meeting some of my favorite Europeans.

Trip Costs

Five components make up your trip cost: airfare, surface transportation, room and board, sightseeing/entertainment, and shopping/miscellany.

Airfare: Don't try to sort through the mess. Get and use a good travel agent. A basic round-trip United States–to–Frankfurt flight should cost $600 to $1,000, depending on where you fly from and when. Always consider saving time and money in Europe by flying "open jaws" (flying into one city and out of another).

Surface Transportation: For a three-week whirlwind trip of all my recommended destinations, allow $650 per person for public transportation (train pass and buses) or $600 per person (based on two people sharing the car) for a three-week car rental, parking, gas, and insurance. Car rental is cheapest when reserved from the United States. Train passes are normally available only outside of Europe. You may save money by simply buying tickets as you go (see Transportation, below).

Room and Board: You can thrive in this region on $60 a day per person for room and board. A $60-a-day budget per person allows $10 for lunch, $15 for dinner, and $35 for lodging (based on two people splitting the cost of a $70 double room that includes breakfast). That's doable. Students and tightwads do it on $40 a day ($15–20 per bed, $20 for meals and snacks). But budget sleeping and eating requires the skills and information covered later in this chapter (and in much more depth in my book *Europe Through the Back Door*).

Sightseeing and Entertainment: In big cities, figure $5 to $10 per major sight, $3 for minor ones, $30 to $40 for bus tours and splurge experiences (e.g., concert tickets, Alpine lifts, conducting the beer-hall band). An overall average of $20 a day works for most. Don't skimp here. After all, this category directly powers most of the experiences all the other expenses are designed to make possible.

Shopping and Miscellany: Figure $1 per postcard and $2 per coffee, beer, and ice-cream cone. Shopping can vary in cost from nearly nothing to a small fortune. Good budget travelers find that this category has little to do with assembling a trip full of lifelong and wonderful memories.

Exchange Rates

I've priced things throughout this book in local currencies.

---

1 deutsche Mark (DM) = 60 cents, and 1.7 DM = $1.
1 Austrian schilling (AS) = 8 cents, and 12 AS = $1.
1 Swiss franc (SF) = 70 cents, and 1.4 SF = $1.
1 Czech Koruna (Kč) = 3 cents, and 32 Kč = $1.

To roughly convert to dollars, subtract one-third from prices in deutsche Marks and Swiss francs (e.g., 60 DM or 60 SF = about $40). For Austrian schillings, drop the last zero and subtract one-fifth (e.g., 450 AS = about $36). Drop the last zero off Czech prices and divide by three. So, that 40-DM cuckoo clock is about $25, the 15-SF lunch is about $10, and the 800-AS taxi ride through Vienna is . . . uh-oh.

Prices, Times, and Discounts

The prices in this book, as well as the hours and telephone numbers, are accurate as of late 1998. Europe is always changing, and I know you'll understand that this, like any other guidebook, starts to yellow even before it's printed.

In Europe—and throughout this book—you'll be using the 24-hour clock. After 12:00 noon, keep going—13:00, 14:00, etc. For anything over 12, subtract 12 and add p.m. (14:00 is 2:00 p.m.)

This book lists peak-season hours for sightseeing attractions.

Off-season, roughly October through April, expect generally shorter hours, longer lunchtime breaks, and fewer activities. Confirm your sightseeing plans locally, especially when traveling between October and April.

While discounts for sightseeing and transportation are not listed in this book, seniors (60 and over), students (only with International Student Identity Cards), and youths (under 18) often get discounts—but only by asking.

When to Go

Summer (peak season) has its advantages: best weather, snow-free Alpine trails, very long days (light until after 21:00), and the busiest schedule of tourist fun.

In "shoulder season" (May, June, September, and early October) travelers enjoy minimal crowds, more comfortable weather, plenty of harvest and wine festivals, and the ability to grab a room almost whenever and wherever they like.

Winter travelers find local concert seasons in full swing, with absolutely no tourist crowds, but many sights and accommodations are either closed or run on a limited schedule. The weather can be cold and dreary, and nighttime will draw the shades on your sightseeing before dinnertime. You may find the climate chart in the Appendix helpful. Pack warm for the Alps no matter when you go.

Sightseeing Priorities

Depending on the length of your trip, here are my recommended priorities.

3 days:	Munich, Bavaria, Salzburg
5 days, add:	Romantic Road, Rhine castles
7 days, add:	Rothenburg, slow down
10 days, add:	Berner Oberland (Swiss Alps)
14 days, add:	Vienna, Hallstatt
17 days, add:	Bern, Danube Valley, Tirol (Reutte)
21 days, add:	West Switzerland, Baden-Baden, Mosel Valley, Köln
24 days, add:	Berlin, Appenzell
30 days, add:	Black Forest, Prague, and slow down

(The map on page 7 and three-week itinerary on page 6 include everything in the top 30 days except Berlin and Prague.)

Prague: Prague is a major detour, both culturally (Slavic rather than Germanic) and geographically (about six hours one-way by train from Berlin, Frankfurt, Munich, or Vienna). But I never met anyone fresh from a visit to Prague who didn't rave

about the city. You have all the information you need for two days
in Prague in this book. If you have the time, go.

Red Tape and Banking

Currently you need a passport, but no visa and no shots, to travel
in Europe (including Prague). Even as borders fade, when you
change countries, you still change money, telephone cards, postage
stamps, and *Unterhosen* (underwear).

Bring traveler's checks in dollars, as well as plastic (ATM,
credit, or debit cards) with a PIN number. Regular banks have the
best rates for cashing traveler's checks. For a large exchange, it
pays to compare rates and fees. Post offices (business hours) and
train stations (long hours) usually change money if you can't get to
a bank. ATMs work fine just about everywhere and are very popular with travelers.

To get a cash advance from a bank machine, you'll need a
four-digit PIN (numbers only, no letters) with your bankcard.
Before you go, verify with your bank that your card will work, then
use it whenever possible. But beware that the distances between
these machines can be great, and bring enough traveler's checks as
backup.

Just like at home, credit (or debit) cards work easily at larger
hotels, restaurants, and shops, but smaller businesses prefer pay-
ment in local currency.

Germany: Banks are generally open Monday through Friday
from 8:00 to noon and from 14:00 to 16:00.

Austria: Bank hours are roughly Monday through Friday
from 8:00 to 15:00 and until 17:30 on Thursday. Austrian banks
charge exorbitant commissions to cash traveler's checks (about $8).
Bring plastic. As a backup, carry American Express checks and
cash them at American Express offices (no commission).

Switzerland: Bank hours are typically Monday through Friday from 8:00 to 17:00.

Czech Republic: Banks are open weekdays from 9:00
to 17:00.

Travel Smart

Upon arrival in a new town, lay the groundwork for a smooth
departure. Reread this book as you travel, and visit local tourist
information offices. Buy a phone card and use it for reservations
and confirmations. Enjoy the hospitality of the Germanic people.
Ask questions. Most locals are eager to point you in their idea of
the right direction. Wear your money belt, pack along a pocket-
size notebook to organize your thoughts, and practice the virtue of
simplicity. Those who expect to travel smart, do. Plan ahead for
banking, laundry, post office chores, and picnics. To maximize
rootedness, minimize one-night stands. Mix intense and relaxed

Germany, Austria, and Switzerland
Best Three-Week Trip

Day	Plan	Sleep in
1	Arrive in Frankfurt	Rothenburg
2	Rothenburg	Rothenburg
3	Romantic Road to the Tirol	Reutte
4	Bavaria and Castle day	Reutte
5	Reutte to Munich	Munich
6	Munich	Munich
7	Salzburg	Salzburg
8	Salzkammergut Lakes District	Hallstatt
9	Mauthausen, Danube to Vienna	Vienna
10	Vienna	Vienna
11	Vienna to the Tirol	Hall
12	Tirol to Swiss Appenzell	Ebenalp
13	Appenzell to Berner Oberland	Gimmelwald
14	Free day in the Alps, hike	Gimmelwald
15	Bern, west to French Switzerland	Murten
16	French Switzerland	Murten
17	Murten to Black Forest	Staufen
18	Black Forest	Baden-Baden
19	Baden-Baden, relax, soak	Baden-Baden
20	Drive to the Rhine, castles	Bacharach
21	The Mosel Valley, Burg Eltz	Bacharach/Zell
22	Köln and Bonn, night train to Berlin, or fly home	

*Note: While this itinerary is designed to be done by car, with slight mod-
ifications it works by train. For the best three weeks by train, sleep in
Füssen rather than Reutte, sleep on the train from Vienna to the Swiss
Alps (skipping Hall and Appenzell), skip French Switzerland, skip the
Black Forest, and add two days in Berlin, connecting it by night trains.*

periods. Every trip (and every traveler) needs at least a few slack
days. Pace yourself. Assume you will return.

As you read through this book, note special days (festivals,
colorful market days, and days when sights are closed). Sundays
have pros and cons, as they do for travelers in the United States

Best Three-Week Trip

(special events, limited hours, shops and banks closed, limited public transportation, no rush hours). Saturdays are virtually weekdays (with most places open until lunchtime). Popular places are even more popular on weekends. Most sights are closed on Monday.

Tourist Information

The tourist information office is your best first stop in any new city. Try to arrive, or at least telephone, before it closes. In this book, I'll refer to a tourist information office as a TI. Throughout Germany, Austria, and Switzerland, you'll find TIs are usually well-organized with English-speaking staff.

As national budgets tighten, many TIs have been privatized. This means they become sales agents for big tours and hotels and their "information" becomes unavoidably colored. While TIs are eager to book you a room, use their room-finding service only as a last resort. TIs can as easily book you a bad room as a good one—they are unable to give hard opinions on the relative value of one place over another. The accommodations stakes are too high to go potluck through the TI. And with the listings in this book, there's no need to do so.

Tourist Offices, U.S. Addresses

Each country's national tourist office in the United States is a wealth of information. Before your trip, get their free general information packet and request any specific information you may want (such as regional and city maps and schedules of upcoming festivals).

German National Tourist Office: 122 E. 42nd St., 52nd floor, New York, NY 10168, tel. 212/661-7200, fax 212/661-7174 Web site: www.germany-tourism.de. Maps, Rhine schedules, events; very helpful.

Austrian National Tourist Office: Box 1142, New York, NY 10108, tel. 212/944-6880, fax 212/730-4568, Web site: www.anto.com. Ask for their "Vacation Kit" map. Fine hikes and Vienna material.

Swiss National Tourist Offices: 608 5th Ave., New York, NY 10020, tel. 212/757-5944, fax 212/262-6116, Web site: www.switzerlandtourism.com; 222 N. Sepulveda Blvd. #1570, El Segundo, CA 90245, tel. 310/640-8900, fax 310/335-0131. Great maps, rail and hiking material.

Czech Tourist Authority: 1109 Madison Ave., New York, NY 10028, tel. 212/288-0830, fax 212/288-0971, Web site: www.czech.cz/new_york. To get a weighty information package (1–2 lbs, no advertising), send a check for $3 to cover postage and specify places of interest.

Recommended Guidebooks

You may want some supplemental information if you'll be traveling beyond my recommended destinations. When you consider the improvements they'll make in your $3,000 vacation, $25 or $35 for extra maps and books is money well spent. Especially for several people traveling by car, the weight and expense are negligible.

Students, backpackers, and those interested in the night scene should consider either the hip Rough Guides (British researchers, more insightful but not updated annually) or the Let's Go guides (by Harvard students, better hotel listings, updated annually). Lonely Planet's Germany, Austria, and Switzerland guides are well-researched and mature. The popular, skinny, green Michelin Guides to Germany, Austria, and Switzerland are excellent, especially if you're driving. They're known for their city and sightseeing maps, dry but concise and helpful information on all major sights, and good cultural and historical background. English editions are sold locally at gas stations and tourist shops.

Rick Steves' Books and Videos

Rick Steves' Europe Through the Back Door 1999 (John Muir Publications) gives you budget travel tips on minimizing jet lag, packing light, planning your itinerary, traveling by car or train, finding budget beds without reservations, changing money, avoiding rip-offs, outsmarting thieves, hurdling the language barrier, staying healthy, taking great photographs, using your bidet, and much more. The book also includes chapters on my 37 favorite "Back Doors."

Rick Steves' Country Guides are a series of eight guide-books—including this book—covering Europe, Britain/Ireland, France/Belgium/Netherlands, Italy, Spain/Portugal, Scandinavia, and Russia/Baltics. All but the last two are updated annually and come out each January.

My new **City Guides** cover Paris and London. With the sleek Eurostar train, London is now just three hours from Paris. Consider combining the two cities (and books) for a great visit.

Europe 101: History and Art for the Traveler (cowritten with Gene Openshaw, John Muir Publications, 1996) gives you the story of Europe's people, history, and art. Written for smart people who were sleeping in their history and art classes before they knew they were going to Europe, *101* really helps Europe's sights come alive.

Rick Steves' Mona Winks (also cowritten with Gene Openshaw, John Muir Publications, 1998) gives you fun, easy-to-follow, self-guided tours of Europe's top 20 museums (in London, Paris, Madrid, Amsterdam, Venice, Florence, and Rome).

Rick Steves' German Phrase Book (John Muir Publications, 1999) is a fun, practical tool for independent budget travelers. With everything from beer-hall vocabulary to sample telephone conversations (for making hotel reservations) to a menu decoder, this book will undoubtedly come in handy.

My television series, *Travels in Europe with Rick Steves*, includes 11 half-hour shows on Germany, Austria, and Switzer-land—including two shows on the Swiss and Austrian Alps and Prague. A new series of 13 shows is planned for 2000. All 52 of the earlier shows are run throughout the United States on public tele-vision stations and on the Travel Channel. The shows are also available as information-packed videotapes, along with my two-hour slideshow lecture on Germany, Austria, and Switzerland (call us at 425/771-8303 for our free newsletter/catalog).

Rick Steves' Postcards from Europe (John Muir, 1999), my new autobiographical book, packs 25 years of travel anecdotes and insights into the ultimate 3,000-mile European adventure. Through my guidebooks, I share my favorite European discoveries with you. *Postcards* introduces you to my favorite European friends.

Maps

The maps in this book, drawn by Dave Hoerlein, are concise and simple. Dave, who is well-traveled in Germany, Austria, and Switzerland, has designed the maps to help you locate recom-mended places and get to the tourist offices, where you can pick up a more in-depth map (usually free) of the city or region. Euro-pean bookstores, especially in tourist areas, have good selections of maps. For drivers, I'd recommend a 1:200,000- or 1:300,000-scale map for each country. Train travelers can usually manage fine with the freebies they get with their train pass and from the local tourist offices.

Transportation

By Car or Train?

The train is best for single travelers, those who'll be spending more time in big cities, and those who don't want to drive in Europe. While a car gives you the ultimate in mobility and freedom, enables you to search for hotels more easily, and carries your bags for you, the train zips you effortlessly from city to city, usually dropping you in the center and near the tourist office. Cars are great in the countryside but a worthless headache in places like Munich, Bern, and Vienna.

Trains

The trains are punctual and cover cities well, but frustrating schedules make a few out-of-the-way recommendations (such as the concentration camp at Mauthausen) not worth the time and trouble for the less determined. For timetables, visit http://bahn .hafas.de/english.html.

If you're doing a whirlwind trip of all of my recommended destinations, a three-week first-class Eurailpass is worthwhile—especially for a single traveler (available from your travel agent or Europe Through the Back Door—call 425/771-8303 for our free newsletter/catalog). You can save about $60 by managing with the "any 10 days out of two months" Eurail Flexipass, but it will require some streamlining. The "Europass," (e.g., five days in two months) which covers Germany and Switzerland with an Austria add-on, is especially good when two travel together (since each person gets a 15 percent discount). Each country has its own individual train passes. Patchworking several second-class country passes together (for example, a 10-day-in-a-month German railpass, a three-days-in-15 Austrian pass, and an eight-day Swiss pass) may be cheaper than a single first-class Eurail-pass for the total traveling time, but the $50 savings isn't substantial and you'll be going second class.

Eurailers should know what extras are included with their pass—such as any German buses marked "Bahn" (run by the train company); city S-Bahn systems; boats on the Rhine, Mosel, and Danube Rivers and Swiss lakes; and a hefty discount on the Romantic Road bus tour. Those traveling in the Swiss Alps can use their Eurailpass to get discounts (but not free passage) on some private trains and lifts in the mountains. If you want to focus on Switzerland (where many scenic rides are not covered by rail-

Major Train Lines

passes), consider the various Alps passes sold at Swiss train stations. The Swiss Family Card allows children under 16 to travel free with their parents (20 SF at Swiss stations or free with Swiss train passes when requested with purchase in the United States).

If you decide to buy train tickets as you go, look into local specials. For instance, Germany offers a wild "Schönes Wochenende" ticket for 35 DM giving any group of up to five people unlimited travel on non-express trains all day Saturday and Sunday. Their "Guten-Abend" pass gives you unlimited travel on non-express trains any evening from 19:00 until 02:00 for 60 DM. Seniors (women over 60, men over 65) and youths (under 26) can enjoy substantial discounts. While Eurailers (over 26) automatically travel first class, those buying individual tickets should remember that second-class tickets provide the same transportation for 33 percent less.

Cost of Public Transportation

1999 GERMAN RAILPASS

	1st cl	1st twin	2nd cl	2nd twin
4 days in a month	$252	$126	$174	$87
Add-on days (max 10)	$32	$16	$22	$11

"Twin" pass is for companion of anyone who buys a full price pass in same class (must travel together). Cheaper youth passes available.* Covers Rhine and Mosel boats, 75% off Romantic Road bus ride.

Switzerland & Germany (Austria below):

All maps show approximate point-to-point one-way 2nd-class rail fares in $US.

1999 EUROPASSES

All Europasses include France, Germany, Italy, Spain and Switzerland.

	1st cl	1st cl Saver	2nd Youth*
5 days in 2 months	$348	$296	$233
6 days in 2 months	$368	$314	$253
8 days in 2 months	$448	$382	$313
10 days in 2 month	$528	$450	$363
15 days in 2 months	$728	$620	$513
With one add-on zone	+$60	+$52	+$45
With two add-on zones	+$100	+$86	+$78

Saverpass prices are per person for 2 or more traveling together.

Europass add-on zones
Choose from: (max 2)
◆ Austria/Hungary
◆ Belgium/Netherlands/ Luxembourg
◆ Portugal
◆ Greece

1999 SWISS PASS AND SWISS FLEXIPASS

	1st cl	1st cl twin	2nd cl	2nd cl twin
4 consec. days	$264	$158	$188	$112
8 consec. days	316	190	238	142
15 consec. days	368	220	288	172
21 consec. days	403	241	320	192
1 month	508	304	400	240
3 days in 15 flexi	264	158	176	106
Add'l rail days (6 max)	30	18	24	14

"Twin" pass is for companion of anyone who buys a full price pass in same class (must travel together). Covers all trains, boats and buses with 25% off on high mountain rides. Kids under 16 free with parent.

1999 AUSTRIAN FLEXIPASS

Austria

	1st cl	2nd cl
Any 3 days out of 15 days	$151	$102
Add-on days (max 5):	22	16

Youth = under 26. Kids 4-11 (4-12 in Austria): half adult fare. Under 4: free.

Standard European Road Signs

Train schedules are generally slick and speedy with synchronized connections. Major German stations now have handy Service Points offering general help to travelers.

Hundreds of local train stations rent bikes for about $5 a day (discounted for train-pass holders, ask for a *Fahrrad am Bahnhof* brochure at any station).

Car Rental

It's cheapest to rent a car through your travel agent well before departure (rather than in Europe). You'll want a weekly rate with unlimited mileage. For three weeks or longer, leasing is cheaper (because it saves you money on taxes and insurance). Comparison shop through your agent. DER, a German company, often has the best rates (tel. 800/782-2424).

Expect to pay about $700 for a small economy car for three weeks with unlimited mileage and CDW (collision damage waiver) insurance. I normally rent a small, inexpensive model (e.g., Ford Fiesta). For a bigger, roomier, and more powerful inexpensive car, move up to the Ford 1.3-liter Escort or VW Polo category. If you drop your car off early or keep it longer, you'll be credited or charged at a fair, prorated price.

For peace of mind, I splurge for the CDW insurance (about $14 a day). A few "gold" credit cards cover CDW; quiz your credit-card company on the worst-case scenario. Travel Guard sells CDW insurance for $6 a day (tel. 800/826-1300). With the luxury of CDW, you'll enjoy the Autobahn knowing you can bring back the car in shambles and just say, "S-s-s-sorry."

Driving

Every long drive between my recommended destinations is via the Autobahn (super-freeway), and nearly every scenic backcountry drive is paved and comfortable.

Drivers over 21 need only their U.S. driver's license. For Austria, you'll need a sticker for your rental car (buy at the border)—70 AS for one week or 150 AS for up to two months. To use the Autobahn in Switzerland, you'll pay a one-time 40-SF fee (at the border, a gas station, or a rental agency).

Learn the universal road signs (explained in charts in most

road atlases and at service stations). Seat belts are required, and two beers under those belts is enough to land you in jail.

Use good local maps and study them before each drive. Learn which exits you need to look out for, which major cities you'll travel toward, where the ruined castles lurk, and so on. For parking, you can pick up the "cardboard clock" (*Parkscheibe*, available free at gas stations, police stations, and *Tabak* shops) and display your arrival time on the dashboard so parking attendants can see you've been there less than the posted maximum stay (blue lines indicate 90-minute zones on Austrian streets).

In Europe the shortest distance between any two points is the Autobahn. Signs directing you to the Autobahn are green in Austria and Switzerland, blue in Germany. To understand the complex but super-efficient Autobahn (no speed limit, toll-free), pick up the *Autobahn Service* booklet at any Autobahn rest stop (free, lists all stops, services, road symbols, and more). Learn the signs: *Dreieck* means a "Y" in the road; *Autobahnkreuz* is an intersection. Exits are spaced about every 20 miles, and often have a gas station, restaurant, a mini-market, and sometimes a tourist information desk. *Bleifrei* means unleaded. Exits and intersections refer to the next major or the nearest small town. Study the map and anticipate which town names to look out for. Know what you're looking for—miss it and you're long Autobahn-gone. When navigating, you'll see *nord, süd, ost, west,* or *mitte.* Don't cruise in the passing lane; stay right.

Get used to metric. A liter is about a quart, four to a gallon; a kilometer is six-tenths of a mile. Convert kilometers to miles by cutting them in half and adding back 10 percent of the original (120 km: 60 + 12 = 72 miles).

Telephones and Mail

Smart travelers learn the phone system and use it daily to reserve or reconfirm rooms, get tourist information, or phone home. Many European phone booths take cards and not coins. Each country sells phone cards good for use only in that country's phones. (For example, a Swiss phone card works for local and international calls from Switzerland, but is worthless in Austria.) Buy a phone card from post offices, newsstands, or tobacco shops. Insert the card into the phone, make your call, and the value is deducted from your card. If you use coins, have a bunch handy. Or look for a metered phone ("talk now, pay later") in the bigger post offices. Avoid using hotel room phones for anything other than local calls and toll-free "U.S.A. Direct" calling-card calls (see below).

Dialing Direct: You'll save money by dialing direct. You just need to learn to break the codes. When calling long-distance within a country, first dial the area code (which starts with zero), then dial the local number. For example, Munich's area code is 089, and the number of my favorite Munich hotel is 264-043. To call it from

Frankfurt, dial 089/264-043. When dialing internationally, dial the international access code (of the country you're calling from), the country code (of the country you're calling to), the area code (without the initial zero), and the local number. To call the Munich hotel from the United States, dial 011 (the U.S. international access code), 49 (Germany's country code), 89 (Munich's area code without the zero), then 264-043. To call my office from Munich, I dial 00 (Germany's international access code), 1 (U.S.A.'s country code), 425 (Edmonds' area code), and 771-8303. European time is six/nine hours ahead of the East/West Coast of the United States. For a listing of international access codes and country codes, see the Appendix. Don't be surprised if local phone numbers have differing numbers of digits within the same city or even the same hotel (e.g., a hotel can have a 6-digit phone number and an 8-digit fax number).

U.S.A. Direct Services: Calling home from Europe is easy from any phone booth with a local phone card. New inexpensive phone booth rates of less than a dollar a minute make the previously economical U.S.A. Direct Services (AT&T, MCI, or Sprint) a relatively bad value.

Still many are comforted by their American phone card and hearing that Yankee operator. Each card company has a toll-free number in each European country that puts you in touch with an English-speaking operator. The operator asks for your card number and the number you want to call, puts you through, and bills your home phone number for the call (at the rate of $3 for the first minute and $1.30 per additional minute, plus a $2.50 service charge). Calling an answering machine is an expensive mistake ($5.50). First use a small-value coin or a German, Austrian, or Swiss phone card to call home for five seconds—long enough to make sure an answering machine is off so you can call back using your U.S.A. Direct number. For a list of AT&T, MCI, and Sprint operators, see the Appendix. Avoid using U.S.A. Direct for calls between European countries; it's far cheaper to call direct using coins or a European phone card.

Mail: To arrange for mail delivery, reserve a few hotels along your route in advance and give their addresses to friends, or use American Express Company's mail services (available to anyone who has at least one Amex traveler's check). Allow 10 days for a letter to arrive. Phoning is so easy that I've dispensed with mail stops altogether.

Sleeping
In the interest of smart use of your time, I favor hotels and restaurants handy to your sightseeing activities. Rather than list hotels scattered throughout a city, I describe two or three favorite neighborhoods and recommend the best accommodations values in each, from $10 bunks to $150 doubles.

Sleep Code

To save space while giving more specific information for people with special concerns, I've described my recommended
hotels with a standard code. Prices listed are per room, not per
person. When a range of prices is listed for a room, the price
fluctuates with room size or season.

  S = Single room or price for one person using a double.

  D = Double or twin room. Double beds are usually two
twins pushed together—comfortable for non-roman-
tic couples.

  T = Three-person room (often a double bed with a single
bed moved in).

  Q = Four-adult room (an extra child's bed is usually
cheaper).

  b = Private bathroom with toilet and shower or tub.

  t = Private toilet only (the shower is down the hall).

  s = Private shower or tub only (the toilet is down the
hall).

  CC = Accepts credit cards (**V** = Visa, **M** = MasterCard,
A = American Express). If no CC, assume they accept
only cash.

  SE = Speaks English. This code is used only when it seems
predictable that you'll encounter English-speaking
staff.

  NSE = Does not speak English. Used only when it's unlikely
you'll encounter English-speaking staff.

  According to this code, a couple staying at a "Db-120 DM,
CC:V, SE" hotel would pay 120 deutsche Marks (around $80)
for a double room with a private bathroom. The hotel accepts
Visa or German cash, and the staff speaks English.

While accommodations in Germany, Austria, and Switzerland
are fairly expensive, they are normally very comfortable and come
with breakfast. Plan on spending $70 to $120 per hotel double in big
cities, and $40 to $70 in towns and in private homes. Swiss beds are
20 percent more expensive than those in Austria and Germany.

A triple is much cheaper than a double and a single. While
hotel singles are most expensive, private accommodations
(*Zimmer*) have a flat per-person rate. Hostels and dorms always
charge per person. Especially in private homes, where the boss
changes the sheets, people staying several nights are most desir-
able. One-night stays are sometimes charged extra.

In recommending hotels, I favor small, family-run places that
are central, inexpensive, quiet, clean, safe, friendly, English-
speaking, and not listed in other guidebooks. I also like local

character and simple facilities that don't cater to American "needs." Obviously, a place meeting every criteria is rare, and all of my recommendations fall short of perfection—sometimes miserably. But I've listed the best values for each price category, given the above criteria. The best values are family-run places with showers down the hall and no elevator.

Any room without a bathroom has access to a bathroom in the corridor (free unless otherwise noted). Except for pensions in Prague, all rooms have a sink. For environmental reasons, towels are often replaced in hotels only when you leave them on the floor. In cheaper places they aren't replaced at all, so hang them up to dry and reuse.

Unless I note otherwise, the cost of a room includes a continental breakfast. The price is usually posted in the room. Before accepting, confirm your understanding of the complete price. The only tip the hotels I've listed would like is a friendly, easygoing guest. The accommodations prices listed in this book should be good through 1999. I appreciate feedback on your hotel experiences.

Making Reservations

It's possible to travel at any time of year without reservations, but given the high stakes, erratic accommodations values, and the quality of the gems I've found for this book, I'd highly recommend calling ahead for rooms a day or two in advance as you travel. If tourist crowds are down, you might make a habit of calling between 9:00 and 10:00 on the day you plan to arrive, when the hotel knows who'll be checking out and just which rooms will be available. I've taken great pains to list telephone numbers with long distance instructions (see the Appendix). Use the telephone and the convenient telephone cards. Most hotels listed are accustomed to English-only speakers. A hotel receptionist will trust you and hold a room until 17:00 (5:00 p.m.) without a deposit, though some will ask for a credit-card number. Honor (or cancel by phone) your reservations. Long distance is cheap and easy from public phone booths. Don't let these people down—I promised you'd call and cancel if for some reason you can't show up. Don't needlessly confirm rooms through the tourist offices; they'll take a commission.

If you know exactly which dates you need and really want a particular place, reserve a room well before you leave home. To reserve from home, call, fax, or e-mail the hotel. Phone and fax costs are reasonable, and simple English is usually fine. To fax, use the form in the Appendix. If you're writing, add the zip code and confirm the need and method for a deposit. A two-night stay in August would be "two nights, 16/8/99 to 18/8/99"—European hotel jargon uses your day of departure. You'll often receive a letter back requesting one night's deposit. A credit-card number and expiration date will usually be accepted as a deposit, though you may need to send a signed traveler's check or a bank draft in the local currency. If your credit card is the deposit, you can pay with your card or cash when you arrive; if you don't show up, you'll be billed for one night. Reconfirm your reservations a day in advance for safety.

Camping and Hosteling

Campers can manage with the Let's Go listings and help from the local TI (ask for a regional camping guide). Your hometown travel bookstore also has guidebooks on camping in Europe. You'll find campgrounds just about wherever you need them. Look for "Campingplatz" signs. You'll meet lots of Europeans—camping is a popular, middle-class–family way to go. Campgrounds are cheap ($4–6 per person), friendly, safe, more convenient than rustic, and rarely full.

Hostelers can take advantage of the wonderful network of hostels. Follow signs marked "Jugendherberge," with triangles or the "tree next to a house" logo. Generally, those without a membership card ($25 per year, sold at hostels in most U.S. cities and through ETBD) are admitted for a $5 extra charge.

Hostels are open to members of all ages (except in Bavaria, where a maximum age of 26 is strictly enforced). They usually cost $10 to $20 per night (cheaper for those under 27, plus $4 sheet rental if you don't have your own) and serve good, cheap meals and/or provide kitchen facilities. If you plan to hostel, bring your own sheet. While many have couples' or family rooms available upon request for a little extra money, plan on beds in segregated dorms—four to 20 per room. Hostels can be idyllic and peaceful, or school groups can raise the rafters. School groups are most common on summer weekends and on school-year weekdays. I like small hostels best. While many hostels may say over the telephone that they're full, most hold a few beds for people who drop in, or they can direct you to budget accommodations nearby.

Eating

Germanic cuisine is heavy and hearty. While it's tasty, it can get monotonous if you fall into the schnitzel or wurst-and-potatoes rut. Be adventurous. My German phrase book has a handy menu decoder that works well for most travelers, but galloping gluttons will prefer the meatier *Marling German Menu Master*. Each region has its specialties, which, while not cheap, are often good values.

There are many kinds of restaurants. Hotels often serve fine food. A *Gaststätte* is a simple, less-expensive restaurant. Ethnic restaurants provide a welcome break from Germanic fare. Foreign cuisine is either the legacy of a crumbled empire (Hungarian and Bohemian—from which Austria gets its goulash and dumplings) or a new arrival to feed the many hungry-but-poor guest workers.

Italian, Turkish, and Greek food are good values. The cheapest meals are found in department-store cafeterias, *Schnell-Imbiss* (fast-food) stands, university cafeterias (*Mensas*), and hostels. For a quick, cheap bite, have a deli make you a *Wurstsemmel*, a meat sandwich.

Most restaurants tack a menu onto their door for browsers and have an English menu inside. Only a rude waiter will rush you. Good service is relaxed (slow to an American). When you want the bill, ask, *"Die Rechnung, bitte."* (In Germany and Austria, you might be charged for bread you've eaten from the basket on the table.) Service is included, although it's common to round the bill up after a good meal. To wish others "Happy eating!" offer a cheery *"Guten Appetit!"*

For most visitors, the rich pastries, wine, and beer provide the fondest memories of Germanic cuisine. The wine (85 percent white) is particularly good from the Mosel, Rhine, Danube, east-ern Austria, and southwestern Switzerland areas. Order wine by the *Viertel* (quarter-liter) or *Achtel* (eighth-liter). You can say, *"Ein Viertel Weisswein* (white wine), *bitte* (please)." Order it *süss* (sweet), *halbe trocken* (medium), or *trocken* (dry). *Rotwein* is red wine and *Sekt* is German champagne.

The Germans enjoy a tremendous variety of great beer. The average German, who drinks 40 gallons of beer a year, knows that *dunkles* is dark, *helles* is light, *Flaschenbier* is bottled, and *vom Fass* is on tap. *Pils* is barley-based, *Weize* is wheat-based, and *Malzbier* is the malt beer that children learn on. *Radler* is half beer and half lemonade. When you order beer, ask for *ein Halbe* for a half-liter (not always available) or *eine Mass* for a whole liter (about a quart). Menus list drink size by the tenth of a liter, or deciliter.

Tipping is generally not expected. But for good service, it's customary to round the bill up to the next silver coin. Rather than leaving coins on the table, Germans pay with paper, saying how much they'd like the bill to be (e.g., for a 9.20-DM meal, give a 20-DM bill and say *"Zehn Mark"*—10 marks).

Send Me a Postcard, Drop Me a Line

If you enjoy a successful trip with the help of this book and would like to share your discoveries, please fill out and send the survey at the end of this book to me at Europe Through the Back Door, Box 2009, Edmonds, Washington 98020. I personally read and value all feedback. Thanks in advance—it helps a lot.

For our latest information, check our Web site: www .ricksteves.com. My e-mail address is rick@ricksteves.com. Anyone can request a free issue of our *Back Door* quarterly newsletter.

Judging from all the happy postcards I receive, it's safe to assume you're on your way to a great vacation—independent, inexpensive, and with the finesse of an experienced traveler.

Thanks, and *gute Reise!*

BACK DOOR TRAVEL PHILOSOPHY
As Taught in *Rick Steves' Europe Through the Back Door*

Travel is intensified living—maximum thrills per minute and one of the last great sources of legal adventure. Travel is freedom. It's recess, and we need it.

Experiencing the real Europe requires catching it by surprise, going casual . . . "Through the Back Door."

Affording travel is a matter of priorities. (Make do with the old car.) You can travel—simply, safely, and comfortably—anywhere in Europe for $60 a day plus transportation costs. In many ways, spending more money only builds a thicker wall between you and what you came to see. Europe is a cultural carnival and, time after time, you'll find that its best acts are free and the best seats are the cheap ones.

A tight budget forces you to travel close to the ground, meeting and communicating with the people, not relying on service with a purchased smile. Never sacrifice sleep, nutrition, safety, or cleanliness in the name of budget. Simply enjoy the local-style alternatives to expensive hotels and restaurants.

Extroverts have more fun. If your trip is low on magic moments, kick yourself and make things happen. If you don't enjoy a place, maybe you don't know enough about it. Seek the truth. Recognize tourist traps. Give a culture the benefit of your open mind. See things as different but not better or worse. Any culture has much to share.

Of course, travel, like the world, is a series of hills and valleys. Be fanatically positive and militantly optimistic. If something's not to your liking, change your liking. Travel is addicting. It can make you a happier American, as well as a citizen of the world. Our Earth is home to nearly 6 billion equally important people. It's humbling to travel and find that people don't envy Americans. They like us, but with all due respect, they wouldn't trade passports.

Globetrotting destroys ethnocentricity. It helps you understand and appreciate different cultures. Travel changes people. It broadens perspectives and teaches new ways to measure quality of life. Many travelers toss aside their hometown blinders. Their prized souvenirs are the strands of different cultures they decide to knit into their own character. The world is a cultural yarn shop. And Back Door Travelers are weaving the ultimate tapestry. Come on, join in!

GERMANY
(DEUTSCHLAND)

- Germany is 136,000 square miles (like Montana).
- Population is 77 million (about 650 per square mile, declining slowly).
- The West was 95,000 square miles (like Wyoming), with 61 million people. The East was 41,000 square miles (like Virginia), with 16 million people.
- 1 deutsche Mark (DM) = 60 cents, and 1.7 DM = $1.

Deutschland is energetic, efficient, and organized, and Europe's muscleman—economically and wherever people are lining up. Its bustling cities hold 85 percent of its people, and average earnings are among the highest on earth. Ninety-seven percent of the workers get one-month paid vacations, and during the other 11 months, they create a gross national product that's about one-third of the United States' and growing. Germany has risen from the ashes of World War II to become the world's fifth-biggest industrial power, ranking fourth in steel output and nuclear power and third in automobile production. Germany shines culturally, beating out all but two countries in production of books, Nobel laureates, and professors.

While its East-West division lasted about 40 years, historically Germany has been divided between north and the south. While northern Germany was barbarian, is Protestant, and assaults life aggressively, southern Germany was Roman, is Catholic, and enjoys a more relaxed tempo of life. The American image of Germany is beer-and-pretzel Bavaria (probably because that was "our" sector after the war). This historic north-south division is less pronounced these days as Germany becomes a more mobile society. The big chore facing Germany today is integrating the wilted economy of what was East Germany into the powerhouse economy of the West. This monumental task has given the West higher taxes (and second thoughts).

Germany's tourist route today—Rhine, Romantic Road, Bavaria—was yesterday's trade route, connecting its most prosperous medieval cities. Germany as a nation is just 120 years old. In 1850 there were 35 independent countries in what is now Germany. In medieval times there were more than 300, each with its own weights, measures, coinage, king, and lotto.

Germans eat lunch and dinner about when we do. Order house specials whenever possible. Pork, fish, and venison are good, and don't miss the bratwurst and sauerkraut. Potatoes are the standard vegetable. The bread and pretzels in the basket on your table often cost extra. Great beers and white wines abound. Go with whatever beer is on tap. Service and tips are included in your restaurant bills. Gummi Bears are local gumdrops with a cult following (beware of imitations—you must see the word "Gummi"), and Nutella is a chocolate-hazelnut spread that may change your life.

MUNICH
(MÜNCHEN)

Munich, Germany's most livable and "yuppie" city, is also one of its most historic, artistic, and entertaining. It's big and growing, with a population of more than 1.4 million. Just a little more than a century ago, it was the capital of an independent Bavaria. Its imperial palaces, jewels, and grand boulevards constantly remind visitors that this was once a political and cultural power-house. And its recently-bombed-out feeling reminds us that 75 years ago it provided a springboard for Nazism, and 55 years ago it lost a war.

Orient yourself in Munich's old center with its colorful pedes-trian mall. Immerse yourself in Munich's art and history—crown jewels, Baroque theater, Wittelsbach palaces, great paintings, and beautiful parks. Munich evenings are best spent in frothy beer halls, with their oompah bunny-hopping and belching Bavarian atmos-phere. Pry big pretzels from no-nonsense, buxom beer maids.

Planning Your Time

Munich is worth two days, including a half-day side trip to Dachau. If necessary, its essence can be captured in a day (walk the center, tour a palace and a museum, and enjoy a beer-filled evening). Those without a car and in a hurry can do the castles of Ludwig as a day trip from Munich by tour. Even Salzburg can be a handy day trip from Munich.

Orientation (tel. code: 089)

The tourist's Munich is circled by a ring road (which was the town wall) marked by four old gates: Karlstor (near the train station, known as the *Hauptbahnhof*), Sendlinger Tor, Isartor (near the river), and Odeonsplatz (near the palace). Marienplatz is the city center. A great pedestrian-only street cuts this circle in half, running nearly from Karlstor and the train station through Marienplatz to Isartor. Orient yourself along this east-west axis. Most sights are within a few blocks of this people-filled walk. Ninety percent of the sights and hotels I recommend are within a 20-minute walk of Marienplatz and each other.

Tourist Information

Munich has two helpful TIs: at the train station (Monday–Saturday 9:00–20:00, Sunday 10:00–18:00, Bahnhofplatz 2, tel. 089/233-30-257) and on Marienplatz (Monday–Friday 10:00–20:00, Saturday 10:00–16:00, closed Sunday, tel. 089/233-30-272, Web site: www.muenchen-tourist.de). Have a list of questions ready, confirm sightseeing plans, and pick up brochures. The excellent Munich city map (use the close-up of downtown, with all bus lines) is one of the handiest in Europe. Consider the *Monatsprogramm* (2.50 DM, a German-language list of sights and events calendar), *Hits for Kids* (1 DM), and the free twice-monthly magazine *In München* (lists in German all the movies and entertainment in town, available at TI or any big cinema till supply runs out). The TI can refer you to hotels for a 10 to 15 percent fee, but you'll get a better value with my recommended hotels—contact them directly. If the line at the TI is bad, go to EurAide (below). The only essential item is the TI's great city map (also available at EurAide and many hotels).

   EurAide: The industrious, eager-to-help EurAide office in the train station is a wonderful aid for Eurailers and budget travelers (daily in summer 7:45–12:00, 13:00–18:00; in winter it closes at 16:00 on weekdays, 12:00 on Saturday, and all day Sunday; Room 3 at track 11; tel. 089/593-889, fax 089/550-3965, Web site: www.cube.net/kmu/euraide.html, e-mail: euraide@compuserve.com). Alan Wissenberg and his staff know your train travel and accommodations questions and have answers in clear American English. The German rail company pays them to help you design your best train travels. They make reservations and sell train tickets, couchettes, and sleepers. They can find you a room for a 7-DM fee, and they offer the city map and a free newsletter. They sell a "Prague Excursion" train pass, convenient for Prague-bound Eurailers—good for train travel from any Czech border station to Prague and back to any border station within seven days (1st class-90 DM, 2nd class-60 DM, youth 2nd-40 DM; a bit cheaper through their U.S. office: 941/480-1555, fax 941/480-1522). Every Wednesday in June and July, EurAide provides an excellent "Two Castle" tour of Neuschwanstein and Linderhof that includes Wieskirche (frustrating without a car, see below). EurAide is my stop for train and couchette reservations.

Arrival in Munich

By Train: Munich's train station is a sight in itself—one of those places that can turn an accountant into a vagabond. For a quick orientation in the station, use the big wall maps showing the train station, Munich, and Bavaria (through the center doorway as you leave the tracks on the left). For a quick rest stop, the Burger King upstairs has toilets as pleasant and accessible as its hamburgers. A classier and more peaceful hangout is the vast, generally empty, old restaurant opposite track 14. Next door, the post office (which has handy metered phones) is open daily. Sussmann's Internationale Presse (across from track 24) is great for English-language books, papers, and magazines, including *Munich Found* (informative English-speaking residents' monthly, 4 DM). You'll also find two TIs (the city TI and EurAide, see above). The station is connected by U-Bahn, S-Bahn, and buses to the rest of the city (though many hotels listed in this book are within walking distance of the station).

By Plane: There are two good ways to connect downtown Munich and its airport. Either take an easy 40-minute ride on S-8 (from Marienplatz, 14 DM or free with train pass), or hop the Lufthansa airport bus to (or from) the train station (15 DM, 3/hrly, 45 min, buy tickets on bus or from EurAide).

Getting Around Munich

Much of Munich is walkable. To reach sights away from the city center, use the fine tram, bus, and subway systems. Taxis are expensive and generally unnecessary (except perhaps to avoid the time-comsuming trip to Nymphenburg).

By Public Transit: Subways are called U- or S-Bahns. Subway lines are numbered (e.g., S-3 or U-5). Eurailpasses are good on the S-Bahn (actually an underground-while-in-the-city commuter railway). Regular tickets cost 3.50 DM and are good for two hours of changes in one direction. For the shortest rides (one or two stops), get the cheapest 1.80-DM ticket (*Kurzstrecke*). The 8.50-DM all-day pass is a great deal (valid until 6:00 the next morning). The Partner Daily Ticket (for 12.50 DM) is good all day for up to two adults, three kids, and a dog. Tickets are available from easy-to-use ticket machines (which take bills and coins), subway booths, and TIs. The entire system (bus/tram/subway) works on the same tickets. You must punch your own ticket before boarding (stamping a date and time on it). Plainclothes ticket-checkers enforce this "honor system," rewarding freeloaders with stiff 60-DM fines.

Important: All S-Bahn lines connect the Hauptbahnhof (main station) with Marienplatz (main square). At either the station or Marienplatz, follow signs to the S-Bahn (U is not for you) and concern yourself only with the direction (*Richtung*: Hauptbahnhof/Pasing or Ostbahnhof/Marienplatz).

By Bike: Munich—level and compact, with plenty of bike paths—feels good on two wheels. Bikes can be rented quickly and easily at the train station at Radius Bikes (daily 10:00–18:00 May–mid-October, near track 30, tel. 089/596-113). The owner, Englishman Patrick Holder, rents three-speed bikes (5 DM/ hour, 25 DM/day, 30 DM/24 hours, 45 DM/48 hours, mountain bikes 20 percent more; credit-card imprint, 100 DM, or passport for a deposit). Patrick organizes Munich and Dachau tours (see below) and dispenses all the necessary tourist information (city map, bike routes), including a do-it-yourself bike tour booklet (5 DM).

Helpful Hints

Most Munich sights (including Dachau) are closed on Monday. If you're in Munich on Monday, here are some suggestions: visit the Deutsches Museum, BMW museum, or churches; take a walking tour or bus tour; climb high for city views (below); stroll the pedestrian streets; have lunch at the Viktualien Markt (see Eating, below); rent a bike for a spin through Englischer Garten; or day-trip to Salzburg or Ludwig's castles.

Helpful phone numbers: pharmacy (at train station, tel. 089/594-119), train information (tel. 089/19419), U.S. consulate (Königinstrasse 5, tel. 089/28880), American Express Company (tel. 089/290-900), taxi (tel. 089/21610).

There's plenty of online access in Munich. In the station consider the Times Square OnLine Bistro (9 DM/30 min).

Sights—Central Munich

▲▲**Marienplatz and the Pedestrian Zone**—Riding the escalator out of the subway into sunlit Marienplatz (Mary's Square) gives you a fine first look at the glory of Munich: great buildings bombed flat and rebuilt, the ornate facades of the new and old city halls (the Neues Rathaus, built in neo-Gothic style from 1867 to 1910—with the *Glockenspiel*, and the grey, pointy Altes Rathaus), outdoor cafés, and people bustling and lingering like the birds and breeze they share this square with. The not-very-old *Glockenspiel* "jousts" on Marienplatz daily through the tourist season at 11:00, 12:00, and 17:00.

From here the pedestrian mall (Kaufingerstrasse and Neuhauserstrasse) leads you through a great shopping area, past carnivals of street entertainers and good old-fashioned slicers and dicers, the twin-towering Frauenkirche (built in 1470, rebuilt after World War II), and several fountains, to Karlstor and the train station. One of Europe's first pedestrian zones, this enraged shopkeepers when it was built in 1972. Today it is "Munich's living room." Nine thousand shoppers pass through it each hour . . . and the shopkeepers are very happy. Imagine this street in hometown U.S.A.

In the pedestrian zone around Marienplatz, there are three

Munich Center

NEUE PINAKOTHEK
ALTE PINAKOTHEK
TO SCHWABING
ENGLISH GARDEN
LENBACH HAUS
GLYPTOTHEK
KÖNIG PLATZ
BRIENNER
OBELISK
ODEONS PLATZ
HAUS DER KUNST
DACHAVER STRASSE
LUISEN STR
BAKER STR
VON DER TANN
LUDWIG STR
STRASSE
TRAIN STATION
THEATINER KIRCHE
HOF GARTEN
MAX - PLATZ
KARLSTOR + PLATZ
FRAUEN KIRCHE
ST. MICHAEL'S
RESIDENZ
SCHATZKAMMER + CUVILLIES THEATER
BAYER STR
RAT-HAUS
HOFBRAU HAUS
BUDGET
LANDWEHR
HOTEL AREA
ASAM KIRCHE
SENDLINGER
OBERAUGER
IM TAL
WIMMER
ISARTOR
TO OKTFEST
PETTENKOFER
SCHULER
SONNEN STR
STADT MUSEUM
FRAUEN STR
ZWEIBRUCKEN STR
GOETHE STRASSE
BLUMEN
SENDLINGER TOR
¼ MILE
VIKTUALIEN MARKT + ST. PETER'S
DEUTSCHES MUSEUM
DCH

HOTELS IN CENTER
❶ BRISTOL   ❸ LINDNER   ★ MARIENPLATZ
❷ MUNCHNER KINDL ❹ SEIBEL ||||| PEDESTRIAN ZONE

noteworthy churches. **St. Michael's Church**, while one of the first great Renaissance buildings north of the Alps, has a brilliantly Baroque interior. You can borrow the tiny English booklet to read in a pew, see the interesting photos of the bombed-out city center near the entry, and go into the crypt to see King Ludwig II's tomb (2 DM, 40 stark royal tombs and one still-loved-by-romantics "mad" king).

The twin onion domes of the 500-year-old **Frauenkirche** (Church of Our Lady) are the symbol of the city. While much of the church was destroyed in World War II, the towers survived. Gloriously rebuilt since, the church is worth a visit. It was built in Gothic style, but money problems meant the domes weren't added until Renaissance times. These domes were inspired by the typical arches of the Venetian Renaissance. And the church domes we think of as "typically Bavarian" were inspired by these.

St. Peter's Church, the oldest in town, overlooks Marienplatz. Built upon the hill where the first monks founded the city in the 12th century, it has a fine interior with photos of the WWII bomb damage near the entrance. It's a long climb to the top of the spire (no elevator), much of it with two-way traffic on a one-way staircase, but the view is dynamite (2.50 DM, Monday–Saturday 9:00–18:00, Sunday 10:00–18:00). Try to be two flights from the top when the bells ring at the top of the hour (and when your friends ask you about your trip, you'll say, "What?").

▲▲**City Views**—Downtown Munich's three best city viewpoints are from the tops of: 1) St. Peter's Church (described above); 2) Frauenkirche—the highest viewpoint at 350 feet (elevator, 4 DM, Monday–Saturday 10:00–17:00, closed Sunday), and 3) the Neues Rathaus (3 DM, elevator from under the Marienplatz glockenspiel, Monday–Friday 9:00–19:00, weekends 10:00–19:00).

▲**Münchner Stadtmuseum**—The Munich city museum has four floors of exhibits: first floor—on life in Munich through the centuries (including World War II) illustrated in paintings, photos, models; second floor—special exhibits (often more interesting than the permanent ones); third floor—historic puppets and carnival gadgets; and fourth floor—a huge collection of musical instruments from around the world (5 DM, 7.50 DM for families, Tuesday–Sunday 10:00–17:00, Wednesday until 20:30, closed Monday, no English descriptions, no crowds, bored and playful guards, three blocks off Marienplatz at St. Jakob's Platz 1, a fine children's playground faces the entry).

▲▲**Alte Pinakothek**—Bavaria's best painting gallery is newly renovated to show off a great collection of European masterpieces (14th–18th centuries, Fra Angelico, Botticelli, da Vinci, Raphael, Dürer, Rubens, Rembrandt, El Greco, and Goya, 7 DM, Tuesday–Sunday 10:00–17:00, closed Monday, U-2 to Königsplatz or tram #27, tel. 089/238-05215).

▲**Neue Pinakothek**—The Alte Pinakothek's hip sister is a twin building across the square showing off paintings from 1800 to 1920: Romantic, Realistic, Impressionism, Jugendstil, Monet, Renoir, van Gogh, Klimt (7 DM, Tuesday–Sunday 10:00–17:00, closed Monday).

▲**Haus der Kunst**—Built by Hitler as a temple of Nazi art, this bold and fascist building now houses modern art, the kind the Führer censored. It's a playful collection—Kandinsky, Picasso, Dalí, and much more from this century (6 DM, Tuesday–Sunday 10:00–17:00, closed Monday, Prinzregentenstrasse 1, at south end of Englischer Garden).

Bayerisches Nationalmuseum—An interesting collection of Riemenschneider carvings, manger scenes, traditional living rooms, and old Bavarian houses (3 DM, Tuesday–Sunday 9:30–17:00, closed Monday, tram #20 or bus #53 or #55 to Prinzregentenstrasse 3).

▲▲▲**Deutsches Museum**—Germany's answer to our Smithsonian Institution, the Deutsches Museum traces the evolution of science and technology. With 10 miles of exhibits—from astronomy to zymurgy—even those on roller skates will need to be selective. Blue dots on the floor mark someone's idea of the top 12 stops, but I had a better time just wandering through well-described rooms of historic bikes, cars (Benz's first car . . . a three-wheeler from the 1880s), trains, airplanes (Hitler's flying bomb from 1944), spaceships (step inside a rocket engine), mining, the harnessing of wind and water power, hydraulics, musical instruments, printing, photography, computers, astronomy, clocks . . . it's the Louvre of science and technology.

Most sections are lovingly described in English. The much-vaunted "high voltage" demonstrations (three per day, 15 minutes, all in German) show the noisy creation of a five-foot bolt of lightning—not that exciting. There's also a state-of-the-art planetarium (German only) and an adjacent IMAX theater (museum entry 10 DM; daily 9:00–17:00; self-serve cafeteria; S-Bahn to Isartor, then walk 300 meters over the river, following signs; tel. 089/217-9369). Save this for a Monday, when virtually all of Munich's museums are closed.

Schwabing—Munich's artsy, bohemian university district, or "Greenwich Village," has been called "not a place but a state of mind." All I experienced was a mental lapse. The bohemians run the boutiques. I think the most colorful thing about Schwabing is the road leading back downtown. U-3 or U-6 will take you to the Münchener-Freiheit Center if you want to wander. Most of the jazz and disco joints are near Occamstrasse. The Haidhausen neighborhood (U-Bahn: Max Weber Platz) is becoming the "new Schwabing."

▲**Englischer Garden**—Munich's "Central Park," the largest on the Continent, was laid out in 1789 by an American. There's a huge beer garden near the Chinese Pagoda. A rewarding respite from the city, it's especially fun on a bike under the summer sun (bike rental at train station). Caution: While a new local law requires sun-worshipers to wear clothes on the tram, this park is sprinkled with nude sunbathers—quite a spectacle to most Americans (they're the ones riding their bikes into the river and trees).

Asam Church—Near the Stadtmuseum, this private church of the Asam brothers is a gooey, drippy masterpiece by Bavaria's top two rococonuts, showing off their popular Baroque-concentrate style. A few blocks away, the small Damenstift Church has a sculptural rendition of the Last Supper so real you feel you're not alone (at intersection of Altheimer Ecke and Damenstiftstrasse, a block south of pedestrian street).

Sights—Residenz
▲**Residenz**—For a long hike through rebuilt corridors of gilded imperial Bavarian grandeur, tour the family palace of the Wittelsbachs, who ruled Bavaria for more than 700 years. With a worthless English guidebook and not a word of English within, it's one of Europe's worst-presented palaces. Think of it as doing laps at the mall, with better art. Follow the "Führungslinie" signs: the first room shows a WWII exhibit. After long, boring halls of porcelain and dishes behind glass, you enter the King's apartments with a little throne-room action. The best Romantic-era dish art is on the top floor (6 DM, Tuesday–Sunday 10:00–16:30, closed Monday, enter on Max-Joseph Platz, three blocks north of Marienplatz).

▲▲**Schatzkammer**—This treasury, next door to the Residenz, shows off a thousand years of Wittelsbach crowns and knickknacks (another 6 DM from the same window, same hours as Residenz, the only English you'll encounter is the "do not touch" signs). Vienna's palace and jewels are better, but this is Bavaria's best, with fine 13- and 14th-century crowns and delicately carved ivory and glass. For a more efficient ramble, consider the eight rooms as one big room and make one long clockwise circle.

▲**Cuvillies Theater**—Attached to the Residenz, this national theater designed by Cuvillies is dazzling enough to send you back to the days of divine monarchs. Visitors see simply the sumptuous interior. There is no real exhibit (3 DM, Monday–Saturday 14:00–17:00, Sunday 10:00–17:00; facing the Residenz entry, go left around the Residenz about a half-block to reach the theater entrance).

Sights—Outer Munich
▲▲**Nymphenburg Palace**—This royal summer palace is impressive only by Bavarian standards. If you do tour it, meditate upon the theme: nymphs. Something about the place feels highly sexed in a Prince Charles kind of way. Two rooms deserve special attention: the riotous rococo Great Hall (at entry, 1756 by Zimmermann) and King Ludwig's Gallery of Beauties. This room (#15, 1825–1848) is stacked with portraits of 36 of Bavaria's loveliest women . . . according to Ludwig. If only these creaking floors could tell a story. Don't miss the photos (in the glass cases) of Ludwig II—the "Mad" King, and his Romantic composer friend Richard Wagner.

The **Amalienburg**—another rococo jewel designed by Cuvillies and decorated by Zimmermann—is 300 meters from the palace. Every rich boy needs a hunting lodge like this. Above the pink and white grand entry notice Diana, goddess of "the chase," flanked by busts of satyrs. Tourists enter around back. Highlights in this tiny getaway include: first room—dog houses under gun cupboards; the fine yellow and silver bedroom—see Vulcan forging arrows for amorous cupids at the foot of the bed; the mini-

Hall of Mirrors—a blue and silver commotion of rococo nymphs and the kitchen with its blue Dutch Bible scene tiles.

The sleigh and coach collection (**Marstallmuseum**, closes from 12:00–13:00) is a huge garage lined with gilded Cinderella coaches. It's especially interesting for "Mad" King Ludwig fans.

The palace park, good for a royal stroll—even better by bike, contains more playful extras such as a bathhouse, pagoda, and artificial ruins (8 DM for everything, less for individual parts, Tuesday–Sunday 9:00–12:30, 13:30–17:00, closed Monday, shorter hours October–March, the 5-DM English guidebook does little to make the palace meaningful; reasonable cafeteria; U-1 direction: West-friedhof to Rotkreuzplatz, then tram or bus #12 to Romanplatz and a 10-minute walk or tram #17 from downtown or the station direct, tel. 089/179-080).

BMW Museum—The BMW headquarters, located in a striking building across the street from the Olympic Grounds, offers a good museum popular with car buffs (5.50 DM, daily 9:00–17:00, last ticket sold at 16:00, closed much of August, U-3 to the end: Olympia-zentrum, tel. 089/382-23-307). BMW fans may ask about factory tours (unreliable hours).

▲**Olympic Grounds**—Expect construction until 2000. Munich's great 1972 Olympic stadium and sports complex is now a lush park offering a tower (5 DM, commanding but so high it's a boring view from 820 feet, daily 8:00–24:00, last trip 23:30), an excellent swimming pool (5 DM, 7:00–22:30, Monday from 10:00, Thursday closed at 18:00), a good look at its striking "cobweb" style of architecture, and plenty of sun, grass, and picnic potential. Take U-3 to Olympia-zentrum direct from Marienplatz.

▲**Müllersches Volksbad**—This elegant Jugendstil (1901) public swimming pool is just across the river from the Deutsches Museum (5 DM, Rosenheimerstrasse 1, tel. 089/2361-3434).

Tours of Munich: By Foot, Bike, and Bus

Walking Tours—Original Munich Walks, run by the folks who started Berlin Walks, offers two tours: an introduction to the old town and "Infamous Third Reich Sites" (both tours are 15 DM, or 10 DM for those under 26, 2.5 hrs, tel. 0177-227-5901, e-mail: 106513.3461@compuserve.com). The old town tour starts daily at 10:30 early April through October (also at 15:30 May–August, not Sunday) and the Third Reich tour is offered at 10:30 Tuesday, Thursday, and Saturday, June through October (less off-season).

Both tours depart from the EurAide office (track 11) in the train station. There may be more frequent tours in 1999; confirm the schedule, but there's no need to register—just show up. Bring along any city transport ticket (like a *Kurzstrecke*) or buy one from your guide. Renate Suerbaum is a good local guide (140 DM for private two-hour walking tour, tel. 089/283-374).

Bike Tours—Radius Bikes organizes serious guided bike tours covering the best of historic and scenic downtown Munich (April weekends at 12:00, daily May–Sept. 5 at 10:30 and 14:30, daily Sept. 6–Oct. 3 at 12:00, 3 hours, 23 DM regular price, 20 DM with this book in 1999—two per book, tel. 089/596-113). Youth hostelers may prefer the hipper Mike's Bike tours (flyers all over town).
City Bus Tour—Panorama Tours offers one-hour city orientation bus tours (17 DM, daily at 10:00, 11:30, 13:00, 14:30, and 16:00 April–October; 10:00 and 14:30 in winter; live guide speaking German and English; near the train station, Arnulfstrasse 8; tel. 089/5490-7560).

Oktoberfest

When King Ludwig I had a marriage party in 1810, it was such a success that they made it an annual bash. These days the Oktoberfest lasts 16 days, ending with the first full weekend in October. It starts (usually on the third Saturday in September) with an opening parade of more than 6,000 participants and fills eight huge beer tents with about 6,000 people each. A million gallons of beer later, they roast the last ox.

It's crowded, but if you arrive in the morning (except Friday or Saturday) and haven't called ahead for a room, the TI can normally find you a place. The fairground, known as the "Wies'n" (a few blocks south of the train station), erupts in a frenzy of rides, dancing, and strangers strolling arm-in-arm down rows of picnic tables while the beer god stirs tons of beer, pretzels, and wurst in a bubbling caldron of fun. The three-loops roller coaster must be the wildest on earth (best before the beer-drinking).

During the fair, the city functions even better than normal, and it's a good time to sightsee, even if beer-hall rowdiness isn't your cup of tea.

Sights—Near Munich

Castle Tours—Two of King Ludwig's castles, Neuschwanstein and Linderhof, are an easy day trip by tour. Without a tour, only Neuschwanstein is easy (two hours by train to Füssen, 10-minute bus ride to Neuschwanstein). Panorama Tours offers all-day bus tours of the two castles with 30 minutes in Oberammergau (78 DM, plus 19 DM for two castle admissions, live guide, two languages, departing 8:30 from north side of Hauptbahnhof at Arnulfstrasse 8, tel. 089/5490-7560). On Wednesdays in June and July, EurAide operates an all-day train/bus Neuschwanstein–Linderhof–Wieskirche day tour (70 DM, 55 DM with a train pass, admissions not included, departs at 7:30 and beats most groups to avoid the long line, tel. 089/593-889). EurAide also sells tickets for Panorama's castle tours (above) at a discount to railpass or ISIC holders. For info on Ludwig's castles, see the Bavaria and Tirol chapter.

Munich Area

Berchtesgaden—This resort, near Hitler's overrated Eagle's Nest getaway, is easier as a day trip from Salzburg (just 20 km away). See Salzburg chapter.

▲**Andechs Monastery**—Where can you find a fine Baroque church in a rural Bavarian setting at a monastery that serves hearty food and perhaps the best beer in Germany, in a carnival atmosphere full of partying locals? It's the Andechs Monastery, crouching quietly with a big smile between two lakes just south of Munich. Come ready to eat tender chunks of pork, huge, soft pretzels, spiraled white radishes, savory sauerkraut, and Andecher monk-made beer that would almost make celibacy tolerable. Everything is served in medieval portions; two people can split a meal. Great picnic center offering first-class views and second-class prices (beer garden open daily 9:45–20:45, dinner until 18:30, church until 19:00, tel. 08152/3760). To reach Andechs from Munich without a car, take the S-5 train to Herrsching and catch a "Rauner" shuttle bus (hourly) or walk two miles from there. Don't miss a stroll up to the church, where you can sit peacefully and ponder the striking contrasts a trip through Germany offers. . . .

▲▲**Dachau**—Dachau was the first Nazi concentration camp (1933). Today it's the most accessible camp to travelers and a very effective voice from our recent but grisly past, warning and pleading "Never Again," the memorial's theme. This is a valuable

Dachau

experience and, when approached thoughtfully, well worth the trouble. In fact, it may change your life. See it. Feel it. Read and think about it. After this most powerful sightseeing experience, many people gain more respect for history and the dangers of not keeping tabs on their government.

Upon arrival, pick up the mini-guide and note when the next documentary film in English will be shown (25 minutes, normally shown at 11:30 and 15:30 and often at 14:00). Both the museum and the movie are exceptional. Notice the Expressionist fascist-inspired art near the theater, where you'll also find English books, slides, and a WC. Outside, see the reconstructed barracks and the memorial shrines at the far end (Tuesday–Sunday 9:00–17:00, closed Monday). For maximum understanding, consider the English guided walk (daily in summer at 12:30, 2 hrs, donation, call 08131/1741 to confirm). It's a 45-minute trip from downtown Munich: take S-2 (direction: Petershausen) to Dachau, then from the station, catch bus #724 or #726, Dachau-Ost, to Gedenkstätte (the camp). The two-zone 7-DM ticket covers the entire trip (one-way); with a train pass, just pay for the bus (1.80 DM one-way). Drivers follow Dachauerstrasse from downtown Munich to Dachau-Ost. Then follow the KZ-Gedenkstätte signs. The town of Dachau (TI tel. 08131/84566) is more pleasant than its unfortunate image.

Radius Touristik at the Munich train station offers tours of the Dachau camp (19 DM plus cost of public transportation, May–September Tuesday–Sunday at 14:00, 3.5 hrs, tel. 089/596-113).

Sleeping in Munich
(1.7 DM = about $1, tel. code: 089)
Sleep Code: **S** = Single, **D** = Double/Twin, **T** = Triple, **Q** = Quad, **b** = bathroom, **t** = toilet only, **s** = shower only, **CC** = Credit Card

(Visa, MasterCard, Amex). English is nearly always spoken, unless otherwise noted. Prices include breakfast and increase with conventions and festivals.

There are no cheap beds in Munich. Youth hostels strictly enforce their 26-year-old age limit, and side-tripping in is a bad value. But there are plenty of decent, moderately priced rooms. I've listed places in three areas: within a few blocks of the Hauptbahnhof (central train station), in the old center, and near the Deutsches Museum. Munich is packed during Oktoberfest (late September–early October) and room prices can triple. While (except for Oktoberfest weekends) rooms can be found through the TI, Oktoberfest revelers are wise to reserve in advance.

Sleeping near the Train Station

Budget hotels (90-DM doubles, no elevator, shower down the hall) cluster in the area immediately south of the station. It's seedy after dark (erotic cinemas, barnacles with lingerie tongues, men with moustaches in the shadows) but dangerous only to those in search of trouble. Still, I've listed places in more polite neighborhoods, generally a five- or 10-minute walk from the station and handy to the center. Places are listed roughly in order of proximity to the station. The nearest Laundromat is at Paul-Heyse Strasse 21, near the intersection with Landswehrstrasse (daily 7:00–23:00, 8-DM wash and dry, English instructions).

Hotel Haberstock, less than a block from the station, is homey, a little worn, old-fashioned, relatively quiet and a classic old European hotel (S-58–75 DM, Ss-82 DM, Sb-102 DM, D-110 DM, Ds-130 DM, Db-170 DM, good breakfast, CC:VMA, TV-5 DM extra, Schillerstrasse 4, 80336 Munich, tel. 089/557-855, fax 089/550-3634, friendly Alfred at the desk). Ask about weekend and winter discounts.

Hotel Europäischer Hof München is a big business hotel with fine rooms and elegant public spaces (S-91 DM, Sb-121 DM, D-111 DM, Db-141 DM, discount with this book, Bayerstrasse 31, 80335 Munich, tel. 089/551-510, fax 089/5515-1222, e-mail: heh_munich@compuserve.com).

Hotel Schweitz Odeon is comfortable for its price, with a fine buffet breakfast and non-smoking rooms (Sb-95 DM, Db-140 DM, Tb-170 DM, 15-DM garage, elevator, CC:VMA, Goethestrasse 26, from the station walk two blocks down Goethestrasse, tel. 089/539-585, fax 089/550-4383).

Jugendhotel Marienherberge is a pleasant, friendly convent offering the best cheap beds in town to young women only (25-year age limit can flex upward a couple of years, S-40 DM, 35 DM per bed in D and T, 30 DM per bed in four- to seven-bed rooms, non-smoking, open 8:00–24:00, a block from the station at Goethestrasse #9, tel. 089/555-805).

Hotels Near Train Station

❶ HOTEL HABERSTOCK & HELVETIA		❼ YMCA (CVJM)
❷ HOTEL EUROPAISCHER HOF MUNCHEN		❽ HOTEL PENSION LUNA
❸ HOTEL SCHWEITZ ODEON		❾ HOTEL UTZELMANN & BRISTOL
❹ JUGENDHOTEL MARIENHERBERGE		❿ HOTEL UHLAND, WESTFALIA & JEDERMAN
❺ KINGS HOTEL		⓫ BIKE RENTAL
❻ HOTEL AMBIENTE		⓬ ROMANTIC ROAD BUS STOP

Hotel Helvetia is a backpacker's favorite (S-53–63 DM, D-78–95 DM, Ds-99–115 DM, T-99–120 DM, laundry service, next to Haberstock at Schillerstrasse 6, 80336 Munich, tel. 089/590-685, fax 089/5906-8570).

Kings Hotel, a fancy old business-class hotel, is an elegant splurge and a very good value on weekends. You'll get carved wooden ceilings, canopy beds, chandeliers, a sauna, and the *Herald Tribune* in your room (Db-265 DM, Friday-Saturday-Sunday "King's Weekend" special: Db-165 DM with this book except during fairs, CC:VMA, some non-smoking rooms, ask about their

"Royal Weekend" special: 200 DM for their 400-DM suite, 150 meters north of station at Dachauer Strasse 13, 80335 Munich, tel. 089/551-870, fax 089/5518-7300, Web site: www.king-group .com, e-mail: kingshotel@aol.com).

Hotel Ambiente has dark halls but clean, bright, newly refurbished rooms with all the comforts and a friendly professional staff (Sb-138–182 DM, Db-150–230 DM depending on season, CC:VMA, a block from station at Schillerstrasse 12, 80336 Munich, tel. 089/545-170, fax 089/5451-7200).

YMCA (CVJM), open to all ages and sexes, has modern rooms (D-86 DM, T-120 DM, a bed in a shared triple-40 DM, those over 26 pay 16 percent more, free showers, elevator, Landwehrstrasse 13, 80336 Munich, tel. 089/552-1410, fax 089/550-4282, Web site: www.cvjm.org/muenchen/hotel/, e-mail: muenchen@cvjm.org). The cafeteria offers 13-DM dinners (Tues–Fri 18:30–22:00).

Hotel Pension Luna is a dumpy building with cheery rooms (S-59 DM, Sb-69 DM, D/twin-90 DM, D-99 DM, Ds-115 DM, T-130 DM, Ts-140 DM, lots of stairs, CC:VA, Landwehrstrasse 5, tel. 089/597-833, fax 089/550-3761).

Hotel Pension Utzelmann has huge rooms, especially the curiously cheap room #6. Each lacy room is richly furnished. It's in a pleasant neighborhood, a 10-minute walk from the station a block off Sendlinger Tor (S-50–65 DM, Ss-85–95 DM, Sb-125 DM, D-90 DM, Ds-110 DM, Db-145 DM, T-125 DM, Ts-150 DM, Tb-175 DM, hall showers-5 DM, Pettenkoferstrasse 6, enter through black iron gate, tel. 089/594-889, fax 089/596-228, Frau Earnst).

Hotel Bristol, nearly next door to Hotel Utzelmann, has renovated, comfortable rooms and is a fine value (Sb-89 DM, Db-129 DM, Tb-160 DM, to get these prices—which are 20–30 DM below the hotel's normal rates—ask for Johannes and mention this book if you call, or show this book if you walk in—and pay cash, non-smoking, hearty buffet breakfast on terrace, bike rental-20 DM/ day, parking available, CC:VMA, Pettenkoferstrasse 2, 80336 Munich, one metro stop on U-1 or U-2 from station, tel. 089/595-151, fax 089/591-451, Web site: www.bristol-muc.com, e-mail: hotel@bristol-muc.com). Johannes also has an apartment (45 DM per person, up to four people).

Hotel Uhland, a veritable mansion, is a worthwhile splurge (Sb-110 DM, Db-140 DM, Tb-180 DM, huge breakfast, elevator, Internet access, free parking, Uhlandstrasse 1, 80336 Munich, near the Theresienwiese Oktoberfest grounds, 10-minute walk from the station, tel. 089/543-350, fax 089/5433-5250, e-mail: Hotel_ Uhland@compuserve.com, SE). Free use of computer, e-mail, and photocopier.

Pension Westfalia overlooks the Oktoberfest grounds from the top floor of a quiet and elegant old building. Well run by Peter and Mary Deiritz, this is a great value if you prefer sanity and personal touches to centrality (S-65 DM, Sb-90 DM, D-90 DM, Db-110–130 DM, cheaper off-season, extra bed 25 DM, hallway showers-3 DM, buffet breakfast, elevator, CC:VA, Mozartstrasse 23, 80336 Munich, easy parking, U-3 or U-6 to Goetheplatz, tel. 089/530-377, fax 089/543-9120). Around the corner, **Pension Schubert** rents four tidy and simple but elegant rooms (S-50 DM, D-85 DM, Db-95 DM, Schubertstrasse 1, tel. 089/535-087.

   Hotel Jederman is a basic well-worn, comfortable old business hotel (S-65–85 DM, Sb-95–160 DM, D-95–145 DM, Db-140–240 DM depending on season, kids' cot-15 DM, CC:VMA, free Internet access, elevator, rental bikes, midway between station and Oktoberfest grounds, tram #18 and #19 at door, Bayerstrasse 95, 80335 Munich, tel. 089/533-617, fax 089/536-506, Web site: www.hoteljederman.cube.net, e-mail: hotel-jederman@cube.net, Jenke family).

Sleeping in the Old Center
Pension Lindner is clean, quiet, and modern, with pastel-bouquet rooms (S-60 DM, D-95 DM, Ds-120 DM, Db-135 DM, elevator, Dultstrasse 1, just off Sendlinger Strasse, 80331 Munich, tel. 089/ 263-413, fax 089/268-760, run by cheery Marion Sinzinger). One floor below, the quirky **Pension Stadt Munich** isn't as homey, but is okay if the Lindner is full (four Ds-120 DM, a tad smoky, Dulstrasse 1, tel. 089/263-417, fax 089/267-548, some English spoken).

   Pension Seibel has cozy rooms and a friendly, family atmosphere a block off the Viktualienmarkt in a fun neighborhood (S-70 DM, Sb-89 DM, D-99 DM, Db-129 DM, Tb-150 DM, these prices are promised though 1999 only with this book, family apartment for up to five people-45 DM each, soft prices, entirely smoke-free, big breakfast, no elevator, CC:VMA, Reichenbachstrasse 8, 80469 Munich, tel. 089/264-043, fax 089/ 267-803, Moe and Kirstin).

   Hotel Münchner Kindl is a jolly place with decent rooms above a friendly local bar (15 rooms, S-80 DM, Sb-110 DM, D-120 DM, Ds-140 DM, Db-160 DM, Tb-195 DM, Qs-200 DM, prices with this book, night noises travel up the central courtyard, no elevator, easy telephone reservations, CC:VM, two blocks off main pedestrian drag from "Thomas" sign at Damenstiftstrasse 16, 80331 Munich, tel. 089/264-349, fax 089/264-526, run by Gunter and English-speaking Renate Dittert, cheery Heinz serves breakfast).

Sleeping near Isartor, the Deutsches Museum, and Beyond
Hotel Isartor is a modern, comfortable, concrete-feeling place beautfully located two minutes' walk from the Isartor S-Bahn stop (26 rooms, Db-160 DM, 10 percent discount with cash in July, August, and slow times, CC:VMA, elevator, refrigerators in rooms, Baaderstrasse 2, 80469 Munich, tel. 089/216-3340, fax 089/298-494, family Pangratz).

Pension Beck is well worn and farther away but a good budget bet (S-from 60 DM, D-82–90 DM, Db-120 DM, rooms for three to five people-42 DM each, free showers; family, youth, and two-night deals; 44 rooms on five floors with no elevator, yellow hall and lots of backpackers, east of Isartor near river and Marienplatz, Thier-schstrasse 36, take streetcar #17 direct from station or any S-Bahn to Isartor and 400-meter walk, tel. 089/220-708, fax 089/220-925).

American **Audrey Bauchinger** rents quiet, tidy rooms and spacious apartments east of the Deutsches Museum in a quiet resi-dential area a 20-minute walk from Marienplatz (Ss-45 DM, D-75 DM, one D with private bath across hall-125 DM, Ds-80–105 DM, spacious Db/Tb with kitchenette-160 DM/200 DM, no breakfast included, CC:VMA accepted at 5 percent charge, corner of Schweigerstrasse, at Zeppelinstrasse 37, 81669 Munich, tel. 089/488-444, fax 089/489-1787, e-mail: 106437.3277 @compuserve.com). From the station, take any S-Bahn to Marien-platz, then bus #52 (the only bus there) to Schweigerstrasse.

Familie Jordan Zimmer—The Jordan family, now with an empty nest, rents two big apartments in their comfortable subur-ban home. This is ideal for those driving between Munich and Salzburg (Db-80 DM, 20 minutes from downtown on the S-5 to Vaterstetten and then a two-minute walk; from the A-99 Auto-bahn, take the Vaterstetten exit on the Salzburg side of town, Luitpoldring 8, 85591 Baterstetten, tel. 08106/358-032, SE).

Hostels and Cheap Beds
Munich's youth hostels charge 25 DM in dorms, and 38 DM in doubles (including breakfast and sheets) and strictly limit admis-sion to YH members who are under 27. **Burg Schwaneck Hostel** is a renovated castle (30 minutes from the center, S-7 to Pullach, then follow signs, walking 10 minutes to Burgweg 4, tel. 089/793-0643).

Munich's **International Youth Camp Kapuzinerhölzl** (a.k.a. "The Tent") offers 400 places on the wooden floor of a huge circus tent with a mattress, blankets, good showers, and free tea in the morning for 13 DM to anyone under 25 (flexible). It's a fun experi-ence—kind of a cross between a slumber party and Woodstock (if anyone under 25 knows what that was). Cool ping-pong-and-frisbee atmosphere throughout the day, no curfew at night (open July and August only, confirm first at TI that it's open, then catch tram #17 from Hauptbahnhof to Botanischer Garten, direction: Amalien-burgstrasse, and follow crowd down Franz-Schrankstrasse).

Eating in Munich
Munich cuisine is best seasoned with beer. For beer halls, you have two basic choices: the Hofbräuhaus with music and tourists or mellower beer gardens with Germans.

The world's most famous and touristy beer hall is the **Hof-bräuhaus** (daily 9:30–24:00, music during lunch and dinner, Platzl 6, five-minute walk from Marienplatz, tel. 089/221-676). Even if you don't eat here, check it out; it's fun to see 200 Japanese people drinking beer in a German beer hall . . . across from a Planet Hollywood. Germans go for the entertainment—to sing "Country Roads," see how Texas girls party, and watch salarymen from Tokyo chug beer. The music-every-night atmosphere is thick; the fat, shiny-leather–bands even get church mice to stand up and conduct three-quarter time with breadsticks. Meals are inexpensive (for a light 10-DM meal, I like the local favorite, *Schweinswurst mit Kraut*); white radishes are salted and cut in delicate spirals; and surly beermaids pull mustard packets from their cleavages. Huge liter beers (called *eine Mass* in German or *"ein* pitcher" in English) cost 10 DM. You can order your beer *helles* (light—but not "lite," what you'll get if you say *"ein* beer"), *dunkeles* (dark), or *Radler* (half lemonade, half light beer). Notice the vomitoriums in the WC. (They have a gimmicky folk evening upstairs in the *Festsaal* nightly at 19:00 for 8 DM, food and drinks are sold from the same menu, tel. 089/290-13-610.)

Weisses Bräuhaus is more local and features good food and the region's fizzy wheat beer (daily 8:00–24:00, Tal 10, between Marienplatz and Isartor, two blocks from Hofbräuhaus). Hitler met with fellow fascists here in 1920 when his Nazi party had yet to ferment.

Augustiner Beer Garden is a sprawling haven for trendy local beer-lovers on a balmy evening (10:00–23:00, across from the train tracks, three loooong blocks from the station, away from the center, on Arnulfstrasse 52). For a true under-the-leaves beer garden packed with locals, this is best.

The tiny **Jodlerwirt** is a woodsy, smart-alecky, yodeling kind of pub. The food is great and the ambience is as Bavarian as you'll find. Avoid the basic ground-floor bar and climb the stairs into the action (accordian act from 19:00, closed Sunday, Altenhofstrasse 4, between the Hofbräuhaus and Marienplatz, tel. 089/221-249). Good food, lots of belly laughs . . . completely incomprehensible to the average tourist.

For a classier evening stewed in antlers and fiercely Bavarian, eat under a tree or inside at the **Nürnberger Bratwurst Glöckl am Dom** (daily 9:30–24:00, 25-DM dinners, Frauenplatz 9, at the rear of the twin-domed cathedral, tel. 089/295-264).

Locals enjoy the **Altes Hackerhaus** for traditional Bayerischer fare with a dressier feel (daily until 24:00, 25–30 DM meals, Sendlingerstrasse 14, tel. 089/260-5026).

For outdoor atmosphere and a cheap meal, spend an evening at the Englischer Garden's **Chinesischer Turm** (Chinese Pagoda) **Biergarten**. You're welcome to BYO food and grab a table or buy from the picnic stall (*Brotzeit*) right there. Don't bother to phone ahead: they have 6,000 seats. For a more intimate place with more local families and fewer tourists, venture deeper into the garden (past the Isarring road) to the **Hirschau Biergarten.**

For similar BYOF atmosphere right behind Marienplatz, eat at **Viktualien Markt**'s beer garden. Lunch or dinner here taps you into about the best budget eating in town. Countless stalls surround the beer garden and sell wurst, sandwiches, produce, and so on. This BYOF tradition goes back to the days when monks were allowed to sell beer but not food. To picnic, choose a table without a tablecloth. This is a good place to grab the most typical meal in town: *Weisswurst* (white sausage) with *süss* (sweet) mustard, a salty pretzel, and *Weissbier.* **Suppenküche** is fine for a small, cozy, sit-down lunch (soup kitchen, 6–9-DM soup meals, in Viktualien Markt near intersection of Frauenkirche and Reichenbachstrasse, everyone knows where it is). For your strudel and coffee, consider the **Marktcafe** (closed Sunday, 7-DM fresh strudel, on a tiny street a block below the market, Heiliggeistrasse 2, tel. 089/227-816).

For a fun and easy (though not cheap) cafeteria meal near Karlstor on the pedestrian mall, try the **Mövenpick Marche.** Climb downstairs into the marketplace fantasy and pick up a card. As you load your tray your card is stamped, choose your table from several typical Munich themes, and pay after you eat (smoke-free zones, reasonable small-plate veggie and salad buffets, distracting men's room, on Neuhauser pedestrian street, across from St. Michael's church, daily 12:00–22:00).

The crown in its emblem indicates that the royal family assembled its picnics in the historic and expensive **Alois Dallmayr** delicatessen (Monday–Friday 9:30–19:30, Saturday 9:00–16:00, closed Sunday, Dienerstrasse 14, behind the Rathaus). An elegant café serves light meals behind the bakery on the ground floor. Explore this dieter's purgatory and put together a royal picnic to munch in the nearby Hofgarten. To save money, browse at Dallmayr's but buy in the basement supermarkets of the Kaufhof stores across Marienplatz or at Karlsplatz.

Transportation Connections—Munich

Munich is a super transportation hub (one reason it was the target of so many WWII bombs).

By train to: Füssen (10/day, 2 hrs, the 8:53 departure is good for a Neuschwanstein castle day trip), **Berlin** (6/day, 8 hrs), **Würzburg** (hrly, 3 hrs), **Frankfurt** (14/day, 3.5 hrs), **Salzburg** (12/day, 2 hrs), **Vienna** (4/day, 5 hrs), **Venice** (2/day, 9 hrs), **Paris** (3/day, 9 hrs), **Prague** (3/day, 7–10 hrs), and just about every other point in western Europe. Munich is three hours from **Reutte**, Austria (every 2 hours, 3 hrs, transfer in Garmisch).

BAVARIA
AND TIROL

Two hours south of Munich, between Germany's Bavaria and
Austria's Tirol, is a timeless land of fairy-tale castles, painted
buildings shared by cows and farmers, and locals who still yodel
when they're happy.

In Germany's Bavaria, tour "Mad" King Ludwig's ornate
Neuschwanstein Castle, Europe's most spectacular. Stop by the
Wieskirche, a textbook example of Bavarian rococo bursting with
curly curlicues, and browse through Oberammergau, Germany's
wood-carving capital and home of the famous Passion Play.

In Austria's Tirol, hike to the Ehrenberg ruined castle,
scream down a nearby ski slope on an oversized skateboard, then
catch your breath for an evening of yodeling and slap-dancing.

In this chapter I'll cover Bavaria first, then Tirol. Austria's
Tirol is easier and cheaper than touristy Bavaria. My favorite
home base for exploring Bavaria's castles is actually in Austria, in
the town of Reutte. Füssen, in Germany, is a handier home base
for train travelers.

Planning Your Time
While locals come here for a week or two, the typical speedy
American traveler will find two days' worth of sightseeing. With a
car and some time you could enjoy the more remote corners, but
the basic visit ranges anywhere from a long day trip from Munich
to a three-night, two-day visit. If the weather's good and you're
not going to Switzerland, be sure to ride a lift to an Alpine peak.

A good schedule for a one-day circular drive from Reutte is:
7:30–breakfast, 8:15–depart, 8:45–arrive at Neuschwanstein, park
and hike to the castle for a tour, 12:00–drive to the Wieskirche (20-
minute stop) and on to Oberammergau for a stroll and lunch,

Highlights of Bavaria and Tirol

14:00–drive to Linderhof, 14:30–tour Linderhof, 16:30–drive along Plansee back into Austria, 17:30–back at hotel, 19:00–dinner at hotel and perhaps a folk evening. In peak season you might arrive later at Linderhof to avoid the crowds. The next morning you could stroll Reutte, hike to the Ehrenberg ruins, and ride the luge on your way to Innsbruck, Munich, Venice, Switzerland, or wherever.

Getting Around Bavaria and Tirol

By Car: This region is ideal by car. All the sights are within an easy 60-mile loop from Reutte or Füssen.

By Train and Bus: It's frustrating by train. Local bus service in the region is spotty for sightseeing. Without wheels, Reutte, the luge ride, and Wieskirche are probably not worth the trouble. Füssen (with a two-hour train ride to and from Munich every hour, transfer in Buchloe) is three miles from Neuschwanstein Castle with easy bus and bike connections. Oberammergau (hourly two-hour trains from Munich with one change) has decent bus connections to nearby Linderhof Castle. Oberammergau to Füssen is a pain.

By Tour: If you're interested only in Bavarian castles, consider an all-day organized bus tour of the Bavarian biggies as a side trip from Munich (see Munich chapter).

By Bike: This is great biking country. Many train stations (including Reutte) and hotels rent bikes for about 15 DM a day.

By Thumb: Hitchhiking, always risky, is a slow-but-possible way to connect the public transportation gaps.

FÜSSEN AND NEUSCHWANSTEIN CASTLE, GERMANY

Füssen has been a strategic stop since ancient times. Its main street sits on the Via Claudia Augusta, which crossed the Alps (over Brenner Pass) in Roman times. The town was the southern terminus of the medieval trade route known among 20th-century tourists as the "Romantic Road." Dramatically situated under a renovated castle on the lively Lech River, Füssen just celebrated its 700th birthday.

Unfortunately, in the summer it's entirely overrun by tourists. Traffic can be exasperating, but by bike or on foot it's not bad. Off-season, the town is a jester's delight.

Apart from Füssen's cobbled and arcaded town center, there's little real sightseeing. The striking-from-a-distance castle houses a boring picture gallery. The mediocre city museum in the monastery below the castle exhibits lifestyles of 200 years ago and the story of the monastery, and offers displays on the development of the violin, for which Füssen was famous (5 DM, Tuesday–Sunday 11:00–16:00, closed Monday, explanations in German only). Halfway between Füssen and the border (as you drive, or a woodsy walk from the town) is the Lechfall, a thunderous waterfall with a handy potty stop.

Orientation (tel. code: 08362)

Füssen's train station is a few blocks from the TI, the town center (a cobbled shopping mall), and all my hotel listings.

Tourist Information: The TI has a room-finding service (look for Kurverwaltung, Monday–Friday 9:30–18:00, weekends 9:00–12:30, shorter hours off-season and closed Sunday, tel. 08362/93850, fax 08362/938-520, www.fuessen.de). After hours, try the little self-service info pavilion, near the front of the TI, which dispenses Füssen maps for 1 DM.

Arrival in Füssen: Exit left as you leave the train station and walk a few straight blocks to the center of town and the TI.

Bike Rental: Rad Zacherl, next to the train station, rents road bikes for 14 DM/day (passport number for deposit, Monday–Friday 9:00–12:00 and 14:00–18:00, Saturday 9:00–12:00, mountain bikes-20 DM, Rupprechtstrasse 8.5, tel. 08362/3292).

Sights—Bavaria, near Füssen

(These are listed in driving order from Füssen.)

▲▲▲**Neuschwanstein Castle**—The fairy-tale castle Neuschwanstein looks medieval, but it's only about as old as the Eiffel Tower and feels like something you'd see at a home show for 19th-century royalty. It was built (1869–1886) to suit the whims of Bavaria's King Ludwig II and is a textbook example of the Romanticism that was popular in 19th-century Europe.

Getting to the castle: It's a steep 20- to 30-minute hike to Neuschwanstein from the parking lot. If you arrive by bus, the quickest (and steepest) way to the castle starts in parking lot D. A more gradual ascent starts at the parking lot near the lake (Parkplatz am Alpsee, best for drivers, all lots cost 6 DM). To minimize hiking, you can take advantage of the shuttle buses (3.50 DM up, 5 DM round-trip; drops you off at Mary's Bridge, a steep 10 minutes above the castle) or horse carriages (8 DM up, 4 DM down; slower than walking, stops five minutes short of the castle) that go constantly (watch your step).

Touring the castle: To beat the crowds, see Neuschwanstein, Germany's most popular castle, either by 9:00 or late in the afternoon. The castle is open every morning at 8:30; by 11:00, it's packed. Rushed 35-minute English-language tours are less rushed early. Tours leave regularly, telling the sad story of Bavaria's "mad" king, who drowned under suspicious circumstances at age 41 after nearly bankrupting Bavaria to build his castles. You'll go up and down more than 300 steps through lavish Wagnerian dream rooms, a royal state-of-the-19th-century-art kitchen, the king's gilded-lily bedroom, and his extravagant throne room. You'll see 15 rooms with their original furnishings and fanciful wall paintings. The rest of the castle is unfinished; the king lived here fewer than 200 days before he died (11 DM, daily 8:30–17:30 April–September, 9:30–16:30 October and March, 10:00–16:00 winter, no photography inside). Guided tours are mandatory. To cut down on lines, the plan for 1999 is give out appointment times for tours; therefore go to the castle's ticket office immediately and pick up a time before hiking up to Mary's Bridge.

After the tour, climb up to Mary's Bridge to marvel at Ludwig's castle, just as Ludwig did. This bridge was quite an engineering accomplishment 100 years ago. From the bridge, the frisky can hike even higher to the "Beware—Danger of Death" signs and an even more glorious castle view. For the most interesting descent (15 minutes longer and extremely slippery when wet), follow signs to the Pöllat Gorge.

▲▲**Hohenschwangau Castle**—Standing quietly below

Neuschwanstein

NOTE: MAP NOT TO SCALE
BORDER TO ALPSEE PARKING = 5 KM DRIVE
ALPSEE PARKING TO NEUSCH. = 20 MIN. WALK

Neuschwanstein, the big yellow Hohenschwangau Castle was Ludwig's boyhood home. It's more lived-in and historic, and actually gives a better glimpse of Ludwig's life. There are only three ways to get an English tour: gather 21 people together; wait in line until 20 English speakers join you; or politely ask your German guide to say a few words in English after her German spiels. (Same hours and price as Neuschwanstein but closed in winter.)

The "village" at the foot of the castles lives off the hungry, shopping tourists who come in droves to Europe's "Disney" castle. The little family-run mini-market (open daily) has the makings for a skimpy picnic and a microwave fast-food machine. Picnic in the lakeside park or in one of the old-fashioned rowboats (rented by the hour in summer). The bus stop, post/telephone office, and helpful TI cluster around the main intersection (TI open daily 9:00–18:00, till 17:00 off-season, tel. 08362/819-840).

To give your castle experience a romantic twist, hike or bike over from Austria (trailhead is at the recommended hotel Gutshof zum Schluxen in Pinswang). When the dirt road forks at the top of the hill, go right (downhill), cross the Austrian-German border (marked by a sign and deserted hut), and follow the paved road to the castles. It's an hour's hike one way (can return by bus) or a great circular bike trip. Signposts and books often refer to these castles in the German: *Königsschlösser*.

Buses run between the Füssen train station and Hohenschwangau (2/hrly, 10 minutes, 4.80 DM round-trip), and between Füssen and Reutte (5/day, 30 min, never on Sunday; schedules at TI).

▲**Tegelberg Gondola**—Just north of Neuschwanstein, hang gliders circle like vultures. They jumped from the top of the Tegelberg Gondola. For 27 DM, you can ride high to the 5,500-foot summit and back down (daily from 9:00, last lift at 17:00, closes earlier in winter, tel. 08362/98360). On a clear day, you get great views of the Alps and Bavaria and the vicarious thrill of watching hang gliders and parasailors leap into airborne ecstasy. Tegelberg is a popular take-off point. Weather permitting, scores of German thrill-seekers line up and leap from their launch ramp at the top of the lift. With one leaving every two or three minutes, it's great spectating. Thrill-seekers with exceptional social skills may talk themselves into a tandem ride with a parasailor. From there, it's a steep 2.5-hour hike down to Ludwig's castle.

Tegelberg Luge—Next to the lift is a luge (like a bobsled on wheels; for details see Sights—Tirol, Near Reutte, below). The track, made of stainless steel, is often open when rainy weather shuts the other luges. It's not as fast or scenic as Bichlbach and Biberwier (below), but it's close and cheap (4 DM per run, 10 percent less when using six-trip cards, can be crowded on sunny summer weekends, tel. 08362/98360). A funky cable system pulls lugers to the top without a ski lift.

▲▲**Wies Church (Wieskirche)**—Germany's greatest rococo-style church, Wieskirche ("the church in the meadow") is newly restored and looking as brilliant as the day it floated down from heaven. Overripe with decoration but bright and bursting with beauty, this church is a divine droplet, a curly curlicue, the final flowering of the Baroque movement. The ceiling depicts the Last Judgment.

This is a pilgrimage church. In the early 1700s a carving of Christ too graphic to be accepted by that generation's church was the focus of worship in a peasant's private chapel. Miraculously, it wept. And pilgrims came from all around.

Bavaria's top rococo architects, the Zimmermann brothers, were then commissioned to build the Wieskirche, which features the amazing carving above its altar and still attracts countless pilgrims. Take a commune-with-nature-and-smell-the-farm detour back through the meadow to the car park.

Wieskirche (donation requested, daily 8:00–20:00, less off-season) is 30 minutes north of Neuschwanstein. The northbound Romantic Road bus tour stops here for 15 minutes. Füssen-Wieskirche buses run several times a day. By car, head north from Füssen, turn right at Steingaden, and follow the signs.

If you can't visit Wieskirche, visit one of the other churches that came out of the same heavenly spray can: Oberammergau's church, Munich's Asam Church, the Würzburg Residenz Chapel, or the splendid Ettal Monastery (free and near Oberammergau).

If you're driving from Wieskirche to Oberammergau, you'll cross the Echelsbacher Bridge, arching 250 feet over the Pöllat Gorge. Drivers should let their passengers walk across and meet them at the other side. Any kayakers? Notice the painting of the traditional village woodcarver (who used to walk from town to town with his art on his back) on the first big house on the Oberammergau side, a shop called Almdorf Ammertal. It has a huge selection of overpriced carvings and commission-hungry tour guides.

▲**Oberammergau**—The Shirley Temple of Bavarian villages and exploited to the hilt by the tourist trade, Oberammergau wears way too much makeup. It's worth a wander only if you're passing through anyway. Browse through the woodcarvers' shops—small art galleries filled with very expensive whittled works—or see folk art at the local Heimatmuseum (TI tel. 08822/2310, closed Saturday afternoon and Sunday off-season).

Visit the church, a poor cousin of the one at Wies. This church looks richer than it is. Put your hand on the "marble" columns. If they warm up, they're painted fakes. Wander through the graveyard. Ponder the deaths that two wars dealt Germany. Behind the church are the photos of three Schneller brothers, all killed within two years in World War II.

Still making good on a deal the townspeople made with God if they were spared devastation by the Black Plague 350 years ago, once each decade Oberammergau performs the Passion Play. The next show is in the year 2000, when 5,000 people a day for 100 summer days will attend Oberammergau's all-day dramatic story of Christ's crucifixion. For the rest of this millennium, you'll have to settle for browsing through the theater's exhibition hall (4 DM, daily 9:30–12:00, 13:30–16:00, closed Monday off-season, tel. 08822/32278), seeing Nicodemus tool around town in his VW, or reading the Book. Oberammergau is connected to Füssen by one direct bus per day (2 hrs).

Gasthaus zum Stern is friendly, serves good food (closed Tuesday in low season), and for this tourist town is a fine value (Sb-45 DM, Db-90 DM, closed November and December, Dorfstrasse 33, 82487 Oberammergau, tel. 08822/867, fax 08822/7027). Oberammergau's modern youth hostel is on the river a short walk from the center (20-DM beds, open all year, tel. 08822/4114).

Driving into town from the north, cross the bridge, take the second left, follow "Polizei" signs, and park by the huge gray Passionsspielhaus. Leaving town, head out past the church and turn toward Ettal on Road 23. You're 20 miles from Reutte via the scenic Plansee.

▲▲**Linderhof Castle**—This was Mad Ludwig's "home," his most intimate castle. It's small and comfortably exquisite, good enough for a minor god. Set in the woods, 15 minutes by car or bus (three per day) from Oberammergau, surrounded by fountains and sculpted, Italian-style gardens, it's the only palace I've toured that actually had me feeling envious. Don't miss the grotto (9 DM, daily 9:00–17:30 April–September, 10:00–16:00 with lunch break off-season, fountains often erupt on the hour, English tours constantly, tel. 08822/3512). Plan for lots of crowds, lots of walking, and a two-hour stop.

▲▲**Zugspitze**—The tallest point in Germany is a border crossing. Lifts from Austria and Germany go to the 10,000-foot summit of the Zugspitze. Straddle two great nations while enjoying an incredible view. There are restaurants, shops, and telescopes at the summit. The 75-minute trip from Garmisch on the German side costs 75 DM round-trip, with family discounts available (buy a combo cogwheel train and cable car ride, tel. 08821/7970). On the Austrian side, from the less crowded Talstation Obermoos, above the village of Erwald, the tram zips you to the top in 10 minutes (420 AS or 61 DM round-trip, daily 8:40–16:40 late May–October, tel. in Austria 05673/2309). The German ascent is easier for those without a car, but buses do connect the Erwald train station and the Austrian lift about hourly. Hikers enjoy the easy 10-km walk around the lovely Elbsee lake (German side, 5 min downhill from cable "Seilbahn").

Sleeping in Füssen, Germany
(1.7 DM = about $1, tel. code: 08362, zip code: 87629)
Sleep Code: **S** = Single, **D** = Double/Twin, **T** = Triple, **Q** = Quad, **b** = bathroom, **t** = toilet only, **s** = shower only, **CC** = Credit Card (**V**isa, **M**asterCard, **A**mex).

Unless otherwise noted, breakfast is included, hall showers are free, and English is spoken. Prices listed are for one-night stays. Some places give a discount for longer stays. Always ask. Competition is fierce, and off-season prices are soft.

Füssen, two miles from Ludwig's castles, is a cobbled, riverside oompah treat, but very touristy (notice das sushi bar). It has just about as many rooms as tourists, though, and the TI has a free room-finding service. All places I've listed (except the hostel) are within a few blocks of the train station and the town center. They are used to travelers getting in after the Romantic Road bus arrives (20:40) and will hold rooms for a telephone promise.

Hotel Kurcafé is deluxe, with spacious rooms and all the modern conveniences. Prices vary wildly with the season (July and August are sky-high). But the hotel's bakery can enjoyably ruin your budget any time of year (Sb-95–139 DM, depending on season, Db-125–189 DM, third or fourth person pays 30 DM extra, CC:VMA, on the tiny traffic circle a block in front of the train station at Bahnhofstrasse 4, tel. 08362/6369, fax 08362/39424, e-mail: hotel.kurcafe@t-online.de). The attached restaurant has good, reasonable daily specials.

Hotel Gasthaus zum Hechten offers all the modern comforts in a friendly, traditional shell right under the Füssen Castle in the old-town pedestrian zone (S-60 DM, Sb-75 DM, D-100 DM, Db-110–130 DM, Tb-150 DM, Qb-180 DM, these prices and free parking promised with this book in 1999, cheaper off-season and for multi-night stays, fun mini-bowling alley in basement; from TI, walk down pedestrian street, take second right to Ritterstrasse 6; tel. 08362/91600, fax 08362/916099; Frau Margaret has taken fine care of travelers for 40 years). The attached restaurant Zum Hechten serves hearty Bavarian specialties and specializes in pike (*Hecht*), caught right out of the Lech River.

Gasthof Krone, a rare bit of pre-glitz Füssen also in the pedestrian zone, has dumpy halls and stairs but bright, cheery, comfy rooms (S-53 DM, D-96 DM, extra bed-48 DM, prices drop 6 DM for two-night stays, CC:VMA, from TI, head down pedestrian street, take first left to Schrannenplatz 17, tel. 08362/7824, fax 08362/37505).

Hotel Bräustüberl has clean, bright, newly renovated rooms in a musty old beer hall–type place (Sb-65 DM, Db-110 DM, depending on season, Rupprechtstrasse 5, a block from the station, tel. 08362/7843, fax 08362/38781).

American-run **Suzanne's B&B** does everything exactly right, from eggs laid right in the backyard to local cheese, a great children's yard, affordable laundry, and feel-good balconies (D-80 DM; large Ds with balcony and fridge—120 DM for two, 135 DM for three, 160 DM for four; non-smoking, 10 DM/day bike rental, backtrack two blocks from station, Venetianerwinkel 3, tel. 08362/38485, fax 08362/921-396, e-mail: svorbrugg@t-online.de).

The funky, old, ornately furnished **Pension Garni Elisabeth** exudes an Addams-family friendliness (S-45 DM, D-80–90 DM, Db-120–170 DM, T-120 DM, Tb-150–180 DM, showers-6 DM, Augustenstrasse 10, two blocks from the station toward town, take second left, tel. 08362/6275). Floors creak, dust balls wander, and the piano is never played.

Haus Peters, across the street, is comfy, smoke-free, and friendly but often closed (Db-86 DM, Tb-120 DM, Augustenstrasse 5, tel. 08362/7171).

Füssen Youth Hostel, a fine, German-run youth hostel, welcomes travelers under 27 (two- to six-bed rooms, 22 DM for bed and breakfast, 9 DM for dinner, 5.50 DM for sheets, laundry facilities-7 DM/load, non-smoking, Mariahilferstrasse 5, tel. 08362/7754, fax 08362/2770). From the station, backtrack 10 minutes along the tracks.

Sleeping in Hohenschwangau, near Neuschwanstein Castle (tel. code: 08362, zip code: 87645)

Inexpensive farmhouse *Zimmer* (B&Bs) abound in the Bavarian countryside around Neuschwanstein and are a good value. Look for signs that say *"Zimmer Frei"* ("room free," or vacancy). The going rate is about 80 DM per double including breakfast. **Pension Weiher** has lots of balconies and flood-lit Neuschwanstein views (S-35–38 DM, D-77 DM, Db-95 DM, Hofwiesenweg 11, tel. & fax 08362/81161). **Pension Schwansee** has clean, basic rooms (Db-100–110 DM, CC:VM, bike rental, 2.5 km from the castle on the road to Füssen at Parkstrasse 9, 87645 Alterschrofen, tel. 08362/8353, family Strössner).

For more of a hotel, try **Alpenhotel Meier**. In a rural setting within walking distance of the castle, its rooms have new furnishings and porches (Sb-88 DM, Db-150 DM, Tb-201 DM, two-night discounts, easy parking, Schwangauerstrasse 37, tel. 08362/81152, fax 08362/987-028).

Eating in Füssen

Infooday is a clever, modern self-service eatery that sells its hot meals and salad bar by weight and offers English newspapers (Monday–Friday 10:30–18:30, Saturday till 14:30, closed Sunday, 8 DM/filling salad, 12-DM meals; under the Füssen Castle in Hotel zum Hechten, Ritterstrasse 6). A couple of blocks away, **Pizza Blitz** offers good take-out or eat-at-counter pizzas and hearty salads for about 8 DM apiece (Monday–Saturday 11:00–23:00, Sunday 12:00–23:00, Luitpoldstrasse 14). For more traditional fare, **Hotel Bräustüberl** (see above) has famous home-brewed beer and a popular kitchen (Tuesday–Sunday 10:00–24:00, closed Monday). For picnicking, try the Plus supermarket on the tiny traffic circle a block from the train station (Monday–Friday 8:30–19:00, Saturday 8:00–14:00, closed Sunday, basement level of shopping complex).

Transportation Connections—Füssen

To: Neuschwanstein (2 buses/hrly, 10 min, 4.8 DM round-trip; taxis cost 15 DM), Reutte (5 buses/day, 30 min, no service on Sunday; taxis cost 35 DM), Munich (hrly, 2 hrs, transfer in Buchloe).

Romantic Road Buses: The northbound Romantic Road bus departs Füssen at 8:00, and the southbound bus arrives at Füssen at 20:40 (bus stops at train station).

REUTTE, AUSTRIA
(12 AS = about $1)
Reutte (ROY-teh, rolled "r"), population 5,500, is a relaxed town, far from the international tourist crowd but popular with Germans and Austrians for its climate. Doctors recommend its "grade 1" air. Reutte isn't in any other American guidebook. Its charms are

subtle. It never was rich or important. Its castle is ruined, its buildings have painted-on "carvings," its churches are full, its men
yodel for each other on birthdays, and lately its energy is spent
soaking its Austrian and German guests in *Gemütlichkeit.* Most
guests stay for a week, so the town's attractions are more time-
consuming than thrilling. If the weather's good, hike to the mysterious Ehrenberg ruins or ride the luge. For a slap-dancing bang,
enjoy a Tirolean folk evening.

Orientation (tel. code: 05672)
Tourist Information: Reutte's helpful TI is a block in front of the
train station (Monday–Friday 8:00–12:00, 13:00–17:00, Saturday
8:30–12:00, tel. 05672/62336 or, from Germany, 0043-5672/62336).
Go over your sightseeing plans, ask about a folk evening, pick up a
city map, and ask about discounts with the hotel guest cards.

    Arrival in Reutte: Head straight out of the station one long
block to the TI. At the TI, turn left to reach the center of town.

    Bike Rental: The train station rents bikes for 150 AS, moun-
tain bikes for 200 AS (50 percent discount if you have a railpass).

    Laundry: Don't ask the TI about a Laundromat. Unless you
can infiltrate the local campground, Hotel Maximilian, or Gutshof
zum Schluxen (see Sleeping, below), the town has none.

Sights—Reutte
▲▲Ehrenberg Ruins—The brooding ruins of Ehrenberg Castle
are a mile outside of Reutte on the road to Lermoos and Innsbruck. This 13th-century rock pile, a great contrast to King Ludwig's "modern" castles, is a super opportunity to let your
imagination off its leash. Hike up from the parking lot at the base
of the hill; it's a 25-minute walk to the castle for a great view from
your own private ruins. (Facing the hill from the parking lot, the
steeper trail is to the right, the easy gravelly road is to the left.)
Imagine how proud Count Meinrad II of Tirol (who built the castle in 1290) would be to know that his castle repelled 16,000
Swedish soldiers in the defense of Catholicism in 1632.

    The easiest way down is via the small road leading from the
gully. The car park, with a café/guest house (Gasthor Klaus closed
Wednesday, offers a German-language flyer about the castle and
has a wall painting of the intact castle), is just off the Lermoos/
Reutte road. Reutte is a pleasant one-hour walk away.

Folk Museum—Reutte's Heimatmuseum, offering a quick look at
the local folk culture and the story of the castle, is more cute than
impressive (20 AS, Tuesday–Sunday 10:00–12:00, 14:00–17:00,
closed Monday and off-season, in the Green House on Untermarkt, around the corner from Hotel Goldener Hirsch).

▲▲Tirolean Folk Evening—Ask the TI or your hotel if there's a
Tirolean folk evening scheduled. About once a week in the sum-

Reutte

mer, Reutte or a nearby town puts on an evening of yodeling, slap-dancing, and Tirolean frolic—usually worth the 80 AS and short drive. Off-season, you'll have to do your own yodeling. There are also weekly folk concerts in the park (ask at TI).

Swimming—Plunge into Reutte's Olympic-sized swimming pool to cool off after your castle hikes (60 AS, daily 10:00–21:00, off-season 14:00–21:00, closed Monday).

Reuttener Bergbahn—This mountain lift swoops you high above the tree line to a starting point for several hikes and to an Alpine flower park with special paths leading you past countless local varieties.

Flying and Gliding—For a major thrill on a sunny day, drop by the tiny airport in Hofen across the river, and fly. A small single-prop plane can buzz the Zugspitze and Ludwig's castles and give you a bird's-eye peek at Reutte's Ehrenberg ruins (two people for 30 minutes 1,350 AS, one hour 2,700 AS, tel. 05672/63207). Or, for something more angelic, how about *Segelfliegen*? For 500 AS, you get 30 minutes in a glider for two (you and the pilot). Just watching the tow-rope launch the graceful glider like a giant, slow-motion rubber-band gun is thrilling (11:00–19:00 late May–October, in good weather only, tel. 05672/71550).

Sights—Tirol, Near Reutte

▲▲**Sommerrodelbahn, the Luge**—Near Lermoos, on the Innsbruck-Lermoos-Reutte road, you'll find two rare and exciting luge courses, or *Sommerrodelbahn*. To try one of Europe's great $5 thrills: take the lift up, grab a sled-like go-cart, and luge down. The concrete course banks on the corners, and even a novice can go very, very fast. Most are cautious on their first run and speed demons on their second. (A woman once showed me her journal illustrated with her husband's dried five-inch-long luge scab. He disobeyed the only essential rule of luging: Keep both hands on your stick.) No one emerges from the course without a windblown hairdo and a smile-creased face. Both places have the same price and hours (70 AS per run, five- and 10-trip discount cards, open weekends from late May and daily mid-June through September or October, weather permitting, 9:00–17:00, closed in wet weather, so call first).

The small and steep luge: Bichlbach, the first course (100-meter drop over 800-meter course), is six kilometers beyond Reutte's castle ruins. Look for a chairlift on the right, and exit on the tiny road at the yellow "Riesenrutschbahn" sign (call first, tel. 05674/5350, or contact the local TI at 05674/5354). If you're without wheels, catch the train from Reutte to Bichlbach (6/day, 20 min) and walk one kilometer to the luge.

The longest luge: The Biberwier Sommerrodelbahn, which is 15 minutes closer to Innsbruck, just past Lermoos in Biberwier (the first exit after a long tunnel), is a better luge and, at 1,300 meters, the longest in Austria. The only drawbacks are its shorter season and that it's open only on weekends until July (9:00–16:30, tel. 05673/2111, local TI tel. 05673/2922). One or two blocks downhill from this luge, behind the Sport und Trachtenstüberl shop, is a wooden church dome with a striking Zugspitze backdrop. If you have sunshine and a camera, don't miss it. Without a car, the bus from Reutte to Biberwier is your best bet (8/day, fewer on Sunday, 30 min, bus stop and posted schedule near Reutte's Hotel Goldener Hirsch on Untermarket). The nearest train station is Lermoos, four kilometers from the luge.

▲**Fallerschein**—Easy for drivers and a special treat for those who may have been Kit Carson in a previous life, this extremely remote log-cabin village is a 4,000-foot-high, flower-speckled world of serene slopes and cowbells. Thunderstorms roll down the valley like it's God's bowling alley, but the pint-sized church on the high ground, blissfully simple in a land of Baroque, seems to promise that this huddle of houses will survive and the river and breeze will just keep flowing. The couples sitting on benches are mostly Austrian vacationers who've rented cabins here. Many of them, appreciating the remoteness of Fallerschein, are having affairs.

For a rugged chunk of local Alpine peace, spend a night in the local Matratzenlager Almwirtschaft Fallerschein, run by Kerle Erwin (120 AS per person with breakfast; open, if weather permits, mid-May–October; 27 cheap beds in a very simple loft dorm, meager plumbing, good, inexpensive meals, 6671 Weissenbach Pfarrweg 18, Reutte, tel. 05678/5142, rarely answered, and then not in English). It's crowded only on weekends. Fallerschein is at the end of a miserable, two-kilometer, fit-for-jeep-or-rental-car-only paved road that looks more closed than it is, near Namlos on the Berwang Road southwest of Reutte.

Sleeping in Reutte, Austria
(12 AS = about $1, tel. code: 05672, zip code: 6600)
For fewer crowds, easygoing locals with a contagious love of life, and a good dose of Austrian ambience, those with a car should home-base in nearby Reutte. (To call Reutte from Germany, dial 0043-5672, then the local number.) You'll drive across the border but probably won't even have to stop. All include breakfast.

Hotels
Reutte is popular with Austrians and Germans who come here year after year for a one- or two-week vacation. The hotels are big and elegant, full of comfy, carved furnishings and creative ways to spend so much time in one spot. They take great pride in their restaurants, and the owners send their children away to hotel management schools.

Hotel Goldener Hirsch, a grand old hotel renovated with a mod Tirolean Jugendstil flair, has sliding automatic doors, minibars, TV with cable in the room, and one lonely set of antlers. The hotel is located right downtown (two blocks from station). For those without a car, this is the most convenient hotel (Sb-550 AS, Db-880 AS, two-night discounts, elevator, grumpy unpredictable management, decent attached restaurant, CC:VMA, 6600 Reutte-Tirol, tel. 05672/62508 and ask for Monika or Helmut, fax 05672/625-087, e-mail: gold.hirsch@netway.at).

Hotel Maximilian, up the river a mile in the village of Ehenbichl, is a fine splurge that includes the use of bicycles, ping-pong, a children's playroom, and the friendly service of the Koch family. Daughter Gabi speaks fine English. There always seems to be a special event here, and the Kochs host many Tirolean folk evenings (Sb-450 AS, Db-900–960 AS, cheaper for families, laundry service, great restaurant, far from the train station in the next village but can often pick up, A-6600 Ehenbichl-Reutte, tel. 05672/62585, fax 05672/625-8554, e-mail: maxhotel@netway.at). You can use their laundry service even if you're not staying at the hotel.

Pension Hohenrainer is a big, friendly, family-run place offering castle-view balconies (Sb-260–300 AS, Db-560–600 AS). The same family runs the simpler **Gasthof Schlosswirt** across the flowery field (S-180–200 AS, D-360 AS, D with view-400 AS, traditional Tirolean-style restaurant). Both are up the road behind Hotel Maximilian (turn right and continue 100 meters to Unterreid 3, A-6600 Ehenbichl, tel. 05672/62544, fax 05672/62052, e-mail: hohenrainer@aon.at).

Gutshof zum Schluxen, run by friendly and helpful Hermann, gets the "remote-old-hotel-in-an-idyllic-setting" award. This working farm offers good food, modern rustic elegance draped in goose down and pastels, and a chance to pet the rabbit. Its picturesque meadow setting will turn you into a dandelion-picker (Sb-460–540 AS, Db-920–1,080 AS, extra person-220 AS, through 1999 only with this book, discounts for multi-night stays, excellent breakfast, self-service laundry, loaner bikes free for guests, free parking, free e-mail service, no credit cards, A-6600 Pinswang-Reutte, between Reutte and Füssen in the village of Unterpinswang, tel. 05677/8903, fax 05677/890-323, e-mail: schluxen@eunet.at). Schluxen is in the village of Pinswang, between Reutte and Füssen.

Gasthof-Pension Waldrast, separating a forest and a meadow, is warmly run by the Huter family. Its big rooms feel like living rooms, many with fine castle views (Db-about 700 AS, on Ehrenbergstrasse, a half-mile out of town toward Innsbruck, past the campground, just under the castle, 6600 Reutte-Ehenbichl, tel. & fax 05672/62443). The Waldrast is a good coffee stop for non-guests hiking into town from the Ehrenberg ruins.

Zimmer

The tourist office has a list of more than 50 private homes that rent out generally elegant rooms with facilities down the hall, pleasant communal living rooms, and breakfast. Most charge 200 AS per person per night, don't like to rent to people staying fewer than three nights, and speak little if any English. Reservations are nearly impossible for one- or two-night stays. But short stops are welcome if you just drop in and fill in available gaps. The TI can always find you a room when you arrive (free service).

The tiny village of Breitenwang, older and quieter than Reutte, has all the best *Zimmer* (a 20-minute walk from the Reutte train station: at the post office roundabout, follow Planseestrasse past the onion dome to the pointy straight dome; unmarked Kaiser Lothar Strasse is the first right past this church). These three places are comfortable, quiet, and kid-friendly, have few stairs, speak some English, and are within two blocks of the Breitenwang church steeple: **Inge Hosp** (S-200 AS, D-380 AS, an old-fashioned place, includes antlers over the breakfast table, Kaiser Lothar Strasse 36, tel. 05672/62401); her cousins **Walter and Emilie Hosp** across the street (D-400 AS for one night, D-380 AS for two or more, third or fourth person pays 160 AS, Kaiser Lothar Strasse 29, tel. 05672/ 65377); and **Helene Haissl** (S-190 AS, D-380 AS, 360 AS for a two-night stay, fine rooms, Planseestrasse 63, tel. 05672/ 67913). *Zimmer* charge 15 AS to 20 AS extra for heat in winter—worth it.

Hostels
Reutte has an excellent hostel. If you've never hosteled and are curious (and have a car), try this one. They accept non-members of any age.

The homey, newly renovated **Jugendgästehaus Graben** has two to six beds per room and includes breakfast and sheets (160 AS per bed, Db-400 AS, self-service laundry; from downtown Reutte, cross the bridge and follow the road left along the river, about two miles from Reutte's station—one bus per hour until 18:00; Graben 1, A-6600 Reutte-Höfen, tel. 05672/62644, fax 05672/626-444, e-mail: jgh-hoefen@tirol.com). Frau Reyman keeps the place traditional, clean, and friendly and serves a great 80-AS dinner. No curfew, smoke-free rooms, bus connection to Neuschwanstein. This is a super value.

Eating in Reutte
Each of the hotels takes great pleasure in earning the loyalty of its return guests by serving fine Austrian food at reasonable prices. Rather than go to a cheap restaurant, I'd order low on a hotel menu. For cheap food, the **Metzgerei Storf Imbiss** (Monday–Friday 8:30–15:00), above the deli across from the Heimatmuseum on Untermarkt Street, is good. **Carina** in Breitenwang is a fine Italian restaurant with decent prices (near *Zimmer*, Bachweg 17).

Transportation Connections—Reutte
To: Füssen (6 buses/day, 30 min, no service on Sunday; taxis cost 35 DM), **Garmisch** (2 trains/hr, 60 min), **Munich** (hrly trains, 3 hrs, transfer in Garmisch).

BADEN-BADEN AND THE BLACK FOREST

Combine Edenism and hedonism as you explore this most romantic of German forests and dip into its mineral spas.

The Black Forest, or "Schwarzwald" in German, is a range of hills stretching 100 miles north-south along the French border from Karlsruhe to Switzerland. Its highest peak is the 4,900-foot-tall Feldberg. Because of its thick forests, people called it black.

Until this century, the Schwarzwald had been cut off from the German mainstream. The poor farmland drove medieval locals to become foresters, glassblowers, and clock-makers. Strong traditions continue to be woven through the thick dialects and thatched roofs. On any Sunday, you will find *Volksmärsche* (group hikes) and traditional costumes coloring the Black Forest.

Popular with German holiday-goers and patients whose doctors have prescribed some serious "R&R," the Black Forest offers clean air, cuckoo clocks, cherry cakes, cheery villages, and countless hiking possibilities.

The area's two biggest tourist traps are the tiny Titisee Lake (not quite as big as its tourist parking lot) and Triberg, a small town filled with cuckoo clock shops. In spite of the crowds, the drives are extremely scenic, hiking is *wunderbar*, and the attractions listed below are well worth a visit. The two major (and very different) towns are Baden-Baden in the north and Freiburg in the south. Freiburg may be the Black Forest's capital, but Baden-Baden is Germany's greatest 19th-century spa resort. Stroll through its elegant streets and casino. Soak in its famous baths.

Planning Your Time

Tour Freiburg, but sleep in charming and overlooked Staufen. By train, Freiburg and Baden-Baden are easy, as is a short foray into

The Black Forest

the forest from either. With more time, do the small-town forest medley between the two. With a car, I'd do the whole cuckoo thing: a night in Staufen, a busy day touring north, and two nights and a relaxing day in Baden-Baden.

A blitz day from Murten or Interlaken (Switzerland) would go like this: 8:30–depart, 11:00–Staufen (stroll town, change money, buy picnic), 12:30–scenic drive to Furtwangen with a scenic picnic along the way, 2:30–tour clock museum, 15:30–drive to Gütach, 16:30–tour open-air folk museum, 18:00–drive into Baden-Baden, 20:00–arrive in Baden-Baden. With an overnight in Staufen, you could spend the morning in Freiburg and arrive in Baden-Baden in time for a visit to the spa (last entry 19:30).

BADEN-BADEN

Of all the high-class resort towns I've seen, Baden-Baden is the easiest to enjoy in jeans with a picnic. This was the playground of

Europe's high-rolling elite 150 years ago. Royalty and aristocracy would come from all corners to take the *Kur*—a soak in the curative (or at least they feel that way) mineral waters—and enjoy the world's top casino. Today this town of 55,000 attracts a more middle-class crowd, both tourists in search of a lower pulse and Germans enjoying the fruits of their generous healthcare system.

Orientation (tel. code: 07221)

Baden-Baden is made for strolling with a poodle. The train station is in a suburb called Baden-Oos, 5 kilometers from the center—easily connected with the center by bus #201. Except for the station and a couple of hotels on the opposite side of town, everything that matters is clustered within a 10-minute walk between the baths and the casino.

Tourist Information: At the TI, behind the fountain on Augustaplatz 8, pick up a map and monthly program (daily 9:30–18:00, tel. 07221/275-200; additional office on B-500 Autobahn exit at Schwartzwaldstrasse 52, longer hours). It has enough recommended walks and organized excursions to keep the most energetic vacationer happy.

Getting Around Baden-Baden: Only one bus matters. Bus #201 runs straight through Baden-Baden, connecting its Oos train station, town center, and the east end of town (runs every 10 minutes; buy tickets from driver: 3-DM ticket per person, or the 8-DM, 24-hour pass good for two people). Tickets are valid for 90 minutes but only in one direction. With bus #201 you don't need to mess with downtown parking.

Sights-Sights—Baden-Baden

▲▲**Strolling Lichtentaler Allee**—Bestow a royal title on yourself and promenade down the famous Lichtentaler Allee, a pleasant 1.5-mile lane through a park along the babbling, brick-lined Oos River, past old mansions, and under hearty oaks and exotic trees (lit until 22:00), to the historic Lichtentaler Abbey (a Cistercian convent founded in 1245). At the mini-golf course (welcomes public) and elitist tennis courts, cross the bridge into the free Art Nouveau rose garden (*Gönneranlage*, 100 labeled kinds of roses, great lounge chairs, best in early summer). Either walk the whole length roundtrip, or take city bus #201 one way (runs between downtown and Klosterplatz, near the abbey). Many bridges cross the river, making it easy to shortcut to bus #201 anytime.

▲**Mini-Black Forest Walks**—Baden-Baden is at the northern end of the Black Forest. If you're not going south but want a taste of Germany's favorite woods, consider one of several hikes from town.

The best is probably the hike that starts from the old town past the Neues Schloss (new castle) to the Altes Schloss (ruined old castle), which crowns a hill above town, past cliffs tinseled

Baden–Baden

TO OOS & TRAIN STATION

TO OLD CASTLE

ROMAN·IRISH BATHS

ALTE BAHNHOF

LANGE STRASSE

NEUES SCHLOSS

HINDENBURG PLATZ

SCHLOSS STR

CARACALLA BATHS

TRINK-HALLE

MARKT PLATZ

SOPHIENSTRASSE

KURHAUS CASINO

POST

LEOPOLDPLATZ

N DCH

GOETHEPLATZ

CONCERT

AUGUSTA PLATZ

MICHAELSTUNNEL

LICHTENTALER

LICHTENTALER

BERT. STR.

BERTHOLD PLATZ

MINI·GOLF

STR

MAXIMILIAN STRASSE

GÖNNER-ANLAGE (ROSE GARDEN)

THALER ALLEE

OOSBACH

RIVER

❶ HOTEL AM MARKT
❷ GASTHAUS NEST
❸ HOTEL DEUTSCHER KAISER

KLOSTER LICHTENTAL

¼ MILE

with rock climbers and on to Ebersteinburg, a village with a ruined castle (catch bus #214 back into town).

For less work and more view, consider riding the cogwheel Merkur Bergbahn (take bus #204 or #205 from Leopoldsplatz to the end of the line and catch 5-DM funicular up, tel. 07221/31640) to the 2,000-foot summit of Merkur, following the trails to the Lichtentaler Abbey, and then along Lichtentaler Allee into town.

▲▲**Casino and Kurhaus**—The impressive building called the Kurhaus is wrapped around a grand casino. Built in the 1850s in wannabe-French style, Marlene Dietrich declared this "the most beautiful casino." Inspired by the Palace of Versailles, it's filled with rooms honoring French royalty who never set foot in the place. But many French did. Gambling was illegal in 19th-century France . . . just over the border. The casino is licenced on the precondition that it pay about 90 percent of its earnings in taxes to fund state-sponsored social programs and public works. It earns $100 million a year . . . and is the toast of Baden-Baden, or at least its bread and butter. The staff of 400 is paid by tips from happy gamblers.

You can visit the casino on a tour (when it's closed to gamblers), or you can drop by after 14:00 to gamble or just observe. (This is no problem—a third of the visitors only observe.) The place is most interesting in action; people-watch under raining chandeliers. The scene is more subdued than at an American casino; anyone showing emotions is a tourist. Lean against a gilded statue and listen to the graceful reshuffling of personal fortunes. Do some imaginary gambling, or buy a few chips at the window near the entry. The casino is open for gambling from 14:00 to 2:00 (5-DM entry, 5-DM minimum bet, 10-DM minimum on weekends, no blue jeans or tennis shoes, tie and coat required and rentable for 20 DM, passport absolutely required, liveliest after dinner and later, pick up English history and game rules as you enter).

Casino Tour: The casino gives 30-minute German-language tours every morning from 9:30 to 12:00 (6 DM, 2/hour, last departure at 11:30, tel. 07221/21060, call to see if there's an English tour scheduled, otherwise organize English-speakers in the group and aggressively lobby for information, pick up the paltry English brochure). Even peasants in T-shirts, shorts, and thongs are welcome on tours.

From the steps of the casino, stand between big white columns #2 and #3 and survey the surroundings (left to right): find the ruined castle near the top of the hill, the rock-climbing cliffs next, the new castle (top of town) next to the red spire of the Catholic church (famous baths are just behind that), the Merkur peak (marked by tower, 2,000 feet above sea level), and the bandstand in the Kurhaus garden. The Baden-Baden orchestra plays here most days (free, usually at 16:00).

Beyond the colonnade on your left is the old **Trinkhalle.** 300-foot-long entrance hall decorated with nymphs and romantic legends (a book inside explains them). In the tacky souvenir shop grab a free glass of mineral water. Enjoy the *Herald Tribune* in the reading room on the side of the hall nearest the casino.

Sights—The Baths

Baden-Baden's two much-loved but very different baths stand side-by-side in a park at the top of the old town. The Roman-Irish Bath is traditional, stately, indoors, not very social, extremely relaxing ...just you, the past, and your body. The perky, fun, and modern baths of Caracalla Baths are half the price, indoor/outdoor, fun, and more social. In each case, your admission ticket works like a subway token—you need it to get out. If you overstay your allotted time, you pay extra. You can relax with your valuables in very secure lockers. Both baths share a huge underground Kur-Garage, which is free only if you validate your parking ticket before leaving either bath. Caracalla is better in the sunshine. Roman-Irish is fine anytime. Most visitors do both. Save 10 to 15 percent by buying tickets from your hotel.

▲▲▲**Roman-Irish Bath (Friedrichsbad)**—The highlight of most Baden-Baden visits is a sober two-hour ritual called the Roman-Irish Bath. Friedrichsbad, on Römerplatz 1, pampered the rich and famous in its elegant surroundings when it opened 120 years ago. Today this steamy world of marble, brass columns, tropical tiles, herons, lily pads, and graceful nudity welcomes gawky tourists as well as locals. For 48 DM you get up to three hours and the works (36 DM without the eight-minute massage; some hotels sell a reduced-admission ticket).

Read this carefully before stepping out naked: In your changing cabin load all your possessions onto the fancy hanger (hang it in locker across the way, slip card into lock, strap key around wrist). As you enter (in the "creme" room), check your weight on the digital kilo scale. Do this again as you leave. You will have lost a kilo...all in sweat. The complex routine is written (in English) on the walls with recommended time—simply follow the room numbers from 1 to 15.

Take a shower; grab a towel and put on plastic slippers before hitting the warm-air bath for 15 minutes and the hot-air bath for five minutes; shower again; if you paid extra, take the soap-brush massage—rough, slippery, and finished with a spank; play Gumby in the shower; lounge under sunbeams in one of several different thermal steam baths; glide like a swan under a divine dome in a royal pool (one of three "mixed" pools); don't skip the cold plunge; dry in warmed towels; and lay cocooned, clean, and thinking prenatal thoughts on a bed for 30 minutes in the mellow, yellow, silent room (don't skip the sleep room). You don't appreciate how really clean you are after this experience until you put your dirty socks back on. (Bring clean ones.)

All you need is money. You'll get a key, locker, and towel (Monday–Saturday 9:00–22:00, Sunday 12:00–20:00, men and women together Wednesday, Saturday, Sunday, and from 16:00–22:00 on Tuesday and Friday, last admission at 19:00 if you'll get a massage, at 19:30 otherwise, tel. 07221/275-920).

About the dress code: it's always nude. During "separate" times, men and women use parallel and nearly identical facilities. "Mixed" is still mostly separate, with men and women sharing only three pools in the center.

Afterward, before going downstairs, browse through the Roman artifacts in the Renaissance Hall, sip just a little terrible but "magic" hot water (*Thermalwasser*) from the elegant fountain, and stroll down the broad royal stairway feeling, as they say, five years younger—or at least 2.2 pounds lighter.

▲▲**Caracalla Therme**—For more of a glorified experience, spend a few hours at the Baths of Caracalla (daily 8:00–22:00, last entry at 20:00), a huge palace of water, steam, and relaxed people.

Bring a towel and swimsuit (shorts are OK for men). Buy a card (19 DM for two hours, 25 DM for three hours, 10 entries—for a group or repeat visits—cost only 155 DM), put the card in the locker to get a key, change, strap the key around your wrist, and go play. Your key gets you into another poolside locker if you want money for a tan or a drink. The Caracalla Therme is an indoor/outdoor wonderland of steamy pools, waterfalls, neck showers, Jacuzzis, hot springs, cold pools, lounge chairs, exercise instructors, saunas, a cafeteria, and a bar. After taking a few laps around the fake river, you can join the kinky gang for water spankings (you may have to wait a few minutes to grab a vacant waterfall). Then join the gang in the central cauldron. The steamy "inhalation" room seems like purgatory's waiting room, with six misty inches of visibility, filled with strange, silently aging bodies.

The spiral staircase leads to a naked world of saunas, tanning lights, cold plunges, and sunbathing. There are three eucalyptus-smelling saunas of varying temperatures: 80, 90, and 95 degrees. Follow the instructions on the wall. Towels are required, not for modesty but to separate your body from the wood bench. The highlight is the Arctic bucket in the shower room. Pull the chain. Only rarely will you feel so good. And you can do this over and over. As you leave, take a look at the Roman bath that Emperor Caracalla soaked in to conquer his rheumatism nearly 2,000 years ago.

Sleeping in Baden-Baden
(1.7 DM = about $1, tel. code: 07221, zip code: 76530)
Sleep Code: **S** = Single, **D** = Double/Twin, **T** = Triple, **Q** = Quad, **b** = bathroom, **t** = toilet only, **s** = shower only, **CC** = Credit Card (**V**isa, **M**asterCard, **A**mex), **SE** = Speaks English, **NSE** = No English.

The TI can nearly always find you a room, but don't use the TI for places listed here or you'll pay more. Go direct! The only tight times are during the horse races (May 15–23 and August 27–September 5 in 1999). If you arrive at Baden-Baden's Oos station, stay near the station (see below) or hop bus #201, which takes you to the center of town (stop at Leopoldplatz, the first stop in the pedestrian zone, for Hotel am Markt, baths, and casino; Augustaplatz for TI and other hotels) and continues to Hotel Deutscher Kaiser (stop: Eckerlestrasse) on the east end of town. Hotel am Markt and Hotel Deutscher Kaiser, clearly the best values, are worth calling in advance.

Unless otherwise noted, assume a fine breakfast is included.

Most hotels give a "guest card" offering small discounts on tourist admissions around town. All hotels and pensions are required to extract an additional 4 DM per-person per-night "spa tax."

Sleeping in the Center

Hotel am Markt is a warm, small, family-run hotel with all the comforts a commoner could want in a peaceful, central, nearly traffic-free location, two cobbled blocks from the baths (S-55 DM, Sb-75–90 DM, Dt-95–110 DM, Db-128–140 DM, Tb-155 DM, extra person-30 DM, CC:VMA, Marktplatz 18, tel. 07221/27040, fax 07221/270-444, Herr und Frau Bogner and Frau Jung all speak English). The church bells blast charmingly through each room every quarter hour from 6:30 until 22:00. Otherwise, quiet rules. The ambience and the clientele make killing time on their small terrace a joy. The daily menu offers a good dinner deal (orders 18:00–19:30, guests only). Walk from central Leopoldsplatz three minutes uphill to the red-spired church on Marktplatz.

Around the corner from Hotel am Markt, **Bratwurstglöckel** is a 16th-century guest house with five cozy rooms and steep stairs (Sb-110 DM, Db-135–150 DM, noisy, cable TV, good meals at attached restaurant but compare prices between their German and English menus, CC:VM, tel. 07221/90610, fax 07221/906-161, Michael Rothe).

Gasthaus Nest is an amazing anomoly—so basic and simple in the heart of this elegant spa resort. They rent six simple rooms (some with no sink) that share one toilet and shower above a popular but smoky restaurant one block off the pedestrian zone's Lichtentalerstrasse (S-40–50 DM, sinkless D-60 DM, D-78 DM, breakfast-10 DM, family room, CC:VMA, free parking, Rettigstrasse 1, tel. 07221/23076, fax 07221/28672).

Gästehaus Löhr is very central but worthwhile only as a last resort (D-90 DM, Db-120 DM, CC:VMA, reception at Café Löhr, 19 Lichtentaler Strasse, rooms two blocks away, tel. 07221/300960).

Hotel Beeg rents 15 attractive and very comfortable rooms, run (without a reception) from a delectable pastry shop/café on the ground floor. It's perfectly located on a little square in a pedestrian zone, facing the baths (Sb-120 DM, Db-160 DM, extra person-45 DM, balcony-10 DM extra, CC:VMA, elevator, on Romerplatz, Gernsbacher Strasse 44, tel. 07221/36760, fax 07221/367-610).

Sleeping on Southeast End of Lichtentaler Allee

Deutscher Kaiser offers some of the best rooms in town for the money. This big, traditional guest house is warmly run by Frau Peter, who enjoys taking care of my readers. Herr Peter cooks fine local-style meals (14–30 DM) in the hotel restaurant. It's right on the bus #201 line (at Eckerlestrasse stop, 30 minutes from train station) or a 20-minute stroll from the city center down polite Licht-entaler Allee—cross the river at "Restaurant Deutscher Kaiser" sign (S-60 DM, Sb-80 DM, D-80–90 DM, Db-110–120 DM, hall showers-3 DM, CC:VMA, some non-smoking rooms, free and easy parking, Hauptstrasse 35, 76534 Baden-Baden–Lichtental, tel. 07221/72152, fax 07221/72154, e-mail: deutscherkaiser@t-online.de). Drivers: From Autobahn, skip town center by following "Congress" signs into Michaelstunnel. Take first exit in tunnel (Lichtental) and another right inside tunnel. Outside, hotel is 300 meters on left. From Black Forest, follow *Zentrum* signs. Ten meters after Aral gas station, turn left down small road to Hauptstrasse.

Gasthof Cäcilienberg is comfortable and beautifully situated even farther out in a quiet area at the end of Lichtentaler Allee (S-58 DM, Sb-68 DM, D-88 DM, Db-98 DM, take bus #201 and get off at Brahmsplatz, Geroldsauer Strasse 2, tel. 07221/ 72297, fax 07221/70459, NSE).

More Baden-Baden Accommodations

Near the Train Station: Gasthof Adler is clean, comfortable, and friendly (25 rooms, S-60 DM, Ss-65 DM, Sb-85 DM, D-100 DM, Ds-110 DM, Db-120–145 DM, CC:VMA, veer right from station, walk three blocks passing post office to stoplight, hotel is on corner, Ooser Hauptstrasse 1, 76532 Baden-Baden Oos, tel. 07221/61858 or 07221/61811, fax 07221/17145). Bus #201 stops across the street.

Hostel: The **Werner Dietz Hostel**, while not cheap, is a good value (beds in two- to six-bed rooms, sheets, and breakfast for 28.50 DM, 33.50 DM if you're 27 or older, add 6 DM if you have no hostel card, Hardbergstrasse 34, bus #201 from the station or downtown to Grosse Dollenstrasse—announced as "Jugendherberge Stop," it's a steep well-marked 10-minute climb from there, tel. 07221/ 52223, SE). They save 25 beds to be doled out at 17:00, give 4.60-DM discount coupons for both city baths, and serve cheap meals. (Drivers, after the freeway to Baden-Baden ends, turn left at first light, and follow signs, winding uphill to the big, modern hostel next to a public swimming pool.)

Eating in Baden-Baden

The recommended hotels **Am Markt** (residents only) and **Deutscher Kaiser** (consider as part of your evening Lichtentaler Allee stroll) both serve fine dinners. For beer garden ambience in the town center, **Löwenbrau Baden-Baden** can't be beat (18 DM to 30 DM meals, leafy outdoors or antlered indoors, nightly, Gernsbacher Strasse 9, tel. 07221/22311). **La Provence**, with an ecletic menu and good food and prices, is popular (daily 12:00–1:00, CC:VMA, from Marktplatz hike up Schloss Strasse to #20, tel. 07221/25550). If you want to spend too much for an elegant 19th-century cup of coffee, **Café Koenig**, on Augustaplatz, is the place.

Transportation Connections—Baden-Baden

By train to: Freiburg (hrly, 60 min), **Triberg** (8/day, 60 min),
Heidelberg (hrly, 60 min, catch Castle Road bus to Rothenburg),
Munich (hrly, 4 hrs, with two changes), **Frankfurt** (2/hrly, 1.5 hrs
with a change), **Koblenz** (hrly, 2.5 hrs with a change), **Mainz am
Rhine** (hrly, 90 min), **Strasbourg** (5/day, 45 min), **Bern** (hrly, 3.5
hrs, transfer in Basel).

FREIBURG

Freiburg (FRY-burg) is worth a quick look. The "sunniest town in
Germany" feels like the university town it is, with 30,000 students.
Freiburg, nearly bombed flat in 1944, skillfully put itself back
together. And it feels cozy, almost Austrian; it was Habsburg terri-
tory for 500 years. It's the "capital" of the Schwarzwald, surrounded by lush forests and filled with environmentally sensitive
people. Enjoy the pedestrian-only old center. Freiburg's trademark
is its system of *Bächle*, tiny streams running down each street.
These go back to the Middle Ages (fire protection, cattle refresh-
ment, constantly flushing disposal system). A sunny day turns any
kid into a puddle-stomper. Enjoy the ice cream and street-singing
ambience of the cathedral square, which has a great produce and
craft market (Monday–Saturday 8:00–14:30).

Orientation (tel. code: 0761)

Tourist Information: Freiburg's busy TI offers a good 6-DM
city guidebook, a room-finding service, a city map, a 1-DM
brochure with a self-guided walking tour, 10-DM German-
English guided walks (several days a week at 10:30 and 14:30),
information on the Black Forest region, and an American Express
booth (Monday–Saturday 9:30–20:00, Sunday 10:00–12:00, less
off-season, WC around the corner, tel. 0761/388-1881).

   Arrival in Freiburg: As you leave the train station, head
straight ahead down Eisenbahnstrasse, the tree-lined boulevard
(passing the post office). Within three blocks you'll take an
underpass under a busy road; as you emerge, the TI is on your left
and the town center is dead ahead.

Sights—Freiburg

▲**Church (Münster)**—This impressive church, completed in 1513,
took more than three centuries to build and ranges in style from late
Romanesque to lighter, brighter Gothic. It was virtually the only
building in town to survive World War II bombs. The lacy tower,
considered by many the most beautiful around, is as tall as the
church is long...and not worth the 329-step ascent. From this lofty
perch, watchmen used to scan the town for fires. While you could
count the 123 representations of Mary throughout the church, most
gawk at the "mooning" gargoyle and wait for rain. Enjoy the market

in the square. The ornate Historisches Kaufhaus, across from the church, was a trading center in the 16th century.

Augustiner Museum—This offers a good look at Black Forest art and culture through the ages. Highlights are downstairs: a close-up look at some of the Münster's original medieval stained glass and statuary (4 DM, Tuesday–Sunday 10:00–17:00, closed Monday).

Schauinsland—Freiburg's own mountain, while little more than an oversized hill, offers the handiest quick look at the Schwarzwald for those without wheels. A gondola system, one of Germany's oldest, was designed for Freiburgers relying on public transportation. At the 4,000-foot summit are a panorama restaurant, pleasant circular walks, and the Schniederli Hof, a 1592 farmhouse museum. A tower on a nearby peak offers a commanding Black Forest view (20 DM round-trip, ride tram #4 from town center to end, then take bus #21 seven stops to lift, tel. 0671/292-930). This excursion will not thrill Americans from Colorado.

Sleeping in Freiburg
(1.7 DM = about $1, tel. code: 0761, zip code: 79098)
I prefer to sleep in Staufen (see below), a pleasant, cheaper, small-town alternative to Freiburg. The first two Freiburg listings are a 15-minute walk or easy bus ride from the station. Prices include breakfast, and English is spoken.

Hotel Alleehaus is tops. Located on a quiet, leafy street in a big house that feels like home, it's thoughtfully decorated and warmly run (S-75 DM, Ss-80 DM, Sb-98 DM, D-105 DM, one small Db-120 DM, Db-140 DM, CC:VM, cable car #4 from station to Holzmarkt, Marienstrasse 7, cross street: Wallstrasse, tel. 0761/387-600, fax 0761/387-6099, phone answered 7:00–18:30).

Hotel am Stadtgarten is also near the old town, with comfortable rooms heavy on beige (S-87 DM, Ss-92 DM, Sb-97 DM, Db-129 DM, Tb-186 DM, Q with kitchenette-228 DM, tram #5 two stops from station to Bernhardstrasse 5, cross street: Karlstrasse, tel. 0761/282-9002, fax 0761/282-9022).

If you're willing to pay dearly to be near the station, stay at **Hotel Barbara**. Its rooms are brighter than its dark lobby (Sb-130 DM, Db-160–170 DM, some non-smoking rooms, CC:VM, on quiet street two minutes from station, head towards TI but turn left to Poststrasse 4, tel. 0761/296250, fax 0761/26688).

City Hotel is business class, with clean, modern rooms, near the station, main shopping street, and old town (Db-160–200 DM, CC:VMA, Weberstrasse 3, tel. 0761/388-070, fax 0761/388-0765).

The big, modern **Freiburg Youth Hostel** is on the east edge of Freiburg on the scenic road into the Black Forest (28 DM per bed with sheets and breakfast, "seniors" over 26 pay 32.50 DM, hostel card required, Kartuserstrasse 151, tram #1 to Römerhof, tel. 0761/67656).

Transportation Connections—Freiburg

By train to: Staufen (hrly, 30 min, 2/day are direct, others require easy change in Bad Krozingen, after 21:00 no trains to Staufen but shared taxis from Bad Krozingen station), **Baden-Baden** (6/day, 45 min), **Munich** (hrly, 4.5 hrs, transfer in Mannheim), **Mainz am Rhine** (6/day, 2.5 hrs), **Basel** (hrly, 45 min), **Bern** (hrly, 2.5 hrs, transfer in Basel).

STAUFEN

Staufen makes a delightful home base for your exploration of Freiburg and the southern trunk of the Black Forest. A mini-Freiburg, it's a perfect combination of smallness and off-the-beaten-pathness with a quiet pedestrian zone of colorful old buildings bounded by a happy creek that actually babbles. There's nothing to do here but enjoy the marketplace atmosphere. Hike through the vineyards to the ruined castle overlooking the town, and savor a good dinner with local wine. A pub at the base of the castle hill offers *Weinprobe* (wine tasting).

Orientation (tel. code: 07633)

Tourist Information: Staufen's TI, on the main square in the Rathaus, can help you find a room (Monday–Friday 8:00–16:30, closed lunchtime, Saturday afternoon and Sunday, tel. 07633/80536).

Arrival in Staufen: At the train station, as you face the Gasthaus Bahnhof (see Sleeping, below), angle right up Bahnhofstrasse. Turn right at the post office on Hauptstrasse for the town center, hotels, and TI.

Sights—Near Staufen

Wine Road (Badische Weinstrasse)—The wine road of this part of Germany staggers from Staufen through the tiny towns of Grunern, Dottingen, Sulzburg, and Britzingen, before sitting down in Badenweiler. If you're in the mood for some tasting, look for "Winzergenossenshaft" signs, which invite visitors in to taste and buy the wines, and often to tour the winery.

▲**Badenweiler**—If ever a town was a park, Badenweiler is it; it's an idyllic, poodle-elegant, and finicky-clean spa town known only to the wealthy Germans who soak there. Its bath, *Markgrafenbad*, is next to the ruins of a Roman mineral bath in a park of imported and exotic trees (including a California redwood). This prize-winning piece of architecture perfectly mixes trees and peace with an elegant indoor/outdoor swimming pool (daily 8:00–18:00, Monday, Wednesday, and Friday until 20:00). The locker procedure, combined with the language barrier, makes getting to the pool more memorable than you'd expect (three hours for 14 DM; towels, required caps, and suits are rentable). Badenweiler is a 20-minute drive south of Staufen.

Sleeping in Staufen
(1.7 DM = about $1, tel. code: 07633, zip code: 79219)
The TI has a list of private *Zimmer* (posted on the window after hours). Prices listed are for one night, but most *Zimmer* don't like one-nighters. You'll usually get a 10-DM discount for stays of three nights or more.

Gasthaus Bahnhof is the cheapest place in town, with a castle out back, a self-service kitchen, and 14-DM dinners (S-30 DM, D-70 DM, no breakfast, across from train station, tel. 07633/6190). It can seem a little depressing during the day, but at night, master of ceremonies Lotte makes it the squeeze-box of Staufen. People come from miles around to party with Lotte. If you want to eat red meat in a wine barrel under a tree, this is the place. For three-night or longer stays, ask her about the rooms next door (Sb-50 DM, Db-80 DM).

Hotel Krone gilds the lily but is still the best value in this price range (Sb-90 DM, Db-130 DM, Tb-170 DM, CC:VMA, Hauptstrasse 30, on the main pedestrian street, tel. 07633/5840, fax 07633/82903). Its restaurant appreciates vegetables and offers wonderful splurge meals (closed Saturday).

Gasthaus Hirschen, which has a storybook location in the old pedestrian center and a characteristic restaurant (closed Monday and Tuesday), is family-run with all the comforts (Sb-80 DM, Db-120 DM, Tb-170 DM, reservations unreliable, Hauptstrasse 19 on the main pedestrian street, tel. 07633/5297, fax 07633/5295). They have a penthouse apartment for four (230 DM).

Hotel Sonne, with eight comfortable rooms, is at the edge of the pedestrian center (Sb-80 DM, Db-110 DM, continue straight past the Hotel Krone, turn right at T-intersection, and take second left on Muhlegasse to reach Albert-Hugard Strasse 1, elevator, tel. 07633/95100).

Sights—Black Forest
▲▲**Short and Scenic Black Forest Joyride**—This pleasant loop from Staufen (or Freiburg) takes you through the most representative chunk of the area, avoiding the touristy, overcrowded Titisee. Leave Staufen on Schwarzwaldstrasse (signs to Donaueschingen), which becomes Scenic Road 31 down the dark Höllental (Hell's Valley) toward Titisee. Turn left at Hinterzarten onto Road 500, follow signs to St. Margen, then to St. Peter—one of the healthy, go-take-a-walk-in-the-clean-air places that doctors actually prescribe for people from all over Germany. There is a fine seven-kilometer walk between these two towns, with regular buses to bring you back. St. Peter's TI, just next to the Benedictine Abbey (private), can recommend a walk (Monday–Friday 8:00–12:00, 14:00–17:00, Saturday 11:00–13:00, tel. 07660/910-224). You can sleep at the traditional old Gasthof Hirschen on the

main square (Db-120 DM, St. Peter/Hochschwarzwald, tel. 07660/204, fax 07660/1557) or Pension Kandelblick (D or Db-70 DM, Schweighofweg, tel. 07660/349). Several morning and late-afternoon buses connect Freiburg and St. Peter.

From St. Peter, wind through idyllic Black Forest scenery up to Kandelhof. At the summit is the Berghotel Kandel. You can park here and take a short walk to the 4,000-foot peak for a great view. Then the road winds steeply through a dense forest to Waldkirch, where a fast road takes you to the Freiburg Nord Autobahn entrance. With a good car and no stops, you'll get from Staufen/Freiburg to Baden-Baden via this route in three hours.

▲▲**Extended Black Forest Drive**—Of course, you could spend much more time in the land of cuckoo clocks and healthy hikes. For a more thorough visit, still connecting with Baden-Baden, try this drive: As described above, drive from Staufen or Freiburg down Höllental. After a short stop in St. Peter, wind up in Furtwangen, with the impressive Deutsches Uhrenmuseum (German Clock Museum, 5 DM, daily April–October 9:00–18:00, less off-season, tel. 07723/920-117). More than a chorus of cuckoo clocks, this museum traces (with interesting English descriptions) the development of clocks from the Dark Ages to the space age. It has an upbeat combo of mechanical musical instruments as well.

Triberg—Deep in the Black Forest, Triberg's famous for its Gutach Waterfall (which falls 500 feet in several bounces, 3 DM to see it) and, more important, the Heimatmuseum, which gives a fine look at the costumes, carvings, and traditions of the local culture (5 DM, daily 8:00–18:00, shorter hours off-season). Touristy as Triberg is, it offers an easy way for travelers without cars to enjoy the Black Forest (TI tel. 07722/953-230).

▲**Black Forest Open-Air Museum (Schwarzwälder Freilichtermuseum)**—This offers the best look at this region's traditional folk life. Built around one grand old farmhouse, the museum is a collection of several old farms filled with exhibits on the local dress and lifestyles (7 DM, 30-DM guided tour with small groups but call first, daily April–October 8:30–18:00, last entry 17:00, north of Triberg, through Hornberg to Hausach/Gutach, tel. 07831/230). The surrounding shops and restaurants are awfully touristy. Try your *Schwarzwald Kirschtorte* (Black Forest cherry cake) elsewhere.

Continue north, through Freudenstadt, the capital of the northern Black Forest, and onto the Schwarzwald-Hochstrasse, which takes you along a ridge through 30 miles of pine forests before dumping you right on Baden-Baden's back porch.

ROTHENBURG AND THE ROMANTIC ROAD

From Munich or Füssen to Frankfurt, the Romantic Road takes you through Bavaria's medieval heartland, a route strewn with picturesque villages, farmhouses, onion-domed churches, Baroque palaces, and walled cities.

Dive into the Middle Ages via Rothenburg (ROE-ten-burg), Germany's best-preserved walled town. Countless travelers have searched for the elusive "untouristy Rothenburg." There are many contenders (such as Michelstadt, Miltenberg, Bamberg, Bad Windsheim, and Dinkelsbühl), but none holds a candle to the king of medieval German cuteness. Even with crowds, overpriced souvenirs, Japanese-speaking night watchmen, and yes, even with *Schneebälle*, Rothenburg is best. Save time and mileage, and be satisfied with the winner.

Planning Your Time

The best one-day look at the heartland of Germany is the Romantic Road bus tour. Eurail travelers, who get a 75-percent discount, pay only 39 DM for the ride (daily, Frankfurt to Munich or Füssen, and vice versa). Drivers can follow the route laid out in the tourist brochures (available at any TI). The only stop worth more than a few minutes is Rothenburg. Twenty-four hours is ideal for this town. Two nights and a day is a bit much, unless you're actually relaxing on this trip.

Rothenburg in a day is easy, with four essential experiences: the Medieval Crime and Punishment Museum, the Riemenschneider wood carving in St. Jacob's Church, the city walking tour, and a walk along the wall. With more time there are several mediocre but entertaining museums, walking and biking in the nearby countryside, and lots of cafés and shops. Make a point to spend at least

Rothenburg

one night. The town is yours after dark, when the groups vacate and the town's floodlit cobbles wring some romance out of any travel partner.

ROTHENBURG

In the Middle Ages, when Frankfurt and Munich were just wide spots on the road, Rothenburg was Germany's second-largest free imperial city, with a whopping population of 6,000. Today it's her best-preserved medieval walled town, enjoying tremendous tourist popularity without losing its charm. Get medievaled in Rothenburg.

Orientation (tel. code: 09861)

To orient yourself in Rothenburg, think of the town map as a human head. Its nose—the castle garden—sticks out to the left, and the neck is the skinny lower part, with the hostel and my favorite hotels in the Adam's apple. The town is a joy on foot. No sight or hotel is more than a 15-minute walk from the train station or each other.

During Rothenburg's heyday, from 1150 to 1400, it was the crossing point of two major trade routes: Tashkent–Paris and Hamburg–Venice. Most of the buildings you'll see were built by 1400. The city was born around its long-gone castle—built in 1142, destroyed in 1356, and now the site of the castle garden. You can see the shadow of the first town wall, which defines the oldest part of Rothenburg, in its contemporary street plan. A few gates from this wall survive. The richest and biggest houses were in this central part. The commoners built higgledy-piggledy (read: picturesquely) farther from the center near the present walls.

Today the great trade is tourism; two-thirds of the townspeople are employed to serve you. Too often Rothenburg brings out the shopper in visitors before they've had a chance to appreciate the historic city. True, this is a great place to do your German shopping, but first see the town. While 2.5 million people visit each year, a mere 500,000 spend the night. Rothenburg is most enjoyable early and late, when the tour groups are gone.

Tourist Information: The TI is on Market Square (Monday–Friday 9:00–12:30, 13:00–18:00, Saturday and Sunday 10:00–15:00 unreliably, shorter hours off-season, tel. 09861/40492, after-hours board lists rooms still available). Pick up a map and the *Sights Worth Seeing and Knowing* brochure (a virtual walking guide to the town). The free "Hotels and Pensions of Rothenburg" map has the greatest detail and names all of the streets. Confirm sightseeing plans and ask about the daily 14:00 walking tour (April–December) and evening entertainment. The best town map is available free at the Friese shop, two doors toward Rothenburg's "nose."

Arrival in Rothenburg: Exit left from the train station, and turn right on the first busy street (Ansbacher Strasse). It'll take you to Rothenburg's Market Square within 10 minutes. Leave luggage in lockers at the station (2 DM). The travel agency in the station is the place to arrange train and *couchette* (sleeper) reservations. Taxis wait at the station and can take you to any hotel for 8 DM.

Tours of Rothenburg

The TI on Market Square offers 60-minute guided **walking tours** in English (6 DM, daily April–October at 14:00 from Market Square). A bit less informative but wonderfully entertaining, the **Night Watchman's Tour** takes tourists on his rounds each evening at 20:00 (6 DM, April–December, in English). This is the best evening activity in town. Or you can hire a private guide. For 85 DM, a local historian—who's usually an intriguing character as well—will bring the ramparts alive. Eight hundred years of history are packed between Rothenburg's cobbles. (Manfred Baumann, tel. 09861/4146, and Anita Weinzierl, tel. 09868/7993, are good guides.) If you prefer riding to walking, **horse-and-buggy rides** last 30 minutes and cost 10 DM per person for a minimum of three people.

Sights—Rothenburg's Town Hall Square

▲▲**Town Hall Tower**—The best view of Rothenburg and the surrounding countryside, and a close-up look at an old tiled roof from the inside are yours for 1 DM and a rigorous (214 steps, 180 feet) but interesting climb (daily 9:30–12:30, 13:00–17:00, off-season weekends from 12:00–15:00 only). Entrance is on Market Square. Women, beware: Some men find the view best from the bottom of the ladder just before the top.

Meistertrunk Show—Be on Market Square at 11:00, 12:00, 13:00, 14:00, 15:00, 20:00, 21:00, or 22:00 for the ritual gathering of the tourists to see the less-than-breathtaking reenactment of the Meistertrunk story. In 1631 the Catholic army took the Protestant town and was about to do its rape, pillage, and plunder thing when, as the story goes, the mayor said, "Hey, if I can drink this entire three-liter tankard of wine in one gulp, will you leave us alone?" The invading commander, sensing he was dealing with an unbalanced people, said, "Sure." Mayor Nusch drank the whole thing, the town was saved, and the mayor slept for three days. Hint: for the best show, don't watch the clock; watch the open-mouthed tourists gasp as the old windows flip open. At the late shows, the square flickers with flash attachments. While you wait for the show, give yourself the spin tour below.

Market Square Spin Tour—Stand at the bottom of Market Square (10 feet below the wooden post) and spin 360 degrees clockwise starting with the city hall tower. Now, do it slower following these notes: 1) The city's tallest tower, at 200 feet, stands atop the old city hall, a white, Gothic, 13th-century building. Notice the tourists enjoying the view from the black top of the tower. 2) When the town had more money and Gothic went out-of-date, a new town hall was built in front of the old one. This is in Renaissance style from 1570. (Access to the old town hall tower is through the middle of the new town hall arcade.) 3) At the top of the square stands the proud Councilors' Tavern (clock tower, from 1466). In its day, the city council drank here. Today it's the tourist office and the focus of all the attention when the little doors on either side of the clock flip open and the wooden figures (from 1910) reenact the Meistertrunk. 4) Across the street, the green building is the oldest pharmacy in town—Löwen Apotheke, from 1374, peek inside. 5) On the bottom end of the square, the grey building is a fine print shop (see Shopping, below, free brandy). 6) Adjoining that is the Baumeister's House with its famous Renaissance facade featuring statues of the seven virtues and the seven vices—the former supporting the latter. 7) The green house below that is the former house of Mayor Toppler, today the fine old Greifen Hotel; next to it is a famous Scottish restaurant. 8) Continue circling to the big 17th-century St. George's fountain. The long metal gutters slid, routing the water into the villagers' buckets. Rothenburg's many fountains had practical functions beyond providing drinking water. The water was used for fighting fires, and the fountains were stocked with fish during times of siege. Two fine buildings behind the fountain show the old-time lofts with warehouse doors and pulleys on top for hoisting. All over town, lofts were filled with grain and corn. A year's supply was required by the city so they could survive any siege. One building is a free art gallery showing off the work of Rothenburg's top artists. The other is another old-time pharmacy. 9) The broad street running under the town hall tower is Herrngasse. The town originated with its castle (1142). Herrngasse leads from the castle (now gone) to Market Square where you stand now.

▲**Historical Town Hall Vaults**—Under the town hall tower is a city history museum that gives a waxy but good look at medieval Rothenburg. With the best English descriptions in town, it offers a look at "the fateful year 1631," a replica of the famous Meistertrunk tankard, and a dungeon complete with three dank cells and some torture lore (3 DM, 9:30–18:00, closed in winter, well described in English).

Sights—Rothenburg

▲▲**Walk the Wall**—Just over a mile around, providing great views and a good orientation, this walk can be done by those under six feet tall and without a camera in less than an hour, and requires no special sense of balance. Photographers go through lots of film, especially before breakfast or at sunset, when the lighting is best and the crowds are fewest. The best fortifications are in the Spitaltor (south end). Walk from there counterclockwise to the "forehead." Climb the Rödertor en route. The names you see along the way are people who donated money to rebuild the wall after World War II.

▲**Rödertor**—The wall tower nearest the train station is the only one you can climb. It's worth the hike up for the view and a fascinating rundown on the bombing of Rothenburg in the last weeks of World War II—the northeast corner of the city was destroyed (2 DM, daily 9:00–17:00, closed off-season, photos, English translation).

▲▲**St. Jacob's Church**—Built in the 14th century, it's been Lutheran since 1544. Take a close look at the Twelve Apostles altar in front (from 1546, left permanently in its open festival day position). Six saints are below Christ. St. James (Jacob in German) is the one with the staff. He's the saint of pilgrims, and this was on the medieval pilgrimage route to Santiago de Compostela in Spain. Study the painted panels. Around the back (upper left) is a great painting of Rothenburg's Market Square in the 15th century—looking like it does today. Before leaving the front of the church, notice the old medallions above the carved choir stalls: the coats of arms of Rothenburg's leading families and portraits of early Reformation preachers.

Next, climb the stairs in the back. Behind the pipe organ stands the artistic highlight of Rothenburg and perhaps the most wonderful woodcarving in all Germany: the glorious 500-year-old, 30-foot-high *Altar of the Holy Blood.* Tilman Riemenschneider, the Michelangelo of German woodcarvers, carved this from 1499 to 1504 to hold a precious rock crystal capsule set in a cross containing a drop of the holy blood (1270). Below, in the scene of the Last Supper, Jesus gives Judas a piece of bread marking him as the traitor while John lays his head on Christ's lap. On the left: Jesus entering Jerusalem. On the right: Jesus praying in the Garden of Gethsemane (2.50 DM, Monday–Saturday 9:00–17:30, Sunday 10:45–17:30, off-season 10:00–12:00 and 14:00–16:00, free helpful English info sheet).

▲▲**Medieval Crime and Punishment Museum**—It's the best of its kind, full of fascinating old legal bits and *Kriminal* pieces, instruments of punishment and torture, even a special cage—complete with a metal gag—for nags. Exhibits are well described in English (5 DM, 8 DM combo includes Imperial City Museum, daily 9:30–17:30, shorter hours in winter, fun cards and posters).

▲**Toy Museum**—Two floors of historic *Kinder*-cuteness is a hit with many (5 DM, 12 DM per family, daily 9:30–18:00, just off Market Square, downhill from the fountain, Hofbronneng 13).

Museum of the Imperial City (Reichsstadt Museum)—This less sensational museum, housed in the former Dominican Convent, gives a more scholarly look at old Rothenburg. Highlights include *The Rothenburg Passion,* a 12-panel series of paintings from 1492 showing scenes leading up to Christ's crucifixion, an exhibit of Jewish culture through the ages in Rothenburg, and a 14th-century convent kitchen (4 DM, daily 9:30–17:30, in winter 13:00–16:00). The convent garden is a peaceful place to work on your tan.

▲▲**Herrngasse and the Castle Garden**—Any town's *Herrngasse,* where the richest patricians and merchants (the *Herren*) lived, is your chance to see its finest old mansions. Wander from Market Square down Herrngasse (past the old Rothenburg official measurement rods on the city hall wall) and drop into the lavish front rooms of a ritzy hotel or two. Pop into the Franciscan Church (free, daily 10:00–12:00, 14:00–16:00, built in 1285—the oldest in town, with a Riemenschneider altarpiece), continue on down past the old-fashioned puppet theater, through the old gate (notice the tiny after-curfew door in the big door and the frightening mask mouth from which hot Nutella was poured onto attackers), through the garden and to the end of what used to be the castle (great picnic spots and Tauber Riviera views at sunset). This is the popular kissing spot for romantic Rothenburg teenagers.

▲**Walk in the Countryside**—Just below the *Burggarten* (castle garden) in the Tauber Valley is the cute, skinny, 600-year-old castle/summer home of Mayor Toppler (2 DM, 13:00–16:00 on Friday, Saturday, and Sunday). On the top floor, notice the photo of bombed-out 1945 Rothenburg. Then walk on past the covered bridge and huge trout to the peaceful village of Detwang. Detwang (from 968, the second-oldest village in Franconia) is actually older than Rothenburg and also has a Riemenschneider altarpiece in its church. For a scenic return, loop back to Rothenburg through the valley along the river, past a café with outdoor tables, great desserts, and a town view to match.

Festivals—Rothenburgers dress up in medieval costumes and beer gardens spill out into the street to celebrate Mayor Nusch's Meistertrunk victory (Whitsun, six weeks after Easter) and 700 years of history in the Imperial City Festival (second weekend in September, with fireworks).

Swimming—Rothenburg has a fine modern recreation center with an indoor/outdoor pool and sauna. It's just a few minutes' walk down the Dinkelsbühl Road (Friday–Wednesday 9:00–20:00, opens at 10:00 on Thursday, tel. 09861/4565).

Sightseeing Lowlights—St. Wolfgang's Church is a fortified Gothic church built into the medieval wall at Klingentor. Its dungeon-like passages and shepherd's dance exhibit are pretty lame (2 DM, daily 10:00–13:00, 14:00–17:00). The cute-looking Bäuerliches Museum (farming museum) next door is even worse. The Rothenburger Handwerkerhaus (tradesman's house, 700 years old) shows the typical living situation of Rothenburg in its heyday (3 DM, daily 9:00–18:00, closed in winter, Alter Stadtgraben 26, near the Markus Tower).

Sights—Near Rothenburg

A Franconian Bike Ride—For a fun, breezy look at the countryside around Rothenburg, rent a bike from Rad & Tat (25 DM/day, Monday–Friday 9:00–18:00, Saturday and Sunday 9:00–14:00, Bensenstrasse 17, outside of town behind the "neck," near corner of Bensenstrasse and Erlbacherstrasse, no deposit except passport number, tel. 09861/87984). Return the bike the next morning before 10:00. For a pleasant half-day pedal, bike south down to Detwang via Topplerschlosschen. Go north along the level bike path to Tauberscheckenbach, then huff and puff uphill about 20 minutes to Adelshofen and south back to Rothenburg.

Franconian Open-Air Museum—A 20-minute drive from Rothenburg in the undiscovered "Rothenburgy" town of Bad

Windsheim is a small, open-air folk museum that, compared with others in Europe, isn't much. But it's trying very hard and gives you the best look around at traditional rural Franconia (6 DM, Tuesday–Sunday 9:00–18:00, closed Monday, March–October).

Shopping

Be careful . . . Rothenburg is one of Germany's best shopping towns. Do it here, mail it home, and be done with it. Lovely prints, carvings, wineglasses, Christmas-tree ornaments, and beer steins are popular.

The Käthe Wohlfahrt Christmas trinkets phenomenon is spreading across the half-timbered reaches of Europe. In Rothenburg tourists flock to two Käthe Wohlfahrt Christmas Villages (on either side of Herrngasse, just off Market Square). This Christmas wonderland is filled with enough twinkling lights to require a special electric hookup, instant Christmas spirit mood music (best appreciated on a hot day in July), and American and Japanese tourists hungrily filling little woven shopping baskets with 5-DM to 10-DM goodies to hang on their trees. (OK, I admit it, my Christmas tree sports a few KW ornaments.) Note: Prices have hefty tour-guide kickbacks built into them. The Käthe Wohlfahrt discount store sells damaged and discontinued items. It's unnamed at Kirchgasse 5 across from the entrance of St. Jacob's Church (weekdays 10:00–18:00, less on weekends, tel. 09861/4090).

The Friese shop offers a charming contrast (just off Market Square, west of the TI on the corner across from public WC). Cuckoo with friendliness, it gives shoppers with this book tremendous service: a 10-percent discount, 16 percent tax deducted if you have it mailed, and a free map. Anneliese, who runs the place with her sons, Frankie and Berni, charges only her cost for shipping, changes money at the best rates in town with no extra charge, and lets tired travelers leave their bags in her back room for free. Her pricing is good, but to comparison shop, go here last.

The Ernst Geissendörfer print shop sells fine prints, etchings, and paintings. If you show this book, they'll offer 10 percent off marked prices for all purchases in cash (or credit card purchases of at least 100 DM) and a free shot of German brandy whether you buy anything or not. The shop is on the corner, where Market Square hits Schmiedgasse.

For characteristic wineglasses and oinkology gear, drop by the Weinladen am Plonlein (Plonlein 27).

Shoppers who mail their goodies home can get handy boxes at the post office (Monday–Friday 9:00–12:30, 14:00–17:00, Saturday 9:00–12:00, Milchmarkt 5).

Those who prefer to eat their souvenirs shop the *Bäckereien* (bakeries). Their succulent pastries, pies, and cakes are pleasantly distracting. Skip the bad-tasting Rothenburger *Schneebälle*.

Sleeping in Rothenburg
(1.7 DM = about $1, tel. code: 09861, zip code: 91541)

Sleep Code: **S** = Single, **D** = Double/Twin, **T** = Triple, **Q** = Quad, **b** = bathroom, **t** = toilet only, **s** = shower only, **CC** = Credit Card (**V**isa, **M**asterCard, **A**mex), **SE** = Speaks English, **NSE** = No English. Unless otherwise indicated, room prices include breakfast.

Rothenburg is crowded with visitors. But when the sun sets, most retreat to the predictable plumbing of their big-city high-rise hotels. Except for the rare Saturday night, room-finding is easy throughout the year. Unless otherwise noted, enough English is spoken.

Many hotels and guest houses will pick up desperate heavy packers at the station. You may be greeted at the station by the *Zimmer* skimmer trying to waylay those on their way to a reserved room. Resist. If you arrive without a reservation, try talking yourself into one of these more desperate bed-and-breakfast rooms for a youth-hostel price. Be warned: These people are notorious for taking you to distant hotels and then charging you for a ride back if you decline a room. There's a handy Laundromat near the station (Johannitergasse 8, tel. 09861/5177).

Hotels

I like **Hotel Goldene Rose**, where scurrying Karin serves breakfast and stately Henni keeps everything in good order. The hotel has only one shower for two floors of rooms, and the streetside rooms can be noisy, but the rooms are clean and airy and you're surrounded by cobbles, flowers, and red-tiled roofs (one small S-25 DM, S-35 DM, D-65 DM, Ds-83 DM, Db-87 DM in classy annex behind the garden, some triples, and a spacious family apartment: for four-190 DM, for five-225 DM, CC:VMA, closed in January and February, kid-friendly, ground-floor rooms in annex, Spitalgasse 28, tel. 09861/4638, fax 09861/86417, Henni SE). The Favetta family also serves good, reasonably priced meals. Remember to keep your key to get in after they close (at the side gate in the alley). The hotel is a 15-minute walk from the station or a seven-minute walk downhill from Market Square.

Gasthof Greifen, once the home of Mayor Toppler, is a big, traditional, 600-year-old place with large rooms and all the comforts. It's family-run and creaks just the way you want it to (small Sb-64, Sb-80 DM, one big D-74 DM with no shower available, Db-115–135 DM, Tb-180 DM, 10 percent off for three-night stay, CC:VMA, laundry self- or full-service, free and easy parking, half a block downhill from Market Square at Obere Schmiedgasse 5, tel. 09861/2281, fax 09861/86374, Brigitte and Klingler family).

Gasthof Marktplatz, right on Market Square, has eight tidy rooms and a cozy atmosphere (S-38 DM, D-70 DM, Ds-80 DM,

Db-88 DM, T-90 DM, Ts-105 DM, Tb-115 DM, Grüner Markt 10, tel. & fax 09861/6722, Herr Rosner SE).

Gästehaus Raidel, a creaky 500-year-old house packed with antiques, offers large rooms with cramped facilities down the hall. Run by grim people who make me want to sing the *Addams Family* theme song, it works in a pinch (S-35 DM, Sb-69 DM, D-69 DM, Db-89 DM, Wenggasse 3, tel. 09861/3115).

Hotel Gerberhaus, a classy new hotel in a 500-year-old building, is warmly run by Inge and Kurt, who mix modern comforts into bright and airy rooms while maintaining the half-timbered elegance. Great buffet breakfasts and pleasant garden in back (Sb-80 DM, Db-100-140 DM depending on size, Tb-165 DM, Qb-185 DM, for five people-210 DM, all with TV and telephones, CC:VM but use cash and you get 5 percent off and a free *Schneeball*, Spitalgasse 25, tel. 09861/ 94900, fax 09861/86555, e-mail: Gerberhaus@t-online.de). Claudia's café, downstairs, serves good salads and sandwiches.

Hotel Klosterstuble, deep in the old town near the castle garden, is even classier. Jutta greets her guests while husband Rudolf does the cooking (Sb-95 DM, Db-120–160 DM, some luxurious family rooms, 10 DM extra on weekends, discounts for families, buffet breakfast, CC:V, Heringsbronnengasse 5, tel. 09861/6774, fax 09861/6474).

Bohemians enjoy the **Hotel Altfränkische Weinstube am Klosterhof**. Mario and Hanne run this dark and smoky pub in a 600-year-old building. Upstairs they rent six *gemütliche* rooms with upscale Monty Python atmosphere, TVs, modern showers, open-beam ceilings, and *"Himmel"* beds—canopied four-poster "heaven" beds (Sb-79 DM, Db-8? DM, Tb-109–119 DM, most rooms have tubs with hand showers, kid-friendly, CC:VM, walk under St. Jacob's church, take second left off Klingengasse at Klosterhof 7, tel. 09861/6404, fax 09861/6410). Their pub is a candlelit classic, serving hot food until 22:30, closing at 1:00. Drop by on Wednesday evening (19:30–24:00) for the English Conversation Club.

Top Private Rooms

For the best real, with-a-local-family, comfortable, and homey experience, stay with **Herr und Frau Moser** (D-65 DM, T-95 DM, no single rooms, Spitalgasse 12, tel. 09861/5971). This charming retired couple speak little English but try very hard. Speak slowly, in clear, simple English. Reserve by phone and you must reconfirm by phone one day ahead of arrival.

Pension Pöschel is friendly with seven cozy rooms on the second floor of a concrete but pleasant building (S-35 DM, D-60 DM, T-90 DM, small kids free, Wenggasse 22, tel. 09861/3430).

Frau Guldemeister rents two simple ground-floor rooms (Ss-40 DM, Ds with twin beds-60 DM, bigger Db-70 DM, breakfast in room, minimum two-night stay, off Market Square behind the Christmas shop, Pfaffleinsgasschen 10, tel. 09861/8988, some English, takes only telephone reservations no more than a day or two in advance).

Last Resort Accommodations

Pension Kreuzerhof has seven big, modern, ground-floor, motel-style rooms with views of parked cars on a quiet street (Sb-40–50 DM, Db-78–87 DM, Millergasse 6, tel. & fax 09861/3424). **Erich Endress** offers five airy, comfy rooms above his grocery store (S-45 DM, D-80 DM, Db-110 DM, non-smoking, Rodergasse 6, tel. 09861/2331). The **Zum Schmolzer** restaurant at Rosengasse 21 rents 14 well-maintained but drab-colored rooms (Sb-55 DM, Db-90 DM, Stollengasse 29, tel. 09861/3371, fax 09861/7204, SE). **Cafe Uhl** offers 10 fine, slightly frayed rooms over a bakery (Sb-55–65 DM, Db-95–110 DM, CC:VA, Plonlein 8, tel. 09861/4895, fax 09861/92820). **Gästehaus Flemming** has seven plain, comfortable rooms behind St. Jacob's Church (Db-86, Klingengasse 21, tel. 09861/92380). **Gästehaus Viktoria** is a peaceful and cheery little place with a tiny garden and two rooms (Ds-75 DM, Klingenschütt 4, tel. 09861/87682, Hanne).

In the modern world, a block from the train station, **Pension Willi und Helen Then** is run by a cool guy who played the sax in a jazz band for seven years after the war and is a regular at the English Conversation Club (D-70 DM, Db-80 DM, tel. 09861/5177, fax 09861/86014).

Hostel

The fine **Rossmühle Youth Hostel** has 180 beds in two buildings. The droopy-eyed building (the old town horse-mill, used when the town was under siege and the river-powered mill was inaccessible) houses groups and the hostel office. The adjacent and newly renovated hostel is mostly for families and individuals (22-DM beds, Db-54 DM, 5.50-DM sheets, breakfast included, 9-DM dinners, Muhlacker 1, tel. 09861/ 94160, fax 09861/941-620, e-mail: JHRothen@aol.com, SE). This popular place takes reservations (even more than a year in advance) and will hold rooms until 18:00. Here in Bavaria, hosteling is limited to those under 27, except for families traveling with children under 18.

Sleeping in Nearby Detwang and Bettwar

The town of Detwang, a 15-minute walk below Rothenburg, is loaded with quiet *Zimmer*. The clean, quiet, and comfortable old **Gasthof zum Schwarzen Lamm** in Detwang (D-85 DM, Db-110–130 DM, tel. 09861/6727, fax 09861/86899) serves good food, as does the popular and very local-style Eulenstube next door. **Gästehaus Alte Schreinerei** offers good food and 18 quiet, comfy, reasonable rooms a little farther down the road in Bettwar (Db-76 DM, 8801 Bettwar, tel. 09861/1541, fax 09861/86710).

Eating in Rothenburg

Most places serve meals only from 11:30 to 13:30 and 18:00 to 20:00. At **Goldene Rose** (see Sleeping, above), Reno cooks up traditional German fare at good prices (11:30–14:00, 17:30–21:00, closed Tuesday and Wednesday, in sunny weather the leafy garden terrace is open in the back, Spitalgasse 28).

Galgengasse (Gallows Lane) has two cheap and popular standbys: **Pizzeria Roma** (11:30–24:00, 10-DM pizzas and normal schnitzel fare, Galgengasse 19) and **Gasthof zum Ochsen** (11:30–13:30, 18:00–20:00, closed Thursday, uneven service but decent 10-DM meals, Galgengasse 26). **Landsknechtstuben**, at Galgengasse 21, is pricey but friendly, with some cheaper schnitzel choices.

Gasthaus Siebersturm serves up tasty, reasonable meals in a bright, airy dining room (Spitalgasse). For a break from schnitzel, **Lotus China** serves good Chinese food daily (two blocks behind TI near the church, Eckele 2, tel. 09861/86886). **Gasthaus Greifen** serves typical Rothenburg cuisine at moderate prices (just below Market Square).

There are two **supermarkets** near the wall at Rödertor (the one outside the wall to the left is cheaper, the one inside is nicer).

Evening Fun and Beer Drinking

For beer garden fun on a balmy summer evening (dinner, or later for beer), you have three fine choices: nearby is **Gasthof Rödertor**, just outside the wall at the Rödertor (red gate). In the valley along the river and worth the 20-minute hike is **Unter den Linden** beer garden. A more central and touristy beer garden is behind **Hotel Eisenhut** (nightly until 22:00, access from Burggasse or through the hotel off Herrngasse).

Trinkstube zur Hölle (Hell) is dark and foreboding, serving good ribs from 18:00 and offering thick wine-drinking atmosphere until late (a block past Criminal Museum on Burggasse, with devil hanging out front, tel. 09861/4229). For mellow ambience, try the beautifully restored **Alte Keller's Weinstube** under walls festooned with old pots and jugs (closed Tuesday, Alter Keller 8). Wine lovers enjoy the Glocke Hotel's Stube (Plonlein 1). And perhaps the most elegant place in town is the courtyard of the Baumeister Haus (behind the statue-festooned facade a few doors below Market Square).

Two popular discos are a few doors farther out near the Sparkasse bank (T.G.I. Friday's at Ansbacher 15, in the alley next to the bank, open Wednesday, Friday, and Saturday; the other is Check Point, around the corner from the bank, open Wednesday and Friday–Sunday).

For a rare chance to mix it up with locals who aren't selling anything, bring your favorite slang and tongue-twisters to the **English Conversation Club** at Mario's Altfränkische Weinstube (Wednesday 19:30–24:00, Anneliese from the Friese shop is a regular). This dark and smoky pub is an atmospheric hangout any night but Tuesday, when it's closed (Klosterhof 7, off Klingengasse, behind St. Jacob's church, tel. 09861/6404).

Transportation Connections—Rothenburg

The Romantic Road bus tour takes you in and out of Rothenburg each afternoon (April–October) heading to Munich, Frankfurt, or Füssen. See the Romantic Road bus schedule on page 86.

A tiny train line runs between Rothenburg and Steinach (almost hrly, 15 min, but only until early evening). **Steinach by train to: Würzburg** (hrly, 30 min), **Munich** (hrly, 2 hrs), **Frankfurt** (hrly, 2 hrs, change in Würzburg). Train connections in Steinach are usually within a few minutes.

Route Tips for Drivers

Rothenburg to Füssen or Reutte, Austria: Get an early start to enjoy the quaint hills and rolling villages of what was Germany's major medieval trade route. The views of Rothenburg from the west, across the Tauber Valley, are magnificent.

After a quick stop in the center of Dinkelsbühl, cross the baby Danube River (Donau) and continue south along the Romantic Road to Füssen. Drive by Neuschwanstein Castle just to sweeten your dreams before crossing into Austria to get set up at Reutte.

If detouring past Oberammergau, you can drive through Garmisch, past Germany's highest mountain (the Zugspitze), into Austria via Lermoos, and on to Reutte. Or you can take the small scenic shortcut to Reutte past Ludwig's Linderhof and along the windsurfer-strewn Plansee.

ROMANTIC ROAD

The Romantic Road (Romantische Strasse) winds you past the most beautiful towns and scenery of Germany's medieval heartland. Once Germany's medieval trade route, now it's the best way to connect the dots between Füssen, Munich, and Frankfurt.

Wander through quaint hills and rolling villages, and stop wherever the cows look friendly or a town fountain beckons. My favorite sections are from Füssen to Landsberg and Rothenburg to Weikersheim. (If you're driving with limited time, you can connect Rothenburg and Munich by Autobahn, but don't miss these two best sections.) Caution: The similarly promoted "Castle Road" sounds intriguing, but is nowhere near as interesting.

Throughout Bavaria, you'll see colorfully ornamented Maypoles decorating town squares. Many are painted in Bavaria's

Romantic Road

colors, blue and white. The decorations that line each side of the pole symbolize the crafts or businesses of that community. Each May Day they are festively replaced. Traditionally, rival communities try to steal each other's Maypole. Locals will guard their new pole night and day as May Day approaches. Stolen poles are ransomed only with lots of beer for the clever thieves.

Getting Around the Romantic Road

By Bus: The Europa Bus Company runs buses daily between Frankfurt and Munich in each direction (April–October). A second route goes between Dinkelsbühl and Füssen daily. Buses leave from train stations in towns served by a train. The 120-DM, 11-hour ride costs only 39 DM with a Eurailpass (including the 10 DM registration fee). Each bus stops in Rothenburg (about 2 hours) and Dinkelsbühl (about an hour) and briefly at a few other attractions, and has a usually mediocre guide who hands out brochures and narrates the journey in English. There is no

1999 Romantic Road Bus Schedule (Daily, April–October)

Frankfurt	8:00	—
Würzburg	9:45	—
Arrive Rothenburg	12:45	—
Depart Rothenburg	14:30	—
Arrive Dinkelsbühl	15:25	—
Depart Dinkelsbühl	16:15	16:15
Munich	19:50	—
Füssen	—	20:40
Füssen	8:00	—
Arrive Wieskirche	8:35	—
Depart Wieskirche	8:55	—
Munich	—	9:00
Arrive Dinkelsbühl	12:50	12:45
Depart Dinkelsbühl	—	14:00
Arrive Rothenburg	—	14:40
Depart Rothenburg	—	16:15
Würzburg	—	18:30
Frankfurt	—	20:30

quicker or easier way to travel across Germany and get such a hearty dose of its countryside. Bus reservations are free, easy, and smart—without one you can lose your seat down the road to someone who has one (especially on summer weekends; call Munich's EurAide office at 089/593-889 at least one day in advance to reserve). You can start, stop, and switch over where you like—but you'll be guaranteed a seat only if you reserve each segment.

By Car: Follow the brown "Romantische Strasse" signs.

Sights—Along the Romantic Road

(These sights are south to north.)

Füssen—This town, the southern terminus of the Romantic Road, is two miles from the startlingly beautiful Neuschwanstein Castle, worthy of a stop on any sightseeing agenda. (See the Bavaria and Tirol chapter for description and accommodations.)

▲▲**Wieskirche**—Germany's most glorious Baroque-rococo church. Heavenly! It's in a sweet meadow and is newly restored. Northbound Romantic Road buses stop here for 15 minutes. (See the Bavaria and Tirol chapter.)

Rottenbuch—Nondescript village with an impressive church in a lovely setting.

▲**Dinkelsbühl**—Rothenburg's little sister is cute enough to merit a short stop. A moat, towers, gates, and a beautifully preserved medieval wall surround this town and its interesting local museum. The Kinderzeche children's festival turns Dinkelsbühl wonderfully on end in mid-July (TI tel. 09851/90240). On Neustädtlein, you'll find 80-DM doubles with bath and TV at friendly Haus Küffner (tel. 09851/1247) and Zur Linde (tel. 09851/3465).

▲▲▲**Rothenburg**—See opening of this chapter for information on Germany's best medieval town.

▲**Herrgottskapelle**—This peaceful church, graced with Tilman Riemenschneider's greatest carved altarpiece (daily 9:15–17:30), is one mile from Creglingen and across the street from the Fingerhut thimble museum (daily 9:00–18:00). The southbound Romantic Road bus stops here for 15 minutes, long enough to see one or the other.

Weikersheim—This untouristy town has a palace with fine Baroque gardens (luxurious picnic spot), a folk museum, and a picturesque town square.

WÜRZBURG

A historic city, though freshly rebuilt since World War II, Würzburg is worth a stop to see its impressive Prince Bishop's Residenz, the bubbly Baroque chapel (Hofkirche) next door, and the palace's sculpted gardens.

Orientation (tel. code: 0931)

Tourist Information: Würzburg has a helpful TI just outside the train station (Monday–Friday 10:00–18:00, Saturday 10:00–14:00, closed Sunday) and another TI on Marktplatz (Monday–Saturday 10:00–18:00, tel. 0931/373-98). Their wonderful little *Visitor's Guide* pamphlet covers the tourists' Würzburg well. The produce market near the Marktplatz TI bustles daily except Sunday. Train information tel. 0931/19419.

Sights—Würzburg

▲▲▲**Residenz**—This Franconian Versailles, with grand rooms, 3-D art, and a tennis-court-sized fresco by Tiepolo, is worth a tour. English tours are on weekends at 11:00 and 15:00 (April–October, confirm at TI or call ahead). During the week, the best strategy is to take the TI's walking tour at 11:00, which includes a tour of the Residenz along with a walk through the "old" city (13 DM, Tuesday–Saturday April–October, two hours, all in English, includes admission to Residenz; meet at the TI on Marktplatz). Or buy the 5-DM guide at the Residenz; it's dry and lengthy, but you can use the pictures to figure out what room you're in. No English labels or descriptions are provided. The top sights are the grand staircase with the Tiepolo ceiling, the reconstructed Room of Mirrors (destroyed during World War II), and the grandly Tiepoloed Imperial Hall (5 DM, April–October Tuesday–Sunday 9:00–17:00, November–March 10:00–16:00, closed Monday, last entry 30 minutes before closing, tel. 0931/355-1712). The elaborate Hofkirche chapel is next door (as you exit the palace, go left) and the entrance to the picnic-worthy garden is just beyond. Easy parking is available. Don't confuse the Residenz (a 15-minute walk from the train station) with the fortress on the hilltop.

Fortress Marienberg—Along with a city history museum, the fortress contains the Mainfränkisches Museum, highlighting the work of Riemenschneider, Germany's top woodcarver and past mayor of Würzburg (3.50 DM, Tuesday–Sunday 10:00–17:00, less off-season, tel. 0931/43016). Riemenschneider fans will find his work throughout Würzburg's many churches (which look closed but are likely open; the sign on the door, *"Bitte Türe schliessen,"* simply means "Please close the doors").

Veitshöchheim—Consider a cruise to Veitshöchheim, five kilometers away, to see the fanciful Baroque gardens and the Summer Residenz (gardens free and open daily 7:00 till dusk; 3 DM for palace, Tuesday–Sunday 9:00–12:00, 13:00–17:00, closed Monday). Catch the boat at the Würzburg dock (13 DM round-trip, leaves hourly, daily 10:00–17:00 April–October) or bus #11 from the Würzburg station (3.20 DM, hourly, 10 min).

Sleeping in Würzburg
(1.7 DM = about $1, tel. code: 0931, zip code: 97070)
All listings include breakfast, and prices are soft off-season.

Hotel-Pension Spehnkuch is the best budget hotel near the station. Overlooking a busy street but quiet behind double-paned windows, it's friendly and comfortable (S-50 DM, D-90 DM, T-130 DM, two minutes' walk from station, exit station and take a right on Rontgenring, at #7, elevator, tel. 0931/54752, fax 0931/54760, SE).
Pension Siegel is a lesser option (S-46 DM, D-89 DM, from station, go straight on Kaiserstrasse and turn left at Muller store, Reisbrubengasse 7, tel. 0931/52941, fax 0931/52967, NSE).

Three fine hotels cluster within a block on Theaterstrasse. Quieter rooms are in back; front rooms have street noise. **Hotel Barbarossa**, tucked away on the fourth floor, has 17 comfortable rooms (Ss-75 DM, Sb-95 DM, one Ds-110 DM, Db-140 DM,

Tb-170 DM, elevator, CC:VMA, Theaterstrasse 2, tel. 0931/321-370, fax 0931/321-3737, e-mail: marchiorello@t-online.de, SE).
Hotel Schönleber is a cheery vision of pastel yellow (S-70–100 DM, Sb-95–110 DM, D-100 DM, Ds-110 DM, Db-150 DM, hall showers-4 DM, elevator, CC:VMA, Theaterstrasse 5, tel. 0931/12068, fax 0931/16012), and the **Altstadt Hotel** is a slight cut above, with a wonderfully fragrant Italian restaurant below (Ss-85 DM, Sb-95 DM, Ds-110 DM, Db-140 DM, CC:VMA, Theaterstrasse 7, tel. 0931/321-640, fax 0931/321-6464, e-mail: marchiorello@t-online.de, SE).

Sankt Josef Hotel has a more Franconian feel, with a woody restaurant on a quieter street (Sb-92 DM, Db-147–167 DM, CC:VMA, Semmelstrasse 28, coming from station, take left off Theaterstrasse, tel. 0931/308-680, fax 0931/308-6860, e-mail: hotelsanktjosef@at-online.de; NSE). Across the street is the elaborately painted **Hotel zur Stadt Mainz**, dating from 1430. You'll pay 40 to 50 DM more for the privilege of sleeping here (CC:VMA, Semmelstrasse 39, tel. 0931/53155, fax 0931/58510).

FRANKFURT
Frankfurt, the northern terminus of the Romantic Road, is actually pleasant for a big city and offers a good look at today's no-nonsense urban Germany.

Orientation (tel. code: 069)
Tourist Information: For a quick look at the city, pick up a 1-DM map at the TI in the train station (Monday–Friday 8:00–21:00, weekends 9:00–18:00, tel. 069/212-38-849). It's a 20-minute walk from the station down Kaiserstrasse past Goethe's house (great man, mediocre sight, Grosser Hirschgraben 23) to Römerberg, Frankfurt's lively Market Square (or you can take subway U-4 or U-5 from the station to Römerberg). The TI's brochure, *Frankfurt Welcome*, describes a self-guided walking tour you can take from this square. A string of museums is just across the river along Schaumainkai (Tuesday–Sunday 10:00–17:00, Wednesday until 20:00, closed Monday). The TI also has info on bus tours of the city (44 DM, 10:00 and 14:00 in summer, 14:00 only off-season, 2.5 hrs).

Near the train station, a browse through Frankfurt's red-light district offers a fascinating way to kill time between trains. Wander down Taunusstrasse two blocks in front of the station and you'll find 20 "eros towers," each a five-story-tall brothel filled with prostitutes. Climbing through a few of these may be one of the more memorable experiences of your European trip. It feels safe, the atmosphere is friendly, and browsing is encouraged (40 DM, daily, tel. 069/32422).

Romantic Road Bus: If you're taking the bus out of Frankfurt, you can buy your ticket either in the Deutsches Touring office at the train station (Monday–Friday 7:30–18:00, Saturday 7:30–15:00, Sunday 7:30–14:00, CC:VMA, entrance at Mannheimer Strasse 4, tel. 069/230-735) or pay cash when you board the bus. Eurail and Europass holders, who get a 75-percent discount, pay only about 30 DM plus 3 DM for one piece of luggage). The bus waits at stall #8 (right of the train station as you leave).

Sleeping in Frankfurt
(1.7 DM = about $1, tel. code: 069, zip code: 60329)
Avoid driving or sleeping in Frankfurt, especially during Frankfurt's numerous trade fairs (about five days a month), which send hotel prices skyrocketing. Pleasant Rhine or Romantic Road towns are just a quick train ride or drive away. But if you must spend the night in Frankfurt, here are some places within a block of the train station (and its handy train to the airport). This isn't the safest neighborhood; be careful after dark. Get a map at the TI, but for a rough idea of directions to hotels, stand with your back to the main entrance of the station: Using a 12-hour clock, Hotel Manhattan is across the street at 10:00, Pension Schneider at 12:00, Hotel Europa and Wiesbaden at 4:00, and the Goldner Stern at 5:00. Breakfast is included in all listings and English is spoken.

Hotel Manhattan, with newly remodeled, sleek, arty rooms, is expensive—best for a splurge on a first or last night in Europe (Sb-135 DM, Db-165 DM, show this book to get a break during non-convention times, elevator, riffraff in front of hotel, CC:VMA, Düsseldorfer Strasse 10, tel. 069/234-748, fax 069/234-532).

Pension Schneider is a strange little oasis of decency and quiet three floors above the epicenter of Frankfurt's red light district, two blocks in front of the train station. The street is safe in spite of the pimps and pushers. Its 10 rooms are big, bright, and comfortable (D-80 DM, Db-100 DM, Tb-110 DM, CC:VMA, elevator, corner of Moselstrasse at Taunusstrasse 43, tel. 069/251071, fax 069/259228).

Hotel Europa, with well-maintained rooms, is a fine value (Sb-80 DM, Db-120 DM, Tb-150 DM, prices soft on weekends, some non-smoking rooms, garage, CC:VMA, Baseler Strasse 17, tel. 069/236-013, fax 069/236-203).

Hotel Wiesbaden has worn rooms and a kind manager (Sb-95 DM, Db-110–135 DM depending on size, Tb-150 DM, a little smoky, elevator, CC:VMA, Baseler Strasse 52, tel. 069/232-347, fax 069/252-845).

Hotel Goldner Stern, a vintage hotel with dim rooms and hallways, is sleepable (S-43–50 DM, D-65–75 DM, hall showers-4 DM, Karlsruherstrasse 8, tel. 069/233-309). It may close before the millennium.

Farther from the station is **Pension Backer** (S-50 DM, D-60 DM, showers-3 DM, near the botanical gardens, Mendelssohn-strasse 92, tel. 069/747992). Take the S-Bahn two stops to Haupt-wache, then transfer to U-6 or U-7 for two stops to Westend.

The **hostel** is open to members of any age (eight-bed rooms, 32 DM per bed with sheets and breakfast, bus #46 from station to Frankenstein Place, Deutschherrnufer 12, tel. 069/619-058).

Transportation Connections—Frankfurt

By train to: Rothenburg (hrly, 3 hrs, changes in Würzburg and Steinach; the tiny Steinach–Rothenburg train often leaves from the "B" section of track, away from the middle of the station, shortly after the Würzburg train arrives; don't miss it; Steinach has no tourism—for good reason), **Würzburg** (hrly, 90 min), **Munich** (hrly, 3.5 hrs), **Baden-Baden** (hrly, 90 min), **Freiburg** (hrly, 2 hrs, change in Mannheim), **Bonn** (hrly, 2 hrs), **Koblenz** (hrly, 90 min), **Köln** (hrly, 2 hrs), **Berlin** (hrly, 5 hrs), **Amsterdam** (8/day, 5 hrs), **Bern** (14/day, 4.5 hrs, changes in Mannheim and Basel), **Brussels** (6/day, 5 hrs), **Copenhagen** (3/day, 10 hrs), **London** (5/day, 9.5 hrs), **Milan** (6/day, 9 hrs), **Paris** (4/day, 6.5 hrs), **Vienna** (7/day, 7.5 hrs).

Frankfurt's Airport

The airport (*Flughafen*) is a 12-minute train ride from downtown (4/hrly, 5.80 DM, ride included in Frankfurt's 8.5-DM, all-day city transit pass or the 13-DM, two-day city pass). The airport is user-friendly, offering showers; baggage check; fair-rate banks with long hours; grocery store; train station; lounge where you can sleep overnight; business lounge (Europe City Club—30 DM to anyone with a plane ticket); easy rental-car pickup; plenty of park-ing; big green meeting-point sign; an information booth; and even McBeer. McWelcome to Germany. Airport English-speaking info: tel. 069/6901 (will transfer you to any of the airlines for booking or confirmation). Lufthansa—069/255-255, American Airlines—069/271-130, Delta—069/664-1212, Northwest—0180/525-4650.

To Rothenburg: Train travelers can validate railpasses or buy tickets at the airport station and catch a train to Würzburg, connecting to Rothenburg via Steinach (hrly, 3 hrs). If driving to Rothenburg, follow Autobahn signs to Würzburg.

Flying Home from Frankfurt: The airport has its own train station, and many of the trains from the Rhine stop there on their way into Frankfurt (e.g., hrly 90-min rides direct from Bonn; hrly 2-hr rides from Bacharach with a change in Mainz, earliest train from Bacharach to Frankfurt leaves just before 6:00). By car, head toward Frankfurt on the Autobahn and follow the little airplane signs to the airport (*Flughafen*).

RHINE AND MOSEL VALLEYS

These valleys are storybook Germany, a fairy-tale world of Rhine legends and robber-baron castles. Cruise the most castle-studded stretch of the romantic Rhine as you listen for the song of the treacherous Loreley. For hands-on castle thrills, climb through the Rhineland's greatest castle, Rheinfels, above the town of St. Goar. Then, for a sleepy and laid-back alternative, mosey through the neighboring Mosel Valley.

In the north you'll find the powerhouse city of Köln (Cologne) with Germany's greatest Gothic cathedral, best collection of Roman artifacts, a world-class art museum, and a good dose of German urban playfulness. Bustling Köln merits a visit, but spend your nights in a castle-crowned village. On the Rhine, stay in St. Goar or Bacharach. On the Mosel, choose Zell.

Planning Your Time

The Rhineland does not take much time. The blitziest tour is an hour at the Köln cathedral and an hour looking at the castles from your train window. For a better look, however, cruise in, tour a castle or two, sleep in a genuine medieval town, and take the train out. With limited time, cruise less and be sure to get into a castle.

Ideally, spend two nights here, sleep in Bacharach, cruise the best hour of the river (from Bacharach to St. Goar), and tour the Rheinfels Castle. Those with more time can bike the river-side bike path. With two days and a car, visit the Rhine and the Mosel. With two days by train, see the Rhine and Köln. With three days, do all three, and with four days include Trier and a sleepy night in the Mosel River Valley.

Rhine and Mosel Valleys

THE RHINE

Ever since Roman times, when this was the Empire's northern boundary, the Rhine has been one of the world's busiest shipping rivers. You'll see a steady flow of barges with 1,000- to 2,000-ton loads. Tourist-packed buses, hot train tracks, and highways line both banks.

Many of the castles were "robber-baron" castles, put there by petty rulers (there were 300 independent little countries in medieval Germany) to levy tolls on passing river traffic. A robber-baron would put his castle on, or even in, the river. Then, often with the help of chains and a tower on the opposite bank, he'd stop each ship and get his toll. There were 10 customs stops between Mainz and Koblenz alone (no wonder merchants were early proponents of the creation of larger nation-states).

Some castles were built to control and protect settlements, and others were the residences of kings. As times changed, so did the lifestyles of the rich and feudal. Many castles were abandoned for more comfortable mansions in the towns.

Most Rhine castles date from the 11th, 12th, and 13th centuries. When the pope successfully asserted his power over the German emperor in 1076, local princes ran wild over the rule of their emperor. The castles saw military action in the 1300s and

1400s, as emperors began reasserting their control over Germany's many silly kingdoms.

The castles were also involved in the Reformation wars, in which Europe's Catholic and "protesting" dynasties fought it out using a fragmented Germany as their battleground. The Thirty Years' War (1618–1648) devastated Germany. The outcome: each ruler got the freedom to decide if his people would be Catholic or Protestant, and one-third of Germany was dead. Production of Gummi Bears ceased entirely.

The French—who feared a strong Germany and felt the Rhine was the logical border between them and Germany—destroyed most of the castles prophylactically (Louis XIV in the 1680s, the revolutionary army in the 1790s, and Napoleon in 1806). They were often rebuilt in neo-Gothic style in the Romantic Age—the late 1800s—and today are enjoyed as restaurants, hotels, hostels, and museums. Check out the Rhine Web site at www.loreleytal.com.

Getting Around the Rhine

While the Rhine flows from Switzerland to Holland, the stretch from Mainz to Koblenz hoards all the touristic charm. Studded with the crenelated cream of Germany's castles, it bustles with boats, trains, and highway traffic. Have fun exploring with a mix of big steamers, tiny ferries, bikes, and trains.

By Boat: While many travelers do the whole trip by boat, the most scenic hour is from St. Goar to Bacharach. Sit on the top deck with your handy Rhine map-guide (or the kilometer-keyed tour in this book) and enjoy the parade of castles, towns, boats, and vineyards.

There are several boat companies, but most travelers sail on the bigger, more expensive, and romantic Köln–Düsseldorf (K-D) line (free with Eurail, otherwise about 15 DM for the first hour, then progressively cheaper per hour, the recommended Bacharach-St. Goar trip costs 15 DM one-way, 18 DM round-trip, tel. 06741/1634 in St. Goar). Boats run daily in both directions from April through October, with fewer boats off-season. Complete, up-to-date schedules are posted in any station, Rhineland hotel, TI, or current Thomas Cook Timetable. Purchase tickets at the dock five minutes before departure. The boat is never full. (Confirm times at your hotel the night before.)

The smaller Bingen-Rüdesheimer line is 25 percent cheaper than K-D (Eurail not valid, buy tickets on the boat, tel. 06721/14140), with three two-hour round-trip St. Goar–Bacharach trips daily in summer (12 DM one-way, 16 DM round-trip; departing St. Goar at 11:00, 14:10, and 16:10; departing Bacharach at 10:10, 12:30, and 15:00).

Drivers have these options: (1) skip the boat; (2) take a

Best of the Rhine

round-trip cruise from St. Goar or Bacharach; (3) draw pretzels and let the loser drive, prepare the picnic, and meet the boat; (4) rent a bike, bring it on the boat for free, and bike back; or (5) take the boat one way and return by train.

By Train: Hourly milk-run trains down the Rhine hit every town: St. Goar-Bacharach, 12 min; Bacharach–Mainz, 60 min; Mainz-Frankfurt, 45 min. (Some train schedules list St. Goar but not Bacharach as a stop, but any schedule listing St. Goar also stops at Bacharach. Tiny stations are unmanned—buy tickets on the train.)

1999 Rhine Cruise Schedule

Koblenz	Boppard	St. Goar	Bacharach →
—	9:00	10:15	11:35
9:00	10:50	12:05	13:15
11:00	12:50	14:05	15:15
14:00	15:50	17:05	18:15
11:05	11:30	11:50	12:10*
←			
13:00	11:40	10:45	10:00
14:20	13:10	12:15	11:30
—	14:00	13:15	12:30
18:00	16:40	15:45	15:00
20:00	18:50	18:00	17:20

Hydrofoil, Koblenz-Bacharach, 30 DM with Eurail, 70 DM without.
Note: *Schedule applies May through September and mostly April and October; no boats run November through March.*

By Bike: In Bacharach try Pension Lettie (15 DM/day, 10 DM/4 hrs, no deposit for guests, otherwise passport or credit-card imprint, tel. 06743/2115), Hotel Gelberhof (20 DM/day for 10-speeds, 25 DM for "trekking" bikes, 5 DM for child's seat, tel. 06743/910-100, ring bell when closed), or Hotel Hillen (15 DM/day, 10 DM/half-day, cheaper for guests, 20 bikes). In St. Goar you can rent bikes at the Golf Pavilion along the Rhine (13 DM/day, 10 DM/4 hrs, 50 DM or passport as deposit, April–October 10:00–21:00, tel. 06741/1360). The best riverside bike path is from Bacharach to Bingen. The path is also good from St. Goar to Bacharach, but it's closer to the highway. Consider sailing to Bingen and biking back, visiting Rheinstein Castle (you're on your own to wander the well-furnished castle) and Reichenstein Castle (admittance with groups), and maybe even taking a ferry across the river to Kaub (where a tiny boat shuttles sightseers to the better-from-a-distance castle on the island). While there are no bridges between Koblenz and Mainz, several small ferries do their job constantly and cheaply.

Sights—The Romantic Rhine
(These sights are north to south, Koblenz to Bingen.)
▲▲▲**Der Romantische Rhein Blitz Zug Fahrt**—One of Europe's great train thrills is zipping along the Rhine in this fast train tour. Here's a quick and easy, from-the-train-window tour

(also works for car, boat, or bike) that skips the syrupy myths and the life story of Dieter von Katzenelnbogen that fill normal Rhine guides. For more information than necessary, buy the handy *Rhine Guide from Mainz to Cologne* (7-DM book with foldout map, at most shops).

Sit on the left (river) side of the train going south from Koblenz. While nearly all the castles listed are viewed from this side, clear a path to the right window for the times I yell, "Crossover!"

You'll notice large black-and-white kilometer markers along the riverbank. I erected these years ago to make this tour easier to follow. They tell the distance from the Rhinefalls where the Rhine leaves Switzerland and becomes navigable. Now the river-barge pilots have accepted these as navigational aids as well. We're tackling just 36 miles of the 820-mile-long Rhine. Your Blitz Rhine Tour starts at Koblenz and heads upstream to Bingen. If you're going the other direction, it still works. Just hold the book upside down.

Km 590: Koblenz—This Rhine Blitz starts with the Romantic Rhine thrills—at Koblenz. Koblenz is not a nice city (it was really hit hard in World War II), but its place as the historic *Deutsche-Ecke* (German corner)—the tip of land where the Mosel joins the Rhine—gives it a certain historic charm. Koblenz, Latin for "confluence," has Roman origins. Walk through the park, noticing the reconstructed memorial to the Kaiser. Across the river, the yellow Ehrenbreitstein Castle now houses a hostel. It's a 30-minute hike from the station to the Koblenz boat dock.

Km 585: Burg Lahneck—Above the modern Autobahn bridge over the Lahn River, this castle (*Burg*) was built in 1240 to defend local silver mines, ruined by the French in 1688 and rebuilt in the 1850s in neo-Gothic style. Burg Lahneck faces the yellow Schloss Stolzenfels (out of view above the train, a 10-minute climb from the tiny car park, open for touring, closed Monday).

Km 580: Marksburg—This castle (black and white with the three modern chimneys behind it, just after town of Spay) is the best-looking of all the Rhine castles and the only surviving medieval castle on the Rhine. Because of its commanding position, it was never attacked. It's now open as a museum with a medieval interior second only to the Mosel's Burg Eltz (9 DM, daily 10:00–17:00, call ahead to see if a rare English tour is scheduled, tel. 02627/206).

Km 570: Boppard—Once a Roman town, Boppard has some impressive remains of fourth-century walls. Notice the Roman tower just after the Boppard train station and the substantial chunk of Roman wall just before. Boppard is worth a stop. Just above the main square are the remains of the Roman wall. Below the square is a fascinating church. Notice the carved Romanesque crazies at the doorway. Inside, to the right of the entrance, you'll

River Trade and Barge Watching

The river is great for barge watching. Since ancient times this has been a highway for trade. Today, the world's biggest port (Rotterdam) waits at the mouth of the river. Barge workers are almost a subculture. Many own their own ships. The captain (and family) live in the stern. Workers live in the bow. The family car often decorates the bow like a shiny hood ornament. In the Rhine town of Kaub, there's even a boarding school for the children of the Rhine merchant marine. The flag of the boat's home country flies in the stern (German, Swiss, Dutch—horizontal red, white, and blue, or French—vertical red, white, and blue). Logically, imports go upstream (Japanese cars, coal, and oil) and exports go downstream (German cars, chemicals, and pharmaceuticals). A clever captain manages to ship goods in each direction.

At this point tugs can push a floating train of up to five barges at once. Upstream it gets steeper and they can push only one at a time. Before modern shipping, horses dragged boats upstream (the faint remains of the tow paths survive at points along the river). From 1873 to 1900 they actually laid a chain from Bonn to Bingen, and boats with cog-wheels and steam engines hoisted themselves slowly upstream. Today, 265 million tons are shipped each year along the 528 navigable miles from Basel on the Swiss border to Rotterdam on the Atlantic.

While riverside navigational aids are ignored by camera-toting tourists, they are of vital interest to captains who don't wish to meet the Loreley. Boats pass on the right unless they clearly signal otherwise with a large blue sign. Since downstream ships can't stop or maneuver as freely, upstream boats are expected to do the tricky do-si-do work. Cameras monitor traffic all along and relay warnings of oncoming ships via large triangular signals posted before narrow and troublesome bends in the river. There may be two or three triangles per sign post, depending upon how many "sectors," or segments, of the river are covered. The lowest triangle indicates the nearest stretch of river. Each triangle tells if there's a ship in that sector. When the bottom side of a triangle is lit, that sector is empty. When the left side is lit, an oncoming ship is in that sector.

see Christian symbols from Roman times. Also notice the painted arches and vaults. Originally most Romanesque churches were painted this way. Down by the river, look for the high water (*Hochwasser*) marks on the arches from various flood years. (You'll find these flood marks throughout the Rhine and Mosel Valleys.)

Km 567: Burg Sterrenberg and Burg Liebenstein—These are the "Hostile Brothers" castles (across from Bad Salzig). Take the wall between the castles (actually designed to improve the defenses of both castles), add two greedy and jealous brothers and a fair maiden, and create your own legend. The castles are restaurants today.

Km 559: Burg Maus—The Maus ("Mouse") got its name because the next castle was owned by the Katzenelnbogen family. ("Katz" means "cat.") In the 1300s it was considered a state-of-the-art fortification . . . until Napoleon had it blown up in 1806 with state-of-the-art explosives. It was rebuilt true to its original plans around 1900.

Km 557: St. Goar and Rheinfels Castle—Cross to the other side of the train. The pleasant town of St. Goar (gwahr) was named for a sixth-century hometown monk. It originated in Celtic times (really old) as a place where sailors would stop, catch their breath, send home a postcard, and give thanks after surviving the seductive and treacherous Loreley crossing. St. Goar is worth a stop to explore its mighty Rheinfels Castle (For information on a guided castle tour and accommodations, see below.)

Km 556: Burg Katz—From the town of St. Goar, you'll see Burg Katz (Katzenelnbogen) across the river. Together, Burg Katz (b. 1371) and Rheinfels Castle had a clear view up and down the river and effectively controlled traffic. There was absolutely no duty-free shopping on the medieval Rhine. Katz got Napoleoned in 1806 and rebuilt around 1900. Today it's a convalescent home.

About km 555: You'll see the statue of the Loreley, the beautiful but deadly nymph (see legend below), at the end of a long spit—built to give barges protection from vicious icebergs that occasionally rage down the river in the winter. The actual Loreley, a cliff, is just ahead.

Km 554: The Loreley—Steep a big slate rock in centuries of legend and it becomes a tourist attraction, the ultimate Rhine-stone. The Loreley (two flags on top, name painted near shoreline), rising 450 feet over the narrowest and deepest point of the Rhine, has long been important. It was a holy site in pre-Roman days. The fine echoes here—thought to be ghostly voices—fertilized the legendary soil.

Because of the reefs just upstream (at km 552), many ships never made it to St. Goar. Sailors (after days on the river) blamed their misfortune on a *wunderbares Fräulein* whose long blonde hair almost covered her body. Heinrich Heine's *Song of Loreley* (the *Cliffs Notes* version is on local postcards) tells the story of a count who sent his men to kill or capture this siren after she distracted his horny son, causing him to drown. When the soldiers cornered the nymph in her cave, she called her father (Father Rhine) for help. Huge waves, the likes of which you'll never see today, rose from the river and carried Loreley to safety. And she has never been seen since.

But alas, when the moon shines brightly and the tour buses are parked, a soft, playful Rhine whine can still be heard from the Loreley. As you pass, listen carefully ("Sailors . . . sailors . . . over my bounding mane").

Km 552: Killer reefs, marked by red-and-green buoys, are called the "Seven Maidens."

Km 550: Oberwesel—Cross to the other side of the train. Oberwesel was a Celtic town in 400 B.C., then a Roman military station. It now boasts some of the best Roman wall and tower remains on the Rhine and the commanding Schönburg castle. Notice how many of the train tunnels have entrances designed like medieval turrets—they were actually built in the Romantic 19th century. OK, back to the riverside.

Km 546: Burg Gutenfels and Pfalz Castle: the Classic Rhine View—Burg Gutenfels (see the white painted "Hotel" sign) and the ship-shape Pfalz Castle (built in the river in the 1300s) worked very effectively to tax medieval river traffic. The town of Kaub grew rich as Pfalz raised its chains when boats came and lowered them only when the merchants had paid their duty. Those who didn't pay spent time touring its prison, on a raft at the bottom of its well. In 1504 a pope called for the destruction of Pfalz, but a six-week siege failed. Notice the overhanging "outhouse" (tiny white room with the faded medieval stains between the two wooden ones). Pfalz is tourable but bare and dull (3-DM ferry from Kaub, 4 DM, Tuesday–Sunday 9:00–13:00, 14:00–18:00, closed Monday, tel. 06774/570).

In Kaub a green statue honors the German General Blücher. He was Napoleon's nemesis. In 1813, as Napoleon fought his way back to Paris after his disastrous Russian campaign, he stopped at Mainz—hoping to fend off the Germans and Russians pursuing him—by controlling that strategic bridge. Blücher tricked Napoleon. By building the first major pontoon bridge of its kind, here at the Pfalz Castle, he crossed the Rhine and outflanked the French. Two years later Blücher and Wellington teamed up to defeat Napoleon once and for all at Waterloo.

Km 544: The "Raft Busters"—Immediately before Bacharach, at the top of the island, buoys mark a gang of rocks notorious for busting up rafts. The Black Forest is upstream. It was poor, and wood was its best export. Black Foresters would ride log booms down the Rhine to the Ruhr (where their timber fortified coal mine shafts) or to Holland (where logs were sold to ship builders). If they could navigate the sweeping bend just before Bacharach and then survive these "raft busters," they'd come home reckless and romantic, the German folkloric equivalent of American cowboys after payday.

Km 543: Bacharach and Burg Stahleck—Cross to the other side of the train. Bacharach is a great stop (see details and accommodations below). Some of the Rhine's best wine is from this town, whose name means "altar to Bacchus." Local vintners brag that the medieval Pope Pius II ordered it by the cartload. Perched above the town, the 13th-century Burg Stahleck is now a hostel.

Km 540: Lorch—This pathetic stub of a castle is barely visible from the road. Notice the small car ferry (3/hrly, 10 min), one of several between Mainz and Koblenz, where there are no bridges.

Km 538: Castle Sooneck—Cross back to the other side of the train. Built in the 11th century, this castle was twice destroyed by people sick and tired of robber-barons.

Km 534: Burg Reichenstein, and Km 533: Burg Rheinstein—Stay on the other side of the train to see two of the first castles to be rebuilt in the Romantic era. Both are privately owned, tourable, and connected by a pleasant trail.

Km 530: Ehrenfels Castle—Opposite Bingerbrück and the Bingen station, you'll see the ghostly Ehrenfels Castle (clobbered by the Swedes in 1636 and by the French in 1689). Since it had no view of the river traffic to the north, the owner built the cute little *Mäuseturm* (Mouse Tower) on an island (the yellow tower you'll see near the train station today). Rebuilt in the 1800s in neo-Gothic style, today it's used as a Rhine navigation signal station.

Km 528: Niederwald Monument—Across from the Bingen station on a hilltop is the 120-foot-high Niederwald monument, a memorial built with 32 tons of bronze in 1877 to commemorate "the re-establishment of the German Empire." A lift takes tourists to this statue from the famous and extremely touristy wine town of Rüdesheim.

Our tour is over. From Bingen, you can continue your journey (or return to Koblenz) by train or boat.

BACHARACH

Bacharach, once prosperous from the wine and wood trade, is now just a pleasant half-timbered village working hard to keep its tourists happy.

The lightweight TI is on the main street—look for the "i" sign (Monday–Friday 9:00–12:30, 13:30–17:00, Saturday 10:00–12:00, tel. 06743/1297). They have a blurry photocopied town map with an English history.

The Jost beer stein "factory outlet" carries everything a shopper could want. It has one shop across from the church in the main square and a slightly cheaper shop a block away on Rosenstrasse 16 (Monday–Friday 8:30–18:00, Saturday 8:30–17:00, Sunday 10:00–17:00, ships overseas, 10 percent discount with this book, CC:VMA, tel. 06743/1224).

Get acquainted with Bacharach by taking a walking tour. You

Bacharach

❶ CASTLE YOUTH HOSTEL
❷ HOTEL KRANENTURM
❸ HOTEL HILLEN
❹ DETTMAR ZIMMER
❺ PENSION LETTIE
❻ ORTH B&B
❼ GELBERHOF
❽ FRITZ BASTIAN'S WINE TASTING
❾ HOTEL ALTKOLNISCHER HOF
❿ PENSION WINZERHAUS

TO STEEG ↑

NOT TO SCALE—
K·D DOCK TO
CASTLE IS A
15-20 MIN. WALK

BURG STAHLECK CASTLE!!

POST

BLÜCHERSTRASSE
ROSENSTRASSE

JOST FACTORY OUTLET

OLD TOWN WALLS

Verkehrsamt

WERNER KAPELLE

STEEP TRAIL
POSTHOF

BAHN-HOF

PHONE

OBER-STRASSE

BAUER

ALTES HAUS

SPAR MKT.

BANK

MÜNZE

LANG-STRASSE

HIGHWAY 9

PHONE

PED. UNDERPASS

TO BINGEN, CAMPGROUND, & FRANKFURT

MEM. PARK

WC

P

TO St GOAR & KOBLENZ

RHINE RIVER

B/R DOCK

K/D DOCK

EURAIL VALID

can hire Herr Rolf Jung, retired headmaster of the Bacharach school (50 DM, 1.5 hrs, tel. 06743/1519, speaks excellent English), or take a self-guided walk, below.

Sights—Bacharach

▲▲**Introductory Bacharach Walk**—Start at the Köln-Düsseldorf ferry dock (next to a fine picnic park). View the town from the parking lot—a modern landfill. The Rhine used to lap against Bacharach's town wall (just over the present-day highway). Every few years, the river floods, covering the highway under several feet of water. The castle on the hill is a youth hostel. Two of its original 16 towers are visible from here (up to five if you look real hard). The huge roadside wine keg declares this town was built on the wine trade.

Reefs up the river forced boats to unload upriver and reload here. Consequently, Bacharach became the biggest wine trader on the Rhine. A riverfront crane hoisted huge kegs of prestigious "Bacharach" wine (which in practice was from anywhere in the region). The tour buses next to the dock and the flags of the biggest spenders along the highway remind you today's economy is basically tourism.

At the big town map and public WC, take the underpass, ascend on the right, and walk under the train tracks through the medieval gate (one out of an original six 14th-century gates) and to the two-tone Protestant church, which marks the town center.

From this intersection, Bacharach's main street (Oberstrasse) goes right to the half-timbered red-and-white Altes Haus (from 1368, the oldest house in town) and left to the TI and train station. To the left (or south) of the church, the golden horn hangs over the old Posthof. (The post horn symbolizes the postal service throughout Europe. In olden days, when the post man blew this, traffic stopped, and the mail sped through.) Step into the courtyard. Notice the fascist eagle (from 1936, on the left doorstep as you enter) and the fine view of a chapel and church. This post station dates from 1724, when stagecoaches ran from Köln to Frankfurt.

Two hundred years ago this was the only road along the Rhine. Napoleon widened it to fit his cannon wagons. The steps alongside the church lead to the castle. Return to the church.

Inside the church you'll find grotesque and brightly painted capitals and a mix of round Romanesque and pointed Gothic arches. In the upper left corner some medieval frescoes survive where an older Romanesque arch was cut by a pointed Gothic one.

Continue down Oberstrasse past the Altes Haus to the old mint (*Münze*), marked by a crude coin in its sign. Across from the mint, the wine garden of Fritz Bastian is the liveliest place in town after dark. Above you in the vineyards stands a ghostly black-and-gray tower—your destination.

Wander 30 meters up Rosenstrasse to the well. Notice the sundial and the wall painting of 1632 Bacharach with its walls intact. Climb the tiny-stepped lane behind the well up into the vineyard and to the tower. The slate steps deposit you at a viewpoint atop the stubby remains of the old town wall just above the tower's base.

A grand medieval town spreads before you. When Frankfurt had 15,000 residents, medieval Bacharach had 6,000. For 300 years (1300–1600) Bacharach was big, rich, and politically powerful.

From this perch you can see the chapel ruins and six of the nine surviving city towers. Visually trace the wall to the castle, home of one of seven electors who voted for the Holy Roman Emperor in 1275. To protect their own power, these elector princes did their best to choose the weakest guy on the ballot. The elector from Bacharach helped select a two-bit prince named Rudolf von Habsburg (from a two-bit castle in Switzerland). The underestimated Rudolf brutally silenced the robber-barons along the Rhine and established the mightiest dynasty in European history. His family line, the Habsburgs, ruled the Austro-Hungarian Empire until 1918.

Plagues, fires, and the Thirty Years' War (1618–1648) finally did Bacharach in. The town has slumbered for several centuries, with a population of about a thousand.

In the mid-19th century, artists and writers such as Victor Hugo were charmed by the Rhineland's romantic mix of past glory, present poverty, and rich legend. They put this part of the Rhine on the old "grand tour" map as the "Romantic Rhine." Victor Hugo pondered the ruined 15th-century chapel, which you can see under the castle. In his 1842 travel book, *Rhein Reise* (*Rhine Travels*), he wrote, "No doors, no roof or windows, a magnificent-skeleton puts its silhouette against the sky. Above it, the ivy-covered castle ruins provide a fitting crown. This is Bacharach, land of fairy tales, covered with legends and sagas."

A path leads along the wall, up the valley, to the next tower, and down onto the street. The road leads under the gate and back into the center. If you're enjoying the Romantic Rhine, thank Victor Hugo and company.

Sleeping on the Rhine
(1.7 DM = about $1)
Sleep Code: **S** = Single, **D** = Double/Twin, **T** = Triple, **Q** = Quad, **b** = bathroom, **t** = toilet only, **s** = shower only, **CC** = Credit Card (Visa, MasterCard, Amex), **SE** = Speaks English, **NSE** = No English. All hotels speak some English. Breakfast is included unless otherwise noted.

The Rhine is an easy place for cheap sleeps. *Zimmer* and *Gasthäuser* with 30-DM beds abound (and *Zimmer* normally discount their prices for longer stays). Several exceptional Rhine-area hostels offer 20-DM beds (for travelers of any age). Each town's helpful TI is eager to set you up, and finding a room should be easy any time of year (except for wine-festy weekends in September and October). Bacharach and St. Goar, the best towns for an overnight stop, are about 10 miles apart, connected by milk-run trains, river boats, and a riverside bike path. Bacharach is less touristy, St. Goar has the famous castle (see St. Goar, below). Parking in Bacharach is simple along the highway next to the tracks (3-hour daytime limit is generally not enforced).

Sleeping in Bacharach
(tel. code: 06743, zip code: 55422)

Hotels

Hotel Kranenturm gives you castle ambience without the climb. It offers the best combination of comfort and hotel privacy with *Zimmer* warmth, central location, and medieval atmosphere. Run by hardworking Kurt Engel, his intense but friendly wife, Fatima, and faithful Schumi (shoo-mee), this hotel is actually part of the medieval fortification. Its former *Kran* (crane) towers are now round rooms—great for medievalists. When the riverbank was higher, cranes on this tower loaded barrels of wine onto Rhine boats. Hotel Kranenturm is five yards from the train tracks, but a combination of medieval sturdiness, triple-paned windows, and included earplugs makes the riverside rooms sleepable (Sb-60–65 DM, Db-90–95 DM, Tb-125–130 DM, Qb-160–165 DM with this book, plus 10 DM for rooms with a TV, cheaper price for stays of two nights, kid-friendly, Rhine views come with train noise, back rooms—some with castle views—are quieter, laundry service, CC:VMA but prefer cash, Langstrasse 30, tel. 06743/1308, fax 06743/1021, e-mail: hotel-kranenturm @t-online.de). Kurt, a great cook, serves fine 15- to 20-DM dinners. Trade travel stories on the terrace with new friends over dinner, letting screaming trains punctuate your conversation. Kurt's big-enough-for-three Kranenturm ice-cream special is a delight (10 DM). For a quick trip to Fiji in a medieval German cellar, check out his tropical bar. Drivers park along the highway at the Kranenturm tower. Eurailers walk down Oberstrasse, then turn right on Kranenstrasse.

Hotel Hillen, a block south of the Hotel Kranenturm, has less charm and more train noise, with friendly owners and lots of rental bikes. To minimize train noise ask for "ruhige Seite," the quiet side, (S-45 DM, Sb-60 DM, D-80 DM, Db-90 DM, Tb-126 DM, 10 percent less for two nights, 10 percent more with CC, Langstrasse 18, tel. 06743/1287, fax 06743/1037).

Hotel Altkölnischer Hof, a grand old building on the main square, rents 20 rooms with modern furnishings and bathrooms, some with balconies. Public rooms are old-time elegant (Sb-90–95 DM, Db-110–130 DM, Db with terrace-140 DM, with balcony-150–160 DM, 10 percent discount for three-night stays, TV and phones in rooms, elevator, attached restaurant, CC:VA, tel. 06743/1339 or 06743/2186, fax 06743/2793).

Hotel Gelberhof has spiffy public spaces but tired rooms (S-55 DM, Sb-75–85 DM, small Db-110 DM, Db-120–140 DM, possible cash or two-night discounts, popular with groups, elevator, bike rental, CC:M, Blücherstrasse 26, tel. 06743/910-100, fax 06743/910-1050, e-mail: gelberhof@fh-bingen.de).

Pensions and Private Rooms

Pension Lettie—Effervescent and eager-to-please Lettie offers four cheery, newly remodeled rooms (Sb-55 DM, Db-75 DM, Tb-110 DM with this book and cash, cheaper price is for longer stays, strictly non-smoking, no train noise, a few doors inland from Hotel Kranenturm, Kranenstrasse 6, tel. & fax 06743/2115, e-mail: pension.lettie@t-online.de). Lettie speaks great English (worked for the U.S. army before we withdrew), does laundry (16 DM per load), and rents bikes (15 DM/day, non-guests leave a passport or credit-card imprint).

Entrepreneurial **Annelie und Hans Dettmar** rent six smoke-free rooms in a modern house on the main drag in the center (big Sb-50 DM, Db-60 DM, Tb-75 DM, Qb-100 DM, free use of two old bikes, laundry-17 DM, Oberstrasse 8, tel. & fax 06743/2661, SE). One room is huge, easily fits a family of four, and has a kitchenette (20 DM to use it). Skip their other building up the hill; it's a long, steep walk away. Readers give this couple mixed reviews, but their place is handy for those who need a smoke-free option. Their son Jürgen runs the adjacent bakery and rents five fine rooms on the main square opposite the Altes Haus at **Pension Braustube** (Db-60 DM, Tb-90 DM, Oberstrasse 64, tel. & fax 06743/1715 or call his parents' B&B, SE).

Ursula Orth offers five small, bright rooms in her home around the corner from the Dettmars' in the town center—perhaps the best cheap beds in town (Sb-30 DM, Db-55–60 DM, Tb-75 DM for one night and less for two, non-smoking, Rooms 4 and 5 on ground floor—easy access, Spurgasse 3, tel. 06743/1557, some English spoken).

The home of **Herr und Frau Theilacker** is a German-feeling *Zimmer* with comfortable rooms and no outside sign. It's likely to have a room when others don't (S-30 DM, D-60 DM, in the town center behind the Altes Haus at Oberstrasse 57, tel. 06743/1248, NSE).

Pension Winzerhaus is a 10-room place run by Herr Petrescu. It's 200 yards up the valley from the town gate, so the location is less charming, but it has no train noise and easy parking. Rooms are simple, clean, and modern (Sb-50 DM, Db-85 DM, Tb-90 DM, Qb-95 DM, 10 percent off with this book, free bikes for guests, Blücherstrasse 60, tel. 06743/1294, fax 069/283-927).

Bacharach's hostel, Jugendherberge Stahleck, is a 12th-century castle on the hilltop, 500 steps above Bacharach, with a royal Rhine view. Open to travelers of any age, this is a newly redone gem with eight beds and a private modern shower and WC in each room. A steep 15-minute climb on the trail from the town church, the hostel is warmly run by Evelyn and Bernhard Falke (FALL-kay), who serve hearty, 9-DM buffet, all-you-can-eat dinners. The hostel pub serves cheap local wine until midnight (24-

DM dorm beds with breakfast and sheets, 6 DM extra without a card or in a double, couples can share rooms, groups pay 32 DM per bed with breakfast and dinner, no smoking in rooms, easy parking, beds normally available but call and leave your name, they'll hold a bed until 18:00, tel. 06743/1266, SE).

Eating in Bacharach

Several places offer good, inexpensive, and atmospheric indoor or outdoor dining in Bacharach. **Hotel Kranenturm** (see above) and **Altes Haus** (the oldest building in town, on main square, 20-DM dinners, closed Wednesday) are both excellent. **Kurpfälzische Münze** serves good 20- to 30-DM dinners nightly (in the old mint, across the street from the Altes Haus, claims to be even older). **Weingut zum Gruner Baum** offers delicious dinners and cold lunches (also next to Altes Haus with good ambience indoors and out). And the **Posthof** beer garden has good, cheap pub grub, served outside in the courtyard.

Wine Tasting: Drop in on entertaining Fritz Bastian's **Weingut zum Grüner Baum** wine bar (just past the Altes Haus, evenings only, closed Thursday, tel. 06743/1208). The president of the local vintner's club, Fritz has a calling to give travelers an understanding of the subtle differences among the Rhine wines. Groups of two to 10 people pay 26 DM for a "carousel" of 15 glasses of 14 different white wines, one lonely red, and a basket of bread. Your mission: team up with others with this book to rendezvous here after dinner. Spin the lazy Susan, share a common cup, and discuss the taste. Fritz insists, "After each wine, you must talk to each other."

ST. GOAR

St. Goar is a classic Rhine town—its hulk of a castle overlooking a half-timbered shopping wonderland and leafy riverside park busy with sightseeing ships and contented strollers. From the boat dock, the main drag—a pedestrian mall—cuts through town before winding up to the castle. Rheinfels castle, once the mightiest on the Rhine, is the single best Rhineland ruin to explore.

The St. Goar TI offers free left-luggage service (Monday–Friday 8:00–12:30, 14:00–17:00, Saturday 10:00–12:00 May–October, closed Sunday and earlier in winter, tel. 06741/383). You can rent a bike at the Golf Pavilion near the river (13 DM/day).

St. Goar's waterfront park is hungry for a picnic. The small EDEKA supermarket on the main street is fine for picnic fixings (Monday–Friday 8:00–19:00, Saturday 8:00–16:00, closed Sunday).

The friendly and helpful Montag family in the shop under Hotel Montag has Rhine guidebooks (Koblenz–Mainz), fine steins, and copies of this year's *Rick Steves' Germany, Austria & Switzerland* guidebook. They also run the cuckoo clock shop across the street (marked by the world's biggest free-hanging cuckoo clock)

St. Goar

① TOURIST INFO
② HOTEL MONTAG
③ HOTEL HAUSER
④ KURZ ZIMMER
⑤ EDEKA SUPERMARKET
⑥ HOTEL AM MARKT
B = BANKS

and offer 10 percent off any of their souvenirs for travelers with this book.

For a good two-hour hike from St. Goar, catch the ferry across to St. Goarshausen, hike to the Katz castle, and traverse along the hillside from there to the top of the Loreley. From the Loreley the trail winds down to the river and then takes you back to the St. Goarshausen-to-St. Goar ferry (4/hrly, 3-DM round-trip).

Sights—St. Goar's Rheinfels Castle

▲▲▲**Self-guided Tour**—Sitting like a dead pit bull above St. Goar, this mightiest of Rhine castles rumbles with ghosts from its hard-fought past. Burg Rheinfels (built in 1245) withstood a siege of 28,000 French troops in 1692. But in 1797 the French Revolutionary army destroyed it.

Rheinfels was huge, the biggest on the Rhine, then used as a quarry. Today this hollow but interesting shell offers your single best, hands-on ruined castle experience on the river (5 DM, daily 9:00–18:00, last entry at 17:00; Saturday and Sunday only in winter; gather 10 English-speaking tourists and get a nearly free English tour, tel. 06741/7753). The cruel castle map is worth .30 DM to help follow the guided tour below. The English booklet is not worth 3.50 DM. If planning to explore the underground passages, bring a flashlight, buy a tiny one (5 DM at entry), or do it by candlelight (museum sells candles with matches, 1 DM). To get to the castle from St. Goar's boat dock or train station, take a steep 15-minute hike, a 7-DM taxi ride (11 DM for a minibus, tel. 06741/93100), or goofy tourist train (3 DM, 3/hrly, from square between station and dock, complete with lusty music).

Rather than wander aimlessly, visit the castle by following this tour: From the ticket gate walk straight and uphill. Pass Grosser Keller on left (where we'll end this tour), walk through an internal gate past "zu den gedeckten Wehrgängen" on right (where we'll pass later) to the museum (daily 9:00–12:00, 13:00–17:00) in the only finished room of the castle.

1. Museum and castle model: The seven-foot tall carved stone ("Keltische Säule von Pfalzfeld") immediately inside the door—a tombstone from a nearby Celtic grave—is from 600 years before Christ. There were people here long before the Romans . . . and this castle. The chair next to the door is an old library chair. Fold it up and it becomes stairs for getting to the highest shelves.

The castle history exhibit in the center of the room is well described in English. At the far end is a model reconstruction of the castle showing how much bigger it was before Louis XIV destroyed it. Study this. Find where you are. This was the living quarters of the original castle, which was only the smallest ring of buildings around the tiny central courtyard (13th century, marked by red well). The ramparts were added in the 14th century. In 1605 the entire fortress was completed. The vast majority of the place was destroyed in 1796. It has had no military value since. While no WWII bombs were wasted on this ruin, it served St. Goar as a quarry for generations. The basement of the museum shows the castle pharmacy and an exhibit on the Rhine icebergs.

(From the museum, walk 30 meters directly out, slightly uphill into the castle courtyard.)

2. Medieval castle courtyard: Five hundred years ago the entire castle circled this courtyard. The place was self-sufficient and ready for a siege with a baker, pharmacy, herb garden, animals, brewery, well (top of yard), and livestock. During peace time, 300 to 600 people lived here—during a siege as many as 4,500. The walls were plastered and painted white. Bits of the original 13th-century plaster survive.

(Continue through courtyard, out "Erste Schildmauer," turn left into the next courtyard below German flag and two old, black, upright posts. Find the pyramid of stone catapult balls.)

3. Castle garden: Catapult balls like these were too expensive not to recycle. If ever used, they'd be retrieved after the battle. Across from the balls is a well: essential for any castle during the age of sieging. The old posts are for the ceremonial baptizing of new members of the local trading league. While this gild goes back centuries, today it's a social club that fills this court with a huge wine party the first weekend of each August.

(If weary, skip to 5; otherwise, climb to the castle's best viewpoint up where the German flag waves.)

4. Highest castle tower lookout: Enjoy a great view of the river, castle, and the forest that was once all part of this castle. Remember, the fortress once covered five times the land it does today. Originally this castle was no bigger than the two you see over the river. Notice how the other castles don't poke above the top of the Rhine canyon. That would make them easy for invading armies to see.

(Return to the catapult balls, walk down the road, through the tunnel, veer left through the arch marked "zu den Gedeckten Wehrgängen," go down two flights of stairs and turn left into the dark covered passageway. We now begin a rectangular walk taking us completely around the perimeter of the castle.)

5. Covered defense galleries: Soldiers—the castle's "minute men"—had a short commute: defensive positions on outside, home in the holes below on the left. Even though these living quarters were padded with straw, life was unpleasant. A peasant was lucky to live beyond age 28.

(Continue straight through the gallery and to the corner of the castle, where you'll see a white painted arrow at eye level.)

6. Corner of castle: Look up. A three-story, half-timbered building originally rose beyond the highest stone fortification. The two stone tongues near the top just around the corner supported the toilet. (Insert joke here.) Turn around. The crossbow slits below the white arrow were once steeper. The bigger hole on the riverside was for hot pitch, etc.

(Follow that white arrow along the outside to the next corner. Midway, you'll pass stairs leading down "zu den Minengängen." Adventurers with flashlights can detour here. You may come out around the next corner. Otherwise, stay with me, walking level to the corner. At the corner, turn left.)

7. Thoop . . . you're dead. Look ahead at the smartly placed crossbow arrow slit. While you're lying there, notice the stone work. The little round holes were for scaffolds used as they built up. They indicate this stonework is original. Notice also the fine stonework on the shoots. More boiling oil . . . now you're toast too. Continue along. At the railing look up the valley and uphill where the fort existed. Below, just outside the wall, is land where attackers would gather. Tunnels filled with explosives ran under the land just outside the walls. With clever thin slate roofs, the force of their detonation went up, killing masses of attackers without damaging the actual castle. In 1626, a handful of underground Protestant Germans blew 300 Catholic Spaniards to—they figured—hell. You can explore these underground passages from the next courtyard.

(Continue along perimeter, jog left, go down five steps and into a huge open field. You may detour here into the passageway marked "13 Hals Graben," or farther to the right and down. The old wooden bridge is actually modern. Continue around the castle through two arches and through the rough entry to "Verliess" on the left.)

8. Prison: This is one of six dungeons. You walked through a door prisoners only dreamed of 400 years ago. They came and went through the little square hole in the ceiling. The holes in the walls supported timbers that politely gave as many as 15 residents something to sit on to keep them out of the filthy slop that gathered on the floor. Twice a day they were given bread and water. Some prisoners actually survived five years in here. The town could torture and execute. The castle had permission only to imprison criminals in these dungeons.

(Continue through next arch, under white arrow, turn left and walk 40 yards to the *Schlachthaus.*)

9. Slaughterhouse: A castle was prepared to survive a six-month siege. With 4,000 people, that's a lot of provisions. The cattle that lived within the walls were slaughtered here. Notice the drainage gutters for water and blood. "Running water" came through from above . . . one bucket at a time.

(Back outside, climb the modern stairs on left. A skinny cool passage leads you into . . .)

10. The big cellar: This "Grosser Keller" was a big pantry. When the castle was smaller, this was the original moat—you can see the rough lower parts of the wall. The original floor was five feet deeper. When the castle expanded, the moat became the cellar. Above the entry, holes mark spots where timbers made a storage loft, perhaps filled with grain. Kegs of wine lined the walls. Part of a soldier's pay was three liters of wine a day. In the back, an arch leads to the wine cellar where finer wine was kept. The castle consumed 200,000 liters of wine a year. The count owned the surrounding farmland. Farmers got to keep 20 percent of their production. Later, in more liberal feudal times, the nobility let them keep 40 percent. Today the German government leaves the workers with 60 percent . . . and provides a few more services.

(Climb out, turn right, and leave. For coffee on a great-view terrace, visit the Rheinfels Castle Hotel, opposite the entrance.)

Sleeping in St. Goar
(tel. code: 06741, zip code: 56329)
Hotel am Markt, well run by Herr and Frau Velich, is a great value. Rustic with all the modern comforts, it features a hint of antler with a pastel flair and bright rooms. It's in the center of town a stone's throw from the boat dock and train station (18 rooms, Ss-65 DM, Sb-80 DM, Db-100 DM, Tb-140 DM, Qb-160 DM, cheaper off-season, open March–November, CC:VMA,

Am Markt 1, tel. 06741/1689, fax 06741/1721, e-mail: hotel_am _markt_st.goar@t-online.de).

Hotel Hauser, facing the boat dock and newly redone, is warmly run by another Frau Velich (S-42 DM, D-88 DM, Db-98 DM, Db with Rhine-view balconies-110 DM, show this book to get these prices, cheaper in off-season, CC:VMA, Heerstrasse 77, telephone reservations easy, tel. 06741/333, fax 06741/1464, SE).

Hotel Silberne Rose is musty with older decor and some with Rhine views (Sb-65 DM, Db-90–100 DM, Tb-120–140 DM, cheaper price for longer stays, CC:VM, across from KD dock, Heerstrasse 63, tel. 06741/7040, fax 06741/2865).

Hotel Montag is on the castle end of town just across the street from the world's largest freehanging cuckoo clock. Manfred Montag, his wife, Maria, and son Mike speak New Yorkish. Even though Montag gets a lot of bus tours, it's friendly, laid-back, and comfortable (Sb-70 DM, Db-130 DM, price can drop if things are slow, CC:VMA, Heerstrasse 128, tel. 06741/1629, fax 06741/2086, Web site: www.loreleyvalley.com/beerstein-center). Check out their adjacent crafts shop (heavy on beer steins).

St. Goar's best *Zimmer* deal is the home of **Frau Kurz,** with a breakfast terrace, fine view, easy parking, and all the comforts of a hotel (S-34 DM, D-60 DM, Db-70 DM, showers-5 DM, one-night stays cost extra, confirm prices, honor your reservation or call to cancel, Ulmenhof 11, tel. & fax 06741/459, some English spoken). From the train station, it's a steep three-minute hike (exit left from station, take immediate left at post office, go under tracks to paved path, take a right partway up stairs, climb a few more stairs to Ulmenhof).

The Germanly run **St. Goar Hostel,** the big beige building under the castle, is a good value, with two to 12 beds per room, a 22:00 curfew, and hearty 9.50-DM dinners (20-DM beds with breakfast, 5-DM sleep sacks, open all day, Bismarckweg 17, tel. 06741/388, SE).

Rheinfels Castle Hotel is the town splurge. Actually part of the castle, but an entirely new building, this luxury place is good for those with money and a car (Db-230–255 DM depending on river views and balconies, CC:VMA, elevator, dress-up restaurant, Schlossberg 47, tel. 06741/8020, fax 06741/802-802, Web site: www.talderloreley.de/html/rheinfelsgoar/html, e-mail: rheinfels .st.goar@t-online.de).

Transportation Connections—Rhine
Milk-run trains stop at all Rhine towns each hour starting around 6:00. Koblenz, Boppard, St. Goar, Bacharach, Bingen, and Mainz are each about 15 minutes apart. From Koblenz to Mainz takes 75 minutes. To get a faster big train, go to Mainz or Koblenz.

From Mainz by train to: Bacharach/St. Goar (hrly, 1 hr), **Cochem** (hrly, 2.5 hrs, changing in Koblenz), **Köln** (3/hr, 90 min), **Baden-Baden** (hrly, 2.5 hrs), **Munich** (hrly, 4 hrs), **Frankfurt** (3/hr, 45 min), **Frankfurt Airport** (3/hr, 25 min).

From Frankfurt by train to: Koblenz (hrly, 90 min), **Rothenburg** (hrly, 3 hrs, transfers in Würzburg and Steinach), **Würzburg** (hrly, 90 min), **Munich** (hrly, 3.5 hrs), **Amsterdam** (8/day, 5 hrs), **Paris** (4/day, 6.5 hrs).

MOSEL VALLEY

The misty Mosel is what many visitors hoped the Rhine would be—peaceful, sleepy, romantic villages slipped between the steep vineyards and the river, fine wine, a sprinkling of castles, and lots of friendly *Zimmer*. Boat, train, and car traffic here is a trickle compared to the roaring Rhine. While the swan-speckled Mosel moseys 300 miles from France's Vosges Mountains to Koblenz, where it dumps into the Rhine, the most scenic piece of the valley lies between the towns of Bernkastel-Kues and Cochem. I'd savor only this section.

Throughout the region on summer weekends and during the fall harvest time, wine festivals with oompah bands, dancing, and colorful costumes are powered by good food and wine.

Getting Around the Mosel Valley

The train zips you to Cochem or Trier in a snap. Regular buses connect the smallest train stations with Mosel villages. The Beilstein-Cochem bus takes 15 minutes (6/day, fewer on weekends, 5.40 DM). Consider a boat ride from Cochem to Zell (KolbLine, 2/day, May–August, except Fridays and Mondays in May and June, 3 hrs, 23 DM one-way, 35 DM round-trip) or Beilstein (5/day, 60 min, 13 DM one-way, 18 DM round-trip, tel. 02673/1515). The K-D (Köln–Düsseldorf) line sails once a day in each direction (May–September, Koblenz to Cochem 10:00–14:30, or Cochem to Koblenz 15:50–20:10, free with Eurail). You can also rent bikes in Cochem from the K-D line kiosk at the dock (summers only) or year-round from Kreutz on Moselstrasse behind the Shell station (7 DM/4 hrs, 14 DM/day, no deposit required, just your passport number). If stranded, many hitchhike.

Sights—Mosel Valley

Cochem—With a majestic castle and picturesque medieval streets, Cochem is the very touristic hub of this part of the river. The Cochem TI has a free town map with history and a walking tour. The pointy Cochem Castle is the work of overly imaginative 19th-century restorers (6 DM, daily mid-March–October 9:00–17:00, 15-minute walk from Cochem, tel. 02671/255). Follow one of the frequent German-language tours (reading English explanation

Mosel Valley

sheets) or call ahead to meet one of the roughly three English tours given daily.

The Cochem TI books rooms (same day only), keeps a thorough 24-hour listing in its window, and offers lots of brochures and concert info (Monday–Friday 10:00–17:00, in summer on Saturday 10:00–15:00 and Sunday 10:00–12:00, off-season closed weekends and at lunch, tel. 02671/3974). The *Moselle Wine Road* flyer is perfect for wine-lovers. Day-trippers can lock or check luggage at the station (2 DM). Many train travelers end up sleeping in Cochem (see Sleeping, below). Stroll along the pleasant paths that line the river. Cochem is right on the train line (to Koblenz, hrly, 60 min; to Trier, hrly, 60 min).

▲▲▲**Burg Eltz**—My favorite castle in all of Europe lurks in a mysterious forest. It's been left intact for 700 years, and is furnished throughout as it was 500 years ago. Thanks to smart diplomacy and clever marriages, Burg Eltz was never destroyed. (It survived one five-year siege.) It's been in the Eltz family for 820 years. The countess arranges for new flowers in each room weekly. The only way to see the castle is with a one-hour tour (included in admission ticket). German tours (with pathetic English fact sheets) go constantly. Organize an English tour. (Corral 20 English-speakers in the inner courtyard—they'll thank you for it. Push the red button on the white porch and politely beg for an English guide. This is well worth a short wait. You can also telephone ahead to see if there's an English-language group scheduled that you could tag along with.)

Reaching Burg Eltz by train, walk one steep hour from Moselkern station (midway between Cochem and Koblenz, no lockers at station; trail is slippery when wet, follow white "park and walk" signs) through a pine forest where sparrows carry crossbows, and maidens, disguised as falling leaves, whisper "watch out."

Drivers often get lost on the way to Burg Eltz. Use your map and do this: leave the river at Moselkern (shortest drive) following the white "Burg Eltz Park & Ride" signs through the towns of Münstermaifeld, then Wierschem. The castle parking lot is two kilometers past Wierschem. From the lot, hike 10 minutes downhill or wait for the red castle shuttlebus (2 DM). There are three "Burg Eltz" parking lots; only the Hatzenport lot is close enough for an easy walk (9 DM, daily April–October 9:30–17:30, tel. 02672/950-500).

▲**Beilstein**—Farther upstream is the quaintest of all Mosel towns (see Sleeping, below). Beilstein is Cinderella land. Check out the narrow lanes, ancient wine cellar, resident (and very territorial) swans, and ruined castle. The small 2-DM ferry goes constantly back and forth. Two shops rent bikes for the pleasant riverside roll (toward Zell is best). The TI is in a café (summer Tuesday–Sunday 9:00–19:00, closed Monday, tel. 02673/1417). Four buses a day connect Zell and Beilstein.

▲**Zell**—This is the best Mosel town for an overnight stop (see Sleeping, below). It's peaceful, with a fine riverside promenade, a pedestrian bridge over the water, plenty of *Zimmer*, and a long pedestrian zone filled with colorful shops, restaurants, *Weinstuben* (wine bars), and a fun oompah folk band on weekend evenings on the main square. Walk up to the medieval wall's gatehouse and through the cemetery to the old munitions tower for a village view. The fine little Wein und Heimatmuseum features Mosel history (Wednesday and Saturday 15:00–17:00). Locals know Zell for its Schwarze Katz (Black Cat) wine. (TI open Monday–Friday 8:00–12:30, 13:30–17:00, Saturday 10:00–13:00, off-season closed Saturday, tel. 06542/4031.)

Franz Josef Weis (who learned his English as a POW in England) gives an entertaining tour of his 40,000-bottle-per-year wine cellar. His witty tour lasts an hour, and you'll want to leave with a bottle or two. (He also rents two luxurious apartments for 95 DM, CC:M) A green flag marks his *Weinkeller* north of town, past the bridge, at Notenau 26 (tel. 06542/5543, fax 06542/5789).

Sleeping on the Mosel
(1.7 DM = about $1)

Sleeping in Cochem
(tel. code: 02671, zip code: 56812)
The little town is strung along the river. Exit right from the station onto Ravenestrasse. A seven-minute walk brings you to the TI (on your left, past the bus lanes). To get to the main square (Markt), continue under the bridge, then angle right and follow Bernstrasse. All rooms come with breakfast.

Gästezimmer Hüsgen is a good and handy value that welcomes one-night stays (Ss-40–45 DM, D-64 DM, Ds-68 DM, Db-82 DM, family deals, ground-floor rooms, small view terrace,

Ravenestrasse 34, 150 meters from the station, tel. 02671/5817, Andrea SE). Across the street, the **Ravene** offers six rooms varying in size and quality from odd to comfortable (Sb-60 DM, Db-80–100 DM, Tb-133 DM, Ravenestrasse 43, tel. 02671/980-177, fax 02671/91119, some English spoken).

The rustic **Hotel Lohspeicher**, just off the main square, is for those who want a real hotel (and much higher prices, Sb-85–95 DM, Db-170 DM, elevator, CC:VMA, Obergasse 1, on tiny-stepped street off main square, tel. 02671/3976, fax 02671/1772, Ingo SE). **Stolz Zimmer**, up the street, has big rooms that look like they were decorated by an elderly aunt (Ss-30 DM, Sb-35 DM, Ds-60 DM, Db-70 DM, less for stays of three nights or more, Obergasse 20, tel. 02671/1509, friendly Mrs. Stolz NSE).

Haus Andreas has small but modern rooms (S-25 DM, Sb-40 DM, Db-60 DM, Schlosstrasse 9 or 16, tel. 02671/1370 or 02671/5155, fax 02671/1370). From the main square, take Herrenstrasse; after a block, angle right uphill on Schlosstrasse.

Sleeping in Zell
(tel. code: 06542, zip code: 56856)

If the Mosel charms you into spending the night, do it in Zell. By car, this is a natural. By train, you'll need to go to Bullay (hourly from Cochem or Trier), where the bus takes you to little Zell (2.60 DM, 2/hrly, 10 min; bus stop is across street from Bullay train station; check yellow MB schedule for times). Its hotels are a disappointment, but its private homes are great. The owners speak almost no English and discount their rates if you stay more than one night. They can't take reservations long in advance for one-night stays; just call a day ahead. My favorites are on the south end of town, a two-minute walk from the town hall square and the bus stop. Breakfast is included.

Gasthaus Gertrud Thiesen is classy, with a TV-living-breakfast room and a river view. The Thiesen house has big, bright rooms and is on the town's first corner overlooking the Mosel from a great terrace (S or D-70 DM, Balduinstrasse 1, tel. 06542/4453, SE). Notice the high-water flood marks on the wall across the street.

Gästezimmer Rosa Mesenich is another friendly little place facing the river a few doors from Thiesen (S-30 DM, Sb-35 DM, D-60 DM, Db-70 DM, Brandenburg 48, tel. 06542/4297).

Friendly **Natalie Huhn**, your German grandmother, has the cheapest beds in town in her simple but comfortable house (S-30 DM, D-60 DM, cheaper for two-night stays, near the pedestrian bridge behind the church at Jakobstrasse 32, tel. 06542/41048).

Weinhaus zum Fröhlichen Weinberg offers cheap, basic rooms (D-70 DM, 60 DM for two or more nights, family *Zimmer*, Mittelstrasse 6, tel. 06542/4308) above a *Weinstube* disco (noisy on

Friday and Saturday nights). **Gästehaus am Römerbad** is also central and a decent value (Db-80 DM, Am Römerbad 5, tel. 06542/41602, Elizabeth Münster).

If you're looking for room service, sauna, pool, and elevator, sleep at **Hotel Grüner Kranz** (Db-160 DM with Mosel views, 140 DM without, elevator, CC:VMA, tel. 06542/98610, fax 06542/986-180). **Weinhaus Mayer**, a classy—if stressed-out—old pension next door, is perfectly central with Mosel-view rooms (13 rooms, Db-120–160 DM, Balduinstrasse 15, tel. 06542/4530, fax 06542/61160).

Sleeping in Beilstein
(tel. code: 02673, zip code: 56814)
Cozier and farther north, Beilstein (BILE-shtine) is very small and quiet (no train; seven buses/day to nearby Cochem, fewer buses on weekends; 15-minute trip). Breakfast is included.

Hotel Haus Lipmann is your chance to live in a medieval mansion with hot showers and TVs. A prizewinner for atmosphere, it's been in the Lipmann family for 200 years. The creaky wooden staircase and the elegant dining hall, with long wooden tables surrounded by antlers, chandeliers, and feudal weapons, will get you in the mood for your castle sightseeing, but the riverside terrace may mace your momentum (five rooms, Db-120–150 DM, tel. 02673/1573, fax 02673/1521).

Gasthaus Winzerschenke an der Klostertreppe is comfortable and a great value, right in the tiny heart of town (Db-75 DM, bigger Db-95 DM, discount for two-night stays, tel. 02673/1354, Frau Sausen).

The half-timbered, riverfront **Altes Zollhaus Gästezimmer** has crammed all the comforts into tight, bright (if a bit musty), and modern rooms (Db-95 DM, deluxe Db-135 DM, 15 DM more on Friday and Saturday, open March–October, tel. 02673/1574 or 02673/1850, fax 02673/1287).

TRIER
Germany's oldest city lies at the head of the scenic Mosel Valley, near the Luxembourg border. An ancient Roman capital, Trier brags that it was inhabited for 1,300 years before the Romans came. A short stop here offers you a look at Germany's oldest Christian church, one of its most enjoyable market squares, and its best Roman ruins.

Founded by Augustus in 15 B.C., Trier was the Roman "Augusta Treverorum" for 500 years. When Emperor Diocletian divided his overextended Roman empire into four sectors in A.D. 285, he made Trier the capital of the West (Germany, France, Spain, and Britain). For most of the fourth century, this city of 80,000, with a four-mile-long wall, four great gates, and 47 round towers, was the favored residence of Roman emperors. Emperor Constantine used the town as the capital of his fading western Roman Empire. Much of the building was built under Constantine before he left for Constantinople. In 480, Trier fell to the Franks. Today Trier's Roman sights include the huge city gate (Porta Nigra), basilica, baths, and amphitheater.

Orientation (tel. code: 0651)

Tourist Information: Trier's TI, next to the Porta Nigra, organizes two-hour, 10-DM town walks in English daily May through October at 13:30 (9:00–18:30, Sunday 9:00–15:30, less off-season, tel. 0651/978-080).

Arrival in Trier: From the train station, walk four boring blocks up Theodor-Heuss Allee to the big black Roman gate, where you'll find the TI. From here the main pedestrian mall leads into the town's charm: the market square, cathedral, and basilica—all within a five-minute walk. Drivers stay on the Autobahn until it ends (don't get off at Trier Verteilerring) and follow signs to "Zentrum." There is parking near the gate and TI.

Sights—Trier

▲**Porta Nigra**—Roman Trier was built as a capital. Its architecture mirrored the grandeur of the empire. Of the four-mile wall's four huge gates, only this north gate survives. This most impressive Roman fortification in Germany was built without mortar—only iron pegs hold the sandstone blocks together. While the other three gates were destroyed by medieval metal and stone scavengers, this "black gate" survived because it became a church. Saint Simeon—a pious Greek recluse—lived inside the gate for seven years. After his death in 1035, the Simeon monastery was established and the gate was made into a two-story church—lay church on the bottom, monastery church on top. While Napoleon had the church destroyed in 1803, the 12th-century Romanesque apse—the round part that you can see at the east end—survived. You can climb around the gate, but there's little to see (4 DM, 9:00–17:30).

Trier's main pedestrian drag, which leads away from the gate, is named for Saint Simeon. The arcaded courtyard and buildings of the monastery of Saint Simeon survive. They now house the (skippable) city museum and TI.

▲▲**Market Square**—Trier's Hauptmarkt square is a people-filled swirl of fruit stands, flowers, painted facades, and fountains—with a handy public WC. This is one of Germany's most in-love-with-life marketplaces. Its centerpiece, a market cross from 958 (with an ancient Roman pedestal), celebrates the trading rights given to the town by King Otto the Great. The adjacent Renaissance St. Peter's Fountain (1595) symbolizes thoughtful city government with allegorical statues of justice (sword and scale), fortitude (broken column), temperance (wine and water), and prudence (snake and mirror). From this square you can survey a textbook of architectural styles. Overlooking it all (as its fire watchman did in medieval times) is the Gothic tower of the church of St. Gangolf.

▲▲**Cathedral**—This church, the oldest in Germany, goes back to Roman times. St. Helena, the mother of Emperor Constantine (who legalized Christianity in the Roman Empire in A.D. 312) and an important figure in early Christian history, let part of her palace be used as the first church on this spot. (A fine Roman-painted ceiling survives under today's altar.) In 326, to celebrate the 20th anniversary of his reign, Constantine began the construction of St. Peter's in Rome and a huge cathedral (*Dom*) in Trier. The cathedral's most important relic is the "Holy Robe" of Christ (rarely on display, found by St. Helena on a pilgrimage to Jerusalem). The treasury (*Schatzkammer*, 2 DM, 9:30–17:00) has huge bishops' rings and "the holy nail" supposedly from the crucifixion.

The Leibfrau Church, connected to the *Dom*, dates from 1235 and claims to be the oldest Gothic church in Germany (daily 8:00–12:00, 14:00–18:00).

▲▲**Basilica**—At 200 feet long and 100 feet high, this is the largest intact Roman building outside of Rome. Picture this hall of justice in ancient times, decorated with golden mosaics, rich marble, colorful stucco, and busts of Constantine and his family filling the niches. The emperor sat in majesty under a canopy on his altar-like throne. The last emperor moved out in 395, and petty kings set up camp in the basilica throughout the Middle Ages. The building became a church in 1856.

Long after its Roman days, Trier was important enough to have a prince "elector" who helped elect the legal successors of the "Holy Roman Emperor." A rococo wing, the Elector's Palace, was added to the basilica in the 18th century. This faces a fragrant garden, which leads to the remains of a Roman bath and a 25,000-seat amphitheater.

Karl Marx's House—Communists can lick their wounds at Karl Marx's house. Early manuscripts, letters, and photographs of the influential economist/philosopher fill several rooms of his birth house. Oblivious to their slide out of a shrinking middle class, people still sneer (3 DM, Tuesday–Sunday 10:00–18:00, Monday 13:00–18:00, lunch breaks in winter, 15-minute film at 20 minutes after each hour, a reasonable amount of English description, from the Market Square walk down Fleischstrasse to Brückenstrasse 10).

Sleeping in Trier
(tel. code: 0651, zip code: 54290)
Kolpinghaus Warsberger Hof is the best value in town. This Catholic Church–run place is super-clean, well managed, and

serves inexpensive meals in its open-to-anyone restaurant (27 DM per bed with sheets and breakfast in two- to six-bed dorm rooms, or 39 DM per person in the S, D, or T hotel rooms, no private showers, a block off Market Square, Dietrichstrasse 42, tel. 0651/975-250, fax 0651/975-2540, e-mail: w-hof @t-online.de).

Hotel Frankenturm, plain, comfortable, and simple, is on the same street, above a classy saloon (S-70 DM, Sb-110 DM, D-90 DM, Db-140 DM, CC:VM, Dietrichstrasse 3, tel. 0651/45712, fax 0651/978-2449). There's a handy self-service Laundromat near the Marx Museum (daily 8:00–22:00, 10 DM for the works, English instructions, Brükenstrasse 19).

Near the train station: Hotel Pieper is family-run and rents 20 comfortable rooms midway between the station and the Roman gate (Sb-75 DM, Db-120 DM, Tb-150 DM, Thebäerstrasse 39, tel. 0651/23008, fax 0651/12839, CC:VMA). **Hotel Monopol** is handy (S-75 DM, Sb-90 DM, D-130 DM, Db-150 DM, buffet breakfast, Bahnhofsplatz 7, tel. 0651/714-090, fax 0651/714-0910). **Hotel zum Christopher** is central and feels Old World (S-50 DM, Sb-75 DM, D-100 DM, Db-130 DM, CC:V, four blocks from the station, facing the TI and Roman gate, tel. 0651/74041, fax 0651/74732).

Transportation Connections—Trier
By train to: Cochem (hrly, 45 min), **Köln** (9/day, 2.5 hrs), **Koblenz** (hrly, 75 min), **Bullay** (hrly, 38 min).

KÖLN (COLOGNE) AND THE UNROMANTIC RHINE
Romance isn't everything. Köln is an urban Jacuzzi that keeps the Rhine churning. The small town of Remagen had a bridge that helped defeat Hitler in World War II, and unassuming Aachen (near the Belgian border) was once the capital of Europe.

Getting Around the Unromantic Rhine
Fast and frequent supertrains connect Köln, Trier, Koblenz, and Frankfurt. All major sights are within a reasonable walk from each city's train station.

KÖLN
Germany's fourth largest city, big, no-nonsense Köln has a compact and lively center. The Rhine was the northern boundary of the Roman Empire and, 1,700 years ago, Constantine—the first Christian emperor—made "Colonia" the seat of a bishopric. Five hundred years later, under Charlemagne, Köln became the seat of an archbishopric. With 40,000 people living within its walls, it was the largest German city and an important cultural and religious

Köln

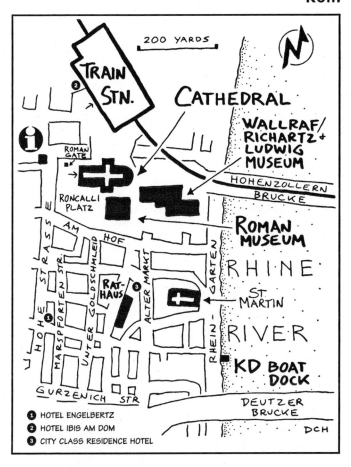

200 YARDS

TRAIN STN.

CATHEDRAL

WALLRAF/ RICHARTZ + LUDWIG MUSEUM

ROMAN GATE

RONCALLI PLATZ

HOHENZOLLERN BRUCKE

ROMAN MUSEUM

RHINE

AM HOF

GOLDSCHMIED

ALTER MARKT

RHEIN-GARTEN

ST. MARTIN

RAT-HAUS

RIVER

HOHE STRASSE

MARSPFORTEN STR.

UNTER GOLDSCHMIED

KD BOAT DOCK

GURZENICH STR

DEUTZER BRUCKE

DCH

❶ HOTEL ENGELBERTZ
❷ HOTEL IBIS AM DOM
❸ CITY CLASS RESIDENCE HOTEL

center throughout the Middle Ages. To many, the city is most famous for its toilet water. "Eau de Cologne" was first made here by an Italian chemist in 1709. Even after World War II bombs destroyed 95 percent of it (population down from 800,000 to 40,000), Köln has remained, after a remarkable recovery, a cultural and commercial center, as well as a fun, colorful, and pleasant-smelling city.

Orientation (tel. code: 0221)
Köln's old town core, bombed out and rebuilt quaint, is traffic free, with a park and bike path along the river. From the

cathedral/TI/train station, Hohe Strasse leads into the shopping action. The Roman arch in front of the cathedral reminds us that even in Roman times this was an important trading street and a main road through Köln. In medieval times, when Köln was a major player in the heavyweight Hanseatic Trading League, two major trading routes crossed here. This "high street" thrived. After complete destruction in World War II, it has emerged—the first pedestrian shopping mall in Germany— once again a thriving trading street. For a quick old town ramble, stroll down Hohe Strasse, go left at the city hall (*Rathaus*) to the river (where K-D Rhine cruises start). Enjoy the quaint old town and waterfront park. The Hohenzollernbrücke (crossing the Rhine at the cathedral) is the busiest railway bridge in the world (30 trains per hour all day long).

Tourist Information: Köln's energetic TI, opposite the church entry, has a list of reasonable private guides and a wealth of brochures (Monday–Saturday 8:00–22:30, Sunday 9:00–22:30, closes at 21:00 in winter, tel. 0221/19433).

Arrival in Köln: Köln couldn't be easier to visit: its three important sights cluster within two blocks of its train station and TI. This super pedestrian zone is a constant carnival of people. There are plenty of 2-DM lockers at the station. If you drive to Köln, follow signs to "Zentrum" and then to the huge Parkhaus Am Dom pay lot under the cathedral.

Sights—Köln's Cathedral

▲▲▲**Cathedral**—The Gothic Dom, or cathedral, Germany's most exciting church, looms immediately up from the train station (daily 7:00–19:00, tel. 0221/9258-4730). The 60-minute English-only tours (7 DM, daily 10:30 and 14:30, not Sunday morning) are reliably excellent. If you are unable to follow a local guide, follow this eight-stop walk:

1. Roman gate and cathedral exterior: The square in front of the cathedral has been a busy civic meeting place since ancient times. A Roman temple stood where the Cathedral stands today. The north gate of the Roman city from A.D. 50 marks the start of Köln's 2,000-year-old main street.

Look for the life-size replica tip of a spire. The real thing is 515 feet above you. The Cathedral facade, while finished according to the original 13th-century plan, is "neo-Gothic" from the 19th century.

(Postcards show the church after the 1945 bombing. The red brick building—to your right as you face the church—is the Diocesan Museum. The Roman museum is beside the church on the right and the art museum is behind that. Step inside the church. Grab a pew in the center of the nave.)

2. Nave: If you feel small, you're supposed to. The 140-feet-

Köln Cathedral

tall ceiling reminds us of our place in the vast scheme of things. Lots of stained glass—enough to cover three football fields—fills the church with light, representing God.

The church was begun in 1248. The choir—the lofty area from the center altar to the far end ahead of you—was finished in 1322. Later, with the discovery of America and routes to the

Indies by sea, trade shifted away from inland ports like Köln. Funds dried up and eventually building stopped. For 300 years the finished end of the church was walled off and functioned as a church while the unfinished torso (where you now sit) waited. For centuries the symbol of Köln's skyline was a huge crane that sat atop the unfinished west spire.

With the rise of German patriotism in the early 1800s, Köln became a symbol of German unity. And the Prussians—the movers and shakers behind German unity—mistakenly considered Gothic a German style. They initiated a national tax that funded the speedy completion of this gloriously Gothic German church. Seven hundred workers (compared to 100 in the 14th century) finished the church in just 38 years (1842-1880). And, for a strong first impression to the city, the great train station was built in the shadow of the cathedral's towering spire.

The glass windows in the front of the church are medieval. The glass surrounding you in the nave is not as old, but it's precious nevertheless. The glass on the left is Renaissance. That on the right is 19th-century Bavarian—a gift from Ludwig I, father of "Mad" King Ludwig of touristic fame.

While 95 percent of Köln was destroyed by WWII bombs, the structure of the cathedral survived fairly well. In anticipation of the bombing, the glass and art treasures were taken to shelters and saved. The new "swallow's nest" organ above you was installed to celebrate the Cathedral's 750th birthday in 1998. Relics (mostly skulls) fill cupboards on each side of the nave.

3. Treasury: The treasury is one room filled with mostly medieval reliquaries (bits of chain, bone, cross, cloth, and so on, in gold-crusted glass capsules—3 DM, daily 9:00–17:00). It's fine medieval art but—with no English descriptions—pretty meaningless. The fine little 6-DM book at the door helps (cheapskates read it on the leash).

4. Gero-Crucifix: The Chapel of the Cross features the oldest surviving monumental crucifix from north of the Alps. Carved in 976 with a sensitivity 300 years ahead of its time, it shows Jesus not suffering and not triumphant—but with eyes closed . . . dead. He paid the price for our sins. It's quite a two-fer: great art and powerful theology in one. The Cathedral has three big pilgrim stops: this crucifix, the Shrine of the Magi, and the *Madonna of Milan* (both coming up).

As you step into the oldest part of the church, look for the mosaic of the ninth-century church on the floor. It shows a saint holding the Carolingian Cathedral, which stood on this spot for several centuries before this one was built.

(Continue to the front end of the church, stopping to look at the glass case behind the high altar.)

5. Shrine of the Magi: Relics were a big deal in the Middle Ages. Köln's acquisition of the bones of the Three Kings in the 12th century put it on the pilgrimage map and brought in enough money to justify the construction of this magnificent place. By some stretch of medieval Christian logic, these relics also justified the secular power of the local king. This reliquary, made in about 1200, is the biggest and most splendid I've seen. It's seven feet of gilded silver, jewels, and enamel. Old Testament prophets line the bottom, and 12 New Testament apostles—with a wingless angel in the center—line the top.

Inside sit the bones of the Magi . . . three skulls with golden crowns. So what's the big deal about these three kings of Christmas carol fame? They were the first to recognize Jesus as the savior and the first to come as pilgrims to worship him. They inspired medieval pilgrims and countless pilgrims since. For a thousand years, a theme of this Cathedral is that life is a pilgrimage . . . a search for God.

6. Chapel of the Three Magi: The center chapel, at the far end, is the oldest with the church's oldest window (center, from 1265). It has the typical design: a strip of Old Testament scenes on the left with a theologically and visually parallel strip of New Testament scenes on the right (e.g., on bottom panels: birth of Eve on left, birth of Mary—with her mother Anne on the bed—on right).

Later, glass (which you saw lining the nave) was painted and glazed. This medieval window is actually colored glass, which is assembled like a mosaic. It was very expensive. The size was limited to what pilgrim donations funded. Notice the plain, budget design higher up.

7. Choir: Try to get into the center zone between the high altar and the carved wooden central stalls. This is surrounded by 13th- and 14th-century art: carved oak stalls, frescoed walls, statues painted as they would have been, and original stained glass high above. Study the fanciful oak carvings. The woman cutting the man's hair is a Samson and Delilah warning to the sexist men of the early Church.

8. Chapel of the Virgin: The nearby chapel faces one of the most precious paintings of the important Gothic "School of Köln." *The Patron Saints of Köln* was painted in 1442 by Stefan Lochner. Notice the photographic realism and believable depth. There are literally dozens of identifiable herbs in the grassy foreground. During the 19th century, the city fought to have it in the museum. The Church went to court to keep it. The judge ruled that it can stay in the Cathedral only as long as a Mass is said before it every day. And for over a hundred years, that has happened at 18:00. Lochner was a leader in the School of Köln art style. (For lots more, see the museum described below.)

Overlooking the same chapel, the *Madonna of Milan* (1290) was associated with miracles and a focus of pilgrims for centuries.

As you head for the exit, find the statue of St. Christopher (with Jesus on his shoulder and the pilgrim's staff). Since 1470, pilgrims and travelers have looked up at him and taken solace in the hope that their patron saint is looking out for them. Go in peace.

Church Spire Climb—For 509 steps and 3 DM, you can enjoy a fine city view from the cathedral's south tower. From the Glockenstube (only 400 steps up) you can see the *Dom's* nine huge bells including Dicke Peter (24-ton "Fat Peter"), claimed to be the largest free-swinging church bell in the world.

Dom Forum—This new visitor center is across from the entry of the church (plenty of info, welcoming lounge with 1-DM coffee, free WC downstairs). They offer an English-language "multivision" video on the history of the church daily at 11:30 and 15:30 (20 minutes—starts slow but gets a little better, 3 DM or included with church tour).

Diocesan Museum—This has some of the cathedral's finest art (free, Friday–Wednesday 10:00–17:00, closed Thursday, English description sheet).

More Sights—Köln

▲▲**Römisch-Germanisches Museum**—Germany's best Roman museum offers not a word of English among its elegant and fascinating display of Roman artifacts: fine glassware, jewelry, and mosaics (5 DM, Tuesday–Friday 10:00–17:00, Saturday and Sunday 11:00–17:00, closed Monday, tel. 0221/4590). The permanent collection is downstairs and upstairs. Temporary exhibits (extra ticket) are on the main floor. Budget travelers can view its prize piece, a fine mosaic floor, free from the front window. Once the dining room floor of a rich merchant, this is actually its original position (the museum was built around it). It shows scenes from the life of Dionysus . . . wine and good times, Roman-style. The tall monument over the Dionysus mosaic is the mausoleum of a first-century Roman army officer. Upstairs you'll see a reassembled, arched original gate to the Roman city with the Roman initials for the town, "CCAA," still legible, and incredible glassware that Roman Köln was famous for producing.

▲▲**Wallraf-Richartz and Ludwig Museums**—Next door and more enjoyable, you'll find three museums in one slick and modern building for one steep ticket price (10 DM, Tuesday 10:00–20:00, Wednesday–Friday 10:00–18:00, Saturday–Sunday 11:00–18:00, closed Monday, exhibits are fairly well described in English, classy but pricey cafeteria with a reasonable salad bar at entry level, tel. 0221/221-2382). Don't worry about which museum you're in—the floor plan is a mess. Just enjoy the art. (In a few years the Wallraf-Richartz collection will be relocated in its own building a few blocks away near the city hall, and the Ludwig will take over this entire building.)

The **Wallraf-Richartz** (upstairs) features a world-class collection of old masters arranged chronologically, from medieval to northern Baroque and Impressionist. You'll see the best collection anywhere of Gothic School of Köln paintings (1300–1550), offering an intimate peek into those times. Then German, Dutch, Flemish, and French with masters such as Dürer, Rubens, Rembrandt, Hals, Steen, van Gogh, Renoir, Monet, Munch, and Cézanne.

The **Ludwig Museum** offers a stimulating trip through the art of our century (upstairs) and American Pop and post-WWII art (in the basement). Artists featured include German and Russian Expressionists, the Blue Rider school, and Picasso.

The **Agfa History of Photography** exhibit is three rooms with no English. (Don't miss the pigeon with the tiny vintage camera strapped to its chest.)

Assorted Museums—The tourist office has information on lots more museums (from Romanesque churches to the Beatles). The Käthe Kollwitz museum offers the largest collection of this woman's powerful Expressionist art, welling from her experiences living in Berlin during the tumultuous first half of this century (Tuesday–Sunday 10:00–17:00, closed Monday, Neumarkt 18, tel. 0221/ 227-2363). Chocoholics love the Chocolate Museum, which takes you on a well-described-in-English tour from the plant to the finished product (an easy walk away on the riverfront between Deutzer and Severins bridges, Rheinauhafen 1a, tel. 0221/931-8880). For a thorough visit, consider Köln's two-day museum and transit pass (20 DM, or 36 DM for the entire family). Two-hour German/ English city bus tours leave from the TI daily (25 DM, at 10:00, 11:00, and 15:00).

Sleeping in Köln
(tel. code: 0221, zip code: 50667)

Köln is *the* convention town in Germany. Consequently, the town is either jam-packed with hotel prices in the 300-DM range or empty and hungry. In 1999, conventions are scheduled for these dates: January 18–24; February 1–7, 12–14, 22–25; March 7–10, 25–28; April 13–17; all of May; June 2–9; July 23–25; much of August; September 5–19; October 22–29; and much of November. Outside of these dates, the TI can always get you a discounted room in a business-class hotel, and the hotels listed below will honor their fair rates.

Hotel Engelbertz is a fine family-run, 40-room place a five-minute walk from the station and cathedral at the end of the pedestrian mall. Herr Ossendorf promises travelers with my book a Db with breakfast for 100 DM through 1999 (normal price is

Db-148–178 DM, CC:VMA, some non-smoking rooms, elevator, just off Hohe Strasse at Obenmarspforten 1–3, tel. 0221/257 8994, fax 0221/257 8924).

Hotel Ibis am Dom, a huge budget chain with a 66-room modern hotel right at the train station, offers all the comforts in a tidy affordable package without the convention price gouge (Db-99–137 DM without breakfast, CC:VMA, some non-smoking rooms, elevator, Hauptbahnhof, tel. 0221/9128580, fax 0221/138194).

City Class Residence Hotel is a modern, practical place buried nicely in the old town (Db-180–210 DM, CC:VMA, elevator, Alter Markt 55, tel. 0221/9201980, fax 92019899).

Transportation Connections—Köln
By train to: Cochem (every 2 hrs, 1.75 hr), **Bacharach** or **St. Goar** (hrly, 1.5 hrs with one change), **Koblenz** (5/hrly, 1 hr), **Bonn** (4/hrly, 20 min), **Trier** (9/day, 2.5 hrs), **Aachen** (3/hrly, 45 min), **Paris** (2/day, 6 hrs), **Amsterdam** (8/day, 2.5 hrs).

Sights—Unromantic Rhine
▲**Bonn**—Bonn was chosen for its sleepy, cultured, and peaceful nature as a good place to plant Germany's first post-Hitler government. Now that Germany is one again, Berlin will resume its position as capital in 1999. Apart from the tremendous cost of switching the seat of government, more than 100,000 jobs are involved, and lots of Bonn families will have some difficult decisions to make.

Today Bonn is sleek, modern, and, by big-city standards, remarkably pleasant and easygoing. Stop here not to see the sparse exhibit at **Beethoven's House** (8 DM, Monday–Saturday 10:00–16:00, Sunday 11:00–16:00, free English brochure, tel. 0228/981-7525) but to come up for a smoggy breath of the real world after the misty, romantic Rhine.

The pedestrian-only old town stretches out from the station and makes you wonder why the United States can't trade in its malls for real, people-friendly cities. The market square and Münster-platz—filled with street musicians—are a joy. People-watching doesn't get much better. The TI faces the station (Monday–Friday 9:00–18:30, Saturday 9:00–17:00, Sunday 10:00–14:00, room-finding service for 5 DM, tel. 0228/773-466).

Hotel Eschweiler is plain but well located, just off the market square on a pedestrian street next to Beethoven's place above a taco joint (S-60 DM, Ss-70 DM, Sb-95 DM, Ds-120 DM, Db-140 DM, show this book for a 10 percent discount, great breakfasts, seven-minute walk from the station, Bonngasse 7, tel. 0228/631-760 or 0228/631-769, fax 0228/694-904).

▲**Remagen**—Midway between Koblenz and Köln are the scant remains of the Bridge at Remagen, of World War II (and movie) fame. But the memorial and the bridge stubs are enough to stir the emotions of Americans who remember when it was the only bridge that remained, allowing the Allies to cross the Rhine and race to Berlin in 1945. The small museum tells the bridge's fascinating story in English. Built during World War I to help supply the German forces on the Western Front, it's ironic that this was the bridge Eisenhower said was worth its weight in gold for its service against Germany. Hitler executed four generals for their failure to blow it up. Ten days after the Americans arrived, it did collapse, killing 28 Americans (2.50 DM, daily March–October 10:00–17:00, on Rhine's west bank, south side of Remagen town, follow "Brücke von Remagen" signs, Remagen TI tel. 02642/2010).

▲Aachen (Charlemagne's Capital)—This city was the capital of Europe in A.D. 800, when Charles the Great (Charlemagne) called it Aix-la-Chapelle. The remains of his rule include an impressive Byzantine/Ravenna-inspired church with his sarcophagus and throne. The city also has a headliner newspaper museum and great fountains, including a clever arrange-'em-yourself version.

Sightseeing Lowlights
Heidelberg—This famous old university town attracts hordes of Americans. Any surviving charm is stained almost beyond recognition by commercialism. It doesn't make it in Germany's top 20 days.
Mainz, Wiesbaden, and Rüdesheim—These towns are all too big or too famous. They're not worth your time. Mainz's Gutenberg Museum is also a disappointment.

BERLIN

No tour of Germany is complete without a look at its historic and newly united capital, a construction zone called Berlin. Stand over ripped-up tracks and under a canopy of cranes and watch the rebirth of a European capital. Enjoy the thrill of walking over what was The Wall and through Brandenburg Gate.

Berlin has shut the door on a tumultuous 50-year chapter in its history. It was devastated in World War II, then divided by the Allied powers, with the American, British, and French sectors being West Berlin, and the Russian sector, East Berlin. The division was set in stone when the East built the Berlin Wall in 1961. In 1989 the Wall fell, and in 1990 Germany was formally reunited. The Berlin Wall lasted only 28 years. Berlin is over 750 years old and striding boldly forward.

Today the city is like a man who had a terrible accident, and half the body was given the best of care and the other was denied therapy. But Dr. Capitalism has arrived, and the East is on the mend.

But unification has a negative side, and the Wall survives in the minds of some people. Some "Ossies" (impolite slang for Easterners) miss their security. Some "Wessies" miss their easy ride (military deferrals, subsidized rent, and tax breaks). To free spirits, walled-in West Berlin was a citadel of freedom within the East.

The new right-wing city government is eager to charge forward with little nostalgia for anything that was "Eastern." Big corporations and the national government have moved in, and the dreary swath of land that was the Wall will soon again be the city center. City planners are boldly taking Berlin's reunification and the return of the national government (the first parliamentary session is slated for May 1999) as a good opportunity to make Berlin a great capital once again.

During the grind of World War II, Hitler enjoyed rolling out the lofty plans for a post war Berlin as capital of a Europe united under his rule. As Europe unites, dominated by a muscular Germany with this shiny new capital in the works, Hitler's dream of a grand post war Berlin seems about to come true . . . .

Planning Your Time

Because of its location, I'd enter and leave by either night train or plane. On a three-week trip through Germany, Austria, and Switzerland, I'd give Berlin two days and spend them this way:

Day 1: Arrive early on the overnight train (or night before by air). Check into a hotel. Do the Bus #100 orientation tour with a walk from Brandenburg Gate down Unter den Linden. (For a guided version of this orientation, consider taking a Berlin Walk followed by a hop-on hop-off city circle tour). After lunch near Alexanderplatz, tour the Pergamon Museum, then spend the afternoon strolling Kurfürstendamm, visiting the Memorial Church and KaDeWe.

Day 2: Check out of hotel but leave bags there. Divide the morning between your choice of the paintings of the Gemäldegalerie (and nearby Kulturforum museums), the Egyptian Museum, Charlottenburg Palace, or the zoo. After lunch, visit the Info Box to survey the Potsdamer Platz construction site, tour the *Topography of Terror* exhibit, see remains of the Wall, tour Haus am Checkpoint Charlie (open late). Spend the evening exploring the trendy area around Oranienburger Strasse. Depart on an overnight train.

Orientation (tel. code: 030)

Berlin is huge, with nearly four million people. But the tourist's Berlin can be broken into four digestible chunks:

1. The area around Bahnhof Zoo and the grand Kurfürstendamm Boulevard (transportation, tours, information, hotel, shopping, and nightlife hub).
2. Former downtown East Berlin (Brandenburg Gate, Unter den Linden Boulevard, Pergamon Museum, and the area around Oranienburger Strasse.
3. The new center: Kulturforum museums, Potsdamer Platz construction zone, and Wall-related sights.
4. Charlottenburg palace and museums.

Chunks 1, 2, and 3 can be done on foot or with bus #100. Catch the U-Bahn to 4.

Tourist Information

The two TI offices are run by a for-profit agency working for the city's big hotels. The main TI office is five minutes from the Bahnhof Zoo train station, in the Europa Center (with Mercedes symbol on top, enter outside to the left, on Budapester Strasse,

Western Berlin

Monday–Saturday 8:00–22:00, Sunday 9:00–21:00, tel. 030/250-025, Web site: www.berlin.de). A smaller TI is in a side wing of Brandenburg Gate (daily 9:30–18:00). The TIs sell city maps (1 DM), the *Berlin Programm* (a German-language monthly listing upcoming events and museum hours, 2.80 DM), and the German-English quarterly *Berlin* magazine (with timely features on Berlin and a partial calendar of events, 3.50 DM), and offer a room-finding service (5 DM). Most hotels have free city maps. TIs also sell the Welcome Card (see Getting Around Berlin, below).

Arrival in Berlin
By Train at Bahnhof Zoo: Berlin's central station is called Bahnhof Zoologischer Garten (because it's near Berlin's famous zoo). Coming from western Europe, you'll probably land at Zoo (rhymes with "toe"). It's small, well organized, and handy. Stop by

Eastern Berlin

the handy EurAide office in the station for maps and answers
(daily 10:00–18:00 in summer, off-season: Monday–Saturday
8:00–12:00, 13:00–16:30, closed Sunday, near post office, tel.
030/2974-9241, great service and opportunity to get all future
couchette reservations nailed ahead of time). EurAide sells city
maps, making a trip to the TI probably unnecessary.

Upon arrival by train, orient yourself like this: Inside the
station, follow signs to Hardenbergplatz. Step into this busy
square filled with city buses, taxis, the transit office, and dere-
licts. Berlin Walks start from the curb immediately outside the
station. Between you and the McDonalds across the street is the
stop for bus #100 (departing to the right for your tour). Turn
right and tiptoe through the riff-raff to the eight-lane highway,
Hardenbergstrasse. Walk to the meridian and stand with your
back to the tracks. Ahead you'll see the black, bombed-out hulk of
the Kaiser Wilhelm Memorial Church and the Europa Center
(Mercedes symbol spinning on roof), which houses the main TI.
Just ahead amid the traffic is the BVG transport information

kiosk. (Buy the 7.50-DM day pass here and pick up a free sub-way map.) After checking into your hotel, return to Hardenberg-platz to catch bus #100 for the intro tour. Facing the church, most of the hotels I recommend are behind you to your right (continue across the street, walk one block to the Karlstadt building and turn right). If you arrive at Berlin's other train sta-tions (Hauptbahnhof or Lichtenberg), no problem: ride the S-Bahn or U-Bahn (runs every few minutes) to Bahnhof Zoo and pretend you arrived here.

By Train from the East: Trains arriving from eastern Europe stop at the Hauptbahnhof. While there was some discus-sion of this resuming its prewar position as the central station, the latest plan is to rename the Hauptbahnhof "Ostbahnhof." In the future, all major trains will use both Ost and Zoo. (For more details, see Transportation Connections, at the end of chapter.)

By Plane: See Transportation Connections.

Getting Around Berlin

Berlin's sights spread far and wide. You'll do a lot of walking. But right from the start, commit yourself to the fine public transit sys-tem. (If you can't, taxis are reasonable.)

By Subway and Bus: The U-Bahn, S-Bahn, and all buses are consolidated into one "BVG" system that uses the same tick-ets. Here are your options:

• Basic ticket (*Gesamtnetz Erwachsener*) for two hours of travel on buses or subways (3.90 DM, *Erwachsener* means adult—anyone 14 or older).

• A day pass (*Tages Karte*) covers zones A and B—the city proper—but not outlying destinations such as Potsdam (7.80 DM, good till 3:00 the morning after). Five adults travel together all day with a 20-DM group day pass.

• Cheap short ride (*Kurzstrecke Erwachsener*) for a single short ride of six bus stops or three subway stations, with one transfer 2.50 DM).

• Berlin/Potsdam WelcomeCard gives you three days of transportation and three days of minor sightseeing discounts (29 DM, valid for an adult and up to three kids).

Buy your tickets or cards from machines at U- or S-Bahn sta-tions, on the tracks, or at any BVG office, such as the little BVG pavilion in front of Bahnhof Zoo. To use the machine, first select the type of ticket you want, then load in the coins or paper. Don't forget to punch your ticket in a red or yellow clock machine to validate it (or risk a 60-DM fine). The double-decker buses are a joy (can buy ticket on bus), and the subway is a snap. The S-Bahn is free with a validated Eurailpass.

By Taxi: Taxis are easy to flag down, and taxi stands are common. A typical ride within town costs 15 DM. A local law designed to help people get safely and affordably home from their subway station late at night is handy for tourists any time of day: a short ride of no more than two kilometers is a flat 5 DM. (Ask for "Kurzstrecke, fünf Mark.")

By Bike: Several places rent bikes in Berlin. The handiest and cheapest is on Schlossplatz (daily 10:00–18:00, 10 DM, 5 DM for students). Or try the Zoo Station (daily 6:00–23:00, 21 DM) or in the east at Hackesche Höfe (17 DM, Monday–Friday 10:00–19:00, Saturday 10:00–16:00, Rosenthaler Strasse 40).

Helpful Hints

City museums are free on the first Sunday of each month. Many sights close on Monday: Pergamon Museum, art museums (Gemäldegalerie and New National Gallery), Charlottenburg sights (palace, museums), and the outlying Sanssouci Palace. Save Monday for Berlin Wall sights, other museums, the do-it-yourself orientation tour (see below), walking/bus tours, churches, zoo, or shopping (Ku'damm, KaDeWe). Grocery stores close on Sunday.

Many Berlin streets are numbered with odd and even numbers on the same side of the street, often with no connection to the other side (i.e., Ku'damm #212 can be across the street from #14). To save steps, check the white street signs on curb corners; many list the street numbers covered on that side of the block.

Do-It-Yourself Orientation Tour

Here's an easy ▲▲▲ introduction to the city. Half the tour is by bus, the other half is on foot. Berlin's bus #100 is a sightseer's dream, stopping at Bahnhof Zoo, Europa Center/Hotel Palace, Siegessaüle, Reichstag, Brandenburg Gate, Unter den Linden, Pergamon Museum, and Alexanderplatz. If you have the 30 DM and 90 minutes for a hop-on hop-off bus tour (described below), take that instead. But this 3.60-DM, 30-minute tour is a winning intro to the city. Buses leave from Hardenbergplatz in front of the Zoo Station (and nearly next door to the Europa Center TI, in front of the Hotel Palace). Jump on and off liberally. Buses come every 10 minutes, and single tickets are good for two hours. Climb aboard, stamp your ticket (giving it a time), and grab a seat on top. You could ride the bus all the way, but I'd get out at the Brandenburg Gate and walk from there.

Part 1: By Bus #100 from Bahnhof Zoo to Brandenburg Gate

(about a 10-minute ride) . . .
• Around the corner, then straight ahead, before descending into the tunnel, you'll see: the bombed-out hulk of the Kaiser-Wilhelm Memorial Church, with its new sister church (described below) and the Europa Center.

• At the stop in front of the Hotel Palace: on the left, the Berlin Zoo entrance and its aquarium (described below).

• Driving down Kurfürstenstrasse, turning left into Tiergarten: the Victory Column, or Siegessäule, (with the gilded angel, described below) towers above a vast city park.

• On the left a block after leaving the Siegessäule: The 18th-century late-rococo Bellevue Palace is the new German "White House," the residence of the federal president. If the flag's out, he's in.

• Driving along the Spree River: This park area was a residential district before World War II. Knowing about all the violent and tragic history that has been bombed and bulldozed in Berlin, locals say "You have to be suspicious when you see the green nice park." Soon it will be filled with the buildings of the new national government. Construction has already started. A Henry Moore sculpture floats in front of the slope-roofed House of World Cultures (left side, nicknamed "the pregnant oyster"). The modern tower (next on left) is a carillon with 68 bells (1987).

• Big glass-domed building on left: The Reichstag Building, while just over 100 years old, is as full of history as its bullet-riddled and patched-up complexion suggests. It was from this Parliament building that the German Republic was proclaimed in 1918. In 1933 Hitler burned this symbol of democracy to frame the Communists and grab power. And it was in here that the last 1,500 Nazis made their last stand, extending World War II in Europe by two days. For its 101st birthday, in 1995, the Bulgarian artist Christo wrapped it up. The Reichstag is newly renovated to serve as the Parliament building. In 1999 Berlin resumes its status as the capital of Germany. The glass cupola rises 48 meters above the ground, a double staircase winds 230 meters to the top for a grand view (open to public in summer of 1999). Inside the dome a cone of 360 mirrors will reflect natural light into the legislative chamber. Lit from inside at night, this will give Berlin a memorable new landmark. The land around the Reichstag is all reserved for future government building.

• From here, things go fast and furiously. While you could continue by bus #100, it's better on foot. After driving along what was The Wall, the bus stops at the Brandenburg Gate. Leap out.

Part 2: Walking Tour from Brandenburg Gate up Unter den Linden to Alexanderplatz
(Allow a comfortable hour for this walk, including dawdling but not museum stops.)
▲▲**Brandenburg Gate**—The historic Brandenburg Gate (1791, the last survivor of 14 gates in Berlin's old city wall), crowned by a majestic four-horse chariot with the Goddess of Peace at the reins, was the symbol of Berlin and then the symbol of divided Berlin.

Napoleon took this statue to the Louvre in Paris in 1806. When the Prussians got it back, she was renamed the Goddess of Victory. The gate sat, part of a sad circle dance called the Wall, for more than 25 years. (The TI, in the gate, has a good English history on display.) Now postcards all over town show the ecstatic day—November 9, 1989—when the world enjoyed the sight of happy Berliners jamming the gate like flowers on a parade float. A carnival atmosphere continues, as tourists stroll past hawkers with "authentic" pieces of the Wall, DDR (East German) flags, and military paraphernalia, to the traditional rhythm of an organ grinder. Step aside for a minute, and think about struggles for freedom—past and present.

Pariser Platz—From Brandenburg Gate face Pariser Platz (into the east). Unter den Linden boulevard leads to the TV tower in the distance (the end of this walk). The space used to be filled with important government buildings, bombed to smithereens, and later replaced by the Wall. Today, Pariser Platz is being restored as much as possible as it was. The U.S. embassy is being built on the right. Beyond the embassy, a Holocaust memorial will be completed by 2000. And beyond that is Potsdamer Platz (one S-Bahn stop or a long walk down Ebertstrasse), formerly the busiest square in Europe, then for decades a vacant lot, now being entirely rebuilt (see below).

Brandenburg Gate, the center of old Berlin, sits on a major city axis. This stretches 10 miles, with a grand boulevard leading past the Siegessäule in one direction to the Charlottenburg Palace. For our walk, we'll follow this axis in the opposite direction, up Unter den Linden, into the heart of old imperial Berlin and what was once the palace of Prussian emperor Frederick the Great. The palace—the reason for just about all you'll see—is a phantom sight . . . long gone.

Ost-algia—Now that the West is rapidly consuming what was the East, some are feeling a wave of nostalgia for the old days of East Berlin. For instance, as the old pedestrian lights in the East burn out, the perky DDR red and green men are being replaced by the standard Western signs (notice these as you walk). Many locals are ost-algic for the old days and want symbols of the DDR such as these to survive.

▲▲Unter den Linden—This is the heart of East Berlin. In Berlin's good old days, Unter den Linden was one of Europe's grand boulevards. In the 15th century, this horseway led from the palace to the hunting lodge. In the 17th century, Hohenzollern princes and princesses moved in, building their palaces here to be near the Prussian emperor.

Named centuries ago for its thousand linden trees, this was the most elegant street of Prussian Berlin before Hitler and the main drag of East Berlin after. Hitler replaced the venerable trees—many 250 years old—with Nazi flags. Popular discontent actually drove him to replant linden trees. Today, the strolling café ambience of Unter den Linden is returning.

Walking toward the giant TV tower, the first big building you will see on your right is the Hotel Adlon. It hosted such notables as Charlie Chaplin, Albert Einstein, and Greta Garbo. (This was where she said, "I want to be alone," during the filming of *Grand Hotel.)* Destroyed in World War II, the grand Adlon was rebuilt in 1996. See how far you can get inside.

On your right, several doors down (at the S-Bahn station), is the Russian embassy (guarded by German police)—not quite as important now as it was a few years ago. It flies the Russian white, red, and blue. Find the hammer-and-sickle motif decorating the window frames. Continuing past the Aeroflot Airline offices, you come to the Komische Oper (comic opera, program posted in window). While the exterior is just an ugly box, the fine old theater survives inside.

A few blocks ahead, the large equestrian statue in the street is of **Frederick II** ("the Great"; possibly gone in 1999 for restoration). Frederick the Great ruled from 1740 to 1786 and established Prussia as a military power. Most of the buildings around you were from his governmental center. Much of the palace actually survived World War II but was torn down by the Communists since it symbolized the imperialist past. It would have been just ahead.

Humboldt University, on the left, was one of Europe's greatest. Marx and Lenin (not the brothers or the sisters) studied here along with 22 Nobel Prize winners. Opposite the university is a square called Bebelplatz, bordered by the German State Opera, former state library, and the round Catholic St. Hedwig's church. It was on this square in 1933 that Hitler built a bonfire of 20,000 newly forbidden books. (Look for the empty-shelves memorial through the glass square in the middle.) The next square on your right holds the Opernpalais (see Eating, below).

On the university side of Unter den Linden, the Greek temple–like building is the **Neue Wache** (New Guardhouse, from 1816). When the Wall fell, this memorial to the victims of fascism became a national memorial for the German victims of war and authoritarianism (from either end of the political spectrum). Look inside where a replica of the Käthe Kollwitz statue, *Mother with Her Dead Son,* is surrounded by thought-provoking silence. A plaque (just outside) tells the story in English.

Just before the bridge (where the German History Museum will reopen in a few years with a new building), wander left along the canal through the tiny but colorful flea market. (Canal boats leave from here for a floating tour of the city.)

Cross the bridge to **Museum Island**, home of Germany's first museums and today famous for its Pergamon Museum (described below). The museum complex starts with the neoclassical facade on the left.

The towering church (ahead, before the next bridge) is the 100-year-old **Berlin Cathedral**, or *Dom* (5 DM, 8 DM including access to the dome, organ concerts are offered most Wednesdays, Thursdays, and Fridays at 15:00 for free with regular admission). Inside, Frederick I lies in an ornate tomb, and the great reformers stand around the brilliantly restored dome like stern saints guarding their theology. The crypt downstairs is not worth a look.

Across the street is the **Palace of the Republic** (with the copper-tinted windows), the grand center and international showcase of East Berlin. While the ost-algic argued it should be preserved, it has a date with the wrecking ball. This trashy "people's palace" of the DDR sits on the spot of the original palace of the Prussian emperor.

Before crossing the next bridge (and leaving Museum Island), look right. The pointy twin spires of the 13th-century Nikolai Church mark the center of medieval Berlin. This *Nikolai-Viertel* (district) was restored by the DDR and was trendy in the last decade of socialism. Today it's dull. With limited time, not worth a visit.

As you cross the bridge, look left in the distance to see the gilded New Synagogue, rebuilt after WWII bombing (described below).

Walk toward the Marien Church (from 1270, interesting but very faded old "Dance of Death" mural inside door) at the base of the TV tower. The big red-brick building past the trees on the right is the city hall, built after the revolution of 1848 and arguably the first democratic building in the city. Next to this was the Communist Party headquarters.

The 1,200-foot-tall **Fernsehturm (TV Tower)** offers a fine view from 600 feet (8 DM, daily 8:00–24:00). Built (with Swedish know-how) in 1969, the tower was meant to show the power of the state at a time when DDR leaders were having the crosses removed from church domes and spires. But when the sun shines on their tower, the greatest spire in East Berlin, a huge cross reflected on the mirrored ball. (Cynics called it "The Pope's Revenge.")

Farther east, pass under the train tracks into . . .
Alexanderplatz—This, especially the Kaufhof, was the commercial pride and joy of East Berlin. Today it's still a landmark, with a major U-Bahn station surrounded by a few Wurst stands. Most of the buildings around the square are slated for destruction.

For a ride through workaday eastern Berlin, with its stark Lego-hell apartments, hop back on bus #100 from here and ride to the end of the line (30-minute round-trip). Are the people different? They are politically free. Are they economically free? How's the future? (At the end of the line, get out. At the same stop, in a

few minutes, another bus will take you back to Alexanderplatz, or
even back to the start at Zoo Station.)

Tours of Berlin

▲▲**City Walking Tours**—Berlin Walks offers a basic three-hour
"Discover Berlin" introductory walk every morning (all year) and
every afternoon (April–October) for 15 DM (or 10 DM if you're
under 26 or have a WelcomeCard; just show up at 10:15 or 14:30
at taxi rank in front of Zoo Station, April–December, confirm
schedule at TI or with Nick or Serena at 030/301-9194, private
tours also available, berlin_walks@compuserve.com). Their quality, fluent-in-English guides also offer tours of "The Third Reich"
(most days at 10:15); "Jewish Life in Berlin" (most Wednesdays
and Sundays at 10:15); and a more youth-oriented 3.5 hour blitz
sightseeing hike (only 10 DM, daily at 9:45 and 14:00 in summer).
Since Nazi sights are so hard to find and really understand, the
Third Reich walk is the best way to cover this slice of Berlin.
Another company, Yellow Walking Tours, offers "Insider Tours"
(walking and on bike) with a more youthful focus (leaving near the
McDonalds across from the Bahnhof Zoo).
▲**City Bus Tours**—For bus tours you have three choices:
1) Full-blown three-hour bus tours. Contact Severin & Kühn (39
DM, live guides in two languages, from Ku'damm 216, 4/day in
summer, tel. 030/880-4190), and BVG buses from Ku'damm 225
(tel. 030/885-9880).
2) Quicky 90-minute orientation tours (25 DM, generally live
guides, departing nearly hourly from the Ku'damm at the Memorial church).
3) Hop-on hop-off circle tours. Four companies do the "City-
Circle Sightseeing" tour offering you unlimited on-and-off privileges for its 12-stop route (30 DM, taped guides, frequent buses).
Guide Friday and Tempelhofer offer a "double circle" with 20
stops for 33 DM (great live guides but buses only twice an hour,
tel. 030/4999-8030). The TI has the brochures. Just hop on where
you like and pay the driver. On a sunny day when the double-
decker buses go topless, they are a photographer's delight.

Sights—Western Berlin

▲**Kurfürstendamm**—In the 1850s, when Berlin became a
wealthy and important capital, her new rich chose Kurfürstendamm as their street. Bismarck made it Berlin's Champs-Élysées.
In the 1920s it became a chic and fashionable drag of cafés and
boutiques. During the Third Reich, as home to the international
community of diplomats and journalists, it enjoyed more freedom
than the rest of Berlin. Throughout the Cold War, economic sub-
sidies from the West made sure that capitalism thrived on
Ku'damm, as western Berlin's main drag is popularly called. And

today, while much of the old charm has been hamburgerized, Ku'-damm is still the place to feel the pulse of the city and enjoy the elegant shops (around Fasanenstrasse), department stores, and people-watching. Ku'damm, starting at Kaiser Wilhelm Memorial Church, does its commercial can-can for two miles.

▲**Kaiser Wilhelm Memorial Church (Gedächtniskirche)**— The church was originally a memorial to the first emperor of Germany, who died in 1888. Its bombed-out ruins have been left standing as a memorial to the destruction of Berlin in World War II. Under a fine mosaic ceiling, a small exhibit features interesting photos about the bombing (free, Monday–Saturday 10:00–16:00). Next to it, a new church (1961) offers a world of 11,000 little blue-glass windows. The blue glass was given by the French as a reconciliation gift. The square between this and the Europa Center (a shiny high-rise shopping center built as a showcase of Western capitalism during the Cold War) is generally a lively busker scene.

▲**Käthe Kollwitz Museum**—This local artist (1867–1945), who experienced much of Berlin's stormiest century, conveys some powerful and mostly sad feelings about motherhood, war, and suffering through the black-and-white faces of her art (8 DM, Wednesday–Monday 11:00–18:00, closed Tuesday, a block off Ku'damm at Fasanenstrasse 24).

▲**Kaufhaus des Westens (KaDeWe)**—The "department store of the West," with a staff of 2,400 to help you sort through its vast selection of 380,000 items, is the biggest department store in Continental Europe. You can get everything from a haircut and train ticket to souvenirs (third floor). A cyber bar is on the fourth floor (5 DM for 30 minutes to surf or e-mail). The theater and concert box office on the sixth floor charges an 18 percent booking fee but they know all your options. The sixth floor is also a world of taste treats. This biggest selection of deli and exotic food in Germany offers plenty of free samples and classy opportunities to sit down and eat. Ride the glass elevator to the seventh floor's glass-domed Winter Garden self-service cafeteria (Monday–Friday 9:30–20:00, Saturday 9:00–16:00, closed Sunday, tel. 030/21210, U-Bahn: Wittenbergplatz). The Wittenbergplatz U-Bahn station (in front of KaDeWe) is a unique opportunity to see an old-time station in Berlin. Enjoy its interior.

Berlin Zoo—More than 1,400 different kinds of animals call Berlin's famous zoo home—or so the zookeepers like to think. Germans enjoy seeing the pandas at play (straight in from the entry). I enjoy seeing the Germans at play (12 DM for zoo or world-class aquarium, 19 DM for both, children half-price, daily 9:00–18:30, feeding times (*Fütterungszeiten*) posted on map just inside entry, enter near Europa Center in front of Hotel Palace, Budapester Strasse 32, tel. 030/254-010).

Erotic Art Museum—This offers three floors of graphic (mostly

18th-century Oriental) art and a tiny theater showing erotic silent movies from the early 1900s. If you're traveling and want only the best, the sex museums in Amsterdam or Copenhagen are far better. This one, while well described in English, is not as imaginative, neglects the history of sex, and is little more than prints and posters (10 DM, daily 9:00–24:00, hard-to-beat gift shop, at corner of Kantstrasse and Joachimstalerstrasse, a block from Zoo Train Station). If you just want to see sex, you'll see much more for half the price in a private video booth next door.

Sights—Central Berlin

Tiergarten/Siegessäule—Berlin's "Central Park" stretches two miles from the Zoo Train Station to Brandenburg Gate. Its centerpiece, the Siegessäule (Victory Column), was built to commemorate the Prussian defeat of France in 1870. The pointy-helmeted Germans rubbed it in, decorating the tower with French cannons and paying for it all with francs received as war reparations. The three lower rings commemorate Bismarck's victories. I imagine the statues of Moltke and other German military greats goose-stepping around the floodlit angel at night. Originally standing at the Reichstag, Hitler moved the Siegessäule to this position to complement his anticipated victory parades. Climbing its 285 steps earns you a fine Berlin-wide view (2 DM, Monday 13:00–18:00, Tuesday–Sunday 9:00–18:00, bus #100). From the tower, the grand Strasse des 17 Juni leads to the Brandenburg Gate.

German Resistance Memorial Center (Gedenkstätte Deutscher Widerstand)—This memorial and museum tell the story of the German resistance to Hitler. The Benderblock was a military headquarters where an ill-fated attempt to assassinate Hitler was plotted. Stauffenberg and his co-conspirators were shot in the courtyard. While explanations are in German only, the spirit that haunts the place is multilingual (free, Monday–Friday 9:00–18:00, weekends 9:00–13:00, printed English translation for sale, just south of the Tiergarten at Stauffenbergstrasse 13, tel. 030/2654-2202).

Potsdamer Platz—The Times Square of Berlin before World War II, arguably the busiest square in Europe, was cut in two by the Wall and left a deserted no-man's-land for 40 years. Sony, Daimler-Benz, Starbucks, and other huge corporations are turning it once again into a center of Berlin. Today it's the busiest construction site in Europe as a new Berlin is rising and East and West are coming together. This huge complex will contain cinemas, restaurants, offices, apartments, retail shops, and a casino. The bright orange-red **Info Box**, perched on black stilts, tells the story and offers a great view. Inside the "Box" are displays of all that's happening on the square (free, daily 9:00–19:00, Thursday till 21:00, at least until 2000, ride elevator or climb inner set of stairs to third floor, lots of photos, models, multimedia shows, well described in English, tel. 030/226-6240). Learn the latest on Germany's magnetic levitation train (Berlin-Hamburg) and the huge transportation tunnel being built under Potsdamer Platz. Climb the outer stairs (2 DM) for a rooftop view of the vast construction site.

Sights—Kulturforum, in Central Berlin

Just off Potsdamer Platz, with several top museums and the concert hall, is the city's cultural center of the 21st century (admission to all sights with the 8-DM day card, S- and U-Bahn: Potsdamer Platz). Gradually the art of the formerly split city is being assembled here in all-new museums.

▲▲**Gemäldegalerie**—Germany's top collection of 13th- through 18th-century European paintings (900 canvases) has been divided since World War II. Finally it's been reunited at its new Kulturforum location. The new building is a work of art in itself with clever use of natural light via its high rotunda. The central hall is part medieval (like three parallel naves) and part Renaissance (pillars converge as they move toward the back wall, giving the place the illusion of greater depth—a trick popular with the Renaissance artists). The heart of the new museum is the octagonal Rembrandt hall with the world's greatest collection of Rembrandts. The North Wing starts with German paintings of the 13th to 16th centuries—with eight by Dürer. Then comes the Dutch and Flemish—Jan van Eyck, Bruegel, Rubens, Van Dyck, Hals, Vermeer—and finishing with English, French, and German 18th-century art—Gainsborough and Watteau. The South Wing is saved for the Italians—Giotto, Botticelli, Titian, Raphael, El Greco, and Caravaggio (4 DM, free on first Sunday of each month, Tuesday–Friday 10:00–18:00, Saturday and Sunday 11:00–18:00, closed Monday, S- and U-Bahn: Potsdamer Platz).

New National Gallery (Neue Nationalgalerie)—This features 20th-century art (4 DM, free on first Sundays, Tuesday–Friday 10:00–18:00, weekends 11:00–18:00, closed Monday, Potsdamer Strasse 50, tel. 030/266-2662).

Kunstgewerbemuseum (Museum of Arts and Crafts)—This shows off a thousand years of applied arts—porcelain, fine Jugendstil furniture, Art Deco, and reliquaries. There are no crowds and no English descriptions. The National Library is across the courtyard (free, huge, English periodicals).

Music Museum—This great hall is filled with 600 exhibits from the 16th to 20th centuries, with old keyboard instruments and funny-looking tubas. There's no English, but it's fascinating if you're into pianos (4 DM, Tuesday–Sunday 9:00–17:00, weekends 10:00–17:00, closed Monday, across the street behind the arabesques of the Philharmonic Concert Hall, tel. 030/254-810).

Poke into the lobby of Berlin's Philharmonic Concert Hall and see if there are tickets available for your stay.

Sights—Eastern Berlin

▲▲**Pergamon Museum**—Of the museums on Museumsinsel (Museum Island), just off Unter den Linden, only the Pergamon Museum is essential. Its fantastic Pergamon Altar, from a second-century B.C. Greek temple, features the Greeks under Zeus and Athena beating the giants in a dramatic pigpile of mythological mayhem. Check out the action spilling out on the stairs. The Babylonian Ishtar Gate (glazed blue tiles from sixth century B.C.) and many ancient Greek and Mesopotamian treasures are also impressive (8 DM, free on first Sundays, Tuesday–Sunday 9:00–18:00, closed Monday, café, tel. 030/2090-5555). Try the excellent audio tours of the museum's highlights (free with admission). To get to the museum from Unter den Linden, walk along the canal. Passing the first bulky neoclassical building on your right, cross a bridge and follow the canal to the next bulky neoclassical building.

▲▲▲**The Museum of the Wall (Haus am Checkpoint Charlie) and a Chunk of the Wall**—The 100-mile "Anti-Fascist Protective Rampart," as it was called by the DDR, was erected almost overnight in 1961 to stop the outward flow of people (3 million leaked out between 1949 and 1961). It was 13 feet high with a 16-foot tank ditch, 30 to 160 feet of no-man's-land, and 300 sentry towers. In its 28 years there were 1,693 cases when border guards fired, 80 deaths, 3,221 arrests, and 5,043 documented successful escapes (565 of these were DDR guards).

Checkpoint Charlie, the famous American military border crossing, has long gone—buried under new construction. The fascinating **Haus am Checkpoint Charlie** museum is a block west of the site of the old checkpoint. It tells the gripping history of the Wall, the many ingenious escape attempts, and includes plenty of video and film coverage of those heady days when people-power tore the Wall down (8 DM, daily 9:00–22:00, U-Bahn to Kochstrasse, Friedrichstrasse 44, tel. 030/253-7250).

When it fell, the Wall was literally carried away by the euphoria. What survived has been nearly devoured by a decade of persistent "wall peckers." From near the museum, Zimmerstrasse leads to a small surviving stretch of wall. The park behind the Wall marks the site of the command center of Hitler's Gestapo and SS (explained by English plaques throughout). It's been left undeveloped as a memorial to the tyranny once headquartered here. At the far edge of this park is . . .

The *Topography of Terror*, built in an excavated air-raid shelter (used as an interrogation room) next to what was the Gestapo headquarters, tells the story of National Socialism in Germany (free, daily 10:00–18:00, English translation 2 DM, tel.

030/2548-6703). Portraits of its most famous victims—who disappeared—line the walls.

East Side Gallery—The biggest remaining stretch of the Wall is now "the world's longest art gallery," stretching for a mile and covered with murals painted by artists from around the world, mostly in celebration of the Wall's demise. While not impressive and in dire need of restoration, it does make for a thought-provoking walk. From Schlesisches Tor (end of Kreuzberg), walk across the river on the bridge, turn left, and follow the Wall to Berlin Hauptbahnhof (a train station two stops from Alexanderplatz).

Kreuzberg—This poorer district along the Wall, with run-down, graffiti-riddled buildings and plenty of student and Turkish street life, offers the best look at melting-pot Berlin in a city where original Berliners are as rare as old buildings. Berlin is the fourth-largest Turkish city in the world, and Kreuzberg is its "downtown." But to call it a "little Istanbul" insults the big one. You'll see mothers wearing scarves, *döner kebab* stands, and spray paint–decorated shops. For a dose of Kreuzberg without getting your fingers dirty, joyride on bus #129. (Take U-8 to Hermannplatz; you'll ascend through the Karstadt department store's great cafeteria; #129 buses wait immediately outside its door, leaving every five minutes. After leaving Kreuzberg, #129 stops at the Checkpoint Charlie Museum and continues to KaDeWe and Ku'damm.) Wander the area between the Kottbusser Tor and Schlesisches Tor subway stops, ideally on Tuesday and Friday afternoons from 12:00–18:00, when the Turkish Market sprawls along the bank of the Maybachufer Canal (U-Bahn: Kottbusser Tor).

Friedrichstrasse—Before the war, the heart of Berlin was the intersection of Friedrichstrasse and Unter den Linden. Friedrichstrasse is emerging once again as a grand boulevard lined with elegant stores. Go inside the slick and immense Galeries Lafayette and marvel at the chrome and glass interior—with its in-your-face, conspicuous-waste-of-space cone design (but resist the temptation to send a coin sliding into the center). American Express Company is across the street. Unfortunately, no one expects the new Friedrichstrasse to have the café/strolling ambience of the old one. It's a no-man's land after dark.

German Cathedral—The Deutscher Dom houses the great and thought-provoking Question of German History exhibit. For a retrospective on this country's tumultuous history, don't miss this (Tuesday–Sunday 10:00–18:00, summer until 19:00, closed Monday, on Gendarmenmarkt just off Friedrichstrasse behind Galleries Lafayette, tel. 030/2273-2141).

▲**Oranienburger Strasse**—Berlin is developing so fast it's impossible to predict what will be "in" next year. For now, the trendy place to be is around Oranienburger Strasse. Here's a quick tour: Ride the S-Bahn to Hackescher Markt. Leaving the station, you might want to browse through the Künst und Trödel Markt (antique market, under tracks on right, 10:00–18:00). Hackesche Höfe—the big, brightly restored curvy building a block ahead—is eight courtyards in a wonderfully restored 1907 Jugendstil building. It's busy with trendy restaurants and theaters.

Nearby, Grosse Hamburger Strasse was known for 200 years as the "street of tolerance" for its many religions. Hitler turned it into the street of death ("Todes Strasse"), bulldozing the city's oldest Jewish cemetery and turning a Jewish old-folks home into a deportation center. Today, candles burn in a memorial on the site of a former Jewish cemetery.

The streets behind Grosse Hamburger Strasse flicker with atmospheric cafes, *Kneipen* (pubs), and art galleries.

At night "techno-prostitutes" line Oranienburger Strasse. Prostitution is legal here but there's a big debate about taxation. Since they don't get unemployment insurance, why should they pay their taxes?

A shiny gilded dome marks the **New Synagogue**, now a museum and cultural center on Oranienburger Strasse. Only the dome and facade have been restored, and a window overlooks a vacant field marking what used to be the synagogue. The largest and finest synagogue in Berlin before World War II, it was vandalized and burned by Nazis on "Crystal Night" in 1938, bombed in 1943, and partially rebuilt in 1990. Inside, past tight security, there's a small but moving exhibit on the Berlin Jewish community through the centuries with some good English descriptions (ground floor and first floor). The "Vergesst es nie" message on its facade means "Never forget"—it was put up by East Berlin Jews in 1966. East Berlin had only a few hundred Jews, but now that the city is united, the Jewish community numbers about 10,000 (5 DM, Sunday–Thursday 10:00–18:00, Friday 10:00–14:00, closed Saturday, at Oranienburger Tor U-Bahn stop). Oren, a popular near-kosher/vegetarian café is next to the synagogue (see Eating, below).

Natural History Museum (Museum für Naturkunde)—Worth a visit just to see the largest dinosaur skeleton ever assembled. While you're there, meet "Bobby," the stuffed ape (5 DM, Tuesday–Sunday 9:30–17:00, closed Monday, U-6 to Zinnowitzer Strasse, at Invalidenstrasse 43).

Sights—Around Charlottenburg Palace

The Charlottenburg District (a short U-Bahn ride from the center) has three visit-worthy sights and makes a good side trip from downtown. Ride U-1 to Sophie-Charlotte Platz and walk 10 minutes (following signs to "Schloss") up the tree-lined boulevard, or catch bus #145 direct from Bahnhof Zoo. For a Charlottenburg lunch, the Luisen Brau is a comfortable brewpub restaurant with a copper and woody atmosphere, a good local "microbeer"—*dunkeles* (dark) or *helles* (light)—and traditional German grub (10 DM meals, daily 9:00–24:00, across from the palace at Luisenplatz 1, tel. 030/341-9388).

▲**Charlottenburg Palace (Schloss)**—This only surviving Hohenzollern Palace is Berlin's top Baroque palace. If you've seen the great palaces of Europe, this one comes in at about tenth place, especially since the main rooms are tourable only with a German guide (8 DM for Royal Apartments, Tuesday–Friday 10:00–18:00, weekends 11:00–18:00, closed Monday, tel. 030/3209-1202). For a quick look at a few royal apartments, the Knöbelsdorff Wing (5 DM) is set up to let you wander on your own, a substantial hike through restored-since-the-war, gold-crusted, white rooms filled with Frederick the Great's not-so-great collection of Baroque paintings.

▲**Galerie der Romantik**—Within the Knöbelsdorff Wing is a separate exhibit of Romantic art (4 DM or part of a bigger combo-ticket). This is a delightful collection of the German answer to the pre-Raphaelites: man against nature, Greek ruins dwarfed in enchanted forests, medieval churches, and powerful mountains.

▲▲**Egyptian Museum**—Across the street from the palace is a little museum of Egyptian treasures. It offers one of the great thrills in art appreciation—gazing into the still-young and beautiful face of 3,000-year-old Queen Nefertiti, the wife of King Akhenaton (8 DM, Tuesday–Friday 10:00–18:00, Thursday until 20:00, weekends 11:00–17:00, Schlosstrasse 70). In a few years, Nefertiti will be moving downtown.

▲**Bröhan Museum**—Wander through a dozen beautifully furnished Art Nouveau (Jugendstil) and art deco living rooms, a curvy organic world of lamps, glass, silver, and posters. While you're there, the second floor holds a fine collection of Impressionist paintings by Karl Hagemeister (8 DM, Tuesday–Sunday 10:00–18:00, closed Monday, next to Egyptian Museum, across street from Charlottenburg Palace).

Sights—Near Berlin

Sanssouci Palace, Potsdam—With a lush park strewn with the extravagant whimsies of Frederick the Great, the sleepy town of Potsdam has long been Berlin's holiday retreat. Frederick's super-rococo Sanssouci Palace is one of Germany's most dazzling. His equally extravagant New Palace (Neues Palais), built to disprove rumors that Prussia was running out of money after the costly Seven Years' War, is on the other side of the park. While Potsdam is easy to get to (30 minutes direct on S-Bahn from Bahnhof Zoo to Potsdam Stadt), Sanssouci Palace can be visited only by German-language tour—which can be booked up for hours. Even though "Sanssouci" means "without a care," get your appointment immediately upon arrival so you know how much time to kill (or if you need to come back and try again tomorrow).

Sanssouci Palace (10 DM, Tuesday–Sunday 9:00–17:00, closed Monday, shorter hours off-season, tel. 0331/969-4190) and the New Palace (8 DM, Wednesday–Monday 9:00–17:00, closed Tuesday, tours not required) are a 30-minute walk apart. The palaces of Vienna, Munich, and even Würzburg offer equal sight-seeing thrills with fewer headaches.

Potsdam's TI offers a handy walking tour from the Film Museum (downtown Potsdam, five-minute walk from S-Bahn stop, 3.5 hours, German/English, 11:00 except on Mondays, 39 DM includes guided tour of palace park and admission and tour of Sanssouci without any wait, book by telephone, tel. 0331/291-100). Otherwise, upon arrival, catch bus #695 from S-Bahn to the palace. Use the same bus (3/hr) to shuttle between the sights in the park. Potsdam's much-promoted Wannsee boat rides are torturously dull.

Late-Night Berlin

Zitty and *Tip* (all German, sold at kiosks) are the top guides to youth and alternative culture. The TI's *Berlin Programm* lists the non-stop parade of concerts, plays, exhibits, and cultural events. Tourists stroll the Ku'damm after dark. Oranienburger Strasse (described above) is an interesting new scene already being eclipsed by the action at Kollwitzplatz a bit farther east.

Visit KaDeWe's ticket office for your music and theater options (sixth floor, 18 percent fee but access to all tickets). Ask about "competitive improvisation" and variety shows.

For jazz (blues and boogie, too) near recommended Savigny-platz hotels, drop by **Ewige Lampe**, the eternal light. Buy a 5-DM drink and enjoy live music in an intimate, friendly atmosphere (Wednesday–Sunday starting at 21:00, Neibuhrstrasse 11a, tel 030/324-3918). Nearby, **Quasimodo Live** is small, fun, and offers good, live jazz nightly (buy a drink or reasonable cover, Kantstrasse 12a, under Delphi Cinema, tel. 030/312-8086).

Sleeping in Berlin
(1.7 DM = about $1, tel. code: 030)

Sleep Code: **S** = Single, **D** = Double/Twin, **T** = Triple, **Q** = Quad, **b** = bathroom, **t** = toilet only, **s** = shower only, **CC** = Credit Card (**V**isa, **M**asterCard, **A**mex). Unless otherwise noted, a buffet break-fast is always included.

Because of the cost of lodging and the distance necessary to travel to Berlin, I try to come and go by night train. My listings are in decent, comfortable neighborhoods generally a couple of flights up in big, run-down buildings. Inside they are clean, quiet, and big enough so that their well-worn character is actually charming. Rooms in back are on quiet courtyards. Prices are often soft in winter and for longer stays.

The city is packed and hotel prices go up on a few days

including: Green Week in mid-January, Easter weekend, first weekend in May, Ascension weekend in May, the Love Parade (a huge techno-Woodstock, second weekend in July), Germany's national holiday October 2–4, Christmas, and New Years.

For the most comforts at the least cost, arrive without a reservation (ideally in the morning) and let the TI book you a room in a fancy hotel on their push list. When there are no conventions or fairs (most of the summer), rather than go empty, business hotels rent rooms through the TI to lowly tourists for around half-price (e.g., 300 DM for 180 DM).

Sleeping near Zoo Station at Savignyplatz
(zip code: 10623, unless otherwise noted)

These hotels and pensions are a five- to 15-minute walk from Bahnhof Zoo (or take S-Bahn to Savignyplatz). Hotels on Kantstrasse have street noise. Ask for a quieter room in back. The area has an artsy charm going back to the cabaret days in the 1920s, when it was the center of Berlin's gay scene. Wasch Salon, a handy Laundromat, is at Leibnizstrasse 72 (near intersection with Kantstrasse, daily 6:00–22:00, 8–16 DM wash and dry). The first eight listings are simple and less expensive. The last four are splurges.

Pension Peters, run by a German-Swedish couple, is sunny and central. Decorated sleek Scandinavian, with every room renovated, it's a winner (S-70–80 DM, Ss-110 DM, D-90–110 DM, Ds-120–130 DM, extra bed-15 DM, kids under 12 free, family room, TVs in rooms, CC:VMA, 10 yards off Savignyplatz, on second floor of Kantstrasse 146, tel. 030/3150-3944, fax 030/312-3519, e-mail: penspeters146@aol.com, Annika and Christoph SE). They rent bikes (10 DM/day). Downstairs in the same building, the **Pension Viola Nova** is similar, but less personable and prompts the question, "Why pay more?" (S-90 DM, Sb-130 DM, D-120 DM, Ds-150 DM, Db-160 DM, breakfast-10 DM, CC:V, tel. 030/313-1457, fax 030/312-3314).

Hotel Crystal Garni is professional, with small comfortable rooms and a *vollkorn* breakfast room (S-70 DM, Sb-80 DM, D-90 DM, Ds-110 DM, Db-130–150 DM, CC:VMA, elevator, a block past Savignyplatz at Kantstrasse 144, tel. 030/312-9047, fax 030/312-6465, run by John and Dorothy Schwartzrock and Herr Glasgow Flasher).

Pension Alexis is a classic old European four-room pension in a stately 19th-century apartment run by Frau and Herr Schwarzer. This, more than any other Berlin listing, has you feeling at home with a far away aunt (S-70 DM, D-100 DM, T-150 DM, Q-200 DM, big rooms, two with balconies over a leafy street, Carmerstrasse 15, tel. 030/312-5144, enough English spoken).

Hotel Carmer 16, newly renovated with 40 big, bright, airy

Berlin's Savignyplatz Neighborhood

❶ PENSION PETERS	❽ HOTEL ASTORIA	⓮ HOTEL BOGOTA
❷ HOTEL CRYSTAL CARNI	❾ PENSION SAVOY	⓯ HOTEL PENSION FUNK
❸ PENSION ALEXIS	❿ HOTEL ATLANTA	⓰ DICKE WIRTIN
❹ HOTEL CARMER 16	⓫ HECKERS HOTEL	⓱ ZILLMARKT RESTAURANT
❺ ALPENLAND HOTEL	⓬ HOTEL AKANISHERHOF	⓲ PAVILLION AM LORETTA
❻ PENSION KNESEBECK	⓭ HOTELS AUSTRIANA, RUGEN	
❼ PENSION SILVA	CURTIS, PARISER ECK, ALEXANDER	

rooms, feels like a big professional hotel (S-80 DM, Sb-100 DM, D-100 DM, Db-160 DM, extra bed-40–60 DM, these discounted prices—except for a few festival/convention times—are promised through 1999, CC:VMA, Carmerstrasse 16, tel. 030/312-5025, fax 030/312-4396).

Alpenland Hotel is a classy hotel with a fine restaurant. The big, bright, but showerless doubles are the best value. It has modern baths, cheap furnishings, and many rooms on the fourth floor, with no elevator (S-75–90 DM, Ss-110 DM, Sb-130–140 DM, D-120 DM, Db-150–200 DM, extra person-65 DM, ground-level rooms upon request, CC:VM, just off Savignyplatz on a quiet street, Carmerstrasse 8, tel. 030/312-3970, fax 030/313-8444).

Pension Knesebeck rents nine comfy, if cheaply furnished, rooms just off Savignyplatz (S-65–75 DM, Ss-85 DM, D-120 DM, Ds-130–140 DM, Ts-180 DM, Qs-200 DM, 8 DM/load laundry service, Knesebeckstrasse 86, tel. 030/312 7255, fax 030/313 9507).

Pension Silva is a basic, new-feeling place just off Savigny-platz (S-55 DM, Sb-90 DM, Db-105 DM, Tb-150 DM, breakfast-

10 DM, Knesebeckstrasse 29, tel. 030/881-2129, fax 030/885-0435, NSE).

Splurges: Hotel Astoria is a three-star business-class hotel with 30 comfortably furnished rooms and affordable summer and weekend rates (high season-Db-269 DM; during low season of July–August, November–February, or any two weekend nights, prices drop: Sb-176 DM, Db-196 DM; CC:VMA, just around corner from Bahnhof Zoo at Fasanenstrasse 2, tel. 030/312-4067, fax 030/312-5027, e-mail: astoriahotel@t-online.de, Web site: http://home.t-online.de/home/astoriahotel).

Pension Savoy, in a very trendy neighborhood just off Ku'-damm, rents big, cheery, newly remodeled rooms with all the amenities. This is the classiest of my pension listings (Sb-135 DM, Db-195 DM, CC:VMA, Meinekestrasse 4, 10719 Berlin, elevator, tel. 030/881-3700, fax 030/882-3746).

Hotel Atlanta is a business hotel in an older building half a block south of Ku'damm. Next to Gucci, on an elegant shopping street, with big leather couches, this hotel has an upscale feel (Sb-130–165 DM, Db-150–195 DM, extra people 20 DM each, family-friendly, some smoke-free rooms, CC:VMA, Fasanenstrasse 74, 10719 Berlin, tel. 030/881-8049, fax 030/881-9872).

Heckers Hotel is an ultra-modern, three-star business hotel with all the sterile Euro-comforts. Its weekend, summer, and Web site rates are almost affordable (July, August, and weekends: Sb-200 DM, Db-250 DM, year-round Web site reservation special without breakfast and not in May: Sb-190 DM, Db-240 DM, high season: Db-310 DM, CC:VMA, some smoke-free rooms, between Savignyplatz and Ku'damm at Grolmanstrasse 35, tel. 030/88900, fax 030/889-0260, Web site: www.heckers-hotel.com).

Sleeping near Zoo Station, South of Ku'damm (zip code: 10707)

Several small hotels are nearby in a charming, café-studded neighborhood 300 yards south of Ku'damm near the intersection of Sächsische Strasse and Pariser Strasse (bus #109 from Bahnhof Zoo). They are less convenient from the station than the Savignyplatz listings above.

Hotel Austriana, with modern and bright rooms, is warmly run by Thomas (S-75 DM, Ss-85 DM, Sb-110 DM, Ds-120 DM, Db-160 DM, cheaper off-season, CC:VMA, Pariser Strasse 39, tel. 030/885-7000, fax 030/8857-0088). Two other pensions are in the same building: the simpler **Hotel Rügen** (Ds-115–125 DM, CC:VM, Pariser Strasse 39, tel. 030/884-3940, fax 030/884-39-437) and **Pension Curtis**, also basic, but hip, with 10 rooms, red comforters, and light-pine furniture (S-70 DM, Ds-110–130 DM, cheaper for those arriving during slow times without reservations, Pariser Strasse 39, tel. 030/883-4931, fax 030/885-0438).

Across the street is **Pension Pariser-Eck**, faded and old fash-
ioned, with 12 big homey rooms (S-60 DM, Ss-90 DM, D-110
DM, Ds-130 DM, Ts-150 DM, extra bed-50 DM, Pariser
Strasse 19, near Sächsische Strasse, tel. 030/881-2145, fax
030/883-6335, e-mail: eventoffice@t-online.de). On the same
street, the almost-too-modern **Hotel Alexander** is an art-deco
splurge with all the comforts (Ss-110–130 DM, Sb-160–210 DM,
Db-180–210 DM, Tb-210 DM, breakfast-20 DM, prices soft on
weekends during slow times, CC:VMA, Pariser Strasse 37, tel.
030/881-6091, fax 030/881-6094).

Hotel Bogota has 125 big, bright, modern rooms in a spacious
old building half a block south off Ku'damm. The service is brisk
and hotelesque (S-78 DM, Ss-100 DM, Sb-130 DM, D-125 DM,
Ds-145 DM, Db-170–190 DM, extra person-45 DM, elevator,
CC:VMA, bus 109 from Bahnhof Zoo to Schlüterstrasse 45, tel.
030/881-5001, fax 030/883-5887, e-mail: hotel.bogota@t-online.de).

Hotel-Pension Funk is the former home of a 1920s silent-
movie star, offering 14 elegant, richly furnished old rooms all on the
first floor and for a great price (S-65 DM, Ss-90 DM, Sb-110 DM,
D-100 DM, Ds-125 DM, Db-140–160 DM, extra person-45 DM,
CC:VMA, reserve early, Fasanenstrasse 69, a long block south of
Ku'damm, tel. 030/882-7193, fax 030/883-3329, fax is best).

Hotel Askanisherhof, a splurge, is the oldest *Zimmer* in
Berlin. Posh as can be, you get porters, valet parking, and antique-
furnished rooms. Photos on the walls brag of famous movie star
guests. Frau Glinicke offers Old World service and old Berlin
atmosphere (Sb-175–210 DM, Db-230–250 DM, CC:VMA, some
non-smoking rooms, elevator, Kurfurstendamm 33, tel. 030/881-
8033, fax 030/881-7206).

More Berlin Hotels

Near Augsburgerstrasse U-Bahn stop: **Hotel-Pension Nürnberger Eck** (D-130 DM, Db-150 DM, Nürnberger Strasse 24a,
tel. 030/235-1780, fax 030/2351-7899). Just upstairs, **Pension Fis-
cher** (D-90 DM, Ds-100 DM, breakfast-8 DM, Nürnberger
Strasse 24a, tel. 030/218-6808, fax 030/213-4225). **Hotel Arco**
(D-125 DM, Db-150–175 DM, Geisbergerstrasse 30, tel.
030/235-1480, fax 030/211-3387).

Near Güntzelstrasse U-Bahn stop: **Hotel Pension München**
(D-80 DM, Db-125 DM, breakfast-9 DM, Güntzelstrasse 62, tel.
030/857-9120, fax 030/8579-1222). At the same address, **Pension
Güntzel** (Ds-120 DM, Db-140 DM, tel. 030/857-9020, fax
030/853-1108). **Pension Finck** (D-90 DM, Ds-110 DM, Güntzelstrasse 54, tel. 030/861-2940, fax 030/861-8158).

In eastern Berlin: **Hotel Unter den Linden** is ideal for those
nostalgic for the days of Soviet rule. Formerly one of the best hotels
in the DDR, this huge blocky hotel, right on Unter den Linden in

the heart of what was East Berlin, is reasonably comfortable and reasonably priced. While built in 1966 with 324 rooms lining its prison-like corridors, the rooms are modern, plain, and comfy (Db-160 DM, some non-smoking rooms, twins are bigger than doubles, at intersection of Friedrichstrasse, Unter den Linden 14, 10117 Berlin, tel. 030/238-110, fax 030/2381-1100).

Studenten Hotel Berlin is open to all, with no curfew (D-84 DM, 38-DM-per-bed quads with sheets and breakfast, near City Hall on JFK Platz, Meiningerstrasse 10, U-Bahn: Rathaus Schoneberg, tel. 030/784-6720, fax 030/788-1532).

Eating in Berlin

Berlin has plenty of fun food places, both German and imported. Colorful pubs, called *Kneipen*, offer light meals and the fizzy local beer, Berliner Weiss. Ask for it *mit Schuss* for a shot of fruity syrup in your suds. If the kraut is getting wurst, try one of the many Turkish, Italian, or Balkan restaurants. Eat cheap at *Imbiss* snack stands, bakeries (sandwiches), and falafel/kebab places. Bahnhof Zoo has several bright, modern fruit-and-sandwich bars and a grocery (daily 6:00–24:00).

Self-Service Cafeterias near Bahnhof Zoo

Check out the big department stores. **KaDeWe's** top floor holds the Winter Garden Buffet view cafeteria, and its sixth-floor deli/food department is a picnicker's nirvana (hours similar to Wertheim's, below). Its arterials are clogged with more than 1,000 kinds of sausage and 1,500 types of cheese. Put together a picnic and enjoy a sunny bench by the Memorial Church. **Wertheim** department store, a half block from the Memorial Church, has cheap basement food counters and a fine Le Buffet self-service cafeteria with a view up six banks of escalators (Monday–Friday 9:30–20:00, Saturday 9:00–16:00, closed Sunday, U-Bahn: Ku'damm). The **Marche,** popping up in big cities all over Germany, is another decent self-service cafeteria within a half block of the church (daily 8:00–24:00, CC:VMA, Ku'damm 14, enter on ground floor of mini-mall).

Eating near Savignyplatz

Four good places are within 100 yards of Savignyplatz: **Dicke Wirtin** has a good *Kneipe* atmosphere and famous *Gulaschsuppe* for 6 DM (opens daily at noon, closes late, feels like a British pub, just off Savigny Platz at Carmerstrasse 9). **Die Zwölf Apostel** restaurant is trendy for leafy candlelit ambience and Italian food. A dressy local crowd packs the place for 20-DM pizzas and 30-DM meals (daily until wee hours, immediately across from Savigny S-Bahn entrance, Bleibtreustrasse 49, tel. 030/312-1433). **Zillemarkt Restaurant** feels like an old-time Berlin beer garden, with seating in the garden or in the rustic candlelit interior, offering traditional Berlin specialties (open daily until past midnight, no English menu (that's good), 20-DM meals, a block from Savigny S-Bahn station, under the tracks at Bleibtreustrasse 48a, tel. 030/881-7040). **Bistrot Hegel** is a mellow little Russian piano bar with light meals and indoor and outdoor seating right on Savignyplatz. Late at night there may be some balalaika action (open from 18:00 on, Savignyplatz 2, tel. 030/312-1948). Colorful eateries abound along nearby Carmerstrasse, Grolmanstrasse, and Knesebeckstrasse.

These places are within a five-minute walk of Savignyplatz: **Pavilion am Loretta** is a leafy, colorful-if-tacky, Munich-style beer garden/food circus with a kid-friendly ferris wheel a block off the Ku'damm, where Knesebeckstrasse hits Lietzenburg Strasse (nightly till late, April–September except in bad weather). **Schildkröte,** the "turtle," is a German-style country inn worth the investment (daily 11:30–24:00, 20–25 DM, CC:A, 100 feet south of Ku'damm on Uhlandstrasse, tel. 030/881-6770). Next door, the **Lindner** deli's sandwiches are perfect (though not cheap) for lazy picnickers. **Ullrich Supermarkt** is the neighborhood grocery store (Monday–Saturday 9:00–20:00, Sunday 9:00–16:00, Kantstrasse 7, under the tracks near Zoo Bahnhof). There's plenty of fast food on Ku'damm and near Zoo Bahnhof.

Eating along Unter den Linden near Pergamon Museum

The **Opernpalais**, preening with fancy pre-war elegance, hosts a number of pricey restaurants. Its Operncafé has the best desserts (longest dessert bar in Europe, across from the university and War Memorial at Unter den Linden 5). The shady beer/tea garden in front has a cheap self-service *Imbiss* (wurst, meatball sandwiches, and so on) and a creperie. More students and fewer tourists eat in the courtyard of Humbolt University across the street.

Oren Restaurant/Cafe is a trendy, stylish, near-kosher/vegetarian place next to the new synagogue. The food is pricey but good, and the ambience is happening (daily 10:00–24:00, north of Museum Island about five blocks away at Oranienburger Strasse 28, tel. 030/282-8228).

Transportation Connections—Berlin

Berlin has three train stations. Bahnhof Zoo was the West Berlin train station and still serves western Europe (Frankfurt, Munich, Hamburg, Paris, Amsterdam). The Hauptbahnhof (former East Berlin's main station) still faces east, serving Prague, Warsaw, Vienna, and Dresden. The Lichtenberg Bahnhof (eastern Berlin's top U- and S-Bahn hub) also handles a few eastbound trains. Expect exceptions. All stations are conveniently connected by subway. Train info: tel. 030/19419.

By train to: Frankfurt (14/day, 5 hrs) **Munich** (8/day, 8.5 hrs), **Köln** (hrly, 6.5 hrs), **Amsterdam** (4/day, 9 hrs), **Budapest** (3/day, 13 hrs), **Copenhagen** (4/day, 8 hrs), **London** (4/day, 15 hrs), **Paris** (6/day, 13 hrs), **Zurich** (12/day, 10 hrs), **Prague** (8/day, 4.5 hrs), **Warsaw** (4/day, 8 hrs), **Vienna** (2/day, 12 hrs via Czech Republic, Eurailers pay an extra 66 DM for second class; otherwise, take the three-hour train to Hannover and sleep through Eurail country to Vienna).

Berlin is connected by overnight trains from Bonn, Köln, Frankfurt, Munich, and Vienna. A *Liegeplatz*, or berth, is money well spent (26 DM in a six-bed cabin; or 45 DM on InterCity night train with breakfast). The beds cost the same whether you have a first- or second-class ticket or railpass. Trains are rarely full, but get your bed reserved a few days in advance from any travel agency or major train station in Europe.

Berlin's Three Airports
Allow 25 DM for a taxi ride to or from any of Berlin's airports. **Tegel Airport** handles most flights from the United States and western Europe (6 km from center, catch bus X9 to Bahnhof Zoo, or bus #109 to Ku'damm and Bahnhof Zoo for 3.90 DM, tel. 030/41011, general airport operator tel. 030/6951-2491). Flights from the east usually arrive at **Schönefeld Airport** (20 km from center, short walk to S-Bahn, catch S-9 to Zoo Station, tel. 030/60910). **Templehof Airport** is getting more domestic and European business (in Berlin, bus #119 to Ku'damm or U-Bahn 6 or 7, tel. 030/6951-2841). British Air (tel. 030/254-0000), Delta (tel. 0180/333-7880), SAS and Lufthansa (tel. 0180/6951-2841).

PRAGUE

It's amazing what 10 years of freedom can do. Prague has always been historic. Now it's fun, too. No place in Europe has become so popular so quickly. And for good reason: The capital of the Czech Republic—the only major city of central Europe to escape the bombs of this century's wars—is Europe's best-preserved Baroque city. It's slinky with sumptuous Art Nouveau facades, offers tons of cheap Mozart and Vivaldi, and brews the best beer in Europe. But more than the architecture and traditional culture, it's an explosion of pent-up entrepreneurial energy jumping for joy after 50 years of Communist rule. And its low prices will make your visit enjoyable and nearly stressless.

Planning Your Time
Two days makes the long train ride in and out worthwhile and gives you time to get beyond the sightseeing and enjoy Prague's fun-loving ambience. Many wish they'd scheduled three days for Prague. From Munich, Berlin, and Vienna, it's a six-hour train ride (during the day) or an overnight ride.

With two days I'd spend a morning seeing the castle and a morning in the Jewish Quarter—the only two chunks of sightseeing that demand any brainpower. Spend your afternoons loitering around the Old Town, Charles Bridge, and the Little Quarter and your nights split between beer halls and live music. Keep in mind that state museums close on Monday, and Jewish sites close on Saturday.

History
Medieval Prague: Prague's castle put it on the map in the ninth century. In the 10th century, the region was incorporated into

Prague

the German "Holy Roman" Empire. The 14th century was
Prague's Golden Age, when it was one of Europe's largest and
most highly cultured cities. During this period Prague built St.
Vitus Cathedral and Charles Bridge and established the first university in central Europe.

Bucking the Pope and Germany: Jan Hus was a local preacher who got in trouble with the Vatican a hundred years before Martin Luther. Like Luther, he preached in the people's language rather than Latin. To add insult to injury, he complained about church corruption. Tried for heresy and burned in 1415, Hus roused nationalist (Bohemian) as well as religious feelings and became a symbol of Czech martyrdom. His followers are Hussites.

Religious Wars: The reformist times of Jan Hus (around 1400, rebelling against both German and Roman control) led to a period of religious wars and ultimately subjugation under Austrian rule. Prague stagnated under the Habsburgs of Austria with the brief exception of Rudolf II's reign.

Under the late 16th-century rule of the Habsburg king Rudolf II, Prague emerged again as a cultural and intellectual center. Johannes Kepler, Tycho Brahe, and others worked here. Much of Prague's great art can be attributed to this Habsburg king who lived not in Vienna but in Prague.

The Thirty Years' War (1618–1648) began in Prague when locals tossed two Catholic/Habsburg officials (Czechs sympathetic to the Germans) out the window of the Prague Castle. Often called "the first world war" because it engulfed so many nations, the 30 years were particularly tough on Prague. During this period, its population dropped from 60,000 to 25,000. The result of this war was 300 years of Habsburg rule: German and Catholic culture, not Czech. Prague was a backwater of Vienna.

Czech Nationalist Revival: The 19th century was a time of nationalism for people throughout Europe, including the Czechs, as the age of divine kings and ruling families was coming to a fitful end. The arts (such as the paintings of Mucha and the building of the massive National Museum atop Wenceslas Square) stirred the national spirit. With the end of World War I the Habsburgs were history, and in 1918 the independent country of Czechoslovakia was proclaimed with Prague as its capital.

Troubled 20th Century: Independence had lasted barely 20 years when the Nazis swept in (1939). Prague escaped the bombs of World War II but went almost directly from the Nazi frying pan into the Communist fire. Almost. A local uprising freed the city from the Nazis on May 8, 1945. The Russians "liberated" them again on May 9.

The Communist chapter of Czech subjugation (1948–1989) was grim. The student and artist-led "Prague Spring" revolt in 1968 was crushed. The charismatic leader Alexander Dubcek was exiled into a job in the back woods, and the years after 1968 were particularly tough. But eventually the Soviet empire crumbled. Czechoslovakia regained its freedom in the 1989 "Velvet Revolution" (so called because there were no casualties). Until 1989, May 9 was the Czech day of liberation. Now Czechs celebrate their liberation on May 8.

In 1993 the Czech and Slovak republics agreed on the "Velvet Divorce" and became two separate countries.

Today, while not without its problems, the Czech Republic is enjoying a growing economy and a strong democracy. Prague has emerged as one of the most popular tourist destinations in Europe. You're about to find out why.

Orientation

Locals call their town "Praha" (pron: pra-ha). It's big, with 1.2 million people, but for the quick visit, think of it as small and focus on the core of the city. I will refer to the tourist landmarks in English (with the Czech name in parentheses). Study the map and learn these key places:

Main Train Station:	*Hlavní Nádraží* (hlav-nee nah-dra-shzee)
Old Town:	*Staré Město* (sta-rey mnyess-toh)
Old Town Square:	*Staroměstské Náměstí* (starro-min-yes-ststi-keh nah-mnyess-tee)
New Town:	*Nové Město* (no-vay mnyess-toh)
Little Quarter:	*Malá Strana* (mah-lah strah-nah)
Jewish Quarter:	*Josefov* (yoo-zef-fohf)
Castle Area:	*Hradčany* (hrad-chah-nee)
Charles Bridge:	*Karluv most* (kar-loov most)
Wenceslas Square:	*Václavske Náměstí* (vah-slawf-skeh nah-mnyess-tee)
The River:	*Vltava* (vul-tah-vah)

The Vltava River divides the west side (castle and Little Quarter) from the east side (train station, Old Town, New Town, and nearly all of the recommended hotels). Prague addresses come with a general zone. Praha 1 is in the old center on either side of the river. Praha 2 is in the new city south of Wenceslas Square. Praha 3 and higher indicates a location farther from the center.

Tourist Information

TIs are at three key locations: at the main train station, on the Old Town Square, and in the West Tower of Charles Bridge (daily 9:00–19:00, until 18:00 on weekends and in winter, tel. 02/2448-2202). They offer maps, information on guided walks and bus tours, and bookings for concerts, hotel rooms, and rooms in private homes. Get the brochure listing all of Prague's museums and hours.

Helpful Hints

Formalities: Travel in Prague is like travel in Western Europe, only it's not covered by the Eurailpass and it seems 15 years behind the times. Americans and Canadians need no visa. Just flash your passport at the border. (U.S. embassy in Prague, tel. 02/5732-0663.)

Rip-offs: Prague's new freedom comes with new scams. There's no particular risk of violent crime, just green, rich tourists getting taken by con artists. Simply be on guard: on trains (thieves on overnight trains and corrupt conductors intimidating Western tourists for a bribe); changing money (tellers anywhere with bad arithmetic and inexplicable pauses while counting back your change); and dealing with taxis (see Getting Around Prague, below). In restaurants, understand the price clearly before ordering.

Telephoning: Czech phones work like any in Europe. For international calls, buy a phone card at a kiosk or your hotel (150 kč). It costs about $1 a minute to call the United States directly (dial 001-area code-number) from a public phone booth that accepts the local phone card. To call Prague from abroad, dial the international code (00 in Europe or 011 in the U.S.), the Czech Republic code (420), then Prague's city code (2), followed by the local number.

Money: 32 Koruna (kč) = about U.S. $1. There is no black market. Assume anyone trying to sell money on the streets is peddling obsolete currency. Buy and sell easily at the station (4 percent fees), banks, or hotels. ATMs are everywhere. Czech money is tough to change in the West. Before leaving the Czech Republic, change your remaining Koruna into your next country's currency (at Prague train station change bureaus).

Local Help: Magic Praha is a tiny travel service run by hard-working English-speaking Lida Steflova. She is a local jack of all trades, helpful with any needs you may have (tel. 02/302-5170, e-mail: mp.ludmila@post.cz).

Best Views: Enjoy "the golden city of a hundred spires" during the early evening when the light is warm and colors rich. Good viewpoints include the castle square, the top of the east tower of Charles Bridge, the Old Town Square clock tower, and the steps of the National Museum overlooking Wenceslas Square.

Language: Czech, a Slavic language, has little resemblance to Western European languages. These days, English is "modern" and you'll find the language barrier minimal. If you speak German, it's helpful. An acute accent means you linger on that vowel. The little carrot above the c, s, or z makes it ch, sh, or zh.

Learn these key Czech words:

Hello/Goodbye (familiar)	*Ahoj* (ah-hoi)
Good day, Hello (formal)	*Dobrý den* (DOH-bree den)
Yes/No	*Ano* (AH-no)/*Ne* (neh)
Please	*Prosím* (proh-zeem)
Thank you	*Děkuji* (dyack-quee)
You're welcome	*Prosím* (proh-zeem)
Where is...?	*Kde je ...?* (gday yeh)
Do you speak English?	*Mluvíte anglicky?*
	(MLOO-vit-eh ANG-litz-key)
krown (the money)	*koruna* (koh-roo-nah)

Arrival in Prague

Prague unnerves many travelers—it's relatively run down, it's behind the former Iron Curtain, and you've heard stories of rip-offs and sky-high hotel prices. But in reality, Prague is charming, safe, and welcomes you with open cash registers and smiles.

By Train: Prague has several train stations. Most travelers coming from and going to the West use the main station (Hlavní Nádraží) or the secondary station (Holešovice Nádraží; if you arrive here, take metro into town: get off at Hlavní Nádraží for main station, or transfer at Muzeum to green line, stops Můstek and Staroměstská are in Old Town). Trains to other points within the country use Masarykovo or Smíchov stations.

Prague's main train station feels like a big metro station. You'll be met at the tracks by room hustlers (snaring tourists for cheap rooms in the center—illegally). A huge highway (Wilson Boulevard) obliterates the front of the formerly elegant station (go upstairs to see its original Art Nouveau interior). The large low-ceilinged main hall is downstairs: filled with travelers, kiosks, loitering teenagers, and older riff-raff.

Upon arrival by train, change money. Rates vary—compare by asking at two windows what you'll get for $100. Count carefully. At the same window, buy a city map (30 kč, with trams and metro lines marked and tiny sketches of the sights for ease in navigating). You'll be constantly referring to this map. Confirm your departure plans at the train information window. Possibly arrange for a room or tour at TI or the AVE travel agency. The left luggage counter is reportedly safer than the lockers.

To reach the Old Town from the train station, you can catch trams 5, 9, or 26 (to find the stop, walk into the park and head two minutes to the right) or take the metro (downstairs in the station, look for the red "M", two directions: Muzeum or Florenc; take metro to Muzeum, then transfer to green line—stops Můstek and Staroměstská straddle the Old Town). The courageous and savvy get a cabby to treat them fairly and get to their hotel fast and sweat-free for no more than 130 kč (see below).

By Plane: A couple of minibus services get you from the airport to downtown (or vice versa). The Cedaz minibus costs 100 kč and runs hourly (5:00–22:00) between the airport and Náměstî Rebulicky.

Getting Around Prague

You can walk nearly everywhere. But the metro is slick, the trams fun, and the taxis quick and easy once you're initiated.

Public Transport: The trams and metro work on the same tickets (buy from machines in metro, kiosks, or hotels). For convenience, buy all the tickets you think you'll need for your stay:

Prague Metro

15-minute ticket—8 kč, 60-minute ticket—12 kč, 24-hour ticket—70 kč, three-day pass—180 kč. The metro closes at midnight.

City maps show the tram/bus/metro lines. The metro system is handy and simple (just three lines) but doesn't get to many hotels and sights. Trams come by every couple of minutes. Get used to hopping on and off. Validate your ticket on the bus by sticking it in the machine (which stamps a time on it).

Taxis: The most infamous taxis in Europe are being tamed. While bandito cabbies still have meters that spin like pinwheels, the city has made great strides in civilizing these thugs. While most guidebooks advise avoiding taxis, this is defeatist. I find Prague is a great taxi town and use them routinely. Get the local rate and they're cheap. Use only registered taxis: these are marked by a roof lamp with the word "TAXI" in black on both sides, and the front doors sport a black-and-white checkered ribbon, the company name, license number, and rates (three rows: drop charge—25 kč, per kilometer charge—17 kč, and wait time per minute—4 kč). The key is the tiny "*sazba*" box on the magic meter showing the rate. This should read "1." If a cabbie tries to rip you off, simply pay 100 kč. Let him follow you into the hotel if he insists you owe him more. (He won't.) The receptionist will defend you. Rip-offs are most likely around tourist sites and the train station. To remind him to turn on the meter, say "*Zapnete taximetr*" (zappa-nyet-ay tax-ah-met-er).

City Tours

Prague Walks offers walking tours of the Old Town, the castle, and Jewish Quarter. Most last two hours and cost 200 kč. Get the current schedule from any TI (e-mail: pwalks@comp.cz).

Cheap big bus orientation tours provide an efficient once-over-lightly look at Prague and a convenient way to see the castle. **Premiant City Tours** offers 15 different tours including: quick city (350 kč, 2 hrs, 5/day), grand city (550 kč, 3.5 hrs, 2/day), Jewish Quarter (590 kč, 2 hrs), Prague by night, Bohemian glass, Terezin Concentration Camp memorial, Karlštejn Castle, český Krumlov (1600 kč, 8 hrs), and a river cruise. The tours feature live guides (in German and English) and depart from near the bottom of Wenceslas Square at Na Príkope 40. Get tickets at an AVE travel agency, hotel, on the bus, or at Na Príkope 23 (tel. 02/0601-212625 or 02/2423-0072, Web site: www.sos.cz/premiant).

Tram #22 makes a fine joyride through town. Consider this as a scenic lead-up to touring the castle. Catch it at metro: Náměstí Míru, roll through a bit of new town, the Old Town, across the river and hop out just above the castle.

Self-Guided Walking Tour

The King's Walk (Královská cesta), the ancient way of coronation processions, is touristy but great. Pedestrian-friendly and full of playful diversions, it connects the essential Prague sites. The king would be crowned in St. Vitus Cathedral in the Prague Castle, walk through the Little Quarter stopping at the Church of St. Nicholas, cross Charles Bridge, and finish at the Old Town Square. If he hurried, he'd be done in 20 minutes. Like the main drag in Venice between St. Mark's and the Rialto bridge, this walk mesmerizes tourists. Use it as a spine, but venture off it—especially to eat.

This walk laces together all the following recommended sights except the Jewish Quarter. From the castle, stairs lead down into the Little Quarter. They dump you into the Little Quarter Square and the Church of St. Nicholas. Farther downhill, a medieval gate announces Charles Bridge. Over the river another gate welcomes you to the Old Town and a well-trod, shop-lined street under glorious Baroque and Art Nouveau facades leads to the Old Town Square. For the sake of completeness, extend the King's Walk from there past the Havelska Market and up Wenceslas Square, where a commanding view awaits from the National Museum steps.

Sights—Prague's Castle Area

▲▲**Prague Castle**—For a thousand years, Czech rulers have ruled from the Prague Castle. It's huge (by some measures, the biggest castle on earth) with a wall more than a kilometer long. And it's confusing with plenty of sights not worth seeing and a newly rebuilt feeling. Rather than worry about rumors that you should spend all day here with long lists of museums within to see, keep things simple. Four stops matter and are explained here: St. Vitus Cathedral, the old Royal Palace, Basilica of St. George, and the Golden Lane. (100 kč for entrance to all sights within, daily 9:00–17:00; the 125 kč audio guide is good but renting it makes it impossible to exit the castle area from the bottom.) To reach the castle by metro, get off at the Malostranská metro stop, climb through the Little Quarter and up the castle steps (Zamecke Schody). Or ride tram #22, which stops above the castle.

Castle Square (Hradčanske Náměstí)—The big square facing the castle offers fine string quartet street music, an awesome city view, and stairs down to the Little Quarter. The National Gallery's collection of European paintings is in the neighboring Sternberg Palace (contains works by Dürer, Rubens, Rembrandt, El Greco, and more—skipable if you're going to Vienna or Munich).

Survey the castle from this square, the tip of a 500-meter-long series of courtyards, churches, and palaces. The offices facing this first courtyard belong to the Czech president, Vaclav Havel (left side). The guard changes on the hour. Walk under the fighting giants, under an arch, and straight into the info center in a small church—buy tickets here.

St. Vitus Cathedral—This cathedral symbolizes the Czech spirit. It was finished in 1929 on about the 1,000th anniversary of the assassination of St. Wenceslas, patron saint of the Czechs. This most important church in Prague houses the crown jewels (thoroughly locked up and out of sight) and the tomb of "Good King" Wenceslas as well as other Czech royalty. Wenceslas's tomb sits in the fancy chapel (on the right). Murals here show scenes of his life. More kings are buried in the royal mausoleum in front of the high altar and in the crypt underneath. The cathedral, a mix of Gothic and neo-Gothic, is 124 meters long and offers a fine view from the top of its spire (daily 9:00–17:00, 287 steps). Notice the fine windows. The rose window above the entry shows the creation. The Art Nouveau window from 1931 is by Czech artist Alfons Mucha (look for Saints Cyril and Methodius, third chapel on left). If you like that, visit the Mucha museum in the Old Town (see below).

Old Royal Palace—This was the seat of the Bohemian princes in the 12th century. While extensively rebuilt, the large hall is late Gothic. It's big enough for jousts—even the spiral staircases were designed to let a mounted soldier gallop up. Look up at the impressive vaulted ceiling, look down on the chapel from the end, and go out on the balcony for a fine Prague view. Is that Paris in the distance? No, it's an observation tower built for an exhibition in 1891 (60 meters tall, a quarter of the height of its big brother in Paris—built in 1889). There's nothing to see downstairs in the palace. Across from palace exit is St. George Basilica.

St. George Basilica and Convent—The first Bohemian convent was established here near the palace in 973. Today the convent houses the Czech Gallery (best Czech paintings from Gothic, Renaissance, and Baroque periods). The basilica is the best-preserved Romanesque church in Prague. St. Ludmila was buried here in 973. Continue walking downhill through the castle grounds. Veer to the left and into a cute lane.

Golden Lane—This street of old buildings, which originally housed goldsmiths, is now filled with gift shops, boutiques, galleries, and cafes. The Czech writer Franz Kafka lived at #22. There's a handy deli/bistro for picnic items at the top and a public WC at the bottom. Beyond that, at the end of the castle, are fortifications beefed up in anticipation of the Turkish attack—the cause for most medieval arms build-ups in Europe—and steps leading down and out into the Little Quarter.

Sights—From the Little Quarter to Charles Bridge

▲▲**Little Quarter (Malá Strana)**—This is the most characteristic fun-to-wander old section of town. It's one of four medieval towns (along with Hradčany, Staré Město, and Nové Město) which eventually grew to become Prague. It centers on the Little Quarter Square (Malostranské Náměstí) with its plague monument and the commanding church.

Church of St. Nicholas—Dominating the Little Quarter, this is the best example of High Baroque in town (daily 9:00–16:00, built 1703–1760, 230-foot-high dome). Normally, every night there are concerts at two venues on this square: in the Church of St. Nicholas and in Lichtenstein Palace across from the church. Charles Bridge is a short walk down Mostecka from the square.

▲▲▲**Charles Bridge (Karluv most)**—This much loved bridge, commissioned by the Holy Roman Emperor Charles IV in 1357, offers one of the most pleasant 500-meter strolls in Europe. Be on the bridge when the sun is low for the warmest people-watching and photography. At one time, the black crucifix (1657) standing near the east end stood alone. The multitude of other saints, near and dear to old Praguers, were added later. Today most are replicas with the originals in museums out of the pollution.

There's a TI at the west end tower (climbable). The tower at the east end is considered one of the finest Gothic gates in existence. Climb it for a fine view but nothing else (30 kč, daily

10:00–18:30). After crossing the bridge, follow the shop-lined street to the Old Town Square.

Sights—Prague's Old Town Square

▲▲▲**Old Town Square**—The focal point for most visits, this has been a market square since the 11th century. It became the nucleus of a town (Staré Město) in the 13th century when its city hall was built. Today the old-time market stalls have been replaced by cafés, touristic horse buggies, and souvenir hawkers.

The Hus Memorial—erected in 1915, 500 years after his burning—marks the center of the square and symbolizes the long struggle for Czech freedom. The Czech reformer Jan Hus stands tall between two groups of people: victorious Hussite patriots and Protestants defeated by the Habsburgs. A mother with her children behind Hus represents the ultimate rebirth of the Czech nation. The steps are a popular local hangout—young Czechs gawking at gawking tourists.

A spin tour from the center gives you a look at architectural styles: Romanesque, Gothic, Renaissance, Baroque, and Art Nouveau.

Spin clockwise from the green domes of the wildly Baroque Church of St. Nicholas. There has been a church on this site since the 12th century. This one, dating from the early 18th century, is now a Hussite church (evening concerts). The Jewish Quarter (Josefov) is a few blocks behind it. Spin to the right past the Hus Memorial and the fine golden and mosaic Art Nouveau facade of the Prague City Insurance Company. Notice the fanciful Gothic Tyn Church with its Disney-esque spires flanking a solid gold effigy of the Virgin Mary. For 200 years after Hus's death, this was the leading Hussite church in Prague (enter through arcade facing the square; a diagram at door locates spots of touristic interest such as the tomb of astronomer Tycho Brahe). Lining the south side of the square is an interesting row of pastel houses. Their Gothic, Renaissance, and Baroque facades are ornamented with interesting statues that symbolize the original use of each building. The pointed 230-foot-tall spire marks the 14th-century Old Town Hall (famous for its astronomical clock—see below). In front of the city hall, 27 white inlaid crosses mark the spot 27 Protestant nobles were beheaded in 1621 after rebelling against Catholic Habsburgs.

▲▲**Old Town Hall Astronomical Clock**—Join the gang, ignoring the ridiculous human sales racks, for the striking of the hour (daily 8:00–20:00) on the 15th-century town hall clock. As you wait for the show, see if you can figure out how the clock works.

With revolving disks and sweeping hands, this clock keeps several versions of time. Two outer rings show the hour: Bohemian time (Gothic numbers, with hours counted from sunset) and our time (24 Roman numerals, XII at the top being noon, XII at the bottom being midnight). Everything revolves around the earth (the fixed middle background, with Prague at the center). Arcing lines and moving spheres combine with the big hand (a sweeping golden sun) and the little hand (the moon showing various stages) to indicate the times of sunset and sunrise. Look for the orbits of the sun and moon as they rise through day (the blue zone) and night (the black zone). If this seems complex today, it must have been a marvel in 1490.

Four statues flank the clock representing 15th-century Prague's four biggest worries: invasion (the Turk), death (skeleton), greed (a moneylender, which used to have "Jewish" features until after World War II, when anti-Semitism became politically incorrect), and vanity (enjoying the mirror).

At the top of the hour, (1) death tips his hourglass and pulls the chord ringing the bell, (2) the windows open and the Twelve Apostles parade by acknowledging the gang of onlookers, (3) the rooster crows, and (4) the hour is rung. The hour is often off because of daylight saving time (which made no sense at all in the 15th century).

Inside the city hall you'll find the main TI, local guides desk, and the opportunity to pay three admissions: for the city hall (by tour only), Gothic chapel (nothing to see except a close-up of the Twelve Apostles and the clock mechanism well-described in English), and the tower (climb for another fine city view).

Sights—Around Wenceslas Square

▲**Havelská Market**—Central Prague's best open-air flower and produce market scene is a block toward the Old Town Square from the bottom of Wenceslas Square. Laid out in the 13th century by King Wenceslas for the German trading community, it keeps hungry locals and vagabonds fed cheaply today.

▲▲**Wenceslas Square (Václavske Náměstí)**—More a broad boulevard than a square, it's named for the statue of King Wenceslas that stands on a horse at the top. The square is a stage for modern Czech history: The Czechoslovak state was proclaimed here in 1918. In 1968 the Soviets put down huge popular demonstrations here. And in 1969 Jan Palach set himself on fire here to protest against the puppet Soviet government. The next day 200,000 local protesters gathered here. Starting at the top (metro: Muzeum), stroll down the square:

The National Museum stands grandly at the top. The only thing exciting about it is the view (60 kč, daily 10:00–18:00, halls of Czech fossils and animals).

St. Wenceslas, commemorated by the statue, is the "good king" of Christmas carol fame. He was never really a king, but the wise and benevolent 10th-century Duke of Bohemia. After being assassinated in 935, he became a symbol of Czech nationalism.

The metro stop (Muzeum) is the crosspoint of two metro lines. From here you could roll a ball straight down the boulevard and through the heart of Prague to Charles Bridge. It is famous locally as the downtown meeting place. They say, "I'll see you under the horse's ass."

Thirty meters below the big horse is a small round garden with a low-key memorial "to the victims of Communism." Pictured here is Jan Palach. The massive demonstrations here in the days following his death led to the overthrow of the Czech Communist government. From the balcony of the Grand Hotel Europa (farther down), Vaclav Havel stood with Alexander Dubcek, hero of the 1968 revolt, and declared the free Republic of Czechoslovakia in December 1989.

Continue people-watching your way downhill. American Express is on the corner (on left, daily 9:00–19:00, money exchange service). The Grand Hotel Europa (halfway down Wenceslas Square) is hard to miss. Notice its Art Nouveau exterior and step inside for the smoky, elegant Old World ambience of its Art Nouveau restaurant (see Sleeping, below).

The bottom of Wenceslas Square meets another fine pedestrian mall. Na Příkope (meaning "the moat") leads from Wenceslas Square right to the Municipal House and the Powder Tower (the Powder Tower sounds interesting but is a dud). City tour buses leave from along this street.

Sights—Prague's Jewish Quarter

▲▲▲Jewish Quarter (Josefov)—The Jewish people were dispersed by the Romans 2,000 years ago. "Time was their sanctuary which no army could destroy" as their culture survived in enclaves throughout the Western world. Jews first came to Prague in the 10th century. The main intersection of Josefov (Maiselova and Siroka Streets) was the meeting point of two medieval trade routes. Jewish traders settled here in the 13th century and built a synagogue.

When the pope declared Jews and Christians should not live together, Jews had to wear yellow badges, and their quarter was walled in, becoming a ghetto. In the 16th and 17th centuries, Prague had the biggest ghetto in Europe with 11,000 inhabitants—nearly half the population of Prague.

The "outcasts" of Christianity relied on profits from money-lending (forbidden to Christians) and community solidarity to survive. While their money protected them, it was also a curse. Throughout Europe, when times got tough and Christian debts to the Jewish community mounted, entire Jewish communities were burned, evicted, or killed.

Within its six gates, Prague's Jewish Quarter was a gaggle of 100 wooden buildings. Someone wrote: "Jews nested rather than dwelled." In the 1780s Emperor Joseph II eased much of the discrimination against Jews. In 1848 the walls were torn down and the neighborhood, named Josefov in honor of the emperor who was less anti-Semitic than the norm, was incorporated as a district of Prague.

In 1897 ramshackle Josefov was razed and replaced with a new modern town—the original 31 streets and 220 buildings became 10 streets and 83 buildings. This is what you'll see today: an attractive neighborhood of fine, mostly Art Nouveau buildings, with a few surviving historic Jewish buildings. In the 1930s some 50,000 Jews lived in Josefov. Today only a couple of thousand remain.

Strangely, the museums of the Jewish Quarter are, in part, the work of Hitler. He preserved Josefov to be his museum of the "exterminated race." Six sites scattered over a three-block area make the tourists' Jewish Quarter. Five, called "the Museum," are treated as one admission. Go early or late, as crowds can be fierce. Your ticket comes with a map locating the sights and five admission appointments: times you'll be let in if it's very crowded. (Without crowds, ignore the times.)

Start at the Maisel Synagogue unless you want to rent the AudioGuide (125 kč, at the Pinkas Synagogue). Westerners pay more than locals: 450 kč (250 kč for the "Museum" and 200 kč for the Old-New Synagogue). The sites are open from Sunday to Thursday 9:00 to 17:30, Friday 9:00 to 14:00 (sometimes later), and closed on Saturday (the Jewish sabbath). The Audio-Guide provides a good historic background and an easy-to-follow orientation for each site. There are also occasional live guided walks (often at 10:00, 40 kč). Most stops are wonderfully described in English. These museums are well presented and profoundly moving: for me, this is the most interesting Jewish site in Europe.

Maisel Synagogue—This shows a thousand years of Jewish history in Bohemia and Moravia. Ironically, the collection was assembled from synagogues throughout the region by Nazis planning to archive the "extinct Jewish culture" here in Josefov with a huge museum. Exhibits include topics such as the origin of the Star of David, Jewish mysticism, and the creation of the Prague Ghetto.

Pinkas Synagogue—A site of Jewish worship for 400 years, today this is a moving memorial to the victims of the Nazis. Of the 120,000 Jews living around here in 1939, only 15,000 lived to see liberation in 1945. The walls are covered with the handwritten names of 77,297 local Jews who were sent from here to the gas chambers of Auschwitz. Family names are in gold, followed by the individuals' first names in black, with birthdays and the last date known to be alive (usually the date of transport). Notice how families generally perished together. Climb six steps into the women's gallery. The names near the ceiling in poor condition are from 1953.

When the Communists moved in, they closed the synagogue and erased everything. With freedom, in 1989, the Pinkas Synagogue was reopened, and all the names rewritten.

Upstairs is the Terezin Children's Art Exhibit. Terezin, near Prague, was a fortified town of 7,000 Czechs. The Nazis moved these people out and moved in 60,000 Jews, creating their model "Jewish town," a concentration camp dolled up for propaganda purposes. The town's medieval walls, which used to prevent people from getting in, were used by Nazis to prevent people from getting out. Jewish culture seemed to thrive in Terezin as "citizens" put on plays and concerts, published a magazine, and raised their families in ways impressive to Red Cross inspectors. Virtually all of the Jews ended up at Auschwitz. The art of the children of Terezin survives as a poignant testimony to the horror of the Holocaust. While the Communists kept the art away from the public, today it's well displayed and described in English.

Terezin is a powerful day trip from Prague for those interested in touring the concentration camp memorial/museum; you can either take a tour bus (see City Tours, above) or public bus (6/day, 60 min, leaves from Prague's Florenc bus station).

Old Jewish Cemetery—From 1439 until 1787, this was the only burial ground allowed for the Jews of Prague. With limited space and over 100,000 graves, tombs were piled atop each other. With as many as 12 layers, the cemetery became a small plateau. The Jewish word for cemetery means "House of Life"; like Christians, Jews believe that death is the gateway into the next world. Today visitors wander among more than 12,000 evocative stones.

Ceremonial Hall—Leaving the cemetery you'll find a neo-Romanesque mortuary house built in 1911 for the purification of the dead. It's filled with an interesting exhibition on Jewish burial traditions with historic paintings of the cemetery.

Klaus Synagogue—This 17th-century synagogue (also at the exit of the cemetery) is the final wing of this museum, devoted to Jewish religious practices.

Old-New Synagogue—For over 700 years, this has been the most important synagogue and central building in Josefov. Standing like a bomb-hardened bunker, it feels like it's survived plenty of hard times. Stairs take you down to the street level of the 13th century and into the Gothic interior. Built in 1270, it's the oldest synagogue in Europe. Originally called "the New Synagogue," it was renamed "Old-New" as other synagogues were built. The Shrine of the Arc in front is the focus of worship. It holds the sacred scrolls of the Torah, the holiest place in the synagogue. The old rabbi's chair to the right is left empty out of respect. Twelve is a popular number (e.g., windows) because it symbolizes the 12 tribes of Israel. The windows on the left are an 18th-century addition allowing women to view the men-only services.

Art Nouveau

▲▲**Mucha Museum**—I find the art of Alfons Mucha (pron. moo-kah, 1860–1939) insistently likeable. Read about this popular Czech artist's posters which were patriotic banners in disguise, see the crucifixion scene he painted as an eight-year-old, and check out the photographs of his models. Prague isn't much on museums, but if you're into Art Nouveau, this one is great. Run by Mucha's grandson, it's two blocks off Wenceslas Square and wonderfully described and displayed on one comfortable floor (150 kč, daily 10:00-18:00, Panska 7, tel. 02/628-4162, Web site: www.mucha.cz). While the exhibit is well described in English, the 50 kč English brochure on the art is a good supplement. The video is also worthwhile (30 minutes, hourly in English, ask upon entry).

More Art Nouveau—Prague is the best Art Nouveau town in Europe. Check out St. Vitus Cathedral (the Mucha stained-glass window), the main train station (dome on top floor), and the Hotel Europa overlooking Wenceslas Square (inside and out). The Municipal House (Obecní Dům, built 1906–1912, near Powder Tower) features Prague's largest concert hall and a great Art Nouveau café with handy cyber access. On the building's striking facade, look for the *Homage to Prague* mosaic, which stoked cultural pride and nationalist sentiment.

Entertainment

Prague booms with live (and inexpensive) theater, opera, classical, jazz, and pop entertainment. Everything's listed in *Test the Best*, Prague's monthly cultural events program (free at TI). The Prague Spring International Music Festival runs the last three weeks in May.

There must be six or eight classical "tourist" concerts a day in the famous Old Town halls and churches. The music is of the crowd-pleasing sort: Vivaldi, Best of Mozart, Most Famous Arias, and works by local boy Anton Dvorak. Leafleteers are everywhere announcing the evening's events. Concerts typically cost 400 kč, start anywhere from 17:00 to 21:00, last 60 minutes, and are usually quartets (e.g., flute, French horn, cello, violin). Common venues are in the Little Quarter Square (Malostranské Náměstí, at the Church of St. Nicholas and the Prague Academy of Music in the Lichtenstein Palace), at the east end of Charles Bridge (St. Francis Church), and on the Old Town Square (another St. Nicholas Church).

Sleeping in Prague

(32 kč = about $1, tel. code: 02)

Sleep Code: **S** = Single, **D** = Double/Twin, **T** = Triple, **Q** = Quad, **b** = bathroom, **t** = toilet only, **s** = shower only, **CC** = Credit Card (**V**isa, **M**asterCard, **A**mex).

Finding a bed in Prague worries Western tourists. It shouldn't.

You have several options. Capitalism is working as Adam Smith promised: with a huge demand, the supply is increasing, and the price is going up. Peak time is May, June, September, October, Christmas, and Easter. July and August are not too bad. Virtually every place listed speaks English. Reserve by telephone first, follow by a fax to confirm. Generally you simply promise to come and need no deposit.

Room-Booking Services: The city is awash with fancy rooms on the push list and private small-time operators with rooms to rent in their apartments. Numerous booking services connect these places with travelers for a small fee.

At the main train station, **AVE** is a helpful and well-organized booking service (daily 6:00–23:00, tel. 02/2422-3226, fax 02/2423-0783, Web site: www.ave.anet.cz, e-mail: avetours@anet.cz). With the railroad tracks at your back, look for the small window on your right. Their main office is by the taxis on the left (at Wilsonova 8; another AVE office is at Holešovice station). Their push-list board displays three-star hotels with $100 rooms available for half-price. They have a slew of private rooms and small pensions available ($50 pension doubles in the old center, $35 doubles a metro ride away). You can reserve by e-mail, using your credit card as a deposit.

Accotour accommodations booking service, 100 meters toward the National Museum from the main train station, has a line on lots of private rooms all over the Old Town. They charge 120 kč per person per booking. Page through their scrapbook, and take your choice of doubles for as little as $20. They claim they always have rooms available and I believe them. For privacy, comfort, and centrality, I'd recommend one of these rooms over a hostel (Thursday–Tuesday 9:00–17:00, closed Wednesday, Wahingtonova 23, tel. 02/2421-5406).

Three-Star Hotels and Agencies

Prague's three-star–rated hotels come with cookie-cutter standards. They're cheap, perfectly professional, and hotelesque, with English-speaking receptionists, comfortable modern furnishings, modern full bathrooms, included buffet breakfasts, and rarely an elevator. These hotels are often beholden to agencies who have a lock on rooms (generally until six weeks in advance). Agencies get a 30-percent discount and can sell the rooms at whatever they like between that and the "rack rate." Because of these agencies, Prague has a reputation of being perpetually booked up. As they rarely use up their allotment, it almost never is. You need to make reservations either very long in advance—when the few rooms not reserved for agencies are still available, or not long in advance—after the agencies have released their rooms.

These recommended three-star hotels all cost about the same

Prague

① PICK UP BUS TOUR (AT #40)
② MUCHA MUSEUM
③ ACCO TOUR ROOM SERVICE
④ HOTEL JULIAN
⑤ HOTEL CENTRAL

⑥ BETHLEM CLUB
⑦ HOTEL U STARE PANI
⑧ HOTEL U KLENOTNIKA
⑨ HOTEL LUNIK
⑩ HOTEL UNION

⑪ HOTEL EUROPA
⑫ PENSION UNITAS
⑬ EXPRESS PENSION
⑭ PENSION U MEDVIDKU

and have rooms any normal person would find pleasant. While I've listed them in order of value for the dollar, characteristics such as location and price need to be considered. Hotel Julian and Hotel Union are away from the center; the rest cluster in the Old Town, mainly near metro: Můstek, unless otherwise noted.

Hotel Julian is an oasis of professional, predictable decency in a quiet neighborhood a five-minute taxi or tram ride from the action. Its 29 spacious, well-furnished rooms and big, homey public spaces hide behind a noble neoclassical facade. The staff is friendly and helpful (Sb-2,680 kč, Db-3,080 kč, suite Db-3,680 kč, extra bed-800 kč, CC:VMA, 5-percent discount off best quoted rate with this book, parking lot, elevator, Internet services, non-smoking rooms, Elisky Peskove 11, Prague 5, tel. 02/5731-1150, reception tel. 02/5731-1144, fax 02/5731-1149, e-mail: casjul@vol.cz).

Hotel Central is likeable like an old horse. I stayed there in the Communist days, and it hasn't changed a lot since. Even Charlie is still at the reception desk. The 62 rooms are proletarian plain, but the place is well run and the location, three blocks east of the old square, is excellent (Sb-2,400 kč, Db-3,100 kč, Tb-3,600 kč, CC:VMA, elevator, Rybna 8, Praha 1, metro: Náměstí Republiky, tel. 02/2481-2041, fax 02/232-8404, e-mail: what?).

Bethlem Club is a shiny jewel of comfort on a charming medieval square in the heart of the Old Town across from the Bethlem Chapel where Jan Hus preached his trouble-making sermons. Its 22 modern comfy rooms face a quiet inner courtyard, and breakfast is served in a Gothic cellar (Sb-2,600 kč, Db-3,400 kč, extra bed-400 kč, elevator, Betlémské Náměstí 9, Praha 1, tel. 02/2421-6872, fax 02/2421-8054).

Hotel U Stare Pani is well located in the Old Town above a jazz club that quits around midnight. The bright rooms are pastel cheery and wicker cozy (Db-3,830 kč, apartment Tb-5,760 kč, apartment Qb-6,660 kč, CC:VMA, no elevator, Michalska 9, Praha 1, two blocks from metro: Můstek, tel. 02/267-267, fax 02/267-9841).

Hotel U Klenotnika, with 10 modern and comfortable rooms in a plain building, is the most central of my recommendations—three blocks off the old square (Sb-2,500 kč, Db-3,600 kč, Tb-4,300 kč, CC:VMA, no elevator, Rytirska 3, Praha 1, tel. 02/2421-1699, fax 02/261-782).

Hotel Lunik is a stately no-nonsense place out of the medieval faux-rustic world and in a normal, pleasant business district two stops by metro from the station or a 10-minute walk from Wenceslas Square. It's friendly, spacious, and rents 35 pleasant rooms (Db-2,500 kč, Tb-2,900 kč, CC:VMA, elevator, Londynska 50, Praha 2, tel. 02/2425-3974, fax 02/2425-3986).

Hotel Union is a grand 1906 Art Nouveau building filling its street corner. Like Hotel Lunik, it's away from the touristic center but in a more laid-back neighborhood a direct 10-minute ride to the station on tram #24 or to Charles Bridge on tram #18 (Db-3,350 kč, Nusle Ostrcilovo Náměstí 1, Praha 2, tel. 02/6121-4812, fax 02/6121-4820).

Hotel Europa is in a class by itself. This landmark place, in all the guidebooks for its wonderful 1903 Art Nouveau facade, is the centerpiece of Wenceslas Square. But someone pulled the plug on the hotel about 50 years ago, and it's a mess, not even meriting its two stars. It offers haunting beauty in all the public spaces with 90 dreary, ramshackle rooms and a weary staff (S-1,300 kč, Sb-2,450 kč, D-2,160 kč, Db-3,400 kč, T-2,800 kč, Tb-4,400 kč, CC:VMA, elevator, Václavské Náměstí 25, Praha 1, tel. 02/2422-8117, fax 02/2422-4544).

Pensions

With the rush of tourists into Prague, small six- to 15-room pensions are popping up everywhere. Most have small, basic, clean rooms with no plumbing at all; sinks, showers, and toilets are down the hall. Breakfast is included in the price. These places take bookings no more than a month in advance. All are within 100 meters of each other in the Old Town, close to the Můstek metro station.

Pension Unitas is best—in every guidebook, right in the center, with lots of modern rooms rented from a convent. It's next to the city police station—site of the old Communist secret police headquarters, which still gives locals the creeps. Unitas shares the building with the classy three-star Cloister Inn (Db-3,400 kč—a great value but nearly always booked by agencies, same address and phone as Unitas). The Pension Unitas' 34 rooms are small and tidy with spartan furnishings and no sinks (S-1,020 kč, D-1,200 kč, T-1,650 kč, Q-2,000 kč, T and Q are cramped with bunks in D-sized rooms, book long in advance, Bartolomejska 9, 11000 Praha 1, tel. 02/232-7700, fax 02/232-7709, Web site: www.cloister-inn.cz, e-mail: unitas@cloister-inn.cz). The place was actually a prison recently—Vaclav Havel spent a night here . . . free.

Express Pension is a creative little place renting 16 simple rooms and serving a lousy continental breakfast in the room (D-1,500 kč, two on ground floor and two on fourth floor, Db-2,300 kč, no elevator, Skorepka 5, Praha 1, tel. 02/2421-1801, fax 02/261-672).

Penzion U Medvidku rents seven big plain rooms with no sinks and an indifferent management (D-1,600 kč, Db-2,860 kč, T-2,400 kč, CC:VMA, Na Perstyne 7, Praha 1, tel. 02/2421-1916, fax 02/2422-0930). They run a popular restaurant that has live music until 23:00 nightly.

Eating in Prague

The beauty of Prague is wandering aimlessly through the winding old quarters marveling at the architecture, people-watching, and sniffing out restaurants. You can eat well and cheaply. What you'd pay for a basic meal in Vienna or Munich will get you an elegant meal in Prague. Your basic decision is: traditional dark Czech beerhall-type ambience, elegant Jugendstil turn-of-the-century atmosphere, or a modern place. For traditional, wander the Old Town (Stare Mesto).

I hesitate to recommend a particular place, but since you asked, here are a few places (between the bottom of Wenceslas Square and Charles Bridge) that I enjoyed:

Plzenska Restaurace U Dvou Kocek has cheap, local, no-nonsense, hearty Czech food, great beer, and a local crowd (150 kč for three courses and beer, serving original Pilsner Urquell with traditional music daily until 23:00, under an arcade, facing the tiny square between Perlova and Skorepka Streets, tel. 02/267-729).

Restaurant U Staré Pani is a good place for Czech or international food (two blocks from metro: Můstek at Michalska 9 in hotel by same name). **Restaurant U Plebana** is a quiet little place with good service, Czech cuisine, and a more modern yet elegant setting (daily until 24:00, Betlemske Square 10, tel. 02/2422-9023). **Restaurant Mucha** is smoky with decent but pricey Czech food in a formal Art Nouveau dining room (300 kč meals, daily until 24:00, Melantrichova 5, tel. 02/263-586). For a basic, very local cafeteria, slide your tray down the line with locals in the Můstek metro station at **37 Patro Fast Food** (extremely cheap, downstairs under the square). Prices go way down when you get away from the tourist areas. At least once, eat in a restaurant with no English menu.

Czech Beer

For many, *pivo* (beer) is the top Czech tourist attraction. After all, the Czechs invented lager in nearby Pilsen. This is the famous Pilsner Urquell, a great lager available on tap everywhere. Budvar, another local beer, is the local Budweiser, but it's not related to the American brew. Czechs are among the world's biggest beer drinkers—adults drink about 80 gallons a year. The big degree on bottles and menus marks the beer's heaviness, not its alcohol content (12 degrees is darker, 10 degrees lighter). The smaller figure shows alcohol content. Order beer from the tap (*sudove pivo*) in either small (.3 liter, *male pivo*) or large (.5 liter, *pivo*). In many restaurants a beer hits your table like a glass of water in the United States. *Pivo* for lunch has me sightseeing the rest of the day on Czech knees.

Transportation Connections—Prague

Getting to Prague: Those with railpasses need to purchase tickets to cover the portion of their journey from the border of the Czech Republic to Prague (buy at station before you board train for Prague). Or supplement your pass with a "Prague Excursion" pass, giving you passage from any Czech border station into Prague and back to any border station within seven days. Ask about this pass (and get reservations) at the EurAide offices in Munich or Berlin (90 DM first class, 60 DM second class, 40 DM for youths under 26). EurAide's U.S. office sells these passes a bit cheaper (tel. 941/480-1555, fax 941/480-1522), or try DER (tel. 847/692-6300) or your travel agent. Direct trains leave Munich for Prague daily around 7:00, 14:00, and 23:00, arriving five or six hours later. Tickets cost about 100 DM from Munich or 30 DM from the border (if you have a railpass covering Germany).

Prague by train to: Berlin (5/day, 5 hrs), **Munich** (3/day, 5 hrs), **Frankfurt** (3/day, 6 hrs), **Vienna** (3/day, 5 hrs), **Budapest** (6/day, 9 hrs). Train information: tel. 02/2422-4200. Czech Rail Agency, tel. 02/800-805.

AUSTRIA
(ÖSTERREICH, THE KINGDOM OF THE EAST)

- 32,000 square miles (the size of South Carolina, or two Switzerlands)
- 7.6 million people (235 per square mile and holding, 85 percent Catholic)
- 12 Austrian schillings (AS) = about $1 (figure 8 cents each)

During the grand old Habsburg days, Austria was Europe's most powerful empire. Its royalty built a giant kingdom of more than 50 million people by making love, not war (having lots of children and marrying them into the other royal houses of Europe).

Today this small, landlocked country does more to cling to its elegant past than any other in Europe. The waltz is still the rage. Austrians are very sociable; it's important to greet people in the breakfast room and those you pass on the streets or meet in shops. The Austrian's version of "Hi" is a cheerful *"Grüss Gott"* ("May God greet you"). You'll get the correct pronunciation after the first volley—listen and copy.

While they speak German and talked about unity with Germany long before Hitler ever said *"Anschluss,"* the Austrians cherish their distinct cultural and historical traditions. They are not Germans. Austria is mellow and relaxed compared to Deutschland. *Gemütlichkeit* is the local word for this special Austrian cozy-and-easy approach to life. It's good living—whether engulfed in mountain beauty or bathed in lavish high culture. The people stroll as if every day were Sunday, topping things off with a cheerful visit to a coffee or pastry shop.

It must be nice to be past your prime—no longer troubled by being powerful, able to kick back and celebrate life in the clean, untroubled mountain air. While the Austrians make less money than their neighbors, they enjoy a short work week and a long life span.

The Austrian schilling (S or AS) is divided into 100 groschen. To convert prices from schillings into dollars, drop the last zero and subtract one-fifth (e.g., 450 AS = about $36). About 8 Austrian schillings equal 1 deutsche Mark (DM). While merchants and waiters near the border are happy to accept DM, you'll save money if you use schillings. Prices in Austria are lower than in Germany and much lower than in Switzerland. Shops are open from 8:00 to 17:00 or 18:00.

Austrians eat on about the same schedule we do. Treats include *Wiener Schnitzel* (breaded veal cutlet), *Knödel* (dumplings), *Apfelstrudel*, and fancy desserts like the *Sachertorte*, Vienna's famous chocolate cake. Bread on the table sometimes costs extra (if you eat it). Service is included in restaurant bills, but it's polite to leave a little extra (less than 5 percent).

"Die Vignette" Motorway Toll Stickers: In Austria, all cars must have a "Die Vignette" toll label stuck to the inside of their windshield. These are sold at all border crossings (24 hours a day) and at big gas stations near borders. Stickers cost 70 AS for one week (150 AS for two months). Not having one earns you a stiff fine.

Most major train stations rent bikes (70 AS half day, 90 AS full day, 50 percent more without a train ticket) and allow you to drop them at other stations for a 45-AS fee.

In this section of the book, I'll cover Austria's top cities *except* for Reutte in Tirol. For this book, Reutte was annexed by Germany. You'll find it in the Bavaria and Tirol chapter.

VIENNA
(WIEN)

Vienna is a head without a body. For 600 years the capital of the once-grand Habsburg Empire, she started and lost World War I and, with it, her far-flung holdings. Today you'll find an elegant capital of 1.6 million people (20 percent of Austria's population) ruling a small, relatively insignificant country. Culturally, historically, and from a sightseeing point of view, this city is the sum of its illustrious past. The city of Freud, Brahms, a gaggle of Strausses, Maria Theresa's many children, and a dynasty of Holy Roman Emperors is right up there with Paris, London, and Rome.

Vienna has always been the easternmost city of the West. In Roman times it was Vindobona, on the Danube facing the Germanic barbarians. In medieval times Vienna was Europe's bastion against the Ottoman Turks (a "horde" of 300,000 was repelled in 1683). While the ancient walls held out the Turks, World War II bombs destroyed 22 percent of the city's buildings. In modern times Vienna took a big bite out of the USSR's Warsaw Pact buffer zone. The truly Viennese person is not Austrian but a second-generation Habsburg cocktail, with grandparents from the distant corners of the old empire—Polish, Serbian, Hungarian, Romanian, Czech, or Italian. Vienna is the melting-pot capital of an empire of 60 million—of which only 8 million are Austrian.

In 1900, Vienna's 2.2 million inhabitants made it the world's fifth-largest city (after New York, London, Paris, and Berlin). But the average Viennese mother has 1.3 children, and the population is down to 1.6 million. (Dogs are the preferred "child.")

Some ad agency has convinced Vienna to make Elisabeth, wife of Emperor Franz Josef—with her narcissism and difficulties with royal life—the darling of the local tourist scene. You'll see Sissy all over town. But stay focused on the Habsburgs who mattered.

Of the Habsburgs who ruled Austria from 1273 to 1918, Maria Theresa (ruled 1740–1765) and Franz Josef (ruled 1848–1916) are the most famous. People are quick to remember Maria Theresa as the mother of 16 children (12 survived). This was actually no big deal back then (one of her daughters had 18 kids, and a son fathered 16). Maria Theresa's reign followed the Austrian defeat of the Turks, when Europe recognized Austria as a great power. She was a strong and effective queen. (Her rival, the Prussian emperor, said, "When at last the Habsburgs get a great man, it's a woman.")

Maria Theresa was a great social reformer. During her reign she avoided wars and expanded her empire by skillfully marrying her children into the right families. With daughter Marie Antoinette's marriage into the French Bourbon family (to Louis XVI), for instance, a country that had been an enemy became an ally. (Unfortunately for Marie, she arrived in time for the Revolution, and she lost her head.)

In tune with her age and a great reformer, Maria Theresa's "Robin Hood" policies helped Austria slip through the "age of revolution" without turmoil. She taxed the church and the nobility and provided six years of obligatory education to all children and free health care to all in her realm. She also welcomed the boy genius Mozart into her court.

As far back as the 12th century, Vienna was a mecca for musicians—both secular (troubadours) and sacred. The Habsburg emperors of the 17th and 18th centuries were not only generous supporters of music but fine musicians and composers themselves. (Maria Theresa played a mean double bass.) Composers like Haydn, Mozart, Beethoven, Schubert, Brahms, and Mahler gravitated to this music-friendly environment. They taught each other, jammed together, and spent a lot of time in Habsburg palaces. Beethoven was a famous figure, walking—lost in musical thought—through Vienna's woods.

After the defeat of Napoleon and the Congress of Vienna in 1815 (which shaped 19th-century Europe), Vienna enjoyed its violin-filled belle époque, which shaped our romantic image of the city—fine wine, chocolates, cafés, and waltzes. The waltz was the rage, and "Waltz King" Johann Strauss and his brothers kept Vienna's 300 ballrooms spinning.

This musical tradition that continues in our century leaves some prestigious Viennese institutions for today's tourists to enjoy: the Opera, the Boys' Choir, and the great Baroque halls and churches, all busy with classical and waltz concerts.

Planning Your Time

For a big city, Vienna is pleasant and laid-back. Vienna is worth two days and two nights. Not only is it packed with great sights, but it's also a joy to spend time in. It seems like Vienna was designed to help people simply meander through a day. To be grand-tour efficient, you could sleep in and sleep out on the train (Berlin, Venice, Rome, the Swiss Alps, Paris, and the Rhine are each handy night trains away). But then you'd miss the Danube and Melk. I'd come in from Salzburg via Hallstatt, Melk, and the Danube and spend two days this way:

Day 1:

9:00	Circle the Ring by tram, following the self-guided tour (below).
10:00	Tour Opera. (Take care of any TI and ticket needs.)
11:00	Horse lovers tour the Lipizzaner Museum and see the horses practicing (at 11:00). Art fans can visit the Academy of Fine Arts or the Art Nouveau sights at Karlsplatz. People-watchers wander Nasch Market.
12:00	Lunch at Buffet Trzesniewski or the Rosenberger Markt Restaurant.
13:00	Tour Hofburg, visiting Augustinian church, royal apartments, treasury, Neue Burg, and Kaisergruft.
16:30	Stroll Kärntner Strasse, tour cathedral, and stroll Graben and Kohlmarkt.
19:00	Choose classical music, *Heurige* wine garden, Prater amusement park, or an opera performance. Spend some time wandering the old center.

Day 2:

9:00	Schönbrunn Palace (drivers: note this is conveniently on the way out of town toward Salzburg).
13:00	Kunsthistorisches Museum after lunch.
15:00	Your choice of the many sights left to see in Vienna.
Evening	See Day 1 evening options.

Orientation (tel. code: 01)

Vienna, or Wien (VEEN) in German, is bordered on three sides by the Vienna Woods (Wienerwald) and the Danube (Donau). To the southeast is industrial sprawl. The Alps, which arc across Europe from Marseilles, end at Vienna's wooded hills. These provide a popular playground for walking and new-wine drinking. This greenery's momentum carries on into the city. You'll notice more than half of Vienna is park land, filled with ponds, gardens, trees, and statue memories of Austria's glory days.

Think of the city map as a target. The bull's-eye is the cathedral, the first circle is the Ring, and the second is the Gürtel. The old town snuggles around towering St. Stephan's Cathedral south of the Donau, bound tightly by the Ringstrasse. The Ring, marking what was the city wall, circles the first district (or *Bezirk*). The Gürtel, a broader ring road, contains the rest of downtown (Bezirkes 2–9).

Addresses start with the *Bezirk*, followed by street and building number. Any address higher than the ninth *Bezirk* is beyond the Gürtel, far from the center. The middle two digits of Vienna's postal codes show the district, or *Bezirk*. The address "7, Lindengasse 4" is in the seventh district, #4 on Linden Street. Its postal code would be 1070. Nearly all your sightseeing will be done in the core first district or along the Ringstrasse. As a tourist, concern yourself only with this small old center, and sprawling Vienna suddenly becomes manageable.

Tourist Information

Beware of "tourist offices" at the train stations, airport, and around town, which are hotel agencies in disguise. Vienna's real tourist office, near the Opera House at Kärntner Strasse 38, is excellent (daily 9:00–19:00, tel. 01/211-140 or 01/513-8892, Web site: http://info.wien.at/). Stop here first with a list of needs and questions. Confirm your sightseeing plans, and pick up the free and essential city map (best of its kind in Europe—use the town center inset, also available at most hotels), the museum brochure (listing hours), the monthly program of concerts, (called "Programm") and the fact-filled *Young Vienna Scene* magazine.

Consider the TI's handy 50-AS *Vienna from A to Z* booklet. Every important building has a numbered flag banner that keys into this guidebook. *A to Z* numbers are keyed into the TI's city map. When lost, find one of the "famous-building flags" and match its number to your map. If you're at a "famous building," check the map to see what other key numbers are nearby, then check the *A to Z* book description to see if you want to go in.

I skip the much promoted 180-AS "Vienna Card," which gives you a three-day transit pass (worth 130 AS) and tiny discounts at museums on the push list (which you probably won't visit).

Arrival in Vienna

By Train at the West Station: Most train travelers arrive at the Westbahnhof. Pick up a free city map at the Reisebüro am Bahnhof. To get to the city center (and most likely, your hotel): catch U-3 subway (buy the 50-AS 24-hour pass from a *Tabak* [tobacco] shop in the station or from a machine—good on all city transit). U-3 signs lead down long escalators to the subway tracks. Catch a train in the direction of U-3-Erdberg. Ride five stops to Stephansplatz, escalate in the exit direction "Stephansplatz," and you hit the cathedral. The TI is a five-minute stroll down the busy Kärntner Strasse pedestrian street.

The Westbahnhof has a grocery store (daily 5:30–23:00), change offices (station ticket windows offer better rates than change offices and are open long hours), storage facilities, and rental bikes (see Getting Around, below).

By Plane: The airport (16 km from town) is connected by 70-AS shuttle buses (3/hr) to either the Westbahnhof (35 min) or the City Air Terminal (20 min) near the river in the old center. Taxis into town cost about 400 AS.

Getting Around Vienna

By Bus, Tram, and Subway: To take simple and economical advantage of Vienna's fine transit system of buses, trams, and sleek, easy subways, buy the 24-hour (50-AS) or 72-hour (130-AS) subway/bus/tram pass at a station machine or at *Tabak* shops near any station. Take a moment to study the eye-friendly city center map on metro station walls to internalize how the metro and tram system can help you. I use it mostly to zip along the Ring (tram #1 or #2) and subway to more outlying sights or hotels. The 15-AS transit map is overkill. All necessary routes are listed on the free tourist city map. Without a pass, either buy individual tickets (17 AS, good for one journey with necessary changes) from metro ticket windows or buy blocks of five tickets for 85 AS (17 AS apiece). Tickets are 20 AS from the driver. Eight-strip, eight-day, 265-AS transit passes, called "8 Tage Umwelt Streifennetzkarte," can be shared (for instance, four people for two days each, a 33 percent savings over the already cheap 24-hour pass).

Stamp a time on your pass as you enter the system or tram (stiff 500-AS fine if caught without a valid ticket). Rookies miss stops because they fail to open the door. Push buttons, pull latches, do whatever it takes. Study your street map before you exit the subway; by choosing the right exit—signposted from the moment you step off the train—you'll save yourself lots of walking.

By Taxi: Vienna's comfortable, honest, and easy-to-flag-down taxis start at 27 AS. You'll pay 90 AS to go from the Opera to the South or West Train Station.

By Bike: Good as the city's transit system is, you may want to rent a bike at any train station (daily 4:00–24:00, 90 AS/day with railpass or train ticket, 150 AS without; rent early in morning before supply runs out). Pedal Power offers rental bikes (350 AS/day for "trekking" bike, 395 AS includes delivery and pickup from your hotel) and 3.5-hour two-language city tours (daily at 10:00, 280 AS includes bike and guide, Austellungsstrasse 3, U-1 to Praterstern and long walk, tel. 01/729-7234).

By Buggy: Rich romantics get around by traditional horse and buggy. You'll see the *Fiakers* clip-clopping tourists on 20-minute (500 AS) or 40-minute (800–1,000 AS) tours.

Helpful Hints

Bank Alert: Banking is expensive in Vienna. Save 3 percent by comparing rates. (Warning: "Rieger Bank" is not a bank; it's an expensive exchange bureau in disguise.) Banks are open weekdays roughly from 8:00 to 15:00 and until 17:30 on Thursday. After hours, you can change money at train stations, the airport, the post office (on Postgasse in city center, open 24 hours daily, also has handy metered phones). Commissions of 100 AS are sadly normal. A happy exception is the American Express Company office, which charges no commissions to change AmExCo checks (Monday–Friday 9:00–17:30, Saturday 9:00–12:00, Kärntner Strasse 21–23, tel. 01/51540). ATMs are abundant.

Post Office: The West and South Train Stations each have full-service post offices (open 4:00–24:00).

English Bookstores: The British Bookshop is at the corner of Weihburggasse and Seilerstätte, and Shakespeare & Co. is at Sterngasse 2, north of the Höher Markt Square (tel. 01/5355-05354).

Telephones: Vienna just changed its 0222 area code to 01. When you encounter 0222 numbers, do the same.

Internet Access: Try Internet Aktiv (8-minute walk from Westbahnhof, small sign, Zieglergasse 29, tel. 01/526-7389).

City Tours

Walks: The *Walks in Vienna* brochure at the TI describes Vienna's many guided walks. Unfortunately, only a few are in English (130 AS, not including admissions, 90 min, tel. 01/894-5363).

Bus Tours: Vienna Line offers hop-on hop-off tours covering the 14 predictable sightseeing stops. Given Vienna's excellent public transportation and this outfit's meager one bus per hour frequency, I'd take this not to hop-on-and-off, but only to get a 2.5-hour narrated (in German and English) orientation drive through town (220 AS, good for two days, for this and more tours, tel: 01/714-1141). Eva Prochaska can book you a private guide who charges 1,230 AS for a half-day (1, Weihburggasse 13–15, tel. 01/513-5294).

Do-It-Yourself Bus Orientation Tour

▲▲**Ringstrasse Tour**—In the 1860s Emperor Franz Josef had the city's ingrown medieval wall torn down and replaced with a grand boulevard 190 feet wide, arcing nearly three miles around the city's core. The road predates all the buildings that line it. So what you'll see is neo-Gothic, neoclassical, and neo-Renaissance. One of Europe's great streets, it's lined with many of the city's top sights. Trams #1 and #2 circle the whole route and so should you.

This self-service tram tour gives you a fun orientation and a ridiculously quick glimpse of the major sights as you glide by (20-AS, 30-minute circular tour). For an actual look at these sights, consider hiking most of the route. Tram #1 goes clockwise; tram #2, counterclockwise. Most sights are on the outside, so tram #2 is best (sit on right). The tour assumes you're sitting in front of the

Vienna

front car. Ideally, start at the Opera House. With a 24-hour ticket, you can jump on and off as you go—trams come every five minutes. (Otherwise, buy your 20-AS one-ride ticket as you board.) Described sights are on the right unless I say "on left." Let's go:

• Just past the Opera (on left): The city's main pedestrian drag, Kärntner Strasse, leads to the zigzag roof of St. Stephan's Cathedral. This tour makes a 360-degree circle, staying about this far from that spire.

• At first bend: Look towards the tall fountain. Schwartzenberg Platz—with its equestrian statue of Prince Charles Schwartzenberg, who battled Napoleon—leads to the Russian monument (behind the fountain). This monument was built in 1945 as a forced thanks to the Soviets for liberating Austria from the Nazis. Formerly a sore point, now it's just ignored.

• Going down Schubertring you reach the huge *Stadtpark* (city park), which honors 20 great Viennese musicians and composers with statues. The white and yellow concert hall behind the trees is the Kursalon, opened in 1867 by the Strauss brothers, who directed many waltzes here (see Music, below).

• Immediately after next stop: In the park, the gilded statue of Waltz King Johann Strauss holds his violin as he did when he conducted his orchestra.

• While at next stop at end of park: On the left, a green statue of Dr. Karl Lueger honors the popular man who was mayor of Vienna until 1910.

• At next bend: The quaint building with military helmets decorating the windows was the Austrian ministry of war, back when that was a serious operation. Field Marshal Radetzky, a military big shot in the 19th century under Franz Josef, still sits on his high horse.

• At next corner: The white-domed building is the Urania, Franz Josef's 1910 observatory. Lean forward and look behind it for a peek at the huge red cars of the giant 100-year-old Ferris wheel in Vienna's Prater Park.

• Now you're rolling along the Danube Canal. This "Baby Danube" is one of the many small arms of the river that once made up the Danube at this point. The rest have been gathered together in a mightier modern-day Danube, farther away. This was the site of the original Roman town, Vindobona. In three long blocks, on the left (opposite the BP station), you'll see the ivy-covered walls and round Romanesque arches of St. Ruprechts, the oldest church in Vienna (built in the 11th century on a bit of Roman ruins). By about 1200, Vienna had grown to fill the area within this ring road.

• Leaving the canal, turning up Schottenring, at first stop: On the left, the pink and white neo-Renaissance temple of money, the Börse, is Vienna's stock exchange.

• Next stop, at corner: The huge frilly neo-Gothic church is a "votive church," built in 1853 as a thanks to God when an assassination attempt on Emperor Franz Josef failed. Ahead on the right is the Vienna University building, which faces (on the left, behind the gilded angel) a chunk of the old city wall.

• At next stop: The neo-Gothic city hall, flying the flag of Europe, towers over Rathaus Platz, a festive site of outdoor movies and concerts. Immediately across the street (on left) is the Hofburg Theater, Austria's national theater.

• At next stop: The neo-Greek temple of democracy houses the Austrian Parliament. The lady with the golden helmet is Athena, goddess of wisdom. Across the street (on left) is the royal park called the "Volksgarten."

• At next stop: Ahead on the right is the Natural History Museum, the first of Vienna's huge twin museums. Next door is the Kunsthistorisches Museum, containing the city's greatest collection of paintings. A statue of Empress Maria Theresa sits between the museums, facing the grand gate to the Hofburg, the emperor's palace (on left). Of the five arches, only the center one was used by the emperor. The gate, a modern addition, is located where Vienna's medieval city wall once stood.

• Fifty yards after next stop, through a gate in the black iron fence: On the left is the statue of Mozart in the Burggarten, which until 1880 was the private garden of the emperor. A hundred yards farther (on left), Goethe sits in a big, thought-provoking chair playing Trivia with Schiller (on right). Behind the statue of Schiller is the Academy of Fine Arts. Vienna had its share of intellectual and creative geniuses.

• Hey, there's the Opera again. Jump out and see the rest of the city.

Sights—Vienna's Old Center

(Sights are listed in a logical walking order.)

▲▲▲**Opera**—The Staatsoper, facing the Ring, just up from Stephansdom and next to the TI, is a central point for any visitor. While the critical reception of the building 130 years ago led the architect to commit suicide, and though it's been rebuilt since the World War II bombings, it's a dazzling place (60 AS, by guided 35-minute tour only, daily in English, July and August at 11:00, 13:00, 14:00, 15:00, and often at 10:00 and 16:00; other months, afternoons only). Tours are often canceled for rehearsals and shows, so check the posted schedule or call 01/51444 or 01/5144-42959.

The Vienna State Opera, with not the Vienna Philharmonic Orchestra but its farm team in the pit (you can't get into the best orchestra in town without doing time here), is one of the world's top opera houses. There are 300 performances a year—nearly nightly, except in July and August (when the singers rest their voices). Expensive seats are normally sold out. Unless Pavarotti is in town, it's easy to get one of 567 *Stehplatz* (standing-room spots, 20 AS for the very top, better 30-AS spots downstairs). If fewer than 567 people are in line, there's no need to line up early. The *Stehplatz* ticket window in the front lobby opens 80 minutes before each performance (*Stehplatz* information tel. 01/5144-42419). Dress is casual (but do your best) at the standing room bar.

Rick's crude tip: For me, three hours is a lot of opera. But just to see and hear the Opera House in action for half an hour is a treat. You can buy a ticket intending to just drop in for part of the show. Ushers don't mind letting tourists with standing-room tickets in for a short look. Ending time is posted in the lobby—you could drop in for just the finale. If you go for the start or finish, you'll see Vienna dressed up. With all the time you save, consider stopping by . . .

Sacher Café, home of every chocoholic's fantasy, the Sachertorte, faces the rear of the Opera (on Philharmoniker Strasse). A coffee and slice of cake here is 100 AS well invested.

Monument against War and Fascism—Behind the Opera

House, on Albertinaplatz, a modern, white split statue is Vienna's monument remembering the victims of the 1938–1945 Nazi rule of Austria. In 1938, Germany annexed Austria, saying Austrians were wanna-be-Germans anyway. Austrians are *not* Germans—never were, never will be. They're quick to tell you that, while Austria was founded in 976, Germany wasn't born until 1870. For seven years (1938–1945), there was no Austria. In 1955, after 10 years of joint occupation by the victorious Allies, Austria regained her independence.

▲**Kärntner Strasse**—This grand mall (traffic-free since 1974) is the people-watching delight of this in-love-with-life city. It points south in the direction of the southern Austrian state of Kärnten (for which it's named). Starting from the Opera, you'll find the TI, city casino (at #41, the former Esterhazy Palace), many fine stores, pastry shops, the American Express Company office (#21–23), and then, finally, the cathedral.

▲▲**St. Stephan's Cathedral**—Stephansdom is the Gothic needle around which Vienna spins. It's survived Vienna's many wars and symbolizes the city's freedom. Locals call it "Steve" (*Steffl*, church open daily 6:00–22:00, tours are in German only, information board near entry has tour schedules and time of impressive 50-minute daily Mass).

Outside, the last bit of the 11th-century Romanesque church can be seen in the west end (above the entry): the portal and the round windows of the towers. The church survived the bombs of World War II but, in the last days of the war, fires from the street-fighting between Russian and Nazi troops leapt to the rooftop; the original timbered Gothic rooftop burnt, and the cathedral's huge bell crashed to the ground. With a financial outpouring of civic pride, the roof of this symbol of Austria was rebuilt in its original splendor by 1952. The ceramic tiles are purely decorative (and each has the name of a local who contributed money to the rebuilding). Photos of the war damage can be seen inside.

The interior is grand in general, but it's hard to get thrilled about any particular bit. An exception is the Gothic sandstone pulpit in the middle of the nave (on left or north). A spiral stairway winds up to the lectern, surrounded and supported by the four Latin Church fathers: St. Ambrose, St. Gerome, St. Gregory, and St. Augustine. The work of Anton Pilgram, this has all the elements of Flamboyant Gothic in miniature. But this was 1515. The Italian Renaissance was going strong in Italy and, while Gothic persisted in the north, the Renaissance spirit had already arrived. Pilgram included a rare self-portrait bust in his work (the guy with sculptor's tools, looking out a window under the stairs). Gothic art was to the glory of God. Artists were anonymous. In the more humanist Renaissance, man was allowed to shine—and artists became famous.

Hundreds of years of history are carved in its walls and buried in its crypt (40 AS, open at odd times, tel. 01/5155-23526). You can ascend both towers, the north (via crowded elevator) and the south (by spiral staircase). The north shows you a big bell (the 21-ton Pummerin, cast from the cannon captured from the Turks in 1683) but a mediocre view (40 AS, daily 9:00–18:00, enter inside). The 450-foot-high south tower, called St. Stephan's Tower, offers a great view—343 tightly wound steps away, up the spiral staircase at the watchman's lookout, 246 feet up (30 AS, daily 9:00–17:30, enter outside and burn about one Sachertorte of calories). From the top, use your *Vienna from A to Z* to locate the famous sights.

The peaceful **Cathedral Museum** (Dom und Diözesen Museum) gives a close-up look at piles of religious paintings, statues, and a treasury (40 AS, Tuesday–Saturday 10:00–16:00, behind the church and past the buggy stand, Stephansplatz 6). Near the church entrance, descend into the Stephansplatz subway stop for a peek into the 13th-century Virgilkapelle.

▲▲**Stephansplatz, Graben, and Kohlmarkt**—The atmosphere of the church square, Stephanplatz, is colorful and lively. At nearby Graben Street (which was once a *Graben* or "ditch"), top-notch street entertainment dances around an exotic plague monument. In medieval times, people did not understand the causes of plagues and figured they were a punishment from God. It was common for survivors to thank God with a monument like this one from the 1600s.

Just beyond the monument is a fine set of Jugendstil public toilets (6 AS). St. Peter's Church faces the toilets. Step into this festival of Baroque (from 1708) and check out the jeweled skeletons—anonymous martyrs donated by the pope.

Kohlmarkt (end of Graben), Vienna's most elegant shopping street (except for "American Catalog Shopping," at #5, second floor), leads left to the palace. Wander down here, checking out the edible window displays at Demel (Kohlmarkt 14). Then drool through the interior (coffee and cake for 100 AS). Shops like this one and the one across the street boast "K. u. K." This means a shop considered good enough for the *König und Kaiser* (king and emperor—same guy).

Kohlmarkt leads to Michaelerplatz. The stables of the Spanish Riding School face this square (left). Notice the Roman excavation in the center. Enter the Hofburg Palace by walking through the gate and into the first square (In der Burg).

Sights—Vienna's Hofburg Palace

▲▲**Hofburg**—The complex, confusing, imposing Imperial Palace, with 640 years of architecture, demands your attention. This first Habsburg residence grew with the family empire from the 13th century until 1913, when the new wing (Neue Burg) was opened.

The winter residence of the Habsburg rulers until 1918, it's still the home of the Spanish Riding School, the Vienna Boys' Choir, the Austrian president's office, and several important museums.

While you could lose yourself in its myriad halls and court-yards, I'd focus on three things: the Imperial Apartments, Treasury, and Neue Berg (New Palace).

Orient from **In der Burg Square**. The statue is of Emperor Franz II (grandson of Maria Theresa and grandfather of Franz Josef). Behind him is a tower with three kinds of clocks (the yellow disc shows the stage of the moon tonight). On the right, a door leads to the Imperial Apartments and Hofburg model. Franz II is facing the oldest part of the palace. The gate (which used to have a drawbridge) leads to the 13th-century Swiss Court (named for the Swiss mercenary guards who used to be stationed here) with the Schatzkammer (treasury) and the Hofburgkappelle (palace chapel) —where the Boys' Choir sings the Mass. Continuing out opposite the way you entered In der Burg, you'll pass through the left-most tunnel (with a handy sandwich bar—Hofburg Stüberl) to the Hero's Square and the Neue Burg. Tour the Imperial Apartments first.

▲▲▲**Imperial Apartments (Kaiserappartements)**—These lavish, Versailles-type "wish-I-were-God" royal rooms are a small, downtown version of the grander Schönbrunn Palace. If rushed, and have time for only one, these suffice. The Imperial Apartments share a ticket booth with the Silver and Porcelain Collection (Silberkammer). You can tour either for 80 AS or get a Kombi-Ticket for 95 AS and see them both (daily 9:00–17:00, from courtyard through St. Michael's Gate, just off Michaeler-platz, tel. 01/533-7570). While combo tickets are cheap, for most, the rooms of plates and fancy silverware are not worth the extra 15 AS or time. (Study the great Hofburg model outside near the ticket line. From there, see enough of the collection through the window.) Palace visits are a one-way romp through 20 rooms. You'll find no English information within, but with the following description, you won't need the 95-AS Hofburg guidebook.

• The first few rooms get you warmed up.

• **The audience chamber:** Three huge paintings would entertain guests waiting here before an audience with the emperor. Every citizen had the right to meet privately with the emperor. Paintings in this room show crowds of commoners enthusiastic about their Habsburg royalty. On the right: The emperor returning to Vienna celebrating news that Napoleon had begun his retreat in 1809. Left: The return of the emperor from the 1814 Peace of Paris, the treaty which ended the Napoleonic wars. (The 1815 Congress of Vienna that followed was the greatest assembly of diplomats in European history. Its goal: to establish peace through a "balance of power" among nations. While rulers ignored nationalism in favor of continued dynastic rule, this worked for about 100 years,

Vienna's Hofburg Palace

CAFE DEMEL →
HERRENGASSE
LOOS HAUS
KOHLMARKT
↑ TO GRABEN
ST. MICHAEL'S CHURCH
100 YARDS
ROMAN RUINS →
SCHAUFFLER
MICHAELER PLATZ
⑤
AUGUSTINER STR.
② ← ⑥
JOSEFS PLATZ →
⑧
IN ❶ DER BURG
❸ ❼
SNACKS
VOLKSGARTEN
HELDEN PLATZ
❹
BURGGARTEN
DCH
BURG - RING
TO OPERA →

❶ IN DER BURG SQUARE	❹ NEW PALACE	❼ CHAPEL WHERE BOYS CHOIR SINGS
❷ IMPERIAL APARTMENTS	❺ LIPIZZANER MUSEUM	❽ AUGUSTINER CHURCH
❸ TREASURY	❻ LINE TO SEE HORSES	

when a colossal war wiped out Europe's royal families.) Center: Less importantly, the emperor makes his first public appearance to adoring crowds after recovering from a life-threatening illness (1826). The chandelier is Baroque of Bohemian crystal.

• **Audience room:** Suddenly you were face to face with the emp. The portrait shows Franz Josef (my vote for the greatest Habsburg emperor) in 1915 when he was over 80 years old. Famously energetic, he lived a spartan life dedicated to duty. He'd stand at the high table here to meet with commoners who came to show gratitude or make a request. (Standing kept things moving.) On the table you see a partial list of 56 appointments he had on June 3, 1910.

• **Conference room:** The emperor presided here over the equivalent of cabinet meetings.

• **Emperor Franz Josef's study:** The desk was originally between the windows. Franz Josef could look up from his work and see his lovely empress Elisabeth's reflection in the mirror. "Sissy's" main purpose in life seemed to be to preserve her reputation as a beautiful empress and maintain her fairy-tale hair. In spite of severe dieting and fanatic exercise, age took its toll. After turning 30, she had no portraits painted and was seen in public generally with a delicate fan covering her face. Notice the trompe l'oeil paintings above each door giving the believable illusion of marble relief.

• The walls between the rooms are wide enough to hide servants' corridors. The emperor lived with a personal staff of 14: "3 valets, 4 lackeys, 2 doormen, 2 manservants, and 3 chambermaids."

• **Emperor's bedroom:** This features his famous spartan iron bed and portable washstand (necessary until 1880 when the palace got running water). A small painted porcelain portrait of the newlywed royal couple sits on the dresser. Franz Josef lived here after his estrangement from Sissy. An etching shows the empress—an avid hunter—riding sidesaddle while jumping a hedge. The big ornate stove in the corner was fed from behind. Through the 19th century, this was a standard form of heating.

• **Large drawing room:** See the paintings of the emperor and empress in grand gala ballroom outfits from 1865.

• **The emperor's smoking room:** This is dedicated to the memory of the assassinated Emperor Maximillian of Mexico (bearded portrait, killed in 1867). A smoking room was necessary in the early 19th century, when smoking was newly fashionable but only for men and not in the presence of women.

• **The empress's bedroom and drawing room:** This was Sissy's, refurbished neo-rococo in 1854. She lived here until her death in 1898.

• **Sissy's dressing room:** This was the marital bedroom of the newlywed couple. The open bathroom door shows her huge copper tub. Servants worked two hours a day on Sissy's famous ankle-length hair here. She'd exercise on the wooden structure. While she had a tough time with people, she did fine with animals. Her favorite circus horses, Flick and Flock, prance on the wall.

• **The empress's large drawing room:** The room is painted with Mediterranean escapes, the 19th-century equivalent of travel posters. The statue is of Elisa, Napoleon's oldest sister (by the neoclassical master Canova).

• Around the corner is a room dedicated to the last emperor (Karl, ruled 1916–1918) and empress (Zita, lived 1892–1989). After the abdication of the last Habsburg, Zita lived in exile until her old age, then returned to Austria.

• **Reception room:** This has Gobelin wall hangings, a 1776 gift from Marie Antoinette and Louis XVI in Paris to their Vienese counterparts.

• **The dining room:** It's dinner time, and Franz Josef has called his large family together. The settings are of modest silver. Gold was saved for formal state dinners. Next to each namecard was a menu with the chef responsible for each dish. (Talk about pressure.) While the Hofburg had tableware for 4,000, feeding 3,000 was a typical day. The cellar was stocked with 60,000 bottles of wine—fit for an emperor. The kitchen was huge—50 birds could be roasted on the hand-driven spits at once.

• **Small salon:** The last room is dedicated to Franz Josef's first two heirs: Rudolf (his troubled son, who committed suicide in 1889) and Franz Ferdinand (his liberal nephew, assassinated in Sarajevo, 1914).

▲▲▲**Treasury**—The Weltliche und Geistliche Schatzkammer (secular and Religious Treasure Room) contains by far the best jewels on the Continent. Slip through the vault doors and reflect on the glitter of 21 rooms filled with scepters, swords, crowns, orbs, weighty robes, a 96-inch-tall and 500-year-old unicorn horn (or maybe the tusk of a narwhal), double-headed eagles, gowns, dangles, and gem-studded bangles. Remember that these were owned by the Holy Roman Emperor—a divine monarch.

Study the Throne Cradle (room 5). Napoleon's son was born in 1811 and made king of Rome. The little eagle at the foot is symbolically not yet able to fly, but glory-bound. "Glory" is the star with his dad's big "N" raised high.

The collection's highlight is the 10th-century crown of the Holy Roman Emperor (room 11). The imperial crown swirls with symbolism "proving" that the emperor is both holy and Roman. The jeweled arch over the top is reminiscent of the parade helmet of ancient Roman emperors whose successors the HRE claimed to be. The cross on top says that the HRE rules as Christ's representative on earth. King Solomon's portrait is Old Testament proof that kings can be wise and good. The crown's eight sides represent the celestial city of Jerusalem's eight gates. The jewels on the front panel symbolize the Twelve Apostles. The honorary 13th stone is the HRE.

Two cases in this room have jewels from the reign of Karl der Grosse (Charlemagne), the greatest ruler of medieval Europe. Notice Charlemagne modeling the crown in the tall painting adjacent. Room 12 features a painting of the coronation of Josef II in 1764, wearing the crown and royal garb you've just seen (80 AS, Wednesday–Monday 10:00–18:00, closed Tuesday, follow "Schatzkammer" signs through the black, red, and gold arch leading from the main courtyard into the Schweizerhof, tel. 01/533-7931). Take advantage of the free and helpful Art-Guide (deposit: passport or 500 AS). Point this infrared computer at display cases to get information.

▲**Neue Burg (New Palace)**—This last grand addition to the palace, from just before World War I, was built for Franz Ferdinand but never used. Its grand facade arches around Heldenplatz, or Hero's Square. Notice statues of the two great Austrian heroes on horseback: Prince Eugene of Savoy (who saved the city from the Turks) and Archduke Charles Schwartzenberg (first to beat Napoleon in a battle, breaking Nappy's image of invincibility and heralding the end of the Napoleonic age). The Neue Burg houses three small but fine museums (same ticket): an armory, historical musical instruments, and classical statuary from ancient Ephesus. The musical instruments are particularly entertaining, and free radio headsets (when they work) play appropriate music in each room. Wait for the German description to finish, and you might hear the instruments you're seeing. Stay tuned in, as graceful period music accompanies your wander through the neighboring halls of medieval weaponry—a killer collection of crossbows, swords, and armor. An added bonus is the chance to wander all alone among those royal Habsburg halls, stairways, and painted ceilings. Gavotte to the music down the royal stairs and out (30 AS for all three collections, Wednesday–Monday 10:00–18:00, closed Tuesday, almost no tourists).

More Sights—Vienna

▲**Lipizzaner Museum**—This is a must for horse lovers. This tidy new museum in the Renaissance Stallburg Palace shows the 400-year history of the famous riding school. Videos show the horses in action (on TVs throughout and in the basement theater—45-minute movie in German, but great horse footage). A highlight for many is the opportunity to view the stable from a museum window and actually see the famous white horses just sitting there looking common (50 AS, daily 9:00–18:00, Reitschulgasse 2 between Josefsplatz and Michaelerplatz, tel. 01/5264-18430). At the end of World War II, knowing that the Soviets were about to take control of Vienna, the U.S. General Patton ordered a raid on the stable to save the horses and insure the survival of their fine old bloodlines.

Seeing the Lipizzaner Stallions: Seats for performances of Vienna's prestigious Spanish Riding School are booked in advance, but standing room is usually available the same day (tickets 250–900 AS, standing room 200 AS, one or two shows per week April–June, September, October). Lucky for the masses, training sessions in a chandeliered Baroque hall are open to the public (100 AS at the door, Tuesday–Friday 10:00–12:00 roughly February–June,

September–December; occasional rehearsals with music on Saturdays are especially entertaining). The gang lines up early at Josefsplatz gate 2. Save money and avoid the wait by buying admission to the training session together with a ticket to the museum. Or, better yet, simply show up late. Tourists line up for hours to get in at 10:00. Anyone can just waltz in with no wait at all after 11:00. Almost no one stays for the full two hours—except for the horses.

▲**Augustinian Church**—Step into the nearby Augustinerkirche (on Josefsplatz), the church where the Habsburg weddings took place. Don't miss the exquisite Canova tomb (neoclassical, 1805) of Maria Theresa's favorite daughter, Maria Christina, with its incredibly sad white-marble procession. The church has the burial vault for the hearts of the Habsburgs (by appointment only).

▲▲**Kaisergruft, the Remains of the Habsburgs**—Visiting the imperial remains is not as easy as you might imagine. These original organ donors left their bodies—147 in all—in the Kaisergruft (Capuchin Crypt), their hearts in St. George Chapel in the Augustinian Church (church open daily, but to see the goods you'll have to talk to a priest; near the Hofburg, Augustinerstrasse 3), and their entrails in the crypt below St. Stephan's Cathedral. Don't tripe.

Upon entering the Kaisergruft (40 AS, daily 9:30–16:00, behind the Opera on Neuer Markt), buy the 5-AS map with a Habsburg family tree and a chart locating each coffin from the Capuchin brother at the door. The double coffin of Maria Theresa and her husband is worth a close look for its artwork. Don't miss the tomb of Franz Josef and—the latest addition— Empress Zita, buried in 1989.

Rather than chasing down all these body parts, remember that the magnificence of this city is the real remains of the Habsburgs. Pan up. Watch the clouds glide by the ornate gables of Vienna.

▲▲▲**Kunsthistorisches Museum**—This exciting museum across the Ring from the Hofburg Palace showcases the great Habsburg art collection—masterpieces by Dürer, Rubens, Titian, Raphael, and especially Brueghel. There's also a fine display of Egyptian, classical, and applied arts, including a divine golden salt bowl by Cellini. The museum sells a pamphlet on the top 21 paintings (20 AS) and offers English tours (30 AS, 1.5 hours, usually at 11:00 and 15:00 Tuesday–Sunday April–October). The paintings are hung on one floor (95 AS, higher depending on special exhibitions, Tuesday–Sunday 10:00–18:00, Thursday until 21:00, closed Monday, tel. 01/525-240).

Natural History Museum—In the twin building facing the art museum, you'll find moon rocks, dinosaur stuff, and the fist-sized Venus of Willendorf—at 30,000 years old, the world's oldest sex symbol, found in the Danube Valley (50 AS, Wednesday– Monday 9:00–18:00, closed Tuesday, off-season 9:00–15:00).

▲**Academy of Fine Arts**—This small but exciting collection includes works by Bosch, Botticelli, and Rubens; a Venice series by Guardi; and a self-portrait by 15-year-old Van Dyck (50 AS, Tuesday–Sunday 10:00–16:00, closed Monday, three blocks from the Opera at Schillerplatz 3, tel. 01/5881-6225).

KunstHausWien—This "make yourself at home" modern-art museum is a hit with lovers of modern art. It features the work of local painter/environmentalist Hundertwasser (90 AS, 45 AS on Monday, daily 10:00–19:00; 3, Weissgerberstrasse 13, nearest metro: U-3 Landstrasse, tel. 01/712-0491). Nearby, the one-with-nature Hundertwasserhaus (at Löwengasse and Kegelgasse) is a complex of 50 lived-in apartments. This was built in the 1980s as a breath of architectural fresh air in a city of boring blocky apartment complexes. It's not open to visitors but worth visiting for its fun-loving and colorful patchwork exterior, the Hundertwasser festival of shops across the street, and for the pleasure of annoying its residents.

▲**Jugendstil**—Vienna gave birth to its own curvaceous brand of Art Nouveau around the turn of the century: Jugendstil. The TI has a brochure laying out Vienna's 20th-century architecture. The best of Vienna's scattered Jugendstil sights: the Belvedere Palace collection; the clock on Höher Markt (which does a musical act at noon); the WC on the Graben; and the Karlsplatz subway stop, where you'll find the gilded-cabbage-domed gallery with the movement's slogan: "To each century its art and to art its liberty." Klimt, Wagner, and friends (who called themselves the Vienna Succession) first exhibited their "liberty style" art here in 1897.

▲**Belvedere Palace**—The elegant palace of Prince Eugene of Savoy (the still-much-appreciated conqueror of the Turks), and later home of Franz Ferdinand, houses the Austrian Gallery of 19th- and 20th-century art. Skip the lower palace and focus on the garden and the top floor of the upper palace (Oberes Belvedere) for a winning view of the city and a fine collection of Jugendstil art, Klimt, and Kokoschka (60 AS, Tuesday–Sunday 10:00–17:00, closed Monday, entrance at Prinz Eugen Strasse 27, tel. 01/795-570). Your ticket includes the Austrian Baroque and Gothic art in the Lower Palace.

▲▲▲**Schönbrunn Palace**—Only Schloss Schönbrunn, among Europe's palaces, rivals Versailles. Located 7 kilometers from the center, it was the Habsburgs' summer residence. It is big—1,441 rooms—but don't worry, only 40 rooms are shown to the public. (The families of 260 civil servants actually rent simple apartments in the rest of the palace.)

While the exterior is Baroque, the interior was finished under Maria Theresa in the let-them-eat-cake rococo style. The chandeliers are either of hand-carved wood with gold-leaf gilding or of Bohemian crystal. Thick walls hid the servants as they ran around stoking the ceramic stoves from the back, and so on. Most of the public rooms are decorated in neo-Baroque as they were under

Franz Josef (ruled 1848–1916). While World War II bombs rained on the city and the palace grounds, the palace itself took only one direct hit. Thankfully, that bomb, which crashed through three floors, including the sumptuous central ballroom, was a dud.

Choose between the Imperial Tour and the bigger Grand Tour. Both come with free headphones that describe the sights in English as you walk through the rooms on your own. The Imperial Tour covers 22 rooms (90 AS, 30 minutes, the Grand Palace rooms plus apartments of Franz Josef and Elisabeth). I'd recommend the Grand Tour, which covers those 22 rooms plus 18 more (120 AS, 45 minutes, adding the apartments of Maria Theresa). Optional guided tours do all 40 rooms in English (departing roughly every two hours, 25 AS extra). The headphones are so good I'd skip the tour.

Schönbrunn suffers from serious crowd problems. To avoid the long delays, simply make a reservation by telephone (01/8111-3239). You'll get an appointment time and ticket number. Upon arrival, go to the first desk reserved for group leaders, give your number, pick up your ticket and jump in ahead of the masses. If you show up without having called first, wait in line, buy your ticket, read the time listed, and wait until then to enter (which could be tomorrow). Kill waiting time in the gardens or coach museum (palace open daily 8:30–17:45—last entry 17:00, off-season until 17:15—last entry 16:30; take tram #58 from West-bahnhof or U-4 to Schönbrunn, tel. 01/8111-3239). Crowds are worst around 10:00 and on weekends; it's least crowded from 12:00–14:00 and after 16:00.

Coach Museum Wagenburg: The Schönbrunn coach museum is a 19th-century traffic jam of 50 impressive royal carriages and sleighs. Highlights include silly sedan chairs, the death-black hearse carriage (used for Franz Josef in 1916 and most recently for Empress Zita in 1989), and an extravagantly gilded imperial carriage—pulled by eight Cinderella horses (30 AS, daily 9:00–18:00, off-season 10:00–16:00 and closes on winter Mondays, 200 meters from the palace).

Palace Gardens: A stroll through the emperor's garden with countless commoners (after strolling through all the Habsburgs tucked neatly into their crypts) is a celebration of the natural (and necessary) evolution of civilization from autocracy into real democracy. We're doing good. The sculpted gardens (with a palm house, 45 AS, 9:30–18:00) lead past Europe's oldest zoo (Tier-garten, 100 AS, built by Maria Theresa's husband for the enter-tainment and education of the court in 1752) up to the Gloriette, a purely decorative monument celebrating an obscure Austrian military victory and offering a fine city view (and an expensive cup of coffee). The park is free and open until dusk.

Honorable Mention—There's much, much more. The city museum brochure lists everything. If you're into butterflies,

Esperanto, undertakers, tobacco, clowns, fire fighting, Freud, or the homes of dead composers, you'll find them all in Vienna. Several good museums that try very hard but are submerged in the greatness of Vienna include: **Historical Museum of the City of Vienna** (Tuesday–Sunday 9:00–16:30, Karlsplatz), **Folkloric Museum of Austria** (8, Laudongasse 15, tel. 01/438-905), and **Museum of Military History**, one of Europe's best if you like swords and shields (Heeregeschichtliches Museum; Saturday–Thursday 10:00–16:00, closed Friday; 3, Arsenal, Objekt 18). The **Albertina Museum**, with its great collection of sketches and graphic art, is closed for a few years. **Shopping:** The best-value shopping street, with more than 2,000 shops, is Mariahilfer Strasse. **Vienna Woods:** For a walk in the Vienna Woods, catch the U-4 subway to Heiligenstadt then bus #38A to Kahlenberg, where there are great city views and a café terrace overlooking the city. From there it's a peaceful 45-minute downhill hike to the *Heurigen* of Nussdorf or Grinzing to enjoy some wine.

Top People-Watching and Strolling Sights

▲**City Park**—Vienna's Stadtpark is a waltzing world of gardens, memorials to local musicians, ponds, peacocks, music in bandstands, and local people escaping the city. Notice the Jugendstil entry at the Stadtpark subway station. The Kursalon orchestra plays Strauss waltzes nightly in summer (see Music, below).

▲**Prater**—Vienna's sprawling amusement park tempts any visitor with its huge 220-foot-high, famous, and lazy Ferris wheel (*Riesenrad*), roller coaster, bumper cars, Lilliputian railroad, and endless eateries. This is a fun, goofy place to share the evening with thousands of Viennese (daily 9:00–24:00 in summer, U-Bahn: Praterstern). For a local-style family dinner, eat at Schweizerhaus (good food, great beer) or Wieselburger Bierinsel.

Sunbathing—Like most Europeans, the Austrians worship the sun. Their lavish swimming centers are as much for tanning as for swimming. For the best man-made island beach scene, head for the "Danube Sea," Vienna's 20 miles of beach along Danube Island (subway: Donauinsel).

▲**Naschmarkt**—Vienna's ye olde produce market bustles daily, near the Opera along Wienzeile Street. It's likably seedy and surrounded by sausage stands, Turkish *döner kebab* stalls, cafés, and theaters. Each Saturday it's infested by a huge flea market where, in olden days, locals would come to hire a monkey to pick little critters out of their hair (Monday–Friday 6:00–18:30, Saturday 6:00–17:00). For a picnic park, walk a block down Schleifmuhlgasse.

Summer Music Scene

Vienna is Europe's music capital. It's music *con brio* from October through June, with things reaching a symphonic climax during the

Vienna Festival each May and June. Sadly, in July and August, the Boys' Choir, the Opera, and many more music companies are—like you—on vacation. But Vienna hums year-round with live classical music. In the summer, you have these basic choices:

Touristy Mozart and Strauss Concerts—If the music comes to you, it's touristy—designed for flash-in-the-pan Mozart fans. Powdered-wig orchestra performances are given almost nightly in grand traditional settings (400–600 AS). Pesky wigged and powdered Mozarts peddle tickets in the streets with slick sales pitches about the magic of the venue and the quality of the musicians. Second-rate orchestras, clad in historic costumes, perform the greatest hits of Mozart and Strauss. While there's not a local person in the audience, the tourists generally enjoy the evening.

Strauss in the Kursalon—Two rival companies offer Strauss concerts inside the Kursalon, where the Waltz King himself directed wildly popular concerts 100 years ago. To accommodate antsy groups, concert tickets are sold in two sections: 20:00–21:00 and 21:30–22:30 (260 AS for one with a glass of wine, 490 AS for both, tel. 01/718-9666; for the other company, tel. 01/710-5580). Or pick up the brochures from racks all over town. Shows are a touristy mix of ballet, waltzing, 15-piece orchestra in wigs and old outfits, and a chance to get on the floor and waltz yourself. On balmy summer evenings, the concert moves into the romantic garden.

Serious Concerts—These events, including the Opera, are listed in the monthly *Programm* (available at the TI). Tickets run from 300 to 700 AS (plus a stiff 25 percent booking fee when booked in advance or through a box office like the one next to the TI behind the Opera). If you call a concert hall directly, they can advise you on the availability of (cheaper) tickets at the door. Vienna takes care of its starving artists (and tourists) by offering cheap standing-room tickets to top-notch music and opera. Locals are amazed at the stiff prices tourists pay to see otherwise affordable concerts.

Vienna's Summer of Music Festival assures that even from June through September you'll find lots of top-notch concerts, choirs, and symphonies (special *Klang Bogen* brochure at TI; tickets at the Wien Ticket pavilion off Kärntner Strasse next to the Opera House, or go directly to the location of the particular event, tel. 01/4000-8410 for information).

▲▲Vienna Boys' Choir—The boys sing (heard but not seen, from a high balcony) at Mass in the Imperial Chapel (Hofburgkapelle) of the Hofburg (entrance at Schweizerhof) at 9:15 on Sundays, except from July through mid-September. Seats must be reserved at least two months in advance (60–280 AS), but standing room inside is free and open to the first 60 who line up. Rather than line up early, you can simply swing by and stand in the narthex just outside, from where you can hear the boys and see the Mass on a TV monitor. Boys' Choir concerts (on stage in the Konzerthaus) are also given

Fridays at 15:30 in May, June, September, and October (390–430 AS, tel. 01/5880-4141, fax 011-431-587-1268 from the United States or write Reisebüro Mondial, Faulmanngasse 4, 1040 Wien). They're nice kids but, for my taste, not worth all the commotion.

Vienna's Cafés and Wine Gardens

▲**Viennese Coffeehouse**—In Vienna the living room is down the street at the neighborhood coffeehouse. This tradition is just another example of the Viennese expertise in good living. Each of Vienna's many long-established (and sometimes even legendary) coffeehouses has its individual character (and characters). They offer newspapers, pastries, sofas, elegance, a smoky ambience, and a "take all the time you want" charm for the price of a cup of coffee. You may want to order *malange* (with a little milk) rather than *schwarzer* (black).

My favorites are: **Café Hawelka**, with a rumpled, "brooding Trotsky" atmosphere, paintings on the walls by struggling artists who couldn't pay, a saloon-wood flavor, chalkboard menu, smoked velvet couches, an international selection of newspapers, and a phone that rings for regulars (8:00–2:00, Sunday from 16:00, closed Tuesday, Dorotheergasse 6, just off the Graben); crowded **Café Central**, with Jugendstil decor and great *Apfelstrudel* (8:00–20:00, closed Sunday, Herrengasse 14); the Jugendstil **Café Sperl**, dating from 1880 (7:00–23:00, closed Sunday in summer, Gumpendorfer 11, just off Naschmarkt); and the basic, untouristy **Café Ritter** (daily 8:00–20:00, Mariahilfer Strasse 73, at the Neubaugasse subway stop near several of my recommended hotels).

▲**Wine Gardens**—The *Heurige* is a uniquely Viennese institution celebrating the *Heurige*, or new wine. It all started when the Habsburgs let Vienna's vintners sell their own wine tax-free for 300 days a year. Several hundred families opened *Heurigen* (wine-garden restaurants) clustered around the edge of Vienna, and a tradition was born. Today they do their best to maintain their old-village atmosphere, serving the homemade new wine (the last vintage, until November 11) with light meals and strolling musicians. For a *Heurige* evening, rather than go to a particular place, tram to the wine-garden district of your choice and wander around, choosing the place with the best ambience.

Of the many *Heurige* suburbs, **Grinzing** (tram #38 or #38A) is the most famous and lively—but it comes with too many tour buses. **Nussdorf** is less touristy but still characteristic and popular with locals (two fine places are right at the end of tram D). Pfarrplatz has many decent spots. **Beethoven's home** in Heiligenstadt comes with crowds and live music (Pfarrplatz, tram #38A or #37 and a 10-minute walk, tel. 01/371-287). While Beethoven lived here in 1817 (to be near a spa he hoped would cure his worsening deafness), he composed his Sixth Symphony (*Pastoral*). These suburbs are all within a 15-minute stroll of each other.

Gumpoldskirchen is a small medieval village farther outside of Vienna with more *Heurige* ambience than tourists. Ride the commuter train from the Opera to Gumpoldskirchen and you'll find plenty of places to choose from.

At any *Heurige*, fill your plate at a self-serve cold-cut buffet (75–125 AS for dinner). Waitresses will then take your wine order (30 AS per quarter-liter). Many locals claim it takes several years of practice to distinguish between *Heurige* and vinegar. For a near-*Heurige* experience right downtown, drop by Gigerl Stadtheuriger (see Eating, below).

Nightlife
If old music or new wine isn't your thing, Vienna has plenty of alternatives. For an up-to-date rundown on fun after dark, get the TI's free *Young Vienna Scene* booklet. An area known as the "Bermuda Dreieck" (Triangle), north of the cathedral between Rotenturmstrasse and Judengasse, is the hot local nightspot, with lots of classy pubs, or *Beisl* (such as Krah Krah, Salzamt, and Kitch, and Bitter) and popular music spots. On a balmy summer evening, the most lively scene is at Danube Island.

Sleeping in Vienna
(12 AS = about $1, tel. code: 01)
Sleep Code: **S** = Single, **D** = Double/Twin, **T** = Triple, **Q** = Quad, **b** = bathroom, **t** = toilet only, **s** = shower only, **CC** = Credit Card (Visa, MasterCard, Amex). English is spoken at each place.

Call accommodations a few days in advance. Most places will hold a room without a deposit if you promise to arrive before 17:00. My recommendations stretch mainly along the likeable Mariahilfer Strasse from the Westbahnhof (West Station) to the town center. Unless otherwise noted, prices include a continental breakfast. Street addresses start with the district. Postal code is 1XX0, with XX being the district.

Sleeping Outside the Ring, along Mariahilfer Strasse
Lively Mariahilfer Strasse connects the West Station with the center. The U-3 subway line, starting at the Westbahnhof, goes down Mariahilfer Strasse to the cathedral. The very Viennese Mariahilfer Strasse is a comfortable and vibrant area filled with local shops and cafés. Most are within a few steps of the subway station just one or two stops from the West Bahnhof. The first three are relatively luxurious splurges followed by you-get-what-you-pay-for good budget values.

Pension Mariahilf is a four-star place offering a clean aristocratic air in an affordable and cozy pension package. Its 12 rooms are spacious and feel new, but with a Jugendstil flair. With four

Vienna: Hotels Outside The Ring

❶ FUNFHAUS	❽ NEUSTIFTGASSE
❷ BUDAI	❾ BELIEVE IT OR...
❸ LINDENHOF	❿ WILD
❹ HARGITA	⓫ ANDREAS
❺ ASTRON SUITE	⓬ IBIS WIEN
❻ QUISISANA	⓭ MARIAHILF
❼ HILDE WOLF	

stars, everything's done right—the latest American magazines and even free Mozart Balls at the reception desk (Sb-800 AS, Db-1,300 AS, Tb-1,700 AS, including an all-you-can eat breakfast, at U-3 Neubaugasse station, Mariahilfer Strasse 49, tel. 01/586-1781, fax 01/5861-78122, warmly run by Frau and Herr Ender).

Hotel Ibis Wien, a modern highrise hotel with American charm, is ideal for anyone tired of quaint old Europe. Its 340 cookie-cutter rooms are bright, comfortable, and modern, with all the conveniences. It has a friendly, spirited staff, lots of smoke-free rooms, some easy-access rooms and air conditioning—rare in this price range (Sb-890 AS, Db-1,090 AS, Tb-1,290 AS, breakfast extra, CC:VMA, elevator, three blocks from the Westbahnhof and metro station at Mariahilfer Gürtel 22–24, A-1060 Wien, tel. 01/59998, fax 01/597-9090, e-mail: mariahilf@hotel-ibis.co.at).

Astron Suite Hotel Wien/Atterseehaus, a new business- and family-friendly place, has 54 suites. Each has a living room, two TVs, bathroom, desk, and kitchenette. Db-1,880 AS, two kids free, breakfast extra, CC:VMA, non-smoking rooms, elevator, at U-3 Sieglergasse subway stop, Mariahilferstrasse 78, A-1070 Wien, tel. 01/5254-6000, fax 01/5254-60015, e-mail: wienattersee-haus@astron-hotels.de). Nearby they have a bigger suite hotel (same prices, Mariahilferstrasse 32, tel. 01/521-720).

Privatzimmer F. Kaled is bright, airy, and homey (S-400 AS Sb-450 AS, D-550 AS, Db-650 AS, T-800 AS, skip breakfast, reserve with CC but pay cash, TVs with CNN; 7, Lindengasse 42, 1070 Wien, near Neubaugasse, tel. & fax 01/523-9013).

Pension Lindenhof is worn but clean, filled with plants, and run with Bulgarian and Armenian warmth (S-370 AS, Sb-470 AS, D-620 AS, Db-840 AS, cheaper in winter, hall showers-20 AS, 7, Lindengasse 4, 1070 Wien, take U-3 Neubaugasse to Stiftgasse, tel. 01/523-0498, fax 01/523-7362).

Pension Hargita, with 19 generally small, bright, and tidy rooms (mostly twins), is handy—right at the U-3 Zieglergasse stop—and next to a sex shop (S-400 AS, Ss-450 AS, D-600 AS, Ds-700 AS, Db-800 AS, Ts-850 AS, Tb-1,050 AS, Qb-1,100 AS, breakfast-40 AS, cheaper for longer stays off-season, U-Bahn: Zieglergasse, on corner of Mariahilfer Strasse and Andreasgasse at 7, Andreasgasse 1, 1070 Wien, tel. 01/526-1928, fax 01/526-0492).

Budai Ildiko has high-ceilinged rooms, classy furnishings, and a warm, homey feeling (three rooms, S-350 AS, D-560 AS, T-820 AS, Q-1,050 AS, no breakfast but free coffee, laundry-20 AS; 7, Lindengasse 39/5, 1070 Wien, tel. & fax 01/526-2595, run by a charming Hungarian woman, Frau Budai SE).

Privatzimmer Hilde Wolf is another homey place one floor above an ugly entry, with four huge rooms like old libraries. Hilde loves her work, will do your laundry if you stay two nights, and even offers to baby-sit if traveling parents need a break. From the Westbahnhof, take tram #6 or #18 five stops to Eichenstrasse, then tram #62 six stops to Paulanergasse. For a real home in Vienna, unpack here (S-450 AS, D-650 AS, T-955 AS, Q-1,225 AS, with a big, friendly, family-style breakfast, prices through 1999; three blocks off Naschmarkt near U-2 Karlsplatz, 4, Schleifmühlgasse 7, 1040 Vienna, tel. 01/586-5103, reserve by phone and CC; if you can't make it, call to cancel).

Pension Quisisana is tired and ramshackle, but cheap and sleepable for vagabonds (S-330 AS, Ss-380 AS, D-520 AS, Ds-600–640 AS, Db-700–740 AS, third person-260 AS, 6, Windmuhl-gasse 6, 1060 Wien, tel. 01/587-7155, fax 01/587-715-633).

Pension Funfhaus is big, clean, stark, and quiet. Although the neighborhood is rundown, this place is a great value (S-390 AS, Sb-470 AS, D-570 AS, Db-650 AS, T-850 AS, Tb-920 AS, two-bedroom apartments for four-1,130 AS, closed mid-November–February; 15, Sperrgasse 12, 1150 Wien, tel. 01/892-3545 or

01/892-0286, fax 01/892-0460, Frau Susi Tersch SE). Half the rooms are in the fine main building and half are in the annex, which has good rooms but is near the train tracks and a bit scary on the street at night. From the station, ride tram #52 or #58 two stops or walk seven blocks away from downtown on Mariahilfer Strasse, to Sperrgasse.

Sleeping Six Blocks North of Mariahilfer Strasse

Jugendherbergen Neustiftgasse is a cheery and well-run youth hostel. They'll hold rooms until 16:00, have a lock-out period from 9:00–16:00, a 1:00 curfew, and 65-AS meals (805 AS per person plus 40 AS for non-members, includes sheets and breakfast, three- to six-bed rooms; 7, Myrthengasse 7, 1070 Wien, tel. 01/523-6316, fax 01/523-5849, e-mail: oejhv-wien-jgh-neustiftg. @oejhv.or.at). They try to accommodate couples and families with private rooms but can make no promises.

   Believe It or Not is across the street—a friendly and basic place with two big coed rooms for up to ten travelers under age 30. It's locked up from 10:30 to 12:30, has kitchen facilities, and no curfew (160 AS per bed, 110 AS November–Easter; 7, Myrthengasse 10, no sign, ring apt. #14, tel. 01/526-4658, run by Gosha).

   Pension Wild has 14 decent rooms (though some have a stale smell) and a good, keep-it-simple-and-affordable attitude (S-450 AS, Ss-550 AS, D-590 AS, Ds-690 AS, Db-890 AS, T-860 AS, Ts-960 AS, reserve with CC:VMA but pay cash, elevator, kitchen privileges, near U-2 Rathaus; 8, Langegasse 10, 1080 Vienna, tel. 01/406-5174, fax 01/402-2168).

   Pension Andreas is past-its-prime classy and quiet, but a bit smoky (40 rooms, St-690 AS, Ds-850 AS, Db-930 AS, big Db-990 AS, big-family room deals, elevator, CC:VMA, near U-2 Rathaus at 8, Schlösselgasse 11, 1080 Wien, tel. 01/405-3488, fax 01/4053-48850).

Sleeping within the Ring, in the Old City Center

These places offer less room per schilling but are comfortable and right in the town center, with elevators and near the subway. The first four are nearly in the shadow of St. Stephan's Cathedral, on or near the Graben, where the elegance of Old Vienna strums happily over the cobbles. The next two listings are near the Opera (subway: Karlsplatz) just off the famous Kärntner Strasse, near the tourist office and five minutes from the cathedral. If you can afford it, staying here gives you the best classy Vienna experience. The last two are past the cathedral, closer to the Danube Canal.

   At **Pension Nossek**, an elevator takes you above any street noise into Frau Bernad's and Frau Gundolf's world, where the children seem to be placed among the lace and flowers by an interior designer. Right on the wonderful Graben, this is the best

Hotels in Central Vienna

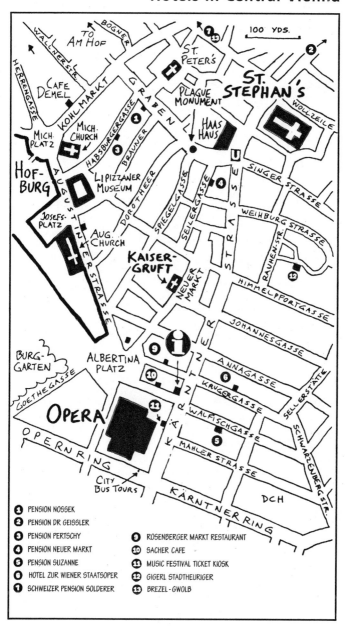

1 PENSION NOSSEK
2 PENSION DR GEISSLER
3 PENSION PERTSCHY
4 PENSION NEUER MARKT
5 PENSION SUZANNE
6 HOTEL ZUR WIENER STAATSOPER
7 SCHWEIZER PENSION SOLDERER
9 ROSENBERGER MARKT RESTAURANT
10 SACHER CAFE
11 MUSIC FESTIVAL TICKET KIOSK
12 GIGERL STADTHEURIGER
13 BREZEL - GWOLB

value of these first three (Ss-700 AS, Sb-850 AS, small Db-1,200 AS, big Db-1,300 AS, apartment-1,600 AS; 1, Graben 17, tel. 01/5337-0410, fax 01/535-3646).

Pension Pertschy is bigger and more hotelesque than the others. Its big rooms are huge (ask to see a couple), and those on the courtyard are quietest (Sb-800 AS, Db-1,180–1,440 AS depending on size, apartments with kitchenette for the same price—just ask, cheaper off-season, extra person-300 AS, CC:VM; 1, Habsburgergasse 5, tel. 01/53449, fax 01/534-4949).

Pension Neuer Markt has narrow halls caused by a mickey-mouse cramming on of bathrooms to each room, but the rooms are comfy and pleasant and the location is great (Ds-1,150 AS, Dt-950 AS, Db-1,400 AS, prices soft when slow, CC:VMA; 1, Seiler-gasse 9, 1010 Wien, tel. 01/512-2316, fax 01/513-9105, Edith SE).

Pension Suzanne, as Baroque and doily as you'll find in this price range, is wonderfully located a few yards from the Opera. Suzanne is quiet, with pink elegance bouncing on every bed (Sb-850–880 AS, Db-1,050–1,300 AS, third person-500 AS, huge discounts in the winter, reserve with CC but cash preferred; a block from the Opera, U-Bahn to Karlsplatz—Opera exit, 1, Walfis-chgasse 4, 1010 Wien, tel. 01/513-2507, fax 01/513-2500, expertly run by Frau Strafinger).

Hotel zur Wiener Staatsoper is quiet, rich, and hotelesque. Its smallish rooms come with high ceilings, chandeliers, and fancy carpets on parquet floors—a good value for this locale and ideal for people whose hotel taste is a cut above mine (Sb-1,100 AS, Db-1,600 AS, Tb-1,900 AS, family deals, CC:VMA; 1, a block from the Opera at Krugerstrasse 11, 1010 Wien, tel. 01/513-1274, fax 01/5131-27415).

Schweizer Pension Solderer, in the family for three generations, is warmly run by two friendly sisters, Monica and Anita. Enjoy the homey feel, 11 big, comfortable rooms, parquet floors, and lots of tourist info (S-450 AS, Ss-700 AS, Sb-800 AS, D-700 AS, Ds-860 AS, Db-980 AS, elevator, laundry-150 AS, non-smoking, Heinrichsgasse 2, 1010 Wien; from West station, take U-3 to Volkstheater, then U-2 to Schottenring; tel. 01/533-8156, fax 01/535-6469).

Pension Dr. Geissler has basic rooms in the center (S-450–580 AS, Sb-650–850 AS, D-600–780 AS, Ds-620–980 AS, Db-800–1,180 AS, prices vary with season, CC:VMA; 1, Postgasse 14, 1010 Wien; U-Bahn: Schwedenplatz; tel. 01/533-2803, fax 01/533-2635).

Eating in Vienna

The Viennese appreciate the fine points of life, and right up there with the waltz is eating. The city has many atmospheric restaurants. As you ponder the Slavic and eastern European specialties on menus, remember that Vienna's diverse empire may be gone, but its flavor lingers.

On nearly every corner, you can find a colorful *Beisl* (Viennese tavern) filled with poetry teachers and their students, couples loving without touching, housewives on their way home from cello lessons, and waiters who thoroughly enjoy serving hearty food and good drink at an affordable price. Ask at your hotel for a good *Beisl*.

All my recommended eateries are within a five-minute walk of the cathedral.

Gigerl Stadtheuriger offers a near-*Heurige* experience (a la Grinzing, see above) without leaving the center. Just point to what looks good. Food is sold by the weight (cheese and cold meats cost about 35 AS/100 grams, salads are about 15 AS/100 grams—price sheet is posted: 10 dag = 100 grams). They also have menu entrees, along with spinach strudel, quiche, *Apfelstrudel,* and, of course, casks of new and local wines. Meals run from 100 AS to 150 AS (daily 11:00–24:00, indoor/outdoor seating, behind cathedral, a block off Kärntner Strasse, a few cobbles off Rauhensteingasse on Blumenstock, tel. 01/513-4431).

Brezel-Gwölb, a wonderfully atmospheric wine cellar with outdoor dining on a quiet square, serves delicious light meals, fine *Krautsuppe,* and old-fashioned local dishes. It's ideal for a romantic late-night glass of wine (daily 11:30–1:00, Ledererhof 9, take Drahtgasse off Am Hof, tel. 01/533-8811). Around the corner, **Zum Scherer Sitz u. Stehbeisl** is just as untouristy, with indoor or outdoor seating, a soothing woody atmosphere, intriguing decor, and local specialties (Monday–Saturday 11:00–1:00, Sunday 17:00–24:00, Judenplatz 7, near Am Hof).

These **wine cellars** are fun and touristic but typical, in the old center of town, with reasonable prices and lots of smoke. **Melker Stiftskeller**, the least touristy, is a *Stadtheurige* in a deep and rustic cellar with hearty, inexpensive meals and new wine (Monday–Saturday 17:00–24:00, closed Sunday, halfway between Am Hof and the Schottentor subway stop at Schottengasse 3, tel. 01/533-5530). Closer to the Graben, **Stadtbeisl** offers a good mix of value, local cuisine, and atmosphere (open nightly, Naglergasse 21, tel. 01/533-3507). **Zu den Drei Hacken** is famous for its local specialties (Monday–Friday 9:00–24:00, Saturday 10:00–24:00, closed Sunday, indoor/outdoor seating, CC:VA, Singerstrasse 28). The touristy **Pürstner** restaurant is pleasantly drenched in Old World atmosphere but doesn't encourage lingering (daily 11:00–24:00, indoor/outdoor seating, 150-AS meals, a block away at Riemergasse 10, tel. 01/512-6357). **Augustinerkeller** is fun, reasonably priced, and touristy with live music nightly (daily 10:00–24:00, next to the Opera under the Albertina Museum on Augustinerstrasse).

For a fast, light, and central lunch, **Rosenberger Markt Restaurant,** a popular highway chain, has an elegant super-branch a block toward the cathedral from the Opera. This place, while not cheap, is brilliant: friendly and efficient, with special theme rooms to dine in, offering a fresh, smoke-free, and healthy cornucopia of food and drink (daily 11:00–23:00, lots of fruits, vegetables, fresh-squeezed juices, just off Kärntner Strasse at Maysedergasse 2, ride the glass elevator downstairs). You can stack a small salad or veggie plate into the tower of gobble for 30 AS.

Buffet Trzesniewski is justly famous for its elegant and cheap finger sandwiches (9 AS) and small beers (9 AS). Three sandwiches and a *kleines Bier* (*Pfiff*) make a fun, light lunch (Monday–Friday 8:30–19:30, Saturday 9:00–17:00, just off the Graben, nearly across from the brooding Café Hawelka, on Dorotheergasse).

Naschmarkt, five minutes beyond the Opera, is Vienna's best Old World market, with plenty of fresh produce, cheap local-style eateries, cafés, and *döner kebab* and sausage stands (Monday–Friday 6:00–18:30, Saturday until 17:00, closed Sunday).

Wherever you're eating, some vocabulary will help. Try the *grüner Veltliner* (dry white wine, any time), *Traubenmost* (a heavenly grape juice on the verge of wine, autumn only, sometimes just called *Most*), and *Sturm* (barely fermented *Most*, autumn only). The local red wine (called *Portuguese*) is pretty good. Since the Austrian wine is often very sweet, remember the word *Trocken* (dry). You can order your wine by the *Viertel* (quarter-liter) or *Achtel* (eighth-liter). Beer comes in a *Krugel* (.5 liter) or *Seidel* (.3 liter).

Transportation Connections—Vienna

Vienna has two main train stations: the Westbahnhof, serving Munich, Salzburg, Melk in Switzerland, and Budapest; and the Südbahnhof, serving Italy, Budapest, and Prague. The third station, Franz Josefs, serves Krems and the Danube Valley (but Melk is served by the Westbahnhof). Subway line U-3 connects the Westbahnhof with the center, tram D takes you from the Südbahnhof and from the Franz Josefs to downtown, and tram #18 connects West and South Stations. Train info: tel. 01/1717.

By train to: Melk (hrly, 75 min), **Krems** (10/day, 1 hr), **Salzburg** (hrly, 3 hrs), **Innsbruck** (3/day, 5.5 hrs), **Budapest** (3/day, 3 hrs), **Prague** (4/day, 5.5 hrs), **Munich** (10/day, 4.5 hrs), **Berlin** (2/day 14 hrs), **Zurich** (4/day, 9 hrs), **Rome** (3/day, 14 hrs), **Venice** (6/day, 9 hrs), **Frankfurt** (7/day, 7.5 hrs), **Amsterdam** (2/day, 14 hrs).

To eastern Europe: Vienna is the springboard for a quick trip to Prague and Budapest—three hours by train from Budapest (360 AS, 580 AS round-trip, free with Eurail) and 5.5 hours from Prague (488 AS one-way, 976 AS round-trip, 652 AS with Eurail). Visas are not required. Purchase tickets at most travel agencies (such as the Austrian National Travel Office at Operngasse 3–5, tel. 01/588-6238, or Intropa, next to the TI on Kärntner Strasse).

DANUBE VALLEY

The Danube is at its romantic best just west of Vienna. Mix a cruise with a bike ride through the Danube's Wachau Valley, lined with ruined castles, beautiful abbeys, small towns, and vineyard upon vineyard. After touring the glorious abbey of Melk, douse your warm, fairy-tale glow with a bucket of Hitler at the Mauthausen concentration camp.

Planning Your Time

For a day trip from Vienna, catch the early train to Melk, tour the abbey, eat lunch and split the afternoon trip along the river from Melk to Krems by boat and rented bike. From Krems, catch the train back to Vienna. Remember, the boat goes faster downstream (east). While this region is a logical day trip from Vienna, with good train connections to both Krems and Melk, spending a night in Melk is a winning idea. Melk is on the main Munich/Salzburg/Vienna train line. Mauthausen, farther away, should be seen en route to or from Vienna. On a three-week trip through Germany, Austria, and Switzerland, I'd see only one concentration camp. Mauthausen is more powerful than the more convenient Dachau.

Cruising the Danube

By car, bike, or boat, the 38-kilometer stretch of the Danube between Krems and Melk is as pretty as they come. You'll cruise along Danube's wine road, seeing wine gardens all along the river. Those hanging out a wreath of straw or greenery are inviting you in to taste. St. Michael has a small wine garden and an old tower you can climb for a view. In local slang, someone who's feeling his wine is "blue." Blue Danube?

By Boat: Boats run between Krems and Melk (3/day in each

Danube Valley

direction, April–October, 170 AS for a day ticket), departing from Melk at 11:00, 13:50, and 16:15 (1.5-hour ride downstream). Boats depart from Krems at 10:15, 13:00, and 15:45 (because of the 6-knot flow of the Donau, the same ride upstream takes three hours). The 16:15 departure from Melk and the 15:45 departure from Krems require an easy transfer in Spitz; the rest are direct. To confirm these times, call the DDSG boat company office (tel. 01/58880 in Vienna), the Melk TI (tel. 02752/523-070), or Krems TI (tel. 02732/82676). On weekends, some boats start or end in Vienna if you'd like a longer cruise (April–October, tel. 01/58880 in Vienna).

By Bike: There's a bike path all the way. Rent a bike at any train station (90 AS with a railpass or ticket, otherwise 150 AS). For 40 AS extra, you can drop off your bike at a different train station. It's a three-hour pedal from Krems to Melk. Pedal along the north bank (just off the main road; the bike-in-a-red-border signs mean "no biking"), following the TI's *Cycle Track* brochure. If you prefer, you can go half and half by cruising to Spitz and then hopping on a bike (or vice versa).

By Bus: The bus between Melk and Krems is a good budget or rainy day-alternative to the boat (70 AS, catch bus at train station, buy ticket on bus, for best views sit on the driver's side from Melk to Krems, non-driver's side from Krems to Melk).

By Train: Trains for Krems depart about hourly from Vienna's Franz Josef Bahnhof. For an easier departure (or return), consider starting or ending your train ride at Spittelau (the train's first stop after the Franz Josef Bahnhof) instead of the Bahnhof. Spittelau has a U-Bahn station and Franz Josef Bahnhof does not. Melk is accessed from Vienna's Westbahnhof.

Sights—The Danube Valley

Krems—This is a gem of a town. From the boat dock, walk a few blocks to the TI (pick up a town map). Then stroll the traffic-free, shopper's-wonderland old town. If nothing else, it's a pleasant 30-minute walk from the dock to the train station (Krems-Vienna trains: hrly, 60 min). The local TI can find you a bed in a private home (D-450 AS, Db-600 AS) if you decide to side-trip into Vienna from this small-town alternative (TI open Monday–Friday 9:00–19:00, weekends 10:00–12:00, 13:00–19:00, less off-season, tel. 02732/82676). Melanie Stasny Gästezimmer is a super place to stay (300 AS per person in Db, Tb, or Qb, friendly with a proud vineyard and shareful wine cellar, 300 meters from dock at Steiner Landstrasse 22, tel. 02732/82843). When they're full, they send travelers to their son's place down the street.

Durnstein—This touristic flypaper lures hordes of visitors with its traffic-free quaintness and its one claim to fame (and fortune): Richard the Lion-Hearted was imprisoned here in 1193. You can probably sleep in his bedroom.

Willendorf—Known among art buffs as the town where the oldest piece of European art was found. A few blocks off the river (follow the signs to "Venus") you can see the monument where the well-endowed, 30,000-year-old fertility symbol, the Venus of Willendorf, was discovered. (The six-inch-tall original is now in Vienna's Natural History Museum.)

▲Melk—Sleepy and elegant under its huge abbey that seems to police the Danube, the town of Melk offers a pleasant stop. The TI, near the traffic-free main square, has info on nearby castles and bike rides along the river (Monday–Saturday 9:00–19:00, Sunday 10:00–14:00, less off-season, good picnic garden with WC behind TI, tel. 02752/523-070).

▲▲Melk Abbey (Benediktinerstift)—The newly restored abbey beaming proudly over the Danube Valley is one of Europe's great sights. The Abbey Church, with its 200-foot-tall dome and symmetrical towers, dominates the complex of abbey buildings. Freshly painted and gilded throughout, it's a Baroque dream, a lily alone. Established as a fortified Benedictine abbey in the 11th century, it was destroyed by fire. What you see today is from the 18th century. Napoleon headquartered here in 1805 and 1809. Its lavish library, palace rooms, church, and the great Danube view from the balcony are highlights of the one-hour tour. Modern frescoes in the courtyard make the point that the abbey is a living institution.

After a grand restoration project (1978–1995), the abbey was completed in time to celebrate the 1996 celebration of the 1,000th anniversary of the first reference to a country named Österreich (Austria).

German tours are available constantly. English tours are offered May through September, daily at 14:55 (65 AS, 80 AS with a tour, daily 9:00–18:00, last entry 17:00, closed in winter, tel. 02752/231-2232). Call to see if you can join a scheduled tour or establish one. They'll schedule an English tour with a nucleus of eight people, then let others join in (400 AS extra for the guide).

It's worth the trouble. The abbey garden, café, and charming village below make waiting for a tour pleasant.

Sleeping in Melk
(12 AS = about $1, tel. code: 02752, zip code: 3390)
Sleep Code: **S** = Single, **D** = Double/Twin, **T** = Triple, **Q** = Quad, **b** = bathroom, **t** = toilet only, **s** = shower only, **CC** = Credit Card **(V**isa, **M**asterCard, **A**mex). Breakfast is included, and at least some English is spoken.

Melk makes a fine overnight stop. **Hotel Fürst** is a fluffy, creaky old place with 15 rooms, run by the Madar family, right on the traffic-free main square with a fountain out your door and the abbey hovering overhead (Db-700–750 AS, Rathausplatz 3-5, tel. 02752/52343, fax 02752/523-434). **Gasthof Goldener Stern**, traditional with a barn-flavored elegance, is also quiet and cozy on a pedestrian street in the center (D-520 AS, cheaper three- to five-bed rooms, Sterngasse 17, tel. 02752/52214, fax 02752/522-144). **Maria Atzmuller** runs a fine and friendly B&B a mile from the abbey (D-400 AS, Kreuzackerstrasse 32, tel. 02752/52163). **Pension Wachau**, near the Autobahn exit, will pick you up at the station (Sb-480 AS, Db-730 AS, Wachberg 157, tel. 02752/52531, fax 02572/525-3113, some English spoken). The modern **hostel** is a few minutes' walk from the station (175-AS beds in quads with sheets and breakfast, easy-going about membership, tel. 02752/52681).

Transportation Connections—Melk
Melk is on the Autobahn and the Salzburg-Vienna train line.
    By train to: Vienna's Westbahnhof (hrly, 1 hr), **Salzburg** (hrly, 2 hrs), **Mauthausen** (nearly hrly, 75 min, transfer at St. Valentin).

MAUTHAUSEN CONCENTRATION CAMP
More powerful and less tourist-oriented than Dachau, this slave-labor and death camp functioned from 1938 to 1945 for the exploitation and extermination of Hitler's opponents. More than half of its 206,000 quarry-working prisoners were killed here. Mauthausen is set in a strangely beautiful setting next to the Danube, in a now still and overgrown quarry (25 AS, daily 8:00-18:00, last entry at 17:00, closes mid-December–January and at 16:00 off-season, tel. 07238/2269 or 07238/3696, TI tel. 07238/3860). Leave your passport to borrow a free tape-recorded 20-minute tour.

    The camp barracks house a worthwhile museum at the far end of the camp on the right (some English labels, but the 35-AS English guidebook gives a complete translation). See the graphic 45-minute movie shown at the top of each hour. Ask for an English showing; if necessary, gather a group of English-speaking visitors. If it's running, just slip in.

The most emotionally moving rooms (described in English) and the gas chamber are downstairs. The spirits of the victims of these horrors can still be felt. Outside the camp each victim's country has erected a gripping memorial. Many yellowed photos sport fresh flowers. Walk to the barbed-wire memorial overlooking the quarry and the "stairway of death."

By visiting a concentration camp and putting ourselves through this emotional wringer, we heed and respect the fervent wish of the victims of this fascism—that we "never forget." Many people forget by choosing not to know.

Sleeping in Enns, near Mauthausen

Hotel am Limes, just off the Autobahn in Enns, has comfortable rooms and an Italian/Austrian restaurant (Sb-500 AS, Db-750 AS, Stadlgasse 2b, tel. 07223/6401, fax 07223/640-164, Reinhard SE). Enns is about 6 km southwest of Mauthausen and 100 km west of Vienna.

Transportation Connections—Mauthausen

Most trains stop at St. Valentin, midway between Salzburg and Vienna, where sporadic trains make the 15-minute ride to the Mauthausen station (get map from station attendant, camp is #9, baggage check-30 AS). To get to the camp, which is 3 miles from the Mauthausen station, you can hike (one hour), bike (90-AS rental at station with railpass or ticket, 150 AS without), or take a mini-bus taxi (100 AS, join other tourists, tel. 07238/2439). Train info: 07238/2207. You can reach Manthausen direct from Vienna's Franz Josef Bahnhof or faster from the Westbahnhof with a transfer in St. Valentin. **St. Valentin by train to: Salzburg** (hrly, 2 hrs), **Vienna** (hrly, 2 hrs).

Route Tips for Drivers

Hallstatt to Vienna, via Mauthausen, Melk, and Wachau Valley (210 miles): Leave Hallstatt early. Follow scenic Route 145 through Gmunden to the Autobahn and head east. After Linz, take exit #155, Enns, and follow Mauthausen signs (8 km from the freeway). Go through Mauthausen town, and follow signs to "Ehemaliges KZ-Lager." From Mauthausen, the speedy route is the Autobahn to Melk, but the curvy, scenic Route 3 along the river is worth the nausea. Cross the bridge and follow the signs, not into town ("Zentrum Melk"), but to "Stift Melk," the Benediktinerstift (Benedictine Abbey).

The most scenic stretch of the Donau is the Wachau Valley, lying between Melk and Krems. From Melk (get a Vienna map at the TI), cross the river again (signs to Donaubrucke) and stay on Route 3. After Krems, it hits the Autobahn (A-22), and you'll barrel right into Vienna's traffic. (See Vienna chapter for details.)

SALZBURG, SALZKAMMERGUT, AND WEST AUSTRIA

Enjoy the sights and sounds of Salzburg, Mozart's hometown, then commune with nature in the Salzkammergut, Austria's *Sound of Music* country. Amid hills alive with the S.O.M., you'll find the tiny town of Hallstatt, as pretty as a postcard (and not much bigger). Farther west, the Golden Roof of Innsbruck glitters—but you'll strike it rich in neighboring Hall, which has twice the charm and none of the tourist crowds.

SALZBURG

With a well-preserved old town, gardens, churches, and lush surroundings, set under Europe's biggest intact medieval castle, its river adding an almost seaside ambience, Salzburg is forever smiling to the tunes of Mozart and *The Sound of Music*.

This town knows how to be popular. Eight million tourists crawl its cobbles each year. That's a lot of Mozart balls. But all that popularity has led to a glut of businesses hoping to catch the tourist dollar, and an almost desperate greediness. The town's creative energy is invested in ways to soak the tourist rather than share its rich cultural heritage. Salzburg makes for a pleasant visit, but for most, a day is plenty. With a few exceptions, it's hard to get English information, and music costs about 350 AS per event.

Planning Your Time

While Vienna measures much higher on the Richter scale of sightseeing thrills, Salzburg is simply a joy—a touristy and expensive joy. If you're going into the nearby Salzkammergut lake country anyway, you don't need to take the *Sound of Music* tour. But this tour kills a nest of sightseeing birds with one ticket (city overview, S.O.M. sights, a luge ride, and a fine drive through the lakes). If you're not planning a detour through the lakes, allow half a day for this tour. That means a minimum of two nights for Salzburg. Of course, the nights are important for concerts and swilling beer in atmospheric local gardens. The actual town sights are mediocre. It's the town itself—a Baroque treat—that you should enjoy. If you like to get away from it all, bike down the river or hike across the Mönchsberg.

Orientation (tel. code: 0662)

Salzburg, a city of 150,000 (Austria's fourth-largest), is divided into old and new. The old town, sitting between the Salzach River and the 1,600-foot-high hill called Mönchsberg, is a bundle of Baroque holding all the charm and most of the tourists.

Tourist Information: Salzburg's tourist offices are helpful (at the train station; on Mozartplatz in the old center—daily 9:00–20:00, less off-season; on freeway entrances; and at airport, tel. 0662/88987, Web site: www.salzburginfo.or.at). Get a city map (10 AS), a list of sights with current hours, and a schedule of events. The TI sells a "Salzburg Card" (200 AS for a 24-hour bus pass and 24 hours free entrance to all the city sights), which pays for itself after two admissions and one bus ride. Book a concert upon arrival. The TIs also book rooms (30-AS fee, or 60 AS for three people or more).

Arrival in Salzburg: The Salzburg station makes it easy. The TI is at track 2A. Downstairs is the place to leave bags, rent bikes, buy tickets, and get train information (at Reisebüro am Bahnhof). This lower street level faces the bus station (where buses #1, #5, #6, and #51 go to the old center; get off at the first stop after you cross the river). To walk downtown (15 minutes), leave the station ticket hall near the Bankomat through the door marked "Zentrum" and walk absolutely straight down Rainerstrasse, which leads you under the tracks past Mirabellplatz, changes its name to Dreitaltigkeitsgasse, and takes you to the *Staatsbrücke* (bridge), which deposits you in the old town. For a more dramatic approach, leave the same way but follow the tracks to the river, turn left, and walk the riverside path toward the castle.

American Express: The Amex office holds mail for their check or credit card users, and doesn't charge a commission for cashing Amex checks (Monday–Friday 9:00–17:30, Saturday 9:00–12:00, Mozartplatz 5, A-5010 Salzburg, tel. 0662/8080).

Getting Around Salzburg

By Bus: Single-ride tickets are sold on the bus for 20 AS. Daily passes (*Tageskarte*) cost 40 AS (good for one calendar day only). Bus information: tel. 0662/872-145.

By Bike: Salzburg is bike friendly. From 7:00 until midnight, the train station rents good road bikes for 50 AS and mountain bikes for 150 AS; without a railpass or train ticket, you'll pay 50

AS more (no deposit required, pay at counter #3, pick it up at "left luggage"). Georg, who runs Velo-Active, rents bikes on Residenz-platz under the Glockenspiel in the old town. He offers carriers of this book a one-day rental for 150 AS (daily 9:00–19:00, less off-season, passport number for security, extra charge for mountain bikes, tel. 0663/868-827). Two companies now offer bike tours of Salzburg (details at TI).

By Funicular and Elevator: The old town is connected to Mönchsberg (and great views) via funicular and elevator. The funicular whisks you up to the imposing Hohensalzburg fortress (69 AS includes fortress admission). The elevator on the east side of the old town propels you to Café Winkler, the recommended Naturfreundehaus (see Sleeping, below), and lots of wooded paths (27 AS round-trip).

Helpful Hints: A good Laundromat is two blocks from rec-ommended Linzergasse hotels (weekdays 7:30–18:00, Saturday 8:00–12:00, self-service or drop-off service, on Wolf-Dietrich Strasse). The post office is just off Rezidenz Platz behind the cathedral.

Sights—Salzburg's Old Town

▲▲**Old Town Walking Tour**—The two-language, one-hour guided walks of the old town are informative and worthwhile if you don't mind listening to a half-hour of German (80 AS, start at TI on Mozartplatz daily at 12:15, not on winter Sundays, tel. 0662/847-568), but you can easily do it on your own. Here's a basic old-town orientation walk (start on Mozartplatz in the old town):

Mozartplatz features a statue of Mozart erected in 1842. Mozart spent most of his first 20 years (1756–1777) in Salzburg. The tourist information office and American Express Company face this square. Salzburg was the greatest Baroque city north of the Alps. Walk to the next square with the huge fountain.

Residenz Platz: Salzburg's energetic Prince-Archbishop Wolf Dietrich (who ruled from 1587–1612) was raised in Rome, counted the Medicis as his buddies, and had grand Renaissance ambitions for Salzburg. After a convenient fire destroyed much of the old town, he set about building "the Rome of the North." This square, with his new cathedral and palace, was the center-piece of his new, Italian-designed Baroque city. A series of inter-connecting squares lead from here through the old town.

For centuries, Salzburg's leaders were both important church leaders and princes of the Holy Roman Empire, hence their title—mixing sacred and secular authority. Wolf Dietrich abused his power and spent his last five years imprisoned in the Salzburg castle.

The fountain is as Italian as can be, with a Triton matching Bernini's famous *Triton Fountain* in Rome. As the north became aware of the exciting things going on in Italy, things Italian were

Salzburg

respected. Local architects even Italianized their names in order to raise their rates.

Dietrich's palace, the **Residenz**, is connected to the cathedral by a skyway. A series of fancy rooms is open to visitors with a headphone guide (60 AS, tel. 0662/8042-2690). The Residenz also has an art gallery.

Opposite the Residenz is the new Residenz, which has long been a government administration building (and post office with a handy bank of pay phones). Atop the new Residenz is the famous **Glockenspiel**, or bell tower. Its carillon of 35 17th-century bells (cast in Antwerp) chimes throughout the day and plays a tune (that changes each month) at 7:00, 11:00, and 18:00. There was a time when Salzburg could afford to take tourists to the top of the tower to actually see the big adjustable barrel turn . . . pulling the right bells in the right rhythm—a fascinating show.

Look back past Mozart's statue to the 4,220-foot-tall Gaisberg (the forested hill with the television tower). A road leads to the top for a commanding view. It's a favorite destination for local bikers.

Opposite the church is a picnic-friendly grocery store with an orange awning (Monday–Friday 8:30–18:00, Saturday 8:00–17:00). Walking under the Prince-Archbishop's skyway, step into Domplatz, the cathedral square.

Salzburg Cathedral, built in the 17th century, claims to be the first Baroque building north of the Alps (free, daily 10:00–18:30). The dates on the iron gates refer to milestones in the church's history: In 774 the previous church (long since destroyed) was founded by St. Virgil, to be replaced in 1628 by the church you see today. In 1959 the reconstruction was completed after a bomb blew through the dome in World War II.

Check out the organ draped over the entrance; it was played only when the archbishop walked in and out of the cathedral. Gape up. The interior is marvelous. Concert and Mass schedules are posted at the entrance; Sunday Mass (10:00) is famous for its music.

Under the skyway, a stairway leads down to the excavation site under the church with a few second-century Christian Roman mosaics and the foundation stones of the previous Romanesque and Gothic churches (20 AS, Wednesday–Sunday 9:00–17:00). The Cathedral (or *Dom*) Museum has a rich collection of church art (entry at portico).

The cathedral square is surrounded by "ecclesiastical palaces." The statue of Mary (1771) is looking away from the church, but if you stand in the rear of the square immediately under the middle arch, you'll see how she's positioned to be crowned by the two angels on the church facade.

From the arch, walk back across the square to the front of the cathedral and turn right (going past the underground public toilets) to the next square, where you'll see locals playing chess on the giant board. Past the chessboard, a small road leads up to the castle (and castle lift). On the right, a gate reading "St. Peter" leads past a traditional old bakery (near the waterfall, hard to beat their rock-like Roggenbrot) and into a cemetery.

St. Peter's Cemetery is a collection of lovingly tended mini-gardens (butted up against the Mönchberg's rock wall). The graves are cared for by relatives; anyone residing in the cemetery for more than 30 years without living kin gets dug up. Early Christian catacombs are carved into the rock wall above the graveyard (12 AS, 10:30–15:30). This was where the von Trapp family hid out in the *S.O.M.* movie. Walk through the cemetery and out the opposite end. Drop into St. Peter's Church, a Romanesque basilica done up beautifully Baroque. Continue (through arch opposite hillside, left at church, second right, pass public WC, another square and church) to Universitätsplatz, with its busy open-air produce market. This is Salzburg at its liveliest and most real (mornings, daily except Sunday). Take one of several covered arcades from here to Getreidegasse.

Getreidegasse was old Salzburg's lively and colorful main drag. Famous for its old wrought-iron signs, it still looks much as it did in Mozart's day. *Schmuck* means jewelry. Wolfgang was born on this street. Find his very gold house.

▲**Mozart's Birthplace (Geburtshaus)**—Mozart was born here in 1756. It was in this building that he composed most of his boy-genius works. This most popular Mozart sight in town, filled with scores of scores, portraits, and old keyboard instruments and violins, is almost a pilgrimage. If you're a fan, you'll have to check it out. It's right in the old town on colorful Getreidegasse #9 (70 AS, or 110 AS for combined ticket to Mozart's *Wohnhaus*—see below, daily 9:00–18:00, shorter hours off-season). Note the cobbled entryway. All Salzburg used to be paved this way.

▲**Hohensalzburg Fortress**—Built on a rock 400 feet above the Salzach River, this castle, one of Europe's mightiest, dominates Salzburg's skyline and offers great views of the city and surrounding hills. The castle interior is so-so unless you catch a tour (35 AS admission plus 30 AS for a tour; confirm that it will be in English as well as German). Check out the sound-and-vision show. The museum has the noisiest floorboards in Europe, but even so, the princess had a chastity belt. You can see it next to other gruesome torture devices that need no explanation. You can walk up to the fortress, but the funicular is effortless (34 AS round-trip, every 10 minutes, 69 AS includes fortress admission, castle open daily 8:00–19:00, 9:00–18:00 off-season, tel. 0662/842-430).

▲**The Hills Are Alive Walk**—For a most enjoyable approach to the castle, consider riding the elevator to the Café Winkler and walking 20 minutes through the woods high above the city to Festung Hohensalzburg (stay on the high paved paths, or you'll have a needless climb back up to the castle).

Sights—Across the River

▲▲**Mozart's Wohnhaus (a.k.a. Mozarts Ton- und Filmmuseum)**—Even better than the birthplace is this newly renovated museum, previously Mozart's second home (his family moved here when he was 17). A headphone, free with admission, lets you hear English throughout. Along with the usual scores and old pianos, the highlight is an intriguing film that leaves you wanting to know more about Mozart and his remarkable family (65 AS, or 110 AS for combined ticket to birthplace, guidebook-59 AS, daily 10:00–18:00, just over the river at Marktplatz 8, tel. 0662/8894040).

▲**Mirabell Gardens and Palace (Schloss)**—The bubbly gardens are always open and free. You may recognize the statues featured in the *S.O.M.* To properly enjoy the lavish Mirabell Palace, get a ticket to a *Schlosskonzert*. Baroque music flying around a Baroque hall is a happy bird in the right cage. Tickets are around 400 AS and are rarely sold out (tel. 0662/848-586).

More Sights—Salzburg

▲▲**Riverside Bike Ride**—The Salzach River has smooth, flat, and scenic bike paths along each side. On a sunny day, I can think of no more shout-worthy escape from the city. Hallein is a pleasant destination (with a salt-mine tour, 9:00–17:00, about 15 kilometers away, the north or new-town side of river is most scenic). Even a quickie ride from one end of town to the other gives you the best possible views of Salzburg. In the evening, it's a hand-in-hand, floodlit-spires world.

▲▲*Sound of Music* **Tour**—I took this tour skeptically (as part of my research chores) and liked it. It includes a quick but good general city tour, stops for a luge ride (in season, fair weather, 35 AS extra), hits all the *S.O.M.* spots (including the stately home, gazebo, and wedding church), and shows you a lovely stretch of the Salzkammergut. The Salzburg Panorama Tours Company charges 350 AS for the four-hour, English-only tour (from Mirabellplatz daily at 9:30 and 14:00, tel. 0662/874-029, Web site: www .panoramatours.at; ask for a reservation and a free hotel pickup if you like; travelers with this book who buy their tickets with cash at the Mirabellplatz ticket booth get a 10 percent discount on this and any other tour they do). This is worthwhile for *S.O.M.* fans without a car, or those who won't otherwise be going into the Salzkammergut. Warning: Many think rolling through the Austrian countryside with 30 Americans singing "Doe, a deer" is pretty schmaltzy. And local Austrians don't understand all the commotion.

There are several similar and very competitive tour companies that offer every conceivable tour of and from Salzburg (Mozart sights, Berchtesgaden, salt mines, Salzkammergut lakes and mountains). Some hotels have their brochures and get a healthy commission. Bob's Tours runs minibus tours (two different tours: *S.O.M.* or Berchtesgaden and Bavarian Alps, Kaigasse 19, tel. 0662/849-511).

▲**Hellbrunn Castle**—The attractions here are a garden full of clever trick fountains and the sadistic joy the tour guide gets from soaking tourists. The archbishop's mediocre 17th-century palace is open by tour only (30 AS, 2/hrly, 20 minutes). His Baroque garden, one of the oldest in Europe, is pretty enough and now features the "I am 16, going on 17" gazebo (70 AS for the 35-minute tour and admission, daily 9:00–17:30, until 22:00 in July and August, until 16:30 in April and October, closed November–March, tel. 0662/ 820-372). The castle is three miles south of Salzburg (bus #55 from the station or downtown, 2/hrly, 20 min). It's most fun on a sunny day or with kids, but, for many, it's a lot of trouble for a few water tricks.

Music Scene

▲▲**Salzburg Festival**—Each summer from late July to the end of August, Salzburg hosts its famous Salzburger Festspiele, founded in 1920 partly to employ Vienna's musicians in the summer. This fun and festive time is crowded, but there are plenty of beds (except for a few August weekends). Except for the big shows, tickets are normally available the day of the concert (ticket office on Mozartplatz, in TI). You can contact the Austrian National Tourist Office in the United States for specifics on this year's festival schedule and tickets (Box 1142, New York, NY 10108, tel. 212/944-6880, fax 212/730-4568, Web site: www.anto.com), but I've never planned in advance and have enjoyed great concerts with every visit.

▲▲**Musical Events outside of Festival Time**—Salzburg is busy throughout the year with 2,000 classical performances in its palaces and churches annually. Pick up the events calendar at the TI (free, comes out monthly). Whenever you visit, you'll have a number of concerts to choose from. There are nearly nightly concerts at the Mirabell Palace and up in the fortress (both with open seating and 400-AS tickets, concerts at 19:30 or 20:30, doors open 30 minutes early). The *Schlosskonzerte* at the Mirabell Palace offer a fine Baroque setting for your Mozart (tel. 0662/848-586). The fortress concerts, called *Festungskonzerte*, are held in the "prince's chamber" (usually chamber music—a string quartet, tel. 0662/825-858 to reserve, you can pick up tickets at the door). This medieval-feeling room atop the castle has windows overlooking the city. The extra 34-AS round-trip lift gives you a chance to enjoy a stroll through the castle courtyard and enjoy the grand city view.

The almost daily "5:00 Concert" next to St. Peter's is cheaper, since it features young artists (120 AS, daily except Wednesday, 45 minutes, tel. 0662/8445-7619). While the series is named after the brother of Joseph Haydn, it features music from various masters.

The Marionette Theater performs operas with fine marionettes and recorded music (350–480 AS, nearly nightly May–September, tel. 0662/872-406).

Sights—Near Salzburg

▲**Bad Dürnberg Salzbergwerke**—Like its salty neighbors, this salt-mine tour and cable-car ride above the town of Hallein (12 kilometers from Salzburg) respects only the German speakers. You'll get information sheets or headphones but none of the jokes. Still, it's a fun experience wearing white overalls, sliding down the sleek wooden chutes, and crossing underground from Austria into Germany (daily 9:00–17:00, easy bus and train connections from Salzburg, tel. 06245/82121 or 06245/852-8515).

▲**Berchtesgaden**—This Alpine resort just across the German border (20 km from Salzburg) flaunts its attractions, and you may find yourself in a traffic jam of desperate tourists trying to turn their money into fun. From the station and TI (tel. 08652/9670), buses go to the salt mines (a 15-minute walk otherwise) and the idyllic Königsee (21.50 DM, two-hour scenic cruises, 2/hrly, stopovers anywhere, tel. 08652/963-618).

At the salt mines, you put on traditional miner's outfits, get on funny little trains, and zip deep into the mountain. For one hour you'll cruise subterranean lakes; slide speedily down two long, slick, wooden banisters; and learn how they mined salt so long ago. Call for crowd-avoidance advice. You can buy a ticket early and browse through the town until your appointed tour time (19.50 DM, daily 9:00–17:00; winter Monday–Saturday 12:30–15:30, tel. 08652/60020).

Hitler's famous (but overrated) Eagle's Nest towered high above Obersalzberg near Berchtesgaden. The site is open to visitors, but little remains of the Alpine retreat Hitler visited only five times. The bus ride up the private road and the lift to the top (a 2,000-foot altitude gain) cost 26 DM from the station, 20 DM from the parking lot. If the weather's cloudy, as it often is, you'll Nazi a thing.

Berchtesgaden is a train ride from Munich (hrly, 2.5 hrs, with one change). From Salzburg, ride the scenic and more-direct-than-train bus (2/hrly, 30 min). Berchtesgaden caters to long-term German guests. During peak season, it's not worth the headaches for the speedy tourist.

Sleeping in Salzburg
(12 AS = about $1, tel. code: 0662, zip code: 5020)
Sleep Code: **S** = Single, **D** = Double/Twin, **T** = Triple, **Q** = Quad, **b** = bathroom, **t** = toilet only, **s** = shower only, **CC** = Credit Card (**V**isa, **M**asterCard, **A**mex).

Finding a room in Salzburg, even during the music festival, is usually easy. Unless otherwise noted, all my listings come with breakfast and at least some English is spoken. The more expensive places charge more during the music festival (late July and August).

Sleeping in (or above) the Old Town
Gasthaus zur Goldenen Ente, run by the family Steinwender, is a great splurge if you'd like to sleep in a 600-year-old building above a fine restaurant as central as you can be on a pedestrian street in old Salzburg. Somehow the 15 modern and comfortable doubles fit into this building's medieval-style stone arches and narrow stairs (Sb-680 AS and Db-980 AS with this book, higher prices in high season, extra person-450 AS, parking deals, CC:VMA, elevator, Goldgasse 10, tel. 0662/845-622, fax 0662/845-6229). The breakfast is buffet-big and their restaurant is a treat (see Eating, below).

Hotel Restaurant Weisses Kreuz is a classy, comfy, family-run place on a cobbled back street near the castle (Sb-700 AS, Db-900-1,200 AS, Tb-1,600, CC:M, reserve ahead, Bierjodlgasse 6, tel. 0662/845-641, fax 0662/845-6419).

Gasthof Hinterbrühl is a smoky, ramshackle old place with a handy location, minimal plumbing, and not a tourist in sight (S-420 AS, D-520 AS, T-600 AS, plus optional 50-AS breakfast, above a bar that can be noisy, workable parking, CC:V, on a village-like square just under the castle at Schanzlgasse 12, tel. 0662/846-798).

Naturfreundehaus, also called "Gasthaus Bürgerwehr," is a local version of a mountaineer's hut. It's a great budget alternative in a forest guarded by singing birds and snuggled in the remains of a 15th-century castle wall overlooking Salzburg, with magnificent town and mountain views (D-280 AS, 120 AS per person in four- to six-bed dorms, breakfast-30 AS, dinner-68–108 AS, curfew-1:00, open May–September, Mönchsberg 19, two minutes from the top of the 27-AS round-trip Mönchsberg elevator, tel. 0662/841-729). High above the old town, it's the stone house to the left of the glass Café Winkler.

Sleeping on Linzergasse and near Kapuzinerberg

All of these listings are a 15-minute walk from the train station in the "new" section of town, across the river from the old town. The first four are on lower Linzergasse, directly across the bridge from Mozartville. Its bustling crowds of shoppers overwhelm the few shy cars that venture onto it. The last two listings are farther from the city center (a 10-minute walk).

Institute St. Sebastian is close to the old town and newly renovated, offering the town's best doubles and dorm beds for the money (Sb-380 AS, Db-660 AS, Tb-900 AS, elevator, Linzergasse 41, enter through arch at #37, tel. 0662/871-386, fax 0662/8713-8685). They usually have rooms available, as well as 210-AS spots in 10-bed dorms (30 AS less if you have sheets, no lock-out time, lockers, free showers). Anyone is welcome to use the self-service kitchen on each floor. Fridge space is free; just ask for a key. This friendly, clean, historic building has lots of spacious public areas and a roof garden. The doubles come with modern baths and head-to-toe twin beds. Some Mozarts are buried in the courtyard.

Hotel Goldene Krone is big, quiet, and creaky-traditional but modern, with comforts rare in this price range (Sb-500–570 AS, D-700–800 AS, Db-850–970 AS, Tb-1,000–1,300 AS, elevator, Linzergasse 48, tel. 0662/872-300).

Hotel zum Jungen Fuchs turns on troglodytes. It's very plain but clean and wonderfully located in a funky, dumpy old building (S-280 AS, D-380 AS, T-480 AS, no breakfast, across from Institute St. Sebastian at Linzergasse 54, tel. 0662/875-496).

Hotel Trumer Stube is a comfy little hotel-pension just off Linzergasse with clean new rooms and a friendly can-do reception (Sb-725 AS, Db-1,250 AS, Tb-1,380 AS, Qb-1,750 AS, higher in August, lower in winter, CC:VMA, elevator, parking-100 AS, Bergstrasse 6, tel. 0662/874-776, fax 0662/874-326, e-mail: hotel.trumer-stube.sbg@eunet.at).

Pension Bergland is a classy oasis of calm, with rustic rooms and musical evenings (Ss-480 AS, Sb-560 AS, two dim D-640 AS, Db-860–920 AS depending on size, Tb-1,060 AS, music room open 17:00–21:30, bike rental, English library, Laundromat nearby, Rupertgasse 15, southeast of the station, tel. 0662/872-318, fax 0662/872-3188, e-mail: pkuhn@sol.at, run by Peter Kuhn).

Gasthaus Ganslhof, three blocks away from the Bergland, is a bit run-down but comfortable and back in the real world with Motel 6 ambience and a parking lot (Sb-480 AS, Db-800 AS, 150 AS more per person in the summer, elevator, TV and phone, CC:VMA, Vogelweiderstrasse 6, tel. 0662/873-853, fax 0662/8738-5323).

Bed-and-Breakfasts

These are generally roomy, modern, comfortable, and come with a good breakfast, easy parking, and plenty of tourist information. Off-season, competition softens prices. They are a bus ride from town, but with a day pass and the frequent service, this shouldn't keep you away. Unsavory *Zimmer* skimmers lurk at the station. If you have a reservation, ignore them. If you need a place . . . they need a customer.

Brigitte Lenglachner fills her big, traditional home with a warm welcome (S-290 AS, D-480 AS, bunk bed D-390 AS, Db-550 AS, T-690 AS, apartment available, two-night minimum, breakfast in room, Scheibenweg 8, tel. & fax 0662/438-044). It's in a chirpy neighborhood a 10-minute walk northwest of the station: from the station, cross the pedestrian Pioneer Bridge, turn right, walk along the river 200 meters, then take a left to Scheibenweg 8. If her place is booked, skip her referrals.

Trude Poppenberger's three pleasant rooms share the same long mountain-view balcony (S-280 AS, D-480 AS, T-720 AS; if you stay two nights she'll do your laundry for 80 AS; Wachtelgasse 9, tel. & fax 0662/430-094). It's a 20-minute walk northwest of the station, near Brigitte's place (or she'll pick you up for free).

Zimmers on Moosstrasse: The street called Moosstrasse, southwest of Mönchsberg, is lined with *Zimmer*. Those farther out are farmhouses. From the station, catch bus #1 and change to bus #60 immediately after crossing the river. From the old town, ride bus #60 (get off after the American High School at Sendleweg). If you're driving from the center, go through the tunnel, straight on Neutorstrasse, and take the fourth left onto Moosstrasse.

Maria Gassner rents 10 sparkling clean, comfortable rooms in her modern house (St-250 AS, Sb-400 AS, D-440 AS, Db-500 AS, big Db-600 AS, 10 percent more for one-night stays, family deals, CC:VM, 60-AS coin-op laundry, Moosstrasse 126-B, tel. 0662/824-990, fax 0662/822-075).

Frau Ballwein offers cozy, charming rooms in an old farmhouse (S-200 AS, Ss-240 AS, D-400 AS, Db-480 AS, farm-fresh breakfasts, Moosstrasse 69A, tel. & fax 0662/824-029).

Haus Reichl also has good rooms (Db-550 AS, Tb-800 AS, Qb-1,000 AS, family deals, Q rooms have balcony and view, between Ballwein and Bankhammer B&Bs at Reiterweg 52, tel. & fax 0662/826-248).

Ziller Family Farm rents three huge rooms with kitchenettes in a kid-friendly, horse-filled environment (Db-600 AS, minimum two nights, Moosstrasse 76, tel. 0662/824-940, Gabi SE).

Helga Bankhammer rents recently renovated, pleasant rooms in a farmhouse with farm animals nearby (D-450 AS, Db-500 AS, Moosstrasse 77, tel. & fax 0662/830-067).

Gästehaus Blobergerhof is rural and comfortable (Sb-350 AS, Db-550 AS, 10 percent more for one-night stays, CC:VM; breakfast buffet, bike rental, laundry service, will pick up at station, Hammerauerstrasse 4, Querstrasse zur Moosstrasse, tel. 0662/830-227, fax 0662/827-061).

Sleeping near the Train Station
Pension Adlerhof, a plain and decent old place, is two blocks in front of the train station but a 15-minute walk from the sightseeing action. It has a quirky staff and well-maintained rooms (S-400–420 AS, Sb-590 AS, D-650 AS, Db-790 AS, Elisabethstrasse 25, tel. 0662/875-236, fax 0662/873-6636).

Gottfried's International Youth Hotel, a.k.a. "the Yo-Ho," is the most fun, handy, and American of Salzburg's many hostels (D-360 AS, Q-160 AS per bed, or six- to eight-bed dorm-140 AS, sheets not required but rentable-20 AS, five blocks from the station toward the center at Paracelsusstrasse 9, tel. 0662/879-649). This easygoing place speaks English first, has cheap meals, lockers, a laundry, tour discounts, and a 1:00 curfew; plays *The Sound of Music* free daily at 13:30; runs a lively bar; and welcomes anyone of any age. Expect a non-stop noisy, smoky, party atmosphere.

Eating in Salzburg
Salzburg boasts many inexpensive, fun, and atmospheric places to eat. I'm a sucker for big cellars with their smoky Old World atmosphere, heavy medieval arches, time-darkened paintings, antlers, hearty meals, and plump patrons. These places are famous with visitors but also enjoyed by the locals.

Gasthaus zum Wilder Mann is the place if the weather's bad and you're in the mood for Hofbräu atmosphere and a hearty, cheap meal at a shared table in one small, well-antlered room (Monday–Saturday 11:00–21:00, closed Sunday, smoky, two minutes from Mozart's place—enter from Getreidegasse 20 or Griesgasse 17, tel. 0662/841-787). For a quick 100-AS lunch, get the *Bauernschmaus*, a mountain of dumplings, kraut, and peasant's meats.

Krimplestätter employs 500 years of experience serving authentic old-Salzburger food in its authentic old-Austrian interior or its cheery garden (10:00–24:00, closed Monday all year and winter Sundays, Müllner Hauptstrasse 31, 10 minutes north of the old town near the river). For fine food with a wild finale, eat here and drink at the nearby Augustiner Bräustübl.

Augustiner Bräustübl, a monk-run brewery, is rustic and crude. On busy nights it's like a Munich beer hall with no music but the volume turned up. When it's cool, you'll enjoy a historic setting with beer-sloshed and smoke-stained halls. On balmy evenings you'll eat under trees in a pleasant outdoor beer garden. Local students mix with tourists eating hearty slabs of schnitzel with their fingers or cold meals from the self-serve picnic counter (daily 15:00–23:30, Augustinergasse 4, head up Müllner Hauptstrasse northwest along the river, and ask for "Müllnerbräu," its local nickname). Don't be fooled by second-rate gardens serving the same beer nearby—this huge, 1,000-seat place is in the Augustiner brewery. Order carefully, prices can sting. Pick up a half-liter (28–32 AS) or full-liter mug (56–64 AS) of the great beer, pay the lady, and give Mr. Keg your empty mug. For dessert, after a visit to the strudel kiosk, enjoy the incomparable floodlit view of old Salzburg from the nearby pedestrian bridge, and then stroll home along the river.

Stiftskeller St. Peter has been in business for more than 1,000 years. It's classier (with strolling musicians), more central, and a good splurge for traditional Austrian cuisine in medieval sauce (daily 11:00–24:00, outdoor and indoor seating, meals 100–200 AS, CC:VMA, next to St. Peter's church at the foot of Mönchsberg, tel. 0662/841-268).

Gasthaus zur Goldenen Ente (see Sleeping, above) serves great food in a classy, subdued hotel dining room. The chef, Robert, specializes in roast duck (*Ente*) and seafood, along with "Salzberger Nockerl," the mountainous sweet soufflé served all over town. It's big enough for four (Monday–Friday 11:00–21:00, closed Saturday and Sunday, Goldgasse 10, tel. 0662/845-622).

Stieglkeller is a huge, atmospheric institution that has several rustic rooms and outdoor garden seating with a great rooftop view of the old town (daily 10:00–22:00, 50 yards uphill from the lift to the castle, Festungsgasse 10, tel. 0662/842-681). They offer the latest *S.O.M.* spin-off—a *Sound of Music* dinner show, featuring songs from the movie and local dances (520 AS includes dinner, 360 AS for show only when booked in advance, daily May–

September, tel. 0662/832-029). Since the Stieglkeller has lots of rooms, you can skip the show and still enjoy the restaurant.

Picnics: The University Square, just behind Mozart's house, hosts a bustling morning **produce market** daily except Sunday.

Lunch: Classy Salzburg delis serve good, cheap, sit-down lunches on weekdays. Have them make you a sandwich or something hot, toss in a carrot, a piece of fruit, yogurt, and a box of milk, and sit at a small table with the local lunch crowd.

Café Glockenspiel, on Mozartplatz 2, does a good, if pricey, lunch (80–160 AS). The following cheaper places are all just across the river from the old town: **Frauenberger** is friendly, picnic-ready, and inexpensive, with indoor or outdoor seating (Monday–Friday 8:00–14:00, across from Linzergasse 16). **Spicy Spices** is a vegetarian-Indian lunch take-out (with a few tables) restaurant serving tasty curry and rice boxes, samosas, organic salads and fresh juices (Wolf-Dietrich Strasse 1). **Mensa Aicherpassage** serves some of Salzburg's cheapest meals in the basement (Monday–Friday 11:30–14:30, go under arch, enter metal door to "Mozarteum," and go down one floor).

Transportation Connections—Salzburg

By train to: Innsbruck (every 2 hrs, 2 hrs), **Vienna** (2/hrly, 3.5 hrs), **Hallstatt** (hrly, 50 min to Attnang Puchheim, 20-minute wait, 1.5 hrs to Hallstatt), **Reutte** (every 2 hrs, 4 hrs, transfer in Innsbruck), **Munich** (hrly, 90 min).

SALZKAMMERGUT LAKE DISTRICT AND HALLSTATT

Commune with nature in Austria's Lake District. "The hills are alive," and you're surrounded by the loveliness that has turned on everyone from Emperor Franz Josef to Julie Andrews. This is *The Sound of Music* country. Idyllic and majestic, but not rugged, it's a gentle land of lakes, forested mountains, and storybook villages, rich in hiking opportunities and inexpensive lodging. Settle down in the postcard-pretty, fjord-cuddling town of Hallstatt.

Planning Your Time

While there are plenty of lakes, Hallstatt is really the only one that matters. One night and two hours to browse is all you'll need to fall in love. To relax or take a hike in the surroundings, give it two nights and a day. It's a good stop between Salzburg and Vienna. A visit here (with a bike ride along the Danube and the two big cites—Salzburg and Vienna) balances out your Austrian itinerary.

Orientation (tel. code: 06134)

Lovable Hallstatt is a tiny town bullied onto a ledge between a selfish mountain and a swan-ruled lake, with a waterfall ripping furiously through its middle. It can be toured on foot in about 10 minutes. The town is one of Europe's oldest, going back centuries before Christ. The charm of Hallstatt is the village and its lakeside setting. Go there to relax, nibble, wander, and paddle. (In August, tourist crowds trample much of Hallstatt's charm.) The lake is famous for its good fishing and pure water (8 km by 2 km, 125 meters deep at 508 meters altitude).

Tourist Information: The TI can always find you a room. Its holiday "guest card" gives you free parking (Monday–Friday 9:00–17:00, weekends 10:00–14:00, less off-season, tel. 06134/8208).

Arrival in Hallstatt: Hallstatt's train station is a wide spot on the tracks across the lake. *Stefanie* (a boat) meets you at the station and glides across the lake into town (23 AS, with each train until 18:40—don't arrive after that). The boat ride is gorgeous. Last departing boat-train connection leaves Hallstatt at 18:15.

Helpful Hints: Laundromat is at the camping place near the bathing island (wash, dry, and soap, 100 AS). Post office is below the TI.

Sights—Hallstatt

Prehistory Museum—The humble Prehistory Museum adjacent to the TI is interesting because little Hallstatt was the important salt-mining hub of a culture that spread from France to the Balkans during what archaeologists call the "Hallstatt Period" (800–400 B.C.). Back then, Celtic tribes dug for precious salt, and Hallstatt was, as its name means, the "home of salt." Your 50-AS Prehistory Museum ticket also gets you into the cute Heimatmuseum of folk culture (daily 10:00–18:00 in summer). Historians like the English booklet that covers both museums (25 AS). The Janu sport shop across from the TI recently dug into a prehistoric site, and now its basement is another small museum (free).

▲▲**Hallstatt Church and Cemetery**—Hallstatt has two churches. The Protestant church is at lake level. The more interesting Catholic church, with a giant St. Christopher (protector of us travelers) on its outside wall, overlooks the town from above. From near the boat dock, hike up the covered wooden stairway to the church. The lovely church has 500-year-old altars and frescoes dedicated to the saints of mining and salt. Space is so limited in Hallstatt that bones have only 12 peaceful buried years in the church cemetery before making way for the freshly dead. The result is a fascinating chapel of bones in the cemetery (*Beinhaus*, 10 AS, daily 10:00–18:00). Each skull is lovingly named, dated, and decorated, with the men getting ivy, and the women, roses. They stopped this practice in the 1960s, about the same time the Catholic Church began permitting cremation.

▲▲**Salt Mine Tour**—If you have yet to do a salt mine, Hallstatt's

Salzkammergut and Hallstatt

is as good as any. You'll ride a steep funicular high above the town (97 AS round-trip), take a 10-minute hike, put on old miners' clothes, take an underground train, slide down the banisters, and listen to an English tape-recorded tour while your guide speaks German (135 AS, daily 9:30–16:30, closes early off-season, no children under age 4, tel. 06134/8251). The well-publicized ancient Celtic graveyard excavation sites nearby are really dead. The scenic 50-minute hike back into town is (with strong knees) a joy.

▲**Boating, Hiking, and Spelunking**—Those into relaxation can rent a sleepy electric motorboat to enjoy town views from the water (75 AS/30 minutes, 120 AS/one hour, one or two people, two speeds: slow and stop, rental place next to the ferry dock).

Mountain lovers, hikers, and spelunkers keep busy for days using Hallstatt as their home base. Get information from the TI on the various caves with their ice formations, the thunderous rivers, mountain lifts, nearby walks, and harder hikes. The best short and easy walk is the two-hour round-trip up the Echerntal Valley to a waterfall and back. With a car, consider hiking around nearby Altaussee (flat, three-hour hike) or along Grundlsee to Tolpitzsee. Regular buses connect Hallstatt with Gosausee for a pleasant walk around that lake. The TI can recommend a great two-day hike with an overnight in a nearby mountain hut.

Sleeping in Hallstatt
(12 AS = about $1, tel. code: 06134, zip code: 4830)
Hallstatt's TI can almost always find you a room. July and August can be tight, and early August is worst. A bed in a private home costs about 200 AS with breakfast. It's hard to get a one-night advance reservation. But if you drop in and they have a spot, they're happy to have you. Prices include breakfast, lots of stairs, and a silent night. "*Zimmer mit Aussicht?*" means "Room with view?"—worth asking for.

Gasthof Simony is my stocking-feet-tidy, 500-year-old favorite, right on the square with a lake view, balconies, creaky wood floors, slip-slidey rag rugs, antique furniture, a lakefront garden, and a huge breakfast. Call friendly Susan Scheutz for a reservation. For safety, reconfirm a day or two before you arrive (Sb-500 AS, Db-850 AS, price can vary according to the plumbing, view, season, and length of stay, 250 AS for third person, cheaper for families, Markt 105, tel. 06134/8231, SE). Downstairs, Frau Zopf runs a traditional Austrian restaurant; try her delicious homemade desserts.

Pension Seethaler is a homey old lodge with 45 beds and a breakfast room mossy with antlers, perched above the lake on the parking-lot side of town (215 AS per person in S, D, T, or Q, 280 AS/person in rooms with private bath, 20 AS cheaper if you stay more than one night, no extra for views, Dr. Morton Weg 22, tel. 06134/8421, fax 06134/84214, Frau Seethaler).

Pension Sarstein has 25 beds, mostly in (sometimes dirty) rooms with flower-bedecked lake-view balconies, in a charming building a few minutes' walk along the lake from the center, run by friendly Frau Fisher. You can swim from her lakeside garden (D-420 AS, Ds-520 AS, Db-620 AS with this book; one-night stays cost 20 AS per person extra; Gosaumühlstrasse 83, tel. 06134/8217). Her sister, friendly **Frau Zimmermann**, runs a small *Zimmer* (as her name implies) in a 500-year-old ramshackle house with low beams, time-polished wood, and fine lake views just down the street (D-400 AS, T-600 AS, can be musty, Gosaumühlstrasse 69, tel. 06134/8309). These elderly women speak almost no English, but you'll find yourself caught up in their charm and laughing together like old friends.

Helga Lenz has a big, sprawling, woodsy house on top of the town with great lake and town views and a neat garden perch. It's ideal for those who sleep well in tree houses (D-360 AS, T-540 AS, Q-720 AS, 20 AS more for one-night stays, high above the paddleboat dock at Hallberg 17, tel. 06134/8508, SE).

Gasthof Zauner is a business machine offering modern pine-flavored rooms with all the comforts on the main square, and a restaurant specializing in grilled meat and fish (Db-1,200 AS, CC:VM, Marktplatz 51, tel. 06134/8246, fax 06134/82468).

Gasthaus Mühle Naturfreunde-Herberge has the best cheap beds in town and is clearly the place to eat well on a budget—great pizzas (145 AS per bed with sheets in two- to 20-bed coed dorms, 110 AS if you BYO hostel sheet, 40-AS breakfast, closed in November, restaurant closed on Wednesday, Kirchenweg 36, below the tunnel car park, tel. & fax 06134/8318, run by Ferdinand Törö). "Nature's friends' houses" are found throughout the Alps. Like mountaineers' huts, they're a good, basic, fun bargain.

The nearby village of Obertraun is a peaceful alternative to Hallstatt in August. You'll find plenty of *Zimmer* and a luxurious hostel (182-AS beds with breakfast, tel. 06131/360).

Transportation Connections—Hallstatt
By train to: Salzburg (hrly, 90 min. to Attnang Puchheim, short wait, 50 min to Salzburg), **Vienna** (hrly, 90 min. to Attnang Puchheim, short wait, 2.5 hrs to Vienna). Daytrippers to Hallstatt can check bags at the Attnang Puchheim station. But connections there and back can be very fast—about five minutes. Have three 10-AS coins ready for the lockers.

INNSBRUCK
Innsbruck is world famous as a resort for skiers and a haven for hikers. When compared to Salzburg and Vienna, it's stale strudel. Still, a quick look is easy and interesting.

Innsbruck was the Habsburgs' capital of the Tirol. Its medieval center, now a glitzy, tourist-filled pedestrian zone, still gives you the feel of a provincial medieval capital. The much ogled Golden Roof (Goldenes Dach) is the centerpiece. Built by Emperor Maximilian in 1496, this balcony (with 2,657 gilded copper tiles) offered an impressive spot to view his medieval spectacles. From this square, you'll see the Golden Roof, the Baroque-style Helblinghaus, and the city tower (climb it for a great view, 22 AS). Nearby are the palace (Hofburg), church (Hofkirche), and Folklife Museum.

Tourist Information: Innsbruck has two TIs; one is downtown (daily 8:00–19:00, three blocks in front of the Golden Roof), and the other is at the train station (open until 21:15, tel. 0512/5356). The

230-AS one-day Innsbruck Card pays for itself only if you take the Mountain Lift (also covers Igls Lift, as well as the buses, trams, museums, zoo, and castle). The TI offers a daily bus and walk tour (in English and German, at noon and 14:00, noon only in winter).

Arrival in Innsbruck: From the train station, it's a seven-minute walk to the old town center. Leave veering right to Brix-nerstrasse. Follow it past the fountain at Boznerplatz and straight until it deadends into Maria-Theresa Strasse. Turn right and go 250 meters into the old town (you'll pass the TI on Burggraben on your right), where you'll see the Golden Roof and Hotel Weisses Kreuz. Tram #3 does the same trip in two stops (21 AS from the driver or 32 AS for an all-day pass from a tobacco shop).

Sights—Innsbruck
▲▲**Folklife Museum (Tiroler Volkskunst Museum)**—This offers the best look anywhere at traditional Tirolean lifestyles. Fascinating exhibits range from wedding dresses and gaily painted cribs and nativity scenes, to maternity clothes and babies' trousers. The upper floors show Tirolean homes through the ages (40 AS, Monday–Saturday 9:00–17:30 in summer, Sunday 9:00–12:00, hard to appreciate without the English guidebook).

Maria-Theresa Strasse—From the medieval center stretches the fine Baroque Maria-Theresa Strasse. St. Anne's Column marks the center of the old marketplace. At the far end, the Triumphal Arch is a gate Maria Theresa built to celebrate the marriage of her son, Leopold II.

▲**Ski Jump View**—The great ski jump of the 1964 and 1976 Olympics is an inviting side trip, overlooking the city just off the Brenner Pass road on the south side of town (follow signs to "Ber-gisel"). For the best view, hike to the Olympic rings under the dish that held the Olympic flame, where Dorothy Hamill and a host of others who brought home the gold are honored. Near the car park is a memorial to Andreas Hofer, the hero of the Tirolean battles against Napoleon.

Mountain Lifts and Hiking—A popular mountain-sports center and home of the 1964 and 1976 Winter Olympics, Innsbruck is sur-rounded by 150 mountain lifts, 1,250 miles of trails, and 250 hikers' huts. If it's sunny, consider riding the lift right out of the city to the mountaintops above (230 AS). Ask your hotel or hostel for an Inns-bruck Club card, which offers overnight guests various discounts, bike tours, and free guided hikes in summer. Hikers meet in front of Congress Innsbruck daily at 8:30; each day it's a different hike in the surrounding mountains and valleys (bring only lunch and water; boots, rucksack, and transport are provided; confirm with TI).

Alpenzoo—This zoo is one of Innsbruck's most popular attrac-tions (understandable when the competition is the Golden Roof). You can ride the funicular up to the zoo (free if you buy your zoo

Innsbruck and Hall

ticket before boarding) and get a look at all the animals that hide out in the Alps: wildcats, owls, elk, vultures, and more (70 AS, cheaper tickets at TI, daily 9:00–18:00).

▲**Slap-Dancing**—For your Tirolean folk fun, Innsbruck hotels offer an entertaining evening of slap-dancing and yodeling nearly every summer night (200 AS includes a drink with the two-hour show, 20:45, tickets at TI). And every summer Thursday the town puts on a free outdoor folk show under the Golden Roof.

▲▲**Alpine Side Trip by Car to Hinterhornalm**—In Gnadenwald, a village sandwiched between Hall and its Alps, pay a 60-AS toll, pick up a brochure, then corkscrew your way up the mountain. Marveling at the crazy amount of energy put into such a remote road project, you'll finally end up at the rustic Hinterhornalm Berg restaurant (crude rooms, often closed, tel. 06641/211-2745). Hinterhornalm is a hang-gliding springboard. On good days, it's a butterfly nest. From there it's a level 20-minute walk to Walderalm, a cluster of three dairy farms with 70 cows that share their meadow with the clouds. The cows—cameras dangling from their thick necks—ramble along ridgetop lanes surrounded by cut-glass peaks. The ladies of the farms serve soup, sandwiches, and drinks (very fresh milk in the afternoon) on rough plank tables. Below you spreads the Inn River Valley and, in the distance, tourist-filled Innsbruck.

Sleeping in Innsbruck
(12 AS = about $1, tel. code: 0512)

Hotel Weisses Kreuz, 50 meters from Innsbruck's Golden Roof, has been housing visitors for 500 years. Rooms are newly renovated and comfortable (S-460-500 AS, Sb-780-880 AS, D-860 AS, Db-1,120-1,400 AS, CC:VMA, elevator, non-smoking rooms, 50 meters from the Golden Roof as central as can be in the old town at Herzog-Friedrichstrasse 31, A-6020 Innsbruck, tel. 0512/59479, fax 0512/594-7990, e-mail: hotel.weisses.kreuz@eunet.at).

Pension Stoi is a clean basic place 200 meters from the train station (S-400 AS, Sb-480 AS, D-590 AS, Db-690 AS, T-730 AS, Tb-830 AS, no breakfast, free parking in alleyway behind #5 at Salurnerstrasse 7, 6020 Innsbruck, tel. 0512/585-434).

Transportation Connections—Innsbruck
To: Hall (4 buses/hrly, 30 min; hrly trains, 15 min), **Salzburg** (hrly trains, 2 hrs), **Vienna** (hrly trains, 5 hrs), **Reutte** (trains every 2 hrs, 2.5 hrs with one change; or by bus: 4/day, 2.5 hrs), **Bregenz** (every 2 hours, 3 hrs), **Zurich** (every 2 hours, 4.5 hrs), **Munich** (every 2 hours, 2 hrs), **Paris** (1 train/day, 11 hrs), **Milan** (every 2 hours, 5.5 hrs), **Venice** (5 trains/day, 5.5 hrs). Train info: tel. 0512/1717.

HALL IN TIROL
Hall was a rich salt-mining center when Innsbruck was just a humble bridge (*Brücke*) town on the Inn River. Hall actually has a larger old town than does its sprawling neighbor, Innsbruck. Hall hosts a colorful morning scene before the daily tour buses arrive, closes down tight for its daily siesta, and sleeps on Sunday. There's a brisk farmers' market on Saturday mornings. The town tries hard and promises much, but in practice, scheduled tours happen only in July and August. (For drivers, Hall is a convenient overnight stop on the long drive from Vienna to Switzerland.)

Orientation (tel code: 05223)
Tourist Information: Hall's TI is just off the main square (Monday–Friday 9:00–18:00, Saturday 9:00–12:00, closed Sunday, tel. 05223/56269).

Bike Rental: Bikes can be rented at the camping grounds (tel. 05223/454-6475). The riverside bike path (11 km from Hall to Volders) is a real treat.

Sights—Hall
Hasegg Castle—This was the town mint. As you walk over the old pedestrian bridge from Gasthof Badl into town, this is the first old building you'll see (you can pick up a town map and a list of sights here).
Parish Church—Facing the town square, this much appended Gothic church is decorated Baroque, with fine altars, a twisted apse, and a north wall lined with bony relics.

Salt Museum (Bergbaumuseum)—Back when salt was money, Hall was loaded. Try catching a tour at this museum, where the town has reconstructed one of its original salt mines, complete with pits, shafts, drills, tools, and a slippery but tiny wooden slide (40 AS, by guided tour only, 30-minute tours depart on the hour from 14:00–17:00 if there are at least two people, English spoken, Monday–Saturday from April–October, closed Sunday, tel. 05223/56269).

Walking Tours—The TI organizes town walks in English (80 AS including admissions, 14:00, two hours, minimum four people, it's best to call first to confirm, tel. 05223/56269).

Swimming—To give your trip a special splash, check out Hall's magnificent Freischwimmbad, a huge outdoor pool with four diving boards, a giant lap pool, a big slide, and a kiddies' pool, all surrounded by a lush garden, sauna, mini-golf, and lounging locals (38 AS).

Sleeping and Eating in Hall
(12 AS = about $1, tel. code: 05223)
Lovable towns that specialize in lowering the pulse of local vacationers line the Inn Valley. Hall, while the best town, has the shortest list of accommodations. Up the hill on either side of the river are towns strewn with fine farmhouse hotels and pensions. Most *Zimmer* charge about 200 AS per person but don't accept one-night stays.

Gasthof Badl is a big, comfortable, friendly place run by sunny Frau Steiner and her daughter, Sonja. It's easy to find: immediately off the Hall Mitte freeway exit, you'll see the orange-lit "Bed" sign straight ahead. I like it for the convenience, quiet, big breakfast, easy telephone reservations, and warm welcome (Sb-455 AS, Db-730 AS, Tb-1,050 AS, Qb-1,360 AS, elevator, CC:VM, Innbrücke 4, A-6060 Hall in Tirol, tel. 05223/56784, fax 05223/567-843, e-mail: badl@tirol.com). Hall's kitchens close early, but Gasthof Badl's restaurant serves excellent dinners until 22:00 (around 120 AS, closed Tuesday). In the Gasthof Badl lobby, you'll find all the essential TI brochures and maps of Hall and Innsbruck in English.

For a cheaper room in a private home, **Frieda Tollinger** rents out three rooms and accepts one-nighters (220 AS per person with breakfast, across the river from Badl and downstream about half a mile, follow Untere Lend, which becomes Schopperweg, to Schopperweg 8, tel. 05223/41366, NSE).

Sleeping near Hall in Gnadenwald
Alpenhotel Speckbacherhof is a grand rustic hotel set between a peaceful forest and a meadow with all the comforts, a pool, mini-golf, and so on (Db-840–880 AS, half-board 170 AS per person

more, ask for 10 percent discount with this book, CC:VMA, A-6060 Gnadenwald/Tirol, tel. 05223/52511, fax 05223/525-1155, family Mayr). Drive 10 minutes uphill from Hall to the village of Gnadenwald. It's across the street from the Hinterhornalm toll road.

Transportation Connections—Hall

Innsbruck is the nearest major train station. Hall and Innsbruck are connected by train and bus. Trains do the trip faster but leave only hourly, and Hall's train station is a 10-minute walk to the town center. The white bus #4 takes a bit longer (30 minutes, 26 AS) but leaves four times per hour and drops you at the edge of town—at the wooden bridge by the Bille Supermarket or the Kurhaus at the top of Hall. Buses go to and from the Innsbruck train station, a seven-minute walk from the old town center. Drivers staying in freeway-handy Hall can smartly side-trip into Innsbruck using bus #4.

Route Tips for Drivers

Into Salzburg from Munich: After crossing the border, stay on the Autobahn, taking the Süd Salzburg exit in the direction of Anif. First you'll pass Schloss Hellbrunn (and zoo), then the TI and a great park-and-ride service. Get sightseeing information and a day-long bus pass from the TI (daily 9:00–20:00), park your car (free), and catch the shuttle bus (20 AS, every five minutes) into town. Mozart never drove in the old town, and neither should you. If you don't believe in park-and-ride, the easiest, cheapest, most central parking lot is the 1,500-car Altstadt lot in the tunnel under the Mönchsberg (160 AS per day, note your slot number and which of the twin lots you're in). Your hotel may have parking discount passes.

From Salzburg to Hallstatt (50 miles): Get on the Munich–Wien Autobahn (blue signs), head for Vienna, exit at Thalgau, and follow signs to Hof, Fuschl, and St. Gilgen. The road to Hallstatt leads first past Fuschlsee (mediocre Sommerrodelbahn summer luge ride, 40 AS, open when dry, April–mid-October 10:00–17:00, at Fuschl an See, tel. 06226/8452), to St. Gilgen (pleasant but touristy), to Bad Ischl (the center of the Salzkammergut with a spa, salt-mine tour, casino, the emperor's villa if you need a Habsburg history fix, and a good tourist office, tel. 06132/23520), and along Hallstattersee to Hallstatt.

Hallstatt is basically traffic-free. Park in the middle of the tunnel at the "P-1" sign and waterfall. If this is full, try the lakeside lot (P-2, a pleasant five-minute lakeside walk from the town center) just after the tunnel. If you're traveling off-season and staying downtown, you can drive in and park by the boat dock (your hotel "guest card" gives you permission).

From Hall into Innsbruck and on to Switzerland: For old

Innsbruck, take the Autobahn from Hall to the Innsbruck Ost exit, and follow the signs to "Zentrum", then "Kongresshaus", and park as close as you can to the old center on the river (Hofgarden).

Just south of Innsbruck is the Olympic ski jump (from the Autobahn take the Innsbruck Süd exit and follow signs to "Bergisel"). Park at the end of the road near the Andreas Hofer Memorial, and climb to the empty, grassy stands for a picnic.

Leaving Innsbruck for Switzerland (from ski jump, go down into town along huge cemetery, thoughtfully placed just beyond the jump landing, and follow blue A12, Garmisch, Arlberg signs), head west on the Autobahn (direction: Bregenz). The 8-mile-long Arlberg tunnel saves you 30 minutes but costs you lots of scenery and 160 AS (Swiss francs and credit cards accepted). For a joyride and to save a few bucks, skip the tunnel, exit at St. Anton, and go via Stuben.

After the speedy Arlberg tunnel, you're 30 minutes from Switzerland. Bludenz, with its characteristic medieval quarter, makes a good rest stop. Pass Feldkirch (and another long tunnel), and exit the Autobahn at Rankweil/Feldkirch Nord, following signs for Altstätten and Meiningen (CH). Crossing the baby Rhine River, you leave Austria.

To side trip to Liechtenstein, follow FL signs at Feldkirch (see Appenzell chapter).

Side trip over Brenner Pass into Italy: A short swing into Italy is fast and easy from Innsbruck or Hall (45-minute drive, easy border crossing, Austrian schillings accepted in border towns). To get to Italy, take the great Europa Bridge over Brenner Pass. It costs about $10, but in 30 minutes you'll be at the border. (Note: Traffic can be heavy on summer weekends.) In Italy drive to the colorful market town of Vipiteno/Sterzing. The **Reifenstein Castle** is just south of town on the west side of the valley, down a small road next to the Autobahn. The lady who lives at the castle gives tours (9:30, 10:30, 14:00, and 15:00, closed Friday) in German, Italian, and a little English. It's a unique and wonderfully preserved medieval castle (5,000L or 35 AS, tel. from Austria 00-39-0472-765-879).

SWITZERLAND
(SCHWEIZ, SUISSE, SVIZZERA)

- 16,000 square miles (half the size of Ireland, or 13 Rhode Islands)
- About 6 million people (400 people per square mile, declining slightly)
- 1 Swiss franc (SF) = about 70 cents, 1.4 SF = about $1

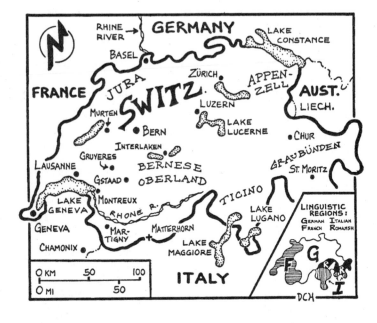

Switzerland is one of Europe's richest, best-organized, and most expensive countries. Like Boy Scouts, the Swiss count cleanliness, neatness, punctuality, tolerance, independence, thrift, and hard work as virtues, and they love pocketknives. Their high income, a great social security system, and the Alps give the Swiss plenty to be thankful for.

Switzerland is Europe's most mountainous country. Forty percent of the country consists of uninhabitable rocks, lakes, and rugged Alps. Its geography has given it distinct cultural regions. Two-thirds of the people speak German, 20 percent French, 10 percent Italian, and a small group in the southeast speak Romansch, a descendant of ancient Latin. The sing-songy Swiss German, the spoken dialect, is quite different from the written High German. Most Swiss are multilingual and English is widely spoken.

Historically, Switzerland is one of the oldest democracies (yet women didn't get the vote until 1971). Born when three states, or "cantons," united in 1291, the Confederation Helvetica, as it was called in Roman times (the "CH" decal on cars doesn't stand for chocolate), grew to the 23 cantons of today. The government is decentralized, and cantonal loyalty is very strong.

Fiercely independent, Switzerland loves its neutrality and stayed out of both world wars. But it's far from lax defensively. Every fit man serves in the army and stays in the reserve. Each house has a gun and a bomb shelter. Switzerland bristles with 600,000 rifles in homes and 12,000 heavy guns in place. Swiss vacuum-packed emergency army bread, which lasts two years, is also said to function as a weapon. Airstrips hide inside mountains behind Batmobile doors. With the push of a button, all road, rail, and bridge entries to the country can be destroyed, changing Switzerland into a formidable mountain fortress. Notice the innocent-looking but explosive patches checkerboarding the roads at key points like tunnel entrances and mountain summits (and hope no one invades until you get past). Sentiments are changing, and Switzerland has come close to voting away its entire military.

Prices are high. More and more locals call sitting on the pavement around a bottle of wine "going out." Hotels with double rooms under $80 are rare. Even dormitory beds cost $15. If your budget is tight, be sure to chase down hostels (many with "family rooms") and keep your eyes peeled for *Matratzenlagers* (literally, "mattress dorms"). Hiking is free, though major Alpine lifts run $20 to $40.

The Swiss eat when we do and enjoy a straightforward, no-nonsense cuisine. Specialties include delicious fondue, rich chocolates, a melted cheese dish called *Raclette*, fresh dairy products (try *müesli* yogurt), 100 varieties of cheese, and *Fendant*, a good, crisp, local white wine. The Co-op and Migros grocery stores are the hungry hiker's best budget bet; groceries are only 50 percent higher than U.S. prices.

You can get anywhere quickly on Switzerland's scenic and efficient trains or its fine road system (the world's most expensive per mile to build). Drivers pay a one-time 40-SF fee for a permit to use Swiss Autobahns (buy at the border, gas station, or rental agency). Anyone caught driving on a Swiss Autobahn without this tax sticker is likely to be cop-stopped and fined.

While Switzerland's booming big cities are cosmopolitan, traditional culture survives in the Alpine villages. Spend most of your time getting high in the Alps. On Sunday you're most likely to enjoy traditional music, clothing, and culture. August 1 is the festive Swiss national holiday.

GIMMELWALD AND THE BERNER OBERLAND

Frolic and hike high above the stress and clouds of the real world. Take a vacation from your busy vacation. Recharge your touristic batteries up here in the Alps, where distant avalanches, cowbells, the fluff of a down comforter, and the crunchy footsteps of happy hikers are the dominant sounds. If the weather's good (and your budget's healthy), ride a gondola from the traffic-free village of Gimmelwald to a hearty breakfast at Schilthorn's 10,000-foot revolving Piz Gloria restaurant. Linger among Alpine whitecaps before riding, hiking, or hang gliding down (5,000 feet) to Mürren and home to Gimmelwald.

Your gateway to the rugged Berner Oberland is the grand old resort town of Interlaken. Near Interlaken is Switzerland's open-air folk museum, Ballenberg, where you can climb through traditional houses from every corner of this diverse country.

Ah, but the weather's fine and the Alps beckon. Head deep into the heart of the Alps and ride the gondola to the stop just this side of heaven—Gimmelwald.

Planning Your Time

Rather than tackling a checklist of famous Swiss mountains and resorts, choose one region to savor—the Berner Oberland. Interlaken is the administrative headquarters (fine transportation hub, banking, post office, laundry, shopping). Use it for business and as a springboard for Alpine thrills. With decent weather, explore the two areas (south of Interlaken) that tower above either side of the Lauterbrunnen Valley: Kleine Scheidegg/Jungfrau and Schilthorn/Mürren. Ideally, home-base three nights in the village of Gimmelwald and spend a day in each area. On a speedy train trip, you can overnight into and out of Interlaken. For the fastest look, consider a night in Gimmelwald, breakfast at the Schilthorn, an afternoon doing the Männlichen-to-Wengen hike, and an evening or night train out. What? A nature lover not spending the night high in the Alps? Alpus-interruptus.

Getting Around the Berner Oberland

For more than 100 years, this has been the target of nature-worshiping pilgrims. And the Swiss have made the most exciting Alpine perches accessible by lift or train. Part of the fun (and most of the expense) here is riding the many lifts. Generally, scenic trains and lifts are not covered on train passes (but a Eurail or Europass gets you a 25 percent discount on even the highest lifts). Ask about discounts for early birds, youths, seniors, families, groups, and those staying awhile. The Family Card pays for itself on the first hour of trains and lifts: children under 16 travel free with parents, children ages 16 to 23 pay half-price (20 SF at Swiss train stations but not gondola stations). Get a list of discounts and the free fare and time schedule at any train station. Study the Alpine Lifts in the Berner Oberland chart in this chapter. Lifts generally go at least twice an hour, from about 7:00 to about 20:00 (sneak preview: www.jungfrau.ch).

INTERLAKEN

When the 19th-century Romantics redefined mountains as something more than cold and troublesome obstacles, Interlaken became the original Alpine resort. Ever since then, tourists have flocked to the Alps "because they're there." Interlaken's glory days are long gone, its elegant old hotels eclipsed by the new, more jet-setty Alpine resorts. Today its shops are filled with chocolate bars, Swiss Army knives, and sunburned backpackers.

Orientation (tel. code: 033)

Efficient Interlaken is a good administrative and shopping center. Take care of business, give the town a quick look, view the live TV coverage of the Jungfrau and Schilthorn weather in the window of the Schilthornbahn office on the main street (at Höheweg 2, also on TV in most hotel lobbies). Then head for the hills. Stay in Interlaken only if you suffer from alptitude sickness (see Sleeping, below).

Tourist Information: The TI has good information for the region, advice on Alpine lift discounts, and a room-finding service (July–September Monday–Friday 8:00–12:00, 13:30–18:30, Saturday 8:00–17:00, Sunday 17:00–19:00; off-season weekdays 8:00–12:00, 14:00–18:00, Saturday 8:00–12:00, closed Sunday, tel. 033/822-2121, on main street, five-minute walk from West station). While the Jungfrau region map costs 2 SF, a good mini-version is included in the free Jungfrau region train timetable. Pick

Interlaken

*Map labels:*

0 KM / 4
0 MI / 1/4

N

FUNICULAR TO HARDERKULM

SLOW ROAD TO BRIENZ →

CASINO, KURSAAL, & BIG, RITZY HOTELS

BRIENZ STRASSE

* 15 MIN. WALK
W TO E STATIONS

BOAT DOCK

← TO THUN

AARE

HOHEWEG

EAST STATION

LAUNDRY

SEE STRASSE

MARKT.

i

HOHEMATTE PARK

LINDENALLEE

POST PHONES

BAHNHOF STRASSE

OELE STRASSE

ALPEN STRASSE

WEST STATION →

CENTRAL STR.

GEN. GUISAN STR.

OB. JUNG.

RUGEN PARK STRASSE

HOTEL LÖTSCHBERG

BALMER'S HERBERGE

→ TO BRIENZ LUZERN & SÜSTENPASS

BOAT DOCK

MIGROS

WALDEGG

WYCHEL STR.

HAUPT STR.

TELL THEATER

N-8 AUTOBAHN

HEIMWEHFLUH

EIGER, MÖNCH & JUNGFRAU

N-8 AUTOBAHN

← TO SPIEZ & BERN

↓ TO LAUTERBRUNNEN

DCH

---

up a Bern map if that's your next destination. The TI organizes daily town walks in English (10 SF, 18:00, 60 minutes, from the TI).

Arrival in Interlaken: Interlaken has two train stations: East and West. Most major trains stop at the Interlaken-West station. The station's train information desk answers tourist questions and has a fair exchange desk (daily 8:00–12:00, 14:00–18:00). Ask at the station about discount passes, special fares, Eurail discounts, and schedules for the scenic mountain trains (tel. 033/826-4750). An open-late Migros supermarket is across the street with a self-service cafeteria upstairs (Monday–Thursday 8:00–18:30, Friday 8:00–21:00, Saturday 7:30–16:00, closed Sunday).

It's a pleasant 15-minute walk between the West and East stations, or an easy, frequent train connection. From the Interlaken-East station, private trains take you deep into the mountainous Jungfrau region (see Transportation Connections, below).

Helpful Hints

Telephone: Phone booths cluster outside the post office in the center of town. Inside the office, you'll find metered phone booths (talk first, pay later; Monday–Friday 7:45–18:15, Saturday 8:30–11:00, closed Sunday). For efficiency, buy a phone card from a newsstand. (There's a card phone—which doesn't take coins—in Gimmelwald.)

Gimmelwald

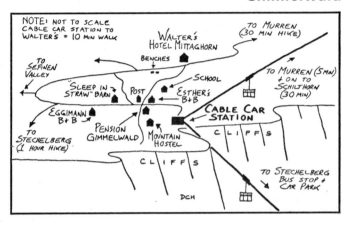

NOTE: NOT TO SCALE
CABLE CAR STATION TO
WALTER'S = 10 MIN WALK

TO MURREN
(30 MIN HIKE)

WALTER'S
HOTEL MITTAGHORN

BENCHES

TO
SEFINEN
VALLEY

TO MURREN (5 MIN)
+ ON TO
SCHILTHORN
(30 MIN)

SCHOOL

"SLEEP IN
STRAW" BARN

POST

ESTHER'S
B+B

CABLE CAR
STATION

EGGIMANN
B+B

PENSION
GIMMELWALD

MOUNTAIN
HOSTEL

C L I F F S

TO
STECHELBERG
(1 HOUR HIKE)

C L I F F S

TO STECHELBERG
BUS STOP +
CAR PARK

DCH

Laundry: Helen Schmocker's *Wäscherei* (laundry) has a change machine, soap, English instructions, and a pleasant riverside locale (daily 7:00–22:00 for self-service, or Monday–Saturday 8:00–12:00, 13:30–18:00 for full service: drop off 10 pounds and 12 SF in the morning and pick up clean clothes that afternoon, from post office, follow Marktgasse over two bridges to Beatenbergstrasse, tel. 033/822-1566).

Activities: For the adventurer with money, Alpin Raft offers high-adrenaline trips such as rafting, canyoning (rappeling down watery gorges), bungee jumping, and paragliding (Postfach 78, tel. 033/823-4100, Web site: www.alpinraft.ch). Most adventure trips cost from 80 to 140 SF.

GIMMELWALD

Saved from developers by its "avalanche zone" classification, Gimmelwald is one of the poorest places in Switzerland. Its economy is stuck in the hay, and its farmers, unable to make it in their disadvantaged trade, are subsidized by the Swiss government (and work the ski lifts in the winter). For some travelers, there's little to see in the village. Others enjoy a fascinating day sitting on a bench and learning why they say, "If heaven isn't what it's cracked up to be, send me back to Gimmelwald."

Take a walk through the town. This place is for real. Most of the 130 residents have the same last name—von Allmen. They are tough and proud. Raising hay in this rugged terrain is labor intensive. One family harvests enough to feed only 15 or 20 cows. But they'd have it no other way, and, unlike absentee landlord Mürren, Gimmelwald is locally owned. (When word got out that urban planners wished to develop Gimmelwald into a town of 1,000,

Lauterbrunnen Valley: West Side Story

locals pulled some strings to secure the town's bogus "avalanche zone" building code.)

Notice the traditional log-cabin architecture and blond-braided children. The numbers on the buildings are not addresses, but fire insurance numbers. The cute little hut near the station is for storing and aging cheese, not hostelers. In Catholic-Swiss towns, the biggest building is the church. In Protestant towns, it's the school. Gimmelwald's biggest building is the school (one teacher, 17 students, and a room that doubles as a chapel when the pastor makes his monthly visit). Do not confuse obscure Gimmelwald with touristy and commercialized Grindelwald just over the Kleine Scheidegg ridge.

Evening fun in Gimmelwald is found at the youth hostel (lots of young Alp-aholics and a good chance to share information on the surrounding mountains) or at the Pension Gimmelwald's terrace restaurant next door (see Sleeping, below).

Walter's bar is a local farmers' hangout. When they've made their hay, they come here to play. They look like what we'd call "hicks" (former city-slicker Walter still isn't fully accepted by the gang), but they speak some English and can be fun to get to know. Sit outside (benches just below the rails, 100 yards down the lane from Walter's), and watch the sun tuck the mountaintops into bed as the moon rises over the Jungfrau.

Alpine Hikes

There are days of possible hikes from Gimmelwald. Many are a fun combination of trails, mountain trains, and gondola rides.

Don't mind the fences, cross at will; a hiker has the right of way in Switzerland. But as late as early June, snow can curtail your hiking plans (the Männlichen lift doesn't even open until June 6). Get advice from a knowledgeable local before setting out on any hike to confirm that it is safe and accessible.

▲▲▲**Hike 1. The Schilthorn: Hikes, Lifts, and a 10,000-Foot Breakfast**—If the weather's good, have breakfast atop the Schilthorn in the slowly revolving, mountain-capping restaurant (of James Bond movie fame). The early bird–special gondola tickets (rides before 9:00) take you from Gimmelwald to the Schilthorn and back at a discount. Nag the Schilthorn station in Mürren for a gondola souvenir decal (Schilthorn info: tel. 033/8231-444).

Breakfast costs from 13.50 SF to 22 SF. Expect slow service, and ask for more hot drinks if necessary. If you're not revolving, ask them to turn it on. Linger on top. Piz Gloria has a souvenir shop, the rocks of the region on the restaurant wall, telescopes, and a "touristorama" film room showing a multi-screen slideshow and explosive highlights from the James Bond thriller that featured the Schilthorn (free and self-serve; push the button for slides or, after a long pause for the projector to rewind, push for 007).

Watch hang gliders set up, psych up, and take off, flying 30 minutes with the birds to distant Interlaken. Walk along the ridge out back. This is a great place for a photo of the "mountain-climber you." For another cheap thrill, ask the gondola attendant to crank down the window, stick your head out, and pretend you're hang gliding, ideally over the bump going down from Gimmelwald.

Lifts go twice an hour, and the ride (including two transfers) to the Schilthorn takes 30 minutes. Watch the altitude meter in the gondola. (The Gimmelwald-Schilthorn hike is free, if you don't mind a 5,000-foot altitude gain.) You can ride up to the Schilthorn and hike down, but I wouldn't (weather can change; have good shoes). For a less scary hike, go halfway down by cable car and walk down from the Birg station. Buy the round-trip excursion early-bird fare (cheaper than the Gimmelwald-Schilthorn-Birg ticket) and decide at Birg if you want to hike or ride down.

Hiking down from Birg is very steep and gravelly. Just below Birg is the Schilthorn-Hutte. Drop in for soup, cocoa, or a coffee schnapps. You can spend the night in the hut's crude loft (40 mattresses, 60 SF for bed, breakfast, and dinner, open July–September, tel. 033/855-1167). Youth hostelers scream down the ice fields on plastic-bag sleds from the Schilthorn. (English-speaking doctor in Mürren.)

The most interesting trail from Birg to Gimmelwald is the high one via Grauseewli Lake and Wasenegg Ridge to Brünli, down to Spielbodenalp, and the Sprutz waterfall. From the Birg lift, hike toward the Schilthorn, taking your first left down to the little, newly made Grauseewli Lake. From the lake a gravelly trail leads down the

Berner Oberland

NOTE: THIS BIRD'S EYE VIEW LOOKS SOUTH...

EIGER 13026' MONCH 13499' JUNGFRAU 13642' SCHILT-HORN 9748'

JUNG-FRAU-JOCH

TUNNEL

KLEINE SCHEIDEGG 6762'

GIMMEL-WALD 4593'

BIRG 8784'

HIKE #1

HIKE #2

W. ALP

MÜRREN 5381'

GRINDEL-WALD 3393'

MÄNN-LICHEN 7317'

STECHEL-BERG 3025'

← NICE WALK

GRUND

GRÜTSCHALP 4879'

R TO FIRST

WENGEN 4180'

LAUTERBRUNNEN 2612'

ISENFLUH

HIKE #3

WILDERSWIL 1916'

ISELT-WALD

SCHYNIGE PLATTE 6454'

SPIEZ

TO LUZERN

E.

W.

LAKE

BRIENZ

BRIENZ

BALLENBERG

INTER-LAKEN 1860'

LAKE THUN

TO BERN

+++ PRIVATE RAIL - EURAIL NOT VALID
+++ OTHER RAIL - EURAIL VALID
o—o MTN. LIFTS

- - - BUS
•••• BOAT
••••• TRAIL

NOT TO SCALE!

— DCH —

rough switchbacks until it levels out. When you see a rock painted with arrows pointing to "Mürren" and "Rotstockhütte," follow the path to Rotstockhütte, traversing the cow-grazed mountainside. Follow Wasenegg Ridge left/down and along the barbed wire fence, which dead-ends at Brünli below. (For maximum thrills, stay on the ridge and climb all the way to the knobby little summit where you'll enjoy an incredible 360-degree view and a chance to sign your name on the register stored in the little wooden box.) A steep trail winds directly down from Brünli towards Gimmelwald, soon hitting a bigger, easy trail. The trail bends right (just before the popular restaurant/mountain hut at Spielbodenalp) leading to Sprutz. Walk under the Sprutz waterfall, and a steep wooded trail deposits you in a meadow of flowers at the top side of Gimmelwald.

For an expensive thrill, you can bungee-jump from the Stechelberg–Mürren service gondola (100 SF for a 330-foot drop, 220 SF for 590 feet, drop head-first or feet-first, have photos taken, daily 8:00–18:00, tel. 033/826-7711).

▲▲▲**Hike 2: The Männlichen–Kleine Scheidegg Hike**—This

Alpine Lifts in the Berner Oberland

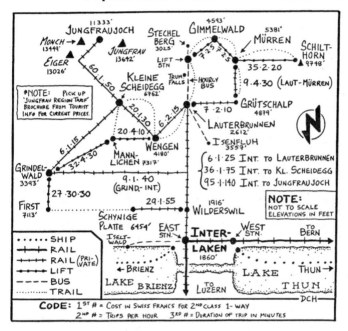

is my favorite easy Alpine hike, entertaining you all the way with glorious Jungfrau, Eiger, and Mönch views. (That's the Young Maiden being protected from the Ogre by the Monk.)

If the weather's good, descend from Gimmelwald bright and early. Catch the post bus to the Lauterbrunnen train station (synchronized to depart with the arrival of each lift—3.60 SF; or drive, parking at the large multi-storied pay lot behind the Lauterbrunnen station). Buy a ticket to Männlichen and catch the train. Ride past great valley views to Wengen, where you'll walk across town (buy a picnic, but don't waste time here if it's sunny), and catch the Männlichen lift (departing every 15 minutes, after June 6) to the top of the ridge high above you.

From the tip of the Männlichen lift, hike 20 minutes north to the little peak for that king- or queen-of-the-mountain feeling. It's an easy hour's walk from there to Kleine Scheidegg for a picnic or restaurant lunch. (For accommodations, see Sleeping, below.) If you've got an extra 100 SF and the weather's perfect, ride the train from Kleine Scheidegg through the Eiger to the towering Jungfraujoch and back. Check for discount trips up to Jungfraujoch (three trips a day—early or late, tel. 033/826-4750, trilingual weather info: tel. 033/855-1022). Jungfraujoch crowds can be frightening. The price has been jacked up to reduce the mobs, but sunny days are still a mess.

From Kleine Scheidegg, enjoy the ever-changing Alpine panorama of the north faces of the Eiger, Jungfrau, and Mönch, probably accompanied by the valley-filling mellow sound of Alphorns and distant avalanches, as you ride the train or hike downhill (30 gorgeous minutes to Wengeralp, 90 more steep minutes from there into the town of Wengen). If the weather turns bad or you run out of steam, catch the train early at the little Wengeralp station along the way. After Wengeralp, the trail to Wengen is steep and, while not dangerous, requires a good set of knees. Wengen is a fine shopping town. (For accommodations, see Sleeping, below.) The boring final descent from Wengen to Lauterbrunnen is knee-killer steep—catch the train. Trails may be snowbound into early June. Ask about conditions at the lift stations or local TI. If the Männlichen lift is closed, take the train straight from Lauterbrunnen to Kleine Scheidegg. Many take the risk of slipping and enjoy the Kleine Scheidegg-to-Wengeralp hike even with a little snow.

▲▲**Hike 3: Schynige Platte to First**—The best day I've had hiking in the Berner Oberland is the demanding six-hour ridge walk high above Lake Brienz on one side and all that Jungfrau beauty on the other. Start at Wilderswil train station (just above Interlaken), where you catch the little train up to Schynige Platte (2,000 meters). Walk through the Alpine flower display garden and into the wild Alpine yonder. The high point is Faulhorn (2,680 meters, with its famous mountaintop hotel). Hike to a small gondola called "First" (2,168 meters), where you descend to Grindelwald and catch a train back to your starting point, Wilderswil—or, if you have a regional train pass or no car but endless money, return to Gimmelwald via Lauterbrunnen from Grindelwald over Kleine Scheidegg. For an abbreviated ridge walk, consider the Panoramaweg, a short loop from Schynige Platte to Daub Peak.

▲▲**Hike 4: Cloudy Day Lauterbrunnen Valley Walk**—For a smell-the-cows-and-flowers lowland walk, ideal for a cloudy day, weary body, or tight budget, follow the riverside trail five kilometers from Lauterbrunnen's Staubach Falls (just after the town church) to the Schilthornbahn station at Stechelberg. Detour to Trümmelbach Falls en route (see below).

If you're staying in Gimmelwald: To get to Lauterbrunnen, walk up to Mürren (30 min), walk or ride the train to Grütschalp (60-min hike), ride the funicular down to Lauterbrunnen (10 min), walk through town, and take the riverside trail ending up at Stechelberg (75 min)—where you can ride the lift back up to Gimmelwald (10 min).

Also consider biking around the valley. Imboden Bike rents bikes on the main street of Lauterbrunnen (20–40 SF/day, tel. 033/855-2114, see Rainy Day Options below).

▲**Other Hikes near Gimmelwald**—For a not-too-tough three-hour walk (but there's a scary 20-minute stretch that comes with ropes) with great Jungfrau views and some mountain farm action, ride the funicular from Mürren to Allmendhübel (1,934 meters), and walk to Marchegg, Saustal, and Grütschalp (a drop of about 500 meters), where you can catch the panorama train back to Mürren. An easier version is the lower Bergweg from Allmenhübel to Grütschalp via Winteregg. For an easy family stroll with grand views, walk from Mürren just above the train tracks to either Winteregg (40 min, restaurant, playground, train station) or Grütschalp (60 min, train station), and catch the panorama train back to Mürren. An easy, go-as-far-as-you-like trail from Gimmelwald is up the Sefinen Valley. Or you can wind from Gimmelwald down to Stechelberg (one hour).

You can get specifics at the Mürren TI. For a description of six diverse hikes on the west side of Lauterbrunnen, pick up the fine and free *Mürren-Schilthorn Hikes* brochure (at stations, hotels, and TIs). The 3-D map of the Mürren mountainside, which includes hiking trails, makes a useful, attractive souvenir (2 SF at TI and lift station). For an extensive rundown on the region, get Don Chmura's fine 5-SF Gimmelwald guidebook (includes info on hikes, flora, fauna, culture, and travel tips; available at Hotel Mittaghorn in Gimmelwald).

Rainy Day Options

If clouds roll in, don't despair. They can roll out just as quickly, and there are some good bad-weather options. There are easy trails and pleasant walks along the floor of the Lauterbrunnen Valley (see above). If all the waterfalls have you intrigued, sneak a behind-the-scenes look at the valley's most powerful one, **Trümmelbach Falls** (10 SF, daily April–November 9:00–17:00, July–August 8:00–18:00, on the Lauterbrunnen-Stechelberg road, tel. 033/855-3232). You'll ride an elevator up through the mountain and climb through several caves to see the melt from the Eiger, Mönch, and Jungfrau grinding like God's band saw through the mountain at the rate of up to 20,000 liters a second (nearly double the beer consumption at Oktoberfest). The upper area, chutes 6 to 10, are the best, so if your legs ache, you can skip the lower ones and ride the lift down.

You can rent bikes at the Interlaken station. For 5 SF extra you can take your bike on the train to the top of Lauterbrunnen Valley and enjoy a scenic ride downhill back into Interlaken via a peaceful bike path over the river from the road.

Lauterbrunnen's **Heimatmuseum** shows off the local folk culture (3 SF, mid-June–September, Tuesday, Thursday, Saturday, and Sunday 14:00–17:30, just over the bridge).

Mürren's slick **Sports Center** (Sportzentrum) offers a world of indoor activities (12 SF for use of the swimming pool and whirlpool, 7 SF for Mürren hotel guests, pool open Monday–Saturday afternoon, mid-June–October). Mürren also has plenty of shops, bakeries, banks, a TI, and accommodations (see Sleeping, below).

Boat Trips from Interlaken—"Interlaken" means "between the lakes." Lazy boat trips explore these lakes (8/day, fewer off-season, free with Eurail, schedules at TI). The Lake Thun boat stops at Beatushöhlen (interesting caves, 30 min from Interlaken) and two visit-worthy towns: Spiez (1 hr from Interlaken) and Thun (1.75 hrs away). The Lake Brienz boat stops at the super-cute and quiet village of Iseltwald (45 min away), and Brienz (1.25 hrs away, near Ballenberg Open-Air Folk Museum).

▲▲Swiss Open-Air Folk Museum at Ballenberg—Near Interlaken, the Swiss Open-Air Museum of Vernacular Architecture, Country Life, and Crafts in the Bernese Oberland is a rich collection of traditional and historic farmhouses from every region of the country. Each house is carefully furnished, and many feature traditional craftspeople at work. The sprawling 50-acre park, laid out roughly as a huge Swiss map, is a natural preserve providing a wonderful setting for this culture-on-a-lazy-Susan look at Switzerland.

The Thurgau house (#621) has an interesting wattle-and-daub (half-timbered construction) display and house #331 has a fun bread museum. Use the 2-SF map/guide. The more expensive picture book is a better souvenir than guide. (14-SF entry, half-price after 16:00, daily mid-April–October 10:00–17:00, houses close at 17:00, park stays open later, craft demonstration schedules are listed just inside the entry, tel. 033/951-1123.) There's a reasonable outdoor cafeteria inside the west entrance, and fresh-baked bread, sausage, mountain cheese, and other goodies on sale in several houses. Picnic tables and grills with free firewood are scattered throughout the park. The little wooden village of Brienzwiler (near the east entrance) is a museum in itself with a lovely little church. Trains run frequently from Interlaken to Brienzwiler, an easy walk from the museum.

Sleeping and Eating in the Berner Oberland
(1.4 SF = about $1, tel. code: 033)
Sleep Code: **S** = Single, **D** = Double/Twin, **T** = Triple, **Q** = Quad, **b** = bathroom, **t** = toilet only, **s** = shower only, **CC** = Credit Card (Visa, MasterCard, Amex), **SE** = Speaks English, **NSE** = No English. Unless otherwise noted, breakfast is included.

Sleeping and Eating in Gimmelwald
(4,500 feet, tel code: 033, zip code: 3826)
To inhale the Alps and really hold it in, sleep high in Gimmelwald. Poor but pleasantly stuck in the past, the village has a creaky

hotel, happy hostel, decent pension, and a couple of B&Bs. The bad news is that the lift costs 7.20 SF each way to get there.

Hotel Mittaghorn, the treasure of Gimmelwald, is run by Walter Mittler, a perfect Swiss gentleman. Walter's hotel is a classic, creaky, Alpine-style place with memorable beds, ancient down comforters (short and fat; wear socks and drape the blanket over your feet), and a million-dollar view of the Jungfrau Alps. The Yodelin' Seniors' loft has a dozen real beds on either side of a divider, with several sinks, down comforters, and a fire ladder out the back window. The hotel has one shower for 10 rooms (1 SF for five minutes). Walter is careful not to let his place get too hectic or big and enjoys sensitive Back Door travelers. He runs the hotel alone with the help of Rosemary from the village, keeping it simple, but with class. This is a good place to receive mail from home (check the mail barrel in entry hall).

To some, Hotel Mittaghorn is a fire waiting to happen—with a kitchen that would never pass code, lumpy beds, teeny towels, and nowhere near enough plumbing—run by an eccentric old grouch. These people enjoy Interlaken, Wengen, or Mürren, and that's where they should sleep. Be warned, you'll see more of my readers than locals here, but it's a fun crowd—an extended family (D-60–70 SF, T-85 SF, Q-105 SF, Yodelin' Seniors' loft beds-25 SF, all with breakfast, 3 SF surcharge for one-night stays, CH-3826 Gimmelwald/Bern, tel. 033/855-1658, closed November–April). Reserve by telephone only, and then you must reconfirm by telephone the day before your arrival. Walter usually offers his guests a simple 15-SF dinner. Off-season only, lofters pay just 20 SF for a bed with breakfast. Hotel Mittaghorn is at the top of Gimmelwald, a five-minute climb up the steps from the village intersection.

Mountain Hostel is goat-simple, as clean as its guests, cheap, and very friendly. Its 50 dorm beds are often taken, so call ahead. Petra only takes reservations the day before or the day of arrival (after 9:30). Simply call and leave your name. The hostel has low ceilings, a self-service kitchen (pack in groceries), and new plumbing. Petra Brunner has filled the place with flowers. This relaxed hostel survives with the help of its guests. Please read the signs, respect Petra's rules, and leave it cleaner than you found it. Guests do a small duty. The place is one of those rare spots where a family atmosphere spontaneously combusts, and spaghetti becomes communal as it softens (15 SF per bed in six- to 15-bed rooms, showers-1 SF, no breakfast and no sheets—bring your own, hostel membership not required, 20 yards from the lift station, tel. & fax 033/855-1704).

Next door, **Pension Restaurant Gimmelwald** serves meals and offers 12 basic rooms under low creaky ceilings (D-90 SF, Db-110 SF) and sheetless backpacker beds (25 SF in D, T, and Q rooms), including breakfast. The pension has a scenic terrace overlooking the Jungfrau and the hostel: great for camaraderie but not for peace (closed November and first half of May, 50 meters from gondola station, non-smoking, CC:VM, tel. & fax 033/855-1730). Nicole speaks English and runs the pension. Her husband, Francois, runs the kitchen. Reserve by phone, obligatory reconfirmation by phone two or three days in advance of arrival.

Maria and Olle Eggimann rent two rooms—Gimmelwald's most comfortable—in their Alpine-sleek chalet. Twelve-year town residents Maria and Olle, who job-share the village's only teaching position and raise three kids of their own, offer visitors a rare inside peek at this community (D-100 SF, Db with kitchenette-180 SF for two or three people, optional breakfast-18 SF, no CC, last check-in 18:30, three-night minimum for advance reservations; from gondola continue straight 100 meters past town's only intersection, B&B on left, CH-3826 Gimmelwald, tel. 033/855-3575, e-mail: oeggimann@bluewin.ch, SE fluently).

Esther's B&B, overlooking the main intersection of the village, rents basic rooms in a creaky old home (St-40 SF, Dt-72 SF, Tt-90 SF, with breakfast, two-night minimum stay, tel. 033/855-5488, fax 033/855-5492, a little English spoken).

Schalf im Stroh ("Sleep in Straw") offers exactly that—in an actual barn. After the cows head for higher ground in the summer, the friendly von Allmen family hoses out their barn and fills it with straw and budget travelers. Blankets are free, but bring your own sheet, sleep sack, or sleeping bag. No beds, no bunks, no mattresses, no kidding (19 SF, 13 SF for kids under 12, breakfast included, showers-2 SF, open mid-June–mid-October, depending on grass and snow levels; from lift, continue straight through intersection, barn marked "1995" on right, tel. 033/855-5488, fax 033/855-5492).

Eating in Gimmelwald: Pension Gimmelwald, the only restaurant in town, serves a hearty breakfast buffet for 11 SF and 15-SF dinners featuring a sampling of organic produce from the local farmers and a fine *Rösti*. The hostel has a decent members' kitchen but serves no food. There are no groceries in town. The wise and frugal pack in food from the Co-op stores in Mürren or Lauterbrunnen or the Migros in Interlaken. Hotel Mittaghorn serves dinner only to its guests (15 SF). Follow dinner with a Heidi Cocoa (cocoa *mit* peppermint schnapps) or a Virgin Heidi. The local farmers sell their produce. Esther (at the main intersection of the village) makes by far Gimmelwald's best yogurt—but only until the cows go up in June.

Sleeping and Eating in Mürren
(5,500 feet, tel. code: 033, zip code: 3825)
Mürren—pleasant as an Alpine resort can be—is traffic-free, filled with bakeries, cafés, souvenirs, old-timers with walking sticks, GE

employees enjoying incentive trips, and Japanese making movies of each other with a Fujichrome backdrop. Its chalets are prefab-rustic. Sitting on a ledge 2,000 feet above the Lauterbrunnen Valley, surrounded by a fortissimo chorus of mountains, it has all the comforts of home and then some, with Alp-high prices. All prices are higher during the ski season and from July 15 to August 15. Mürren has an ATM.

Mürren's TI can find you a room, give hiking advice, rent mountain bikes (20 SF/half-day, 30 SF/full day), and change money (in Sportzentrum, open mid-July–mid-September 9:00–12:00, 13:00–18:30, Thursday until 20:30, Saturday 13:00–18:00, Sunday 13:00–17:30, less off-season, tel. 033/856-8686, Web site: www.muerren.ch, e-mail: info@muerren.ch).

Guesthouse Belmont offers good budget rooms. This is a friendly, creaky, very wooden home away from home (S-45 SF, D-90 SF, Db-130 SF, 39-SF beds in two-, four- and six-person bunkrooms, with sheets and breakfast, closed November, CC:VMA, across from the train station, tel. 033/855-3535, fax 033/855-3531, well-run by Verena). The Belmont serves good, reasonably-priced dinners and its poolroom is a popular local hangout.

Hotel Alpina is a simple modern place with comfortable rooms and a concrete feeling—comforting, given its cliff-edge position (Sb-75 AS, Db-130 AS with awesome cliff-hanging Jungfrau views and balconies, "no view" special: Db-90 SF with this book, CC:VMA, exit left from station, walk two minutes downhill, tel. 033/855-1361, fax 033/855 1049, Frau Taugwalder).

Chalet Fontana, run by an Englishwoman, Denise Fussell, is worn and basic (the rooms, not Denise) but a rare budget option in Mürren (35–45 SF per person in small doubles or triples with break-fast, 5 SF cheaper without breakfast, one three-bed room with kitch-enette-45 SF per person, open mid-May through October, across street from Stägerstübli restaurant in town center, tel. 033/855-2686, e-mail: 106501.2731@compuserve.com). If no one's home, check at the Ed Abegglen shop next door (tel. 033/855-1245).

Hotel Jungfrau offers an array of options: **Hotel** with pricey, modern, and comfortable rooms (Db-160 SF with view, 140 SF without, elevator); **Lodge** in a basic, blocky 20-room annex with well-worn but fine rooms and actually better Jungfrau views (Db-110 SF, family apartments); and the **Staff House.** Outside of ski season, half the industrial-strength employees' quarters are empty and rented to budget travelers—stark and basic with only sinks in the rooms (S-48 SF, D-76 SF). All rooms include the same fancy buffet breakfast and free entrance to the Sports Center pool. Without breakfast deduct 10 SF per person (CC:VMA, near TI and Sportzentrum, tel. 033/855-4545, fax 033/855-4549, Web site: www.muerren.ch/jungfrau, e-mail: jungfrau@muerren.ch).

Hotel Alpenruh—expensive and yuppie-rustic—is about the only hotel in Mürren open year-round. The comfortable rooms come with views and some balconies (Sb-80–100 SF, Db-140–200 SF depending on season, elevator, attached restaurant, sauna, free tickets for breakfast atop Schilthorn, CC:VMA, 10 yards from gondola station, tel. 033/856-8800, fax 033/856-8888, e-mail: alpruh@tcnet.ch). **Hotel Bellevue-Crystal** also offers reasonable rooms (Db-110 SF, tel. 033/855-1401).

Eating in Mürren: For a rare bit of ruggedness, eat at the **Stägerstübli** (10–30 SF lunches and dinners, closed Tuesday). The **Kandhar Snack Bar** at the Sport Center has fun, creative, and inexpensive light meals and a good selection of teas and pastries. Mürren's bakery is excellent. For picnic fixings, shop at the **Co-op** (normally open 8:00–12:00, 14:00–18:30, closed afternoons on Tuesday and Saturday and all day Sunday).

Sleeping in Wengen
(4,200 feet, tel. code: 033, zip code: 3823)

Wengen, a fancy Mürren on the other side of the valley, has more tennis courts than budget beds. This traffic-free resort is an easy train ride above Lauterbrunnen and halfway up to Kleine Scheidegg and Männlichen.

Reasonable beds can be found at: **Hotel Bernerhof** (D-90 SF, Db-130 SF, includes breakfast, dorm bed-29 SF with sheets and breakfast, 17 SF without breakfast, tel. 033/855-2721, fax 033/855-3358). **Chalet Bergheim** (some doubles and six 28-SF dorm beds with sheets, opens in June, tel. 033/855-2755). **Chalet Schweizerheim Garni** (Db-120 SF, summer only, tel. 033/855-1581). **Hotel Eden** (S-62 SF, D-116 SF, Db-144 SF, tel. 033/855-1634, fax 033/855-3950, Kerstin Bucher SE); the same hotel runs **Eddy's Hostel**, a block away, with 33-SF dorm beds. **Clare and Andy's B&B Chalet** (Chalet Trogihalten, one Db-74SF, one Qb-156SF, breakfast 7-SF, four night minimum preferred, tel. & fax 033/855-1712, Clare's English, Andy's Swiss).

Sleeping in Kleine Scheidegg
(6,762 feet, tel. code: 033, zip code: 3801)

For dorm beds with breakfast high in the mountains, sleep at Kleine Scheidegg's **Bahnhof Buffet** (D-106 SF, 38 SF per bed in dorm, breakfast included, tel. 033/855-1151) or at **Restaurant Grindelwaldblick** (32 SF for bed in 12-bed room, no sheets, open June–October, tel. 033/855-1374). Confirm price and availability before ascending.

Sleeping near the Stechelberg Lift
(2,800 feet, tel. code: 033, zip code: 3824)

Stechelberg is a hamlet at the end of the valley (bus stop at the post office). **Nelli Beer**, renting three rooms in a quiet, scenic, and folksy setting, is your best Stechelberg option (S-27 SF, D-50 SF, minimum two nights, over river behind Stechelberg post office at big "Zimmer" sign, tel. 033/855-3930, some English spoken). **Hotel Stechelberg** has 20 clean and quiet rooms (S-45 SF, D-78 SF, Db-112 SF, CC:VMA, tel. 033/855-2921, fax 033/855-4438, e-mail: hotel.stechelberg@tcnet.ch). The local **Naturfreundehaus Alpenhof** is a rugged Alpine lodge for hikers (60 co-ed beds, four to eight per room, 17.60 SF per bed, breakfast-8 SF, dinner-14 SF, no sheets, closed November, tel. 033/855-1202).

Here's a wild idea: **Mountain Hotel Obersteinberg** is a working Alpine farm—cheese, cows, a mule shuttling up food once a day, and an American (Vickie) who fell in love with a mountain man. It's a 2.5-hour hike either from Stechelberg or from Gimmelwald. They rent 12 primitive rooms and a bunch of loft beds: no shower, no hot water, meager solar-panel electricity. Candles light up the night, and you can take a hot-water bottle to bed if necessary (S-74 SF, D-148 SF, including linen, breakfast, and dinner, dorm beds without sheets-17 SF or 57 SF with dinner and breakfast, open June–September, tel. 033/855-2033). The place is filled with locals and Germans on weekends but all yours on weekdays. Why not hike there from Gimmelwald and leave the Alps a day later?

Sleeping in Lauterbrunnen
(2,600 feet, tel. code: 033, zip code: 3822)
Lauterbrunnen—with a train station, TI (tel. 033/855-1955), bank, shops, and lots of hotels—is the valley commercial center. This is the jumping-off point for Jungfrau and Schilthorn adventures. It's idyllic in spite of the busy road and big buildings.

Valley Hostel is new, concrete, and practical, offering cheap and comfortable beds two blocks up the valley from the Lauterbrunnen station (D-44 SF, beds in larger family-friendly rooms-20 SF each, breakfast extra, non-smoking, laundry service, tel. & fax 033/855-2008, Martha and Alfred Abegglen).

Crystal Gästehaus is another new, concrete-feeling hotel offering comfort at a good price and location (Db-120 SF, 50 SF per bed in larger rooms, two blocks up valley from station, tel. 033/856-9090, fax 033/856-9099).

Chalet im Rohr is a creaky old fire-waiting-to-happen place offering 26-SF beds in one- to four-bed rooms and plenty of character (near the church, tel. 033/855-1507).

Masenlager Stocki is rustic and humble with the cheapest beds in town (12 SF with sheets in an easygoing little 30-bed co-ed dorm with a kitchen, tel. 033/855-1754).

Two campgrounds just south of town provide 15- to 25-SF beds (in dorms, two-, four-, and six-bed bungalows, no sheets, kitchen facilities, and big English-speaking tour groups). **Camping**

Jungfrau, romantically situated beyond Staubach Falls, is huge and well organized (tel. 033/855-2010). It also has fancier cabins (18 SF per person). **Schützenbach Campground**, on the left just past Lauterbrunnen toward Stechelberg, is simpler (tel. 033/855-1268).

Sleeping in Isenfluh
(3,560 feet, tel. code: 033, zip code: 3807)
In the tiny hamlet of Isenfluh, which is smaller than Gimmelwald and offers even better views, **Pension Waldrand** rents six reasonable rooms (Db-110 SF, tel. 033/855-1227, hourly shuttle bus from Lauterbrunnen).

Sleeping in Interlaken
(tel. code: 033, zip code: 3800)
I'd head for Gimmelwald. Interlaken is not the Alps. But if you must stay, here are some good choices.

Hotel Lotschberg, with a sun terrace and wonderful rooms, is run by English-speaking Susi and Fritz and is the best real hotel value in town. Information abounds, and Fritz organizes wonderful adventures (Sb-100 SF, Db-145–180 SF, extra bed 20–25 SF, family deals, cheaper November–May, CC:VMA, elevator, bar, laundry service-8 SF, free e-mail access, non-smoking, four-minute walk from the West Station, on General Guisanstrasse 31, tel. 033/822-2545, fax 033/822-2579, Web site: www.beoswiss .ch/lotschberg, e-mail: lotschberg@interlakentourism.ch).

Guest House Susi's B&B is Hotel Lotschberg's no-frills annex, run by the same people (same address and phone number). It has simple, cozy, cheaper rooms (Db-110 SF, apartments with kitchenettes for two people-100 SF; for four to five people-175 SF, cheaper off-season).

Villa Margaretha B&B, warmly mothered by English-speaking Frau Kunz-Joerin, offers the best cheap beds in town for those staying two nights and wishing to be in a private home. It's a big house in a garden on a quiet residential street three blocks directly in front of the West Station (D-75 SF, T-115 SF, minimum two night stay, no breakfast but kitchenette, Aarmühlestrasse 13, tel. 033/822-1813).

Hotel Aarburg offers 13 plain peaceful rooms in a beautifully located but run-down old building five minutes' walk from the West Station (D-80 SF, Db-100 SF, near recommended Laundromat at Beatenbergstrasse 1, tel. 033/822-2615, fax 033/822-6397).

Backpackers' Villa Sonnenhof is a new, creative guesthouse run by a Methodist Church group. It's fun and youthful but without the frat-party ambience of Balmer's. Rooms are comfortable, and most come with Jungfrau-view balconies (D-86 SF, dorm beds in four- to six-bed rooms with individual lockers and sheets-30 SF each, cheaper if you provide your own sheets, breakfast included, kitchen, garden, Internet access, game room, no curfew, 10-minute walk from either station, Alpenstrasse 16, tel. 033/826-7171, fax 033/ 826-7172, Web site: www.villa.ch, e-mail: backpackers@villa.ch).

Happy Inn Lodge has cheap rooms a five-minute walk from the West Station (D-60 SF, dorm bed-20 SF, breakfast-7 SF, their bar is a dive, Rosenstrasse 17, tel. 033/822-3225, fax 033/822-3268).

For many, **Balmer's Herberge** is backpacker heaven. This Interlaken institution comes with movies, ping-pong, a Laundromat, bar, restaurant, swapping library, Internet stations, tiny grocery, bike rental, currency exchange, rafting excursions, a shuttle-bus service (which meets every arriving train), and a friendly, hardworking, mostly American staff. This little Nebraska is home for those who miss their fraternity (20-SF dorm beds, 22–28 SF in D, T, or Q, 12 SF in overflow on-the-floor accommodations, all with breakfast and sheets, no reservations, nonsmoking, open year-round, CC:VMA, Hauptstrasse 23, in Matten, 15-minute walk from either Interlaken station, tel. 033/822-1961, fax 033/823-3261, SE).

Transportation Connections—Interlaken

By train to: Spiez (2/hrly, 15 min), **Brienz** (hrly, 20 min), **Bern** (hrly, 1 hr). While there are a few long trains from Interlaken, you'll generally connect from Bern.

By train from Bern to: Lausanne (hrly, 70 min) **Zurich** (hrly, 75 min), **Salzburg** (4/day, 8 hrs, transfers include Zurich), **Munich** (4/day, 5.5 hrs), **Frankfurt** (hrly, 4.5 hrs, transfers in Basel and Mannheim), **Paris** (4/day, 4.5 hrs).

Interlaken to Gimmelwald: Take the train from the Interlaken East (Ost) Station to Lauterbrunnen, then cross the street to catch the funicular to Mürren. You'll ride up to Grütschalp, where a special scenic train (*Panorama Fahrt*) rolls you along the cliff into Mürren. From there, either walk an easy, paved 30 minutes downhill to Gimmelwald or walk 10 minutes across Mürren to catch the gondola (7.20 SF and a five-minute steep uphill backtrack) to Gimmelwald. A good bad-weather option (or vice versa) is to ride the post bus from Lauterbrunnen (hourly departure generally coordinated with arrival of train) to Stechelberg and the base of the Schilthornbahn (a big, gray gondola station, tel. 033/823-1444 or 033/555-2141), which will whisk you in five thrilling minutes up to Gimmelwald.

By car it's a 30-minute drive from Interlaken to Stechelberg. The pay parking lot (5 SF/day) at the gondola station is safe. Gimmelwald is the first stop above Stechelberg on the Schilthorn gondola (7.20 SF, two trips/hrly at :25 and :55; get off at first stop). Note that for a week in early May and from mid-November through early December, the Schilthornbahn is closed for servicing.

APPENZELL

Welcome to cowbell country. In moo-mellow and storybook-friendly Appenzell, you'll find the warm, intimate side of the land of staggering icy Alps. Savor Appenzell's cozy small-town ambience.

Appenzell is Switzerland's most traditional region—and the butt of much local humor because of it. This is *Landgemeinde* country, where entire villages would meet in town squares to vote (an event featured on most postcard racks). Until 1991 the women of Appenzell couldn't vote on local issues.

A gentle beauty blankets the region overlooked by the 8,200-foot peak Säntis. As you travel, you'll enjoy an ever-changing parade of finely carved chalets, traditional villages, and cows moaning "milk me." While farmers' daughters make hay in bikinis, old ladies walk the steep roads with scythes, looking as if they just pushed the Grim Reaper down the hill. When locals are asked about their cheese, they clench their fists as they answer, "It's the best." (It is, without any doubt, the smelliest.)

If you're here in early September, there's a good chance you'll get in on—or at least have your road blocked by—the ceremonial procession of flower-bedecked cows and whistling herders in traditional, formal outfits. The festive march down from the high pastures is a spontaneous move by the herding families, and when they finally do burst into town (a slow-motion Swiss Pamplona), the people become children again, running into the streets.

Planning Your Time
The area's charms are subtle, prices are brutal, and its public transportation disappointing. For many on a fast trip with no car, the area is not worth the trouble. But by car it's a joy.

Appenzell Region

Ideally it's an interesting way for drivers to connect Tirol and Bavaria with the Berner Oberland (Jungfrau region): Drive in from Tirol in time to get up the lift to Ebenalp (for the most memorable overnight), descend the next morning and spend the day sampling the charms of Appenzell town, and get to the Interlaken area that night.

Getting Around Appenzell

Those with a car have the region by the tail. Those without will need more time and patience. The center of the Appenzell region is Appenzell town. An hourly train connects Appenzell with Wasserauen (20 min) and Herisau (40 min), from where bigger trains go hourly to St. Gallen (20 min) and Luzern (2 hrs). Regional buses connect all towns several times a day.

Sights—Appenzell Region

Appenzell Town—In this traditional town, kids play "barn" instead of "house" while mom and dad watch yodeling on TV. The TI is on the main street, Hauptgasse, next to the city hall (Monday–Friday 9:00–12:00, 14:00–18:00, Saturday 9:00–12:00, 14:00–17:00, tel. 071/788-9641). In Appenzell the post office is in front of the train station. Expensive laundry services are at Zielstrasse 23 and Riedstrasse 32. Bikes can be rented at the train station (19 SF per half-day, 25 SF all day).

▲Folk Music—Local restaurants sponsor folk-music concerts at

restaurants about twice a week (most Saturday nights, July–
September, often free, dinner sometimes optional) and a big tent
music show about 10 nights in summer. Get specifics at TI.
▲**Appenzeller Folk Museum**—The new folk museum next to
the TI is good. Ride the elevator up to the sixth floor and work
your way down through traditional costumes, living rooms, art,
and crafts (5 SF, daily in summer 10:00–12:00, 14:00–17:00, less in
winter, ask for free loaner book in English). The Appenzeller beer
is famous, good, and about the only thing cheap in the region.
(For accommodations, see Sleeping, below.)
▲▲**Ebenalp**—This cliff-hanging hut is a thin-air alternative to
Appenzell town. Ride the lift from Wasserauen, 8 kilometers south
of Appenzell town, to Ebenalp (5,000 feet). On the way up, you'll
get a sneak preview of Ebenalp's cave church and the cliffside
boardwalk that leads to the guest house. From the top, enjoy a
sweeping view all the way to Lake Constance (Bodensee).
     From the top of the lift, take a 12-minute hike downhill
through a prehistoric cave (it's slippery and dimly lit—descend
holding the railing and you'll come to daylight), past a hermit's
home (now a tiny museum, always open) and the 400-year-old
Wildkirchi cave church (hermit monks lived there from 1658–
1853), to a 150-year-old guest house built precariously into the
cliffside. Originally used by pilgrims, Berggasthaus Ascher now
welcomes tourists (see Sleeping, below).
     From Ebenalp's sunny cliff perch, you can almost hear the
cows munching on the far side of the valley. Only the parasailers,
like neon jellyfish, tag your world 20th-century. In the distance,
nestled below Säntis Peak, is the Seealpsee (lake). The one-hour
hike down to the lake (Seealpsee) is steep but a pleasure (take left
at first fork below guesthouse, watch for nettles, pull up socks).
     The Ebenalp lift runs twice hourly until 19:00 in July and
August, 18:00 in June and September; 17:00 in spring and fall (22
SF round-trip, 17 SF up, free hiking brochure, tel. 071/799-1212).
▲**Stein**—The town of Stein has the Appenzell Showcase Cheese
Dairy (Schaukäserei, daily 8:00–19:00, cheese-making normally
9:00–14:00). It's fast, free, and well-explained in a 15-minute
English video and the free English brochure (with cheese
recipes). The lady at the cheese counter loves to cut it so you can
sample it. They also have yogurt and cheap boxes of cold iced tea
for sale. Stein's TI and a great folk (*Volkskunde*) moo-seum are
next door. This cow-culture museum, with old-fashioned cheese-
making demonstrations, peasant houses, fascinating embroider-
ing machinery, lots of cow art, and folk-craft demonstrations, is
not worth the 7 SF if you've seen the similar museum in Appenzell (Monday 13:30–17:00, Tuesday–Sunday 10:00–12:00,
13:30–17:00, may open early if you ask nicely, closed in winter,
tel. 071/368-5056).

▲Urnäsch—This appealing one-street town has Europe's cutest museum. The Appenzeller Museum, on the town square, brings this region's folk customs to life. Warm and homey, it's a happy little honeycomb of Appenzeller culture (4 SF, daily in summer 13:30–17:00, less in spring and fall, closed in winter, good English description brochure, will open for groups of five or more if you call the director at 071/364-1487 or 071/364-2322). Gasthaus Ochsen is a fine traditional hotel with good food, low ceilings, and wonderful atmosphere (D-80 SF, three doors down from the museum, tel. 071/364-1117). Peek into its old restaurant.

Sleeping in Appenzell
(1.4 SF = about $1, tel. code: 071, zip code: 9050)
Sleep Code: **S** = Single, **D** = Double/Twin, **T** = Triple, **Q** = Quad, **b** = bathroom, **t** = toilet only, **s** = shower only, **CC** = Credit Card (Visa, MasterCard, Amex), **SE** = Speaks English, **NSE** = No English. My top choice for a place to stay is Ebenalp (below).

Sleeping in the Town of Appenzell
The town is small but quite touristy. Hotels are expensive and central; the *Zimmer* are a six-block walk from the center.

Gasthaus Hof offers 25-SF beds in its modern *Matratzenlager* (six- to eight-bed rooms with breakfast, sheets-6 SF, just off the central Landgemeindeplatz, tel. 071/787-2210, Herr Dörig). Outside of peak times, you'll be sleeping alone in a warehouse of bunkbeds. They also have a few reasonable doubles. Gasthaus Hof serves a 20-SF *Rösti*, the area's cheesy potato specialty.

Hotel Adler, above a delicious café in a fine location, offers three kinds of rooms: modern; newly refurbished traditional Appenzeller; or old and basic (D-90–110 SF, Db-140–150 SF, elevator, CC:VMA, between TI and bridge, tel. 071/787-1389, fax 071/787-1365, e-mail: adlerhotel@bluewin.ch, Franz Leu SE).
Hotel Taube is also good (D-120 SF, Db-140 SF, CC:VM, elevator, between the station and main street, Hirschengasse 8, tel. 071/787-1149, fax 071/787-5633).

Haus Lydia is an Appenzell-style home filled with tourist information and a woodsy folk atmosphere, on the edge of town with a garden and a powerful mountain view. This wonderful six-room *Zimmer* is run by friendly Frau Mock-Inauen (D-75 SF, great breakfast; east of town over bridge, past Mercedes-Esso station, take next right; Eggerstandenstrasse 53, CH 9050 Appenzell, tel. 071/787-4233). **Gästezimmer Koller-Rempfler** is a comfy traditional place a few blocks before Haus Lydia (D-72 SF, Db-82 SF for one night stays, Eggerstandenstrasse 9, tel. 071/787-2117). **Johann Ebneter** runs a friendly and modern *Zimmer* in the same area (D-80 SF, Mooshaldenstrasse 14, tel. 071/787-3487, SE).

Sleeping in Ebenalp

There's no reason to sleep in Appenzell town. The Ebenalp lift, across from the tiny Wasserauen train station, is a few minutes' drive (or a 20-minute bus ride) south. For a memorable experience, stay in **Berggasthaus Ascher.** Their 150-year-old house has only rainwater and no shower. Friday and Saturday nights often have great live music but are crowded with groups and noisy with up to 40 people (literally four hikers to three mattresses) and parties going into the wee hours. Otherwise you'll normally get a small woody dorm to yourself. The hut is actually built into the cliffside; its back wall is the rock. From the toilet you can study this Alpine architecture. Sip your coffee on the deck, behind drips from the gnarly overhang a 100 yards above. The goats have their cliff hut adjacent. The guestbook goes back to 1941, and the piano in the comfortable dining/living room was brought in by helicopter. For a great 45-minute pre-dinner check-out-the-goats hike, take the high trail toward the lake; circle clockwise back up the peak to the lift and down the way you originally came. Claudia can show you the rock-climbing charts (15 SF dorm beds, blankets but no sheets required or provided, breakfast-10 SF, *Rösti* dinners-14 SF, open May–October, 12 minutes by steep trail below top of lift, 9057 Weissbad, tel. 071/799-1142, run by Claudia and Bennie Knechtle-Wyss, their five little children, three pigs, four goats, two donkeys, and 40 sheep).

The less atmospheric and more normal **Berg Gasthaus Ebenalp** sits atop the mountains just above the lift. It's booked long in advance on Saturdays but wide open otherwise (26-SF dorm bed with blankets but no sheets, breakfast included, D-84 SF, coin-op shower, tel. 071/799-1194, Sutter family).

From Wasserauen at the base of the lift, you can hike up the private road to **Berggasthaus Seealpsee**, situated on an idyllic alpine lake, Seealpsee (D-80 SF, loft dorm beds with sheets-11 SF plus 11 SF for breakfast, CC:VMA, 9057 Weissbad, tel. 071/799-1140, fax 071/799-1820, Dörig family).

WEST SWITZERLAND

Enjoy urban Switzerland at its best in the charming, compact capital of Bern. Ramble the ramparts of Murten, Switzerland's best-preserved medieval town, and resurrect the ruins of an ancient Roman capital in nearby Avenches. The Swiss countryside offers up chocolates, Gruyères cheese, and a fine folk museum. On Lake Geneva, the Swiss Riviera, explore the romantic Château Chillon and stylishly syncopated Montreux. South of Murten, the predominant language is French, *s'il vous plaît*, and, as you'll see, that means more than language.

Planning Your Time

The region doesn't merit a lot of time on a quick trip. Bern, Lake Geneva, and Murten are each worth half a day. Bern is easily seen en route to Murten—"Morat", if you're speaking French. I'd establish a home base in Murten from which to explore the southwest in a day by car. Without a car, use a better transportation hub such as Bern, Montreux, or Lausanne.

For a day by car from Murten: 8:45-depart; 10:00-tour Château Chillon; 11:30-quick visit or drive through Montreux, Vevey, and the Corniche de Laveau; 14:00-cheese-making demo in Gruyères or Moleson; 15:30-Gruerien folk museum in Bulle; 18:00-Roman ruins in Avenches; 19:00-home in Murten for salad by the sea.

BERN

Stately but human, classy but fun, the Swiss capital gives you the most (maybe even the only) enjoyable look at urban Switzerland. User-friendly Bern is packed into a peninsula bounded by the Aare River.

West Switzerland

Orientation

Tourist Information: Start your visit at the TI inside the train station (daily 9:00–20:30, until 18:30 in winter, tel. 031/328-1212). Pick up a map of Bern (and any other Swiss cities you'll be visiting), and a list of city sights. There's a second TI at the Bear Pits (daily 10:00–17:00).

Getting Around Bern: Bern is easy. From the train station it's all downhill through the heart of town to the bear pits and Rose Garden (a 30-minute stroll), then catch trolley #12 back up to the station (buy cheapest ticket from machine at stop, 1.50 SF). *Vancher*, the city newspaper, offers loaner 21-speed bikes (free, leave passport and 20-SF deposit at Casinoplatz blue box in the old town, tel. 031/311-2234).

Sights—Bern

▲▲**Old Town**—Window-shopping and people-watching through dilly-dally arcaded streets and busy market squares are Bern's top attractions. There are over three miles of arcades in this tiny capital of 130,000 people. This is my kind of shopping town: prices are so high there's no danger of buying (shops open Monday–Friday 9:00– 18:30, Thursday until 21:00, Saturday 8:00–16:00, closed Sunday).

Clock Tower (Zytglogge-turm)—The clock performs a few

Bern

minutes before each hour. Apparently this slowmoving five-minute non-event was considered entertaining in 1530. To pass the time during the performance, read the TI's brochure explaining what's so interesting about the fancy old clock. Enthusiasts can tour the medieval mechanics daily at 16:30 (6 SF, May–October).

▲**Cathedral**—The 1421 Swiss late-Gothic *Münster*, or cathedral, is worth a look (Tuesday–Sunday 10:00–17:00, closed Monday, shorter hours off-season). Climb the spiral staircase 100 yards above the town for the view, exercise, and a chance to meet a live church watchman. Peter Probst and his wife, Sigi, live way up there, watching over the church, answering questions, and charging tourists 3 SF for the view.

Parliament (Bundeshaus)—You can tour Switzerland's imposing Parliament building (free 45-minute tours most days at 9:00, 10:00, 11:00, 14:00, 15:00, and 16:00; closed most of March, June, September, and December when in session, tour canceled if less than five people show up, tel. 031/322-8522 to confirm). Don't miss the view from the Bundeshaus terrace. You may see some national legislators, but you wouldn't know it—everything looks very casual for a national capital.

Einstein's House—Einstein did much of his most important thinking while living in this house on the old town's main drag. It was just another house to me, but I guess everything's relative (3 SF, Tuesday–Friday 10:00–17:00, Saturday 10:00–16:00, closed Sunday, Monday, December, and January, Kramgasse 49).

▲**Bear Pits and Rose Garden**—The symbol of Bern is the bear, and some lively ones frolic (8:00–18:00) to the delight of locals and tourists alike in the big, barren, concrete pits (*Graben*) just over the river. You may see graffiti from the B.L.M. (Bear Liberation Movement) which, through its terrorist means, has forced a reluctant city government to give the bears better living conditions. The Old Tram Depot next to the pits is a slick new tourist center with a "Multi-vision" show showing off the wonders of Bern. Up the pathway is the Rosengarten, a restaurant, and a great city view.

▲▲**The Berner Swim**—For something to write home about, join the local merchants, students, and carp in a float down the Aare River. The Bernese, proud of their very clean river and their basic ruddiness, have a tradition—sort of a wet, urban paseo. On summer days, they hike upstream five to 30 minutes and float back down to the excellent (and free) riverside baths and pools (*Aarebad*) just below the Parliament building. While the locals make it look easy, this is dangerous—the current is swift. If you miss the last pole, you're history. If the river is a bit much, you're welcome to enjoy just the Aarebad. If the river is not enough, a popular day trip is to raft all the way from Thun to Bern.

▲▲**Museum of Fine Arts (Kunstmuseum)**—While it features 1,000 years of local art and some Impressionism, the real hit is its fabulous collection of Paul Klee's playful paintings. If you don't know Klee, I'd love to introduce you (6 SF, Tuesday 10:00–21:00, Wednesday–Sunday 10:00–17:00, closed Monday, four blocks from station, Holdergasse 12, tel. 031/311-0944).

Other Bern Museums—Across the bridge from the Parliament building on Helvetiaplatz are several museums (Alpine, Berner History, Postal) that sound more interesting than they are (most open 10:00–17:00, closed Monday).

Sleeping in Bern
(1.4 SF = about $1, tel. code: 031)
Sleep Code: **S** = Single, **D** = Double/Twin, **T** = Triple, **Q** = Quad, **b** = bathroom, **t** = toilet only, **s** = shower only, **CC** = Credit Card (Visa, MasterCard, Amex), **SE** = Speaks English, **NSE** = No English. These are in the old town, within 10-minutes from the station.

   Hotel National has bright, well-furnished rooms with big windows and street noise (S-60–75 SF, Sb-85–110 SF, D-100–120 SF, Db-130–150 SF, apartment-170–260 SF, elevator, CC:VMA, near station and old town, Hirschengraben 24, 3011 Bern, tel. 031/381-1988, fax 031/381-6878).

Hotel Goldener Schlüssel is an old, basic, comfortable, crank-'em-out hotel in the center (S-75 SF, Sb-99 SF, D-110 SF, Db-142 SF, Tb-178 SF, elevator, CC:VMA, Rathausgasse 72, 3011 Bern, tel. 031/311-0216, fax 031/311-5688).

Hotel zum Goldenen Adler has comfy (but worn and smoky) rooms with all the amenities (Sb-120 SF, Db-160 SF, CC:VMA, elevator, Gerechtigkeitsgasse 7, 3011 Bern, tel. 031/311-1725, fax 031/311-3761).

Bern's big, newly renovated, sterile, well-run **IYHF hostel** has four- to 26-bed rooms and provides an all-day lounge, laundry machines, and cheap meals (dorm beds-20 SF, non-members-25 SF, breakfast 6-SF, CC:VM, office open 7:00–9:30 and 15:00–24:00, down the stairs from the Parliament building, by the river at Weihergasse 4, 3005 Bern, tel. 031/311-6316, fax 031/312 5240).

Transportation Connections—Bern
By train to: Murten (hrly, 30 min, change in Kerzers), **Lausanne** (2/hrly, 70 min), **Interlaken** (hrly, 1 hr), **Zurich** (2/hr, 75 min), **Fribourg** (2/hr, 30 min), **Munich** (4/day, 5.5 hrs), **Frankfurt** (hrly, 4.5 hrs), **Paris** (4/day, 4.5 hrs).

MURTEN
The finest medieval ramparts in Switzerland surround the 5,000 people of Murten. We're on the lingua-cusp of Switzerland: 25 percent of Murten speaks French; a few miles to the south and west, nearly everyone does. Murten is a mini-Bern with three parallel streets, the middle one nicely arcaded with breezy outdoor cafés and elegant shops (many closed Monday). Its castle is romantically set, overlooking the cute Murtensee and the rolling vineyards of gentle Mount Vully in the distance. Try some Vully wine. Murten is touristic but seems to be enjoyed mostly by its own people. Nearby Avenches, with its Roman ruins, glows at sunset.

The only required sightseeing is to do the rampart ramble (free, always open, easy stairway access on east side of town). Notice the old town clock reconstructed in the base of the tower (behind the Hotel Ringmauer) and be glad you have a watch. The town history museum in an old mill is boring (closed Monday).

The lakefront offers a popular but pricey restaurant (Des Bains), a swimming pool with a sauna, a lovely promenade path along the lake, and one-hour lake cruises (free with train passes, daily in summer at 15:40). Rent a bike at the train station for a lakeside ride (15 SF/half-day, 19 SF/full day). The Migros and Co-op supermarkets, just outside three of the town gates, have cafeterias (closed Sunday). The post office is in front of the station. Murten has no Laundromat.

Orientation (tel. code: 026)
Tourist Information: Murten's TI tries to be helpful, but there's not much to say (May–September, Monday–Friday 10:00–12:00, 14:00–18:00, Saturday 10:00–12:00, closed Sunday, tel. 026/670-5112). Ask about their free town walks (10:30 in the summer).

Arrival in Murten: Exit right from the station, angle left uphill on Bahnhofstrasse, and turn right through the town gate (a three-minute walk).

Sights—Near Murten
Avenches—This town, four miles south of Murten, was once Aventicum, the Roman capital of the Confederation Helvetica. Back then its population was 50,000. Today it could barely fill the well-worn ruins of its 15,000-seat Roman amphitheater. You can tour the Roman museum (Tuesday–Sunday 10:00–12:00, 13:00–17:00, closed Monday, near dinky amphitheater in town center), but the best experience is some quiet time at sunset pondering the evocative Roman amphitheater in the fields, a half-mile walk out of town (free, always open). Avenches, with a pleasant, small-French-town feel, is a quieter, less expensive place to stay than Murten. It also makes an easy day trip. The TI is a seven-minute uphill walk from the station (TI tel. 026/675-1159).
Murtensee Cruise—Tourist boats circle the tiny Murtensee several times daily (departing Murten 7:55, 13:40, 15:45, 18:35—no morning boat on weekends). The scenic trip takes an hour. Praz, a small town on the French-speaking shore, is a good stop. From there you can hike through vineyards up Mount Vully, where a bench and fine lake and Alp views await.

Sleeping in Murten and Avenches
(1.4 SF = about $1, tel. code: 026)

Sleeping in or near Murten
Hotel Ringmauer (German for "ramparts") is characteristic, a block from the center, with showers and toilets within a dash of each room (S-60 SF, D-105 SF, attached restaurant, near wall on the side farthest from the lake, CC:VM, Deutsche Kirchgasse 2, tel. 026/670-1101, fax 026/672-2083).

Hotel Murtenhof is a worthwhile splurge with all the comforts and a lake view (Sb-90–155 SF, Db-130–210 SF, extra person-50 SF, CC:VMA, next to castle on Rathausgasse, tel. 026/670-5656, fax 026/670-5059, SE). I eat on Hotel Murtenhof's terrace for their salad bar (summer only): 7.50 SF for a small plate, 15 SF for the big one; the small one—carefully stacked—is plenty and comes with wonderful bread and a sunset over the lake. The small plate is meant as a side dish, but, if you can handle the ridicule and don't mind being seated in back or outside, the big boss assured me you can eat just a small salad plate stacked high, and the waiters will even bring you a piece of bread and free water. The terrace is a good place to try the Vully wine—just point to the vineyards across the lake (restaurant open 6:30–23:30, closed Monday).

Hotel Bahnhof, just across the street from the Murten train station, is a last resort (S-60 SF, Ss-70 SF, D-100 SF, Ds-120 SF, CC:VMA, Bahnhofstrasse 14, tel. 026/670-2256, NSE).

Hotel Bel Air is across the Murten lake in lazy Praz, where hotel values are better than in ritzy Murten. Bel Air has seven flowery, in-love-with-life rooms and balconies—many with breath-taking lake views (D-90 SF, Tb-120, closed Thursday, Route Principale 145, 1788 Praz-Vully, tel. 026/673-1414). Henry, who speaks English, runs a fine restaurant here specializing in fish. While this is easy for drivers, train travelers will need to catch the boat from Murten (see above). They can depart weekday mornings at 8:15. The Sugiez train station (on the main Bern line) is a kilometer away.

Oasis Neuchatel is a new 38-bed hostel just outside the town of Neuchatel (bus #1 from center or dock). Beds in two- to six-bed rooms cost 23-28 SF with breakfast (CC:V, non-smoking, vegetarian meals, small kitchen available, creative and young management, Rue du Suchiez 35, 2000 Neuchatel, call to reserve, office open 8:00–10:00, 17:00–21:00, tel. 032/731-3190, fax 032/730-3709).

Sleeping in and near Avenches

The Avenches **IYHF hostel**, the only hostel in the area, is a beauty. It's run by the Dhyaf family, with four- to eight-bed rooms, a homey TV room, ping-pong, a big backyard, and a very quiet setting near the Roman theater (24 SF for bed, sheets, and breakfast, more for non-members, office open 7:00–9:30, 17:00–22:30, three blocks from the center at the medieval *lavoir* or laundry, Rue du Lavoir 5, 1580 Avenches, tel. 026/675-2666, fax 026/675-2717).

Friendly **Elisabeth Clement-Arnold** rents out a room in her house (Sb-30 SF, Db-50 SF, Rue Centrale 5, 1580 Avenches, tel. & fax 026/675-3031 e-mail: kadima@com.mcnet.ch).

Auberge de l'Ecusson Vaudois is the only hotel in the small village of Oleyres, 3 km from Avenches (Sb-60 SF, Db-92 SF, dorm bed-24 SF, all with breakfast, 1580 Oleyres, tel. & fax 026/675-1087). It's run by Madame Glauser, a big Elvis fan who makes frequent trips to Memphis.

Transportation Connections—Murten

By train to: Avenches (hrly, 10 min), **Bern** (hrly, 30 min, change in Kerzers), **Fribourg** (hrly, 30 min), **Lausanne** (hrly, 75 min, transfer in Fribourg).

SOUTHWEST SWISS COUNTRYSIDE

The French Swiss countryside is sprinkled with tasty chocolates, summer skiing, smelly cheese, and sleepy cows. If you're traveling between Murten, Montreux, and Interlaken, take in a few of the countryside's sights, tastes, and smells.

Getting Around the Countryside

Cross-country buses use Fribourg and Bulle as hubs: **Bulle–Gruyères** (7/day, 15 min), **Fribourg–Bulle** (hrly, 45 min), **Avenches–Fribourg** (7/day, 30 min), **Murten–Fribourg** (hrly, 30 min).

Sights—Swiss Countryside

Caillers Chocolate Factory—The Caillers factory, in the town of Broc, welcomes visitors with a hygenic peek through a window at their factory churning out chocolates, a 15-minute movie, and free melt-in-your-hands samples (free, 9:00–11:00 and 13:30–16:00, closed Saturday, Sunday and Monday mornings, closed July and off-season, follow signs to "Nestlé" and "Broc Fabrique", even individuals need to call a day in advance to reserve, tel. 026/921-5151). Broc town is just the sleepy, sweet-smelling home of the chocolate makers. It has a small, very typical hotel, the Auberge des Montagnards (D-70 SF, great Gruyères view, elegant dining room, tel. 026/921-1526). From Bulle, trains run hourly to Broc (10 min).

▲▲**Musée Gruèrien**—Somehow the unassuming little town of Bulle built a refreshing, cheery folk museum that manages to teach you all about life in these parts and leave you feeling very good. (5 SF plus 1 SF for the English guidebook; Tuesday–Saturday 10:00–12:00, 14:00–17:00, Sunday 14:00–17:00, closed Monday, tel. 026/912-7260). When it's over, the guide reminds you, "The Golden Book of Visitors awaits your signature and comments. Don't you think this museum deserves another visit? Thank you!"

▲**Gruyères**—This ultra-touristy town, famous for its cheese, fills its fortified little hilltop like a bouquet. Its ramparts are a park, and the ancient buildings serve the tourist crowds. The castle is mediocre, and you don't need to stay long, but make a short stop for the setting. Minimize your walk by driving up to the second parking lot. Hotels in Gruyères are expensive.

▲▲**Gruyères Fromagerie**—There are two very different cheese-making exhibits to choose from. Five miles above Gruyères, a dark and smoky 17th-century farmhouse in Moleson gives a fun look at the old and smelly craft (3 SF, daily 9:30–18:30, cheese actually being made 10:00–11:00 and 15:00–16:00, mid-May–mid-October, TI tel. 026/921-2434). Closer, slicker, and modern, the cheese-production center at the foot of Gruyères town (follow "Fromagerie" signs) opens its doors to tourists with a good continuous English audiovisual presentation (free, daily 8:00–18:30). The cute cheese shop in the modern center has lunches and picnic goodies (closed from 12:00–13:30).

Glacier des Diablerets—For a grand Alpine trip to the tip of a 10,000-foot peak, take the three-part lift from Reusch or Col du Pillon. A quick trip takes about 90 minutes and costs 40 SF (July and August only). You can stay for lunch. From the top, you can see the Matterhorn and even a bit of Mont Blanc, Europe's highest mountain. This is a good chance to do some summer skiing. Normally expensive and a major headache, summer skiing isn't bad here. A lift ticket and rental skis, poles, boots, and coat cost about 65 SF. The slopes close at 14:00. The base of the lift is a two-hour drive from Murten or Gimmelwald. From Montreux it's a two-hour bus ride (7/day, transfer in Gstaad Bahnhof).

▲▲**Taveyanne**—This remote hamlet is a huddle of log cabins used by cowherds in the summer. The hamlet's old bar is a restaurant serving a tiny community of vacationers and hikers. Taveyanne is two miles off the main road between Col de la Croix and Villars. A small sign points down a tiny road to a jumble of huts and snoozing cows stranded at 5,000 feet. The inn is Refuge de Taveyanne (1882 Gryon), where the Seibenthal family serves meals in a prize-winning rustic setting with no electricity, low ceilings, and a huge charred fireplace. Consider sleeping in their primitive loft (10 SF, five mattresses, access by a ladder outside, urinate with the cows, open May–October, closed Tuesday except in July and August, tel. 024/498-1947). A fine opportunity to really know prize-winning cows.

LAKE GENEVA (LAC LEMAN)

This is the Swiss Riviera. Separating France and Switzerland, surrounded by Alps, and lined with a collage of castles, museums, spas, resort towns, and vineyards, Lake Geneva's crowds are understandable. This area is so beautiful that Charlie Chaplin and Idi Amin both chose it as their second home.

Getting Around Lake Geneva

Buses connect towns along Lake Geneva every 15 minutes. Boats carry visitors comfortably to all sights of importance. The boat ride from Lausanne to Chillon takes two hours with stops in Vevey and Montreux (19 SF, Eurailers sail free, four trips daily in each direction, tel. 021/614-0444). The short Montreux–Château Chillon cruise is fun even for those with a car (6 SF, 15 min). Trains connect Lausanne, Montreux, and Villeneuve hourly.

Sights—Lake Geneva

▲▲▲**Château Chillon**—This wonderfully preserved 13th-century castle, set wistfully at the edge of Lake Geneva, is a joy. Follow the excellent free English brochure from one fascinating room to the next, enjoying tingly views, the dank prison, battle-scarred weapons, mobile furniture, and 700-year-old toilets.

The 130-step climb to the top of the keep (#25 in the brochure) isn't worth the time or sweat. Stroll the patrol ramparts, then curl up on a window sill to enjoy the lake (7 SF, 1.50 SF extra to join a tour, daily 9:00–18:00, less off-season, easy parking, tel. 021/966-8910, call to see if an English tour group is scheduled). Coming by train, get off at Veytaux-Chillon, and walk a few minutes along the lake to the castle.

Villeneuve—This is a relatively run-down little resort a 30-minute walk beyond Château Chillon. The train station is a block from the beach promenade, main street (Grand-Rue), and TI (Monday 13:30–18:00, Tuesday–Friday 9:00–12:30, 13:30–18:00, Saturday 9:00–12:30, closed Sunday, tel. 021/960-2286). Visit here only if you need an affordable place to sleep (see Sleeping, below).

Montreux—This expensive resort has a famous jazz festival each July. The Montreux TI has a list of moderate rooms in the center (TI tel. 021/962-8484). Hotel-Restaurant du Pont offers decent rooms and great spaghetti (Db-120 SF, Rue du Pont 12, tel. 021/963-2249). Near Montreux, Vevey is a smaller and more comfortable resort town.

Corniche de Lavaux—The rugged Swiss Wine Road swerves through picturesque towns and the stingy vineyards that produce most of Switzerland's tasty but expensive *Fendant* wine. Hikers can take the boat to Cully and explore on foot from there. A car tour is quick and frightening (from Montreux, go west along the lake through Vevey, following blue signs to Lausanne along the waterfront, taking the Moudon/Chexbres exit). Explore some of the smaller roads.

Geneva—This big city bores me. It's sterile, cosmopolitan, expensive, and full of executives, diplomats, and tourists.

LAUSANNE

This is the most interesting city on the lake. Peek in its impressive cathedral, and stroll through the, colorful town—the ritzy shopping street is Rue Bourg and the liveliest square is Place de la Palud (mechanical puppet show above the *Pharmacie* tells a story in French on the hour). Open-air markets sprawl every Wednesday and Saturday morning from St. Francis Church to the town hall. Climb up to the 13th-century cathedral for the view (2 SF to climb the tower, but the view from the terrace is free).

Orientation (tel. code: 021)

Tourist Information: Lausanne has two TIs, one in the train station (daily 9:00–20:00) and the other at Ouchy (Monday–Friday 8:00–19:00, weekends 9:00–18:00, tel. 021/613-7373-93). Skip the museum pass. Ask if there are free concerts at the cathedral and any walking tours in English (the twice-daily walking tours offered

May–September are "subject to the availability of an English-speaking guide," 10 SF, tel. 021/321-7766).

Helpful Hints: The Laundromat closest to the train station is Quick-Wash (open Monday–Saturday 8:00–21:30, Sunday 11:00–21:00, Boulevard de Grancy 44).

Getting Around Lausanne

The city is steeper than it is big. A five-stop metro connects the upper part of Lausanne (called the old town, vielle ville, or centre ville) with the train station (about mid way) and ends at Ouchy (OO-shee), the lakefront district. The cost is 2.20 SF (tickets good for one hour on buses, too). You can walk, but even locals use the metro. Buy your ticket from the ticket window or TI. The train station's metro stop is directly across the street from the station. If you take a bus, buy your ticket from the blue machine at the bus stop before boarding (2.20 SF; the cheaper 1.30-SF ticket is good for only three stops). The 24-hour pass, which covers both the metro and the bus, is a good deal if you take three trips or more (6.5 SF).

The train station rents bikes (15 SF/half-day, 19 SF/full day, plus 10 SF to take bike on a train and drop off at another station, no deposit needed except address and passport number).

Sights—Lausanne

Collection de l'Art Brut—This thought-provoking collection of art was produced by untrained artists—about a quarter of it by people labeled criminal or crazy by society (6 SF, Tuesday–Sunday 11:00–13:00, 14:00–18:00, closed Monday, bus #3 from the station, follow signs to "Palais de Beaulieu", Avenue des Bergieres 11, tel. 021/647-5435).

Olympics Museum—This new high-tech museum includes an extensive film archive of thrilling moments in the history of the games (14 SF, daily 9:00–19:00, tel. 021/621-6511).

City History Museum—This museum traces life in Lausanne from Roman times with many fun interactive displays and CD-ROM demos. It's notable for its 1:200-scale model of Lausanne in the 17th century, accompanied by an audiovisual presentation (Tuesday–Sunday 11:00–18:00, Thursday until 20:00, closed Monday, English handouts in each room). The museum is right next to the cathedral and the viewpoint terrace.

Sleeping in Lausanne

(1.4 SF = about $1, tel. code: 021, zip code: 1007)

Breakfast is included unless otherwise noted.

Jeunotel, clean and affordable, has concrete walls and cell-block rooms. You know it's not a minimum-security prison because they give you a key (dorm bed-27 SF, S-56 SF, Sb-80 SF,

D-84 SF, Db-102 SF, T-99 SF, easy parking, any age welcome, CC:VMA, Chemin du Bois-de-Vaux 36, tel. 021/626-0222, fax 021/626-0226, SE). Take the Metro to Ouchy, then bus #2 to the Bois-de-Vaux stop (you'll see signs for the hotel, a block away).

Hotel Regina, on a pedestrian street in the old town, is newly remodeled with comfy rooms and an energetic management (S-70 SF, Sb-95–120 SF, D-100 SF, Db-130–160 SF, CC:VMA, Rue Grand Saint-Jean 18, tel. 021/320-2441, fax 021/320-2529, e-mail: hotel-regina@gve.ch).

Hotel du Raisin, with dingy, faded furnishings, has a great but noisy location on a popular square in the old town (S-60 SF, D-120 SF, attached restaurant with sidewalk café, CC:VMA, Place de la Palud 19, tel. & fax 021/312-2756).

Hotel du Port, in a peely building, has small rooms but some lakefront views (S-42 SF, D-80 SF, Db-106 SF, Tb-130 SF, breakfast-9 SF, CC:VMA, closed non-summer Tuesdays, a block from Ouchy metro stop at Place du Port 5, tel. 021/616-4930, fax 021/616-8368, NSE).

Sleeping in Villeneuve, near Montreux and Château Chillon
(1.4 SF = about $1, tel. code: 021, zip code: 1844)
Villeneuve, 3 miles east, has Montreux's palmy lakeside setting without the crowds or glitz. Its main drag runs parallel to the shore, a block inland. Stroll 30 minutes along the waterfront promenade to the château. Don't count on speaking English at these hotels. Leaving the train station, take a left on Main Street to find the TI and first two hotels, or walk straight ahead to find the lakefront listing.

La Romantica, with dark, narrow, cheap-feeling rooms, is a decent value with a frumpy, very French bar scene downstairs (Sb-50 SF, Db-100–120 SF, breakfast-5 SF, CC:VMA, Grand-Rue 34, tel. 021/960-1540, fax 021/960-3791).

Hotel du Soleil is expensive but comfortable (Sb-70 SF, Db-100–120 SF, CC:VMA, Grand-Rue 20, tel. 021/960-4206, fax 021/960-4208). **Hotel du Port** is the town's hotel on the waterfront (Db-150 SF, family deals, elevator, CC:VMA, Rue du Quai 6, tel. 021/960-4145, fax 021/960-3967, Msr. Raneda SE).

Haut Lac Hostel is at the edge of Montreux, on the lake, a 10-minute stroll north of the château (dorm bed, sheets, and breakfast-27.40 SF, D-73 SF, non-members pay 5 SF extra, closed 10:00–16:00, cheap meals served, Passage de l'Auberge 8, 1820 Territet town, tel. 021/963-4934). Train noise can be a problem.

Transportation Connections—Lake Geneva
Lausanne by train to: Montreux (hrly, 20 min), **Geneva** (3/hr, 40 min), **Bern** (hrly, 70 min), **Basel** (direct every two hours, 2.5 hrs), **Milan** (hrly, 3.5 hrs).

APPENDIX

Let's Talk Telephones

Dialing Direct

Calling between Countries: First dial the international access code, then the country code, the area code (if it starts with zero, drop the zero), and then the local number.

Calling Long Distance within a Country: First dial the area code (including its zero), then the local number.

Europe's Exceptions: Some countries do not use area codes, such as Italy, Spain, France, Norway, and Denmark. To make an international call to these countries, dial the international access code (usually 00), the country code (see chart below), then the local number in its entirety (okay, so there's one exception; for France, drop the initial zero of the local number). To make long-distance calls within any of these countries, simply dial the local number.

International Access Codes

When dialing direct, first dial the international access code of the country you're calling from. For most countries, it's "00." Only the exceptions are noted below.

Estonia—800	Russia—810
Finland—990	Spain—07
Latvia—800	Sweden—009
Lithuania—810	U.S.A./Canada—011

Country Codes

After you've dialed the international access code, then dial the code of the country you're calling.

Austria—43	Germany—49	Portugal—351
Belgium—32	Greece—30	Russia—7
Britain—44	Ireland—353	Spain—34
Czech Rep.—420	Italy—39	Sweden—46
Denmark—45	Latvia—371	Switzerland—41
Estonia—372	Lithuania—370	U.S.A./Canada—1
Finland—358	Netherlands—31	
France—33	Norway—47	

U.S.A. Direct Services: Calling Card Operators

	AT&T	MCI	SPRINT
Austria	022-903-011	022-903-012	022-903-014
Germany	0130-0010	0800-888-8000	0130-0013
Switzerland	0800-89-0011	0800-89-0222	0800-89-9777
Czech Republic	00420-00101	00420-00112	00420-87187

Directory Assistance

Austria: national–16, international–08
Switzerland: national–111, international–191
Swiss info for Germany/Austria: 192
Germany: national–01188, international–00118
German tourist offices: local code then 19433
German train information: local code then 19419

Numbers and Stumblers

- Europeans write a few of their numbers differently than we do. 1 = 1, 4 = 4, 7 = 7. Learn the difference or miss your train.
- In Europe, dates appear as day/month/year, so Christmas is 25/12/99.
- Commas are decimal points, and decimals are commas. A dollar and a half is 1,50 and there are 5.280 feet in a mile.
- When pointing, use your whole hand, palm downward.
- When counting with fingers, start with your thumb. If you hold up your first finger to request one item, you'll get two.
- What we Americans call the second floor of a building is the first floor in Europe.
- Europeans keep the left "lane" open for passing on escalators and moving sidewalks. Keep to the right.

Climate

First line, average daily low; second line, average daily high; third line, days of no rain.

	J	F	M	A	M	J	J	A	S	O	N	D
Frankfurt Germany	29°	31°	35°	41°	48°	53°	56°	55°	51°	43°	36°	31°
	37°	42°	49°	58°	67°	72°	75°	74°	67°	56°	45°	39°
	22	19	22	21	22	21	21	21	21	22	21	20
Vienna Austria	26°	28°	34°	41°	50°	56°	59°	58°	52°	44°	36°	30°
	34°	38°	47°	57°	66°	71°	75°	73°	66°	55°	44°	37°
	23	21	24	21	22	21	22	21	23	23	22	22
Geneva Switzerland	29°	30°	35°	41°	48°	55°	58°	57°	52°	44°	37°	31°
	39°	43°	51°	58°	66°	73°	77°	76°	69°	58°	47°	40°
	20	19	21	19	19	19	22	21	20	20	19	21

German Survival Phrases

Hello (good day).	Guten Tag.	**goo**-ten tahg
Do you speak English?	Sprechen Sie Englisch?	**shprekh**-en zee **eng**-lish
Yes. / No.	Ja. / Nein.	yah / nīn
I'm sorry.	Entschuldigung.	ent-**shool**-dee-goong
Please. / Thank you.	Bitte. / Danke.	**bit**-teh / **dahng**-keh
Goodbye.	Auf Wiedersehen.	owf **vee**-der-zayn
Where is...?	Wo ist...?	voh ist
...a hotel	...ein Hotel	īn hoh-**tel**
...a youth hostel	...eine Jugend-herberge	ī-neh **yoo**-gend-hehr-behr-geh
...a restaurant	...ein Restaurant	īn res-tow-**rahnt**
...a supermarket	...ein Supermarkt	īn **zoo**-per-markt
...the train station	...der Bahnhof	dehr **bahn**-hohf
...the tourist information office	...das Touristen-informationsbüro	dahs **too**-ris-ten-in-for-maht-see-**ohns**-bew-roh
...the toilet	...die Toilette	dee toh-**leh**-teh
men / women	Herren / Damen	**hehr**-ren / **dah**-men
How much is it?	Wieviel kostet das?	vee-**feel** kos-tet dahs
Cheap / Cheaper.	Billig / Billiger.	**bil**-lig / **bil**-lig-er
Included?	Eingeschlossen?	**īn**-geh-shlos-sen
Do you have...?	Haben Sie...?	**hah**-ben zee
I would like...	Ich hätte gern...	ikh **het**-teh gehrn
...just a little.	...nur ein bißchen.	noor īn **bis**-yen
...more.	...mehr.	mehr
...a ticket.	...ein Karte.	īn **kar**-teh
...a room.	...ein Zimmer.	īn **tsim**-mer
...the bill.	...die Rechnung.	dee **rekh**-noong
one	eins	īns
two	zwei	tsvī
three	drei	drī
four	vier	feer
five	fünf	fewnf
six	sechs	zex
seven	sieben	**zee**-ben
eight	acht	ahkht
nine	neun	noyn
ten	zehn	tsayn
At what time?	Um wieviel Uhr?	oom vee-**feel** oor
now / soon / later	jetzt / bald / später	yetzt / bahld / **shpay**-ter
today / tomorrow	heute / morgen	**hoy**-teh / **mor**-gen

For more survival phrases, check out *Rick Steves' German Phrase Book and Dictionary* or *Rick Steves' French, Italian & German Phrase Book and Dictionary.*

Faxing Your Hotel Reservation

Most hotel managers know basic "hotel English." Faxing is the preferred method for reserving a room. It's more accurate and cheaper than telephoning and much faster than writing a letter. Use this handy form for your fax. Photocopy and fax away.

One-Page Fax

To: _____ @ _____
             hotel   *fax*

From: _____ @ _____
             name   *fax*

Today's date: ____ /_____ /____
                     day *month* *year*

Dear Hotel _____,

Please make this reservation for me:

Name: _____

Total # of people: _____   # of rooms: _____   # of nights: _____

Arriving: ____ /_____ /____   My time of arrival (24-hr clock): _____
               day *month* *year*   (I will telephone if I will be late)

Departing: ____ /_____ /____
                 day *month* *year*

Room(s):   Single___   Double___   Twin___   Triple___   Quad___

With: Toilet___   Shower___   Bath___   Sink only___

Special needs: View___   Quiet___   Cheapest Room___

Credit card: Visa___   MasterCard___   American Express___

Card #: _____

Expiration Date:_____

Name on card: _____

You may charge me for the first night as a deposit. Please fax or mail me confirmation of my reservation, along with the type of room reserved, the price, and whether the price includes breakfast. Thank you.

_____
Signature

_____
Name

_____
Address

_____
City   *State*   *Zip Code*   *Country*

_____
E-mail Address

Road Scholar Feedback for
Germany, Austria & Switzerland 1999

*We're all in the same travelers' school of hard knocks. Your feedback
helps us improve this guidebook for future travelers. Please fill this out
(attach more info or any tips/favorite discoveries if you like) and send it
to us. As thanks for your help, we'll send you our quarterly travel
newsletter free for one year. Thanks!* **Rick**

**Of the recommended accommodations/restaurants used,
which was:**

Best _____

    Why? _____

Worst _____

    Why? _____

**Of the sights/experiences/destinations recommended by this
book, which was:**

Most overrated _____

    Why? _____

Most underrated _____

    Why? _____

Best ways to improve this book:

_____

I'd like a free newsletter subscription:

___ Yes   ___ No   ___ Already on list

_____

Name

_____

Address

_____

City, State, Zip

_____

E-mail Address

Please send to: ETBD, Box 2009, Edmonds, WA 98020

Jubilee 2000—Let's Celebrate the Millennium by Forgiving Third World Debt

Let's ring in the millennium by convincing our government to forgive the debt owed to us by the world's poorest countries. Imagine spending over half your income on interest payments alone. You and I are creditors and poor countries owe us more than they can pay.

Jubilee 2000 is a worldwide movement of concerned people and groups—religious and secular—working to cancel the international debts of the poorest countries by the year 2000.

Debt ruins people: In the poorest countries, money needed for health care, education, and other vital services is diverted to interest payments.

Mozambique, with a per capita income of $90 and life expectancy of 40, spends over half its national income on interest. This poverty brings social unrest, civil war, and often costly humanitarian intervention by the U.S.A. To chase export dollars, desperate countries ruin their environment. As deserts grow and rain forests shrink, the world suffers. Of course, the real suffering is among local people born long after some dictator borrowed (and squandered) that money. As interest is paid, entire populations go hungry.

Who owes what and why? Mozambique is one of 41 countries defined by the World Bank as "Heavily Indebted Poor Countries." In total, they owe $200 billion. Because these debts are unlikely to be paid, their market value is only a tenth of the face value (about $20 billion). The U.S.A.'s share is under $2 billion.

How can debt be canceled? This debt is owed mostly to the U.S.A., Japan, Germany, Britain, and France either directly or through the World Bank. We can forgive the debt owed directly to us and pay the market value (usually 10 percent) of the debts owed to the World Bank. We have the resources. (Norway, another wealthy creditor nation, just unilaterally forgave its Third World debt.) All America needs is the political will . . . people power.

While many of these poor nations are now democratic, corruption is still a concern. A key to Jubilee 2000 is making certain that debt relief reduces poverty in a way that benefits ordinary people: women, farmers, children, and so on.

Let's celebrate the new millennium by giving poor countries a break. For the sake of peace, fragile young democracies, the environment, and countless real people, forgiving this debt is the right thing for us in the rich world to do.

Tell Washington, DC.: If our government knows this is what we want, it can happen. Learn more, write letters, lobby legislators, or even start a local Jubilee 2000 campaign. For details, contact Jubilee 2000 (tel. 202/783-3566, www.j2000usa.org). For information on lobbying Congress on J2000, contact Bread for the World (tel. 800/82-BREAD, www.bread.org).

INDEX